Landscape Architecture for Sea

This book assesses and illustrates innovative and practical worldwide measures for combating sea level rise from the profession of landscape architecture. The work explores how the appropriate mixture of integrated, multi-scalar flood protection mechanisms can reduce risks associated with flood events including sea level rise.

Because sea level rise is a global issue, illustrative case studies performed from the United States, Korea, Australia, New Zealand, Thailand, Japan, China, and the Netherlands identify the structural (engineered), non-structural (nature-based), and hybrid mechanisms (mixed) used to combat sea level rise and increase flood resilience. The alternative flood risk reduction mechanisms are extracted and analyzed from each case study to develop and explain a set of design-based typologies to combat sea level rise which can then be applied to help proctor new and existing communities.

It is important for those located within the current or future floodplain considering sea level rise and those responsible for land use, developmental, and population-related activities within these areas to strategically implement a series of integrated constructed and green infrastructure-based flood risk reduction mechanisms to adequately protect threatened areas. As a result, this book is beneficial to both academics and practitioners related to multiple design professions such as urban designers, urban planners, architects, real estate developers, and landscape architects.

Galen D. Newman is Associate Professor and Interim Department Head in the Department of Landscape Architecture and Urban Planning at Texas A&M University. He also serves as the Director of the Center for Housing and Urban Development. Dr. Newman's research overlaps the fields of community resilience, land use science, urban analytics, landscape performance and advanced visualization. He has published over 70 peer reviewed articles in high-quality journals and has received over 31 million dollars in interdisciplinary funded research projects.

Zixu Qiao has a Master of Landscape Architecture from Texas A&M University. She is a professional landscape architect, guest speaker at University of Guelph, and the founder of Land.Space Architecture. Her work includes research, design, and planning on a variety of site planning and landscape architecture projects in the US and China. Her design is committed to improving cities' economic and environmental sustainability, resilience, and quality of life. She founded Land. Space Architecture in 2019, an online educational platform committed to improving young professionals' visualization skills in landscape architecture.

Landscape Architecture for Sea Level Rise

Innovative Global Solutions

Edited by Galen D. Newman and Zixu Qiao

NEW YORK AND LONDON

First published 2022
by Routledge
605 Third Avenue, New York, NY 10158

and by Routledge
4 Park Square, Milton Park, Abingdon, Oxon, OX14 4RN

Routledge is an imprint of the Taylor & Francis Group, an informa business

Library of Congress Cataloging-in-Publication Data
Names: Newman, Galen D., editor.
Title: Landscape architecture for sea level rise : global innovative
solutions / edited by Galen D. Newman and Zixu Qiao.
Description: New York, NY : Routledge, 2022. | Includes bibliographical
references and index.
Identifiers: LCCN 2021048249 (print) | LCCN 2021048250 (ebook) |
ISBN 9781032024578 (hardback) | ISBN 9781032024561 (paperback) |
ISBN 9781003183419 (ebook)
Subjects: LCSH: Landscape architecture—Climatic factors. | Landscape
architecture—Environmental aspects. | Flood damage prevention. | Sea
level—Environmental aspects. | Climate change.
Classification: LCC SB475.9.C55 L36 2022 (print) | LCC SB475.9.C55
(ebook) | DDC 712—dc23/eng/20211202
LC record available at https://lccn.loc.gov/2021048249
LC ebook record available at https://lccn.loc.gov/2021048250

ISBN: 978-1-032-02457-8 (hbk)
ISBN: 978-1-032-02456-1 (pbk)
ISBN: 978-1-003-18341-9 (ebk)

DOI: 10.4324/9781003183419

Typeset in Corbel
by Apex CoVantage, LLC

Contents

Foreword

Kate Orff

This book traces design approaches and case studies for sea level rise adaptation in cities, and it comes at a pivotal moment in design culture. We are moving beyond broad calls to action into a space requiring detailed design, funding, implementation, and maintenance. Chapter contributors from New Orleans to Baltimore to New Zealand describe herein a range of contexts and adaptation strategies that can expand options for urban managers, Mayors, and regional authorities beyond "business as usual" – vertical steel bulkhead walls, 25′ H levees, and underdrainage. With essays, papers, and contextual information, it provides a comparative context that landscape architects can draw from to expand the problem-solving mix.

Sea levels are not rising everywhere but are appearing to do so, nonetheless. In Greenland, for example, the land itself is rising and sea level is falling off due to the shedding of ice and the lifting of the land in a geologic process called isostatic rebound. Rising, falling, changing, advancing . . . to become climate designers, we must embrace dynamism itself and develop open, iterative, and grounded projects that embed the changing nature of natural systems and social life into future forms and structures.

It's also time to embrace the life-giving power of water itself and look beyond engineered outcomes to a different measure of success based on a living planet index. The space where water meets land propagates our most ecologically and culturally productive zones and has been consistently eroded in the last century as expansive riverbanks have been canalized, flows severed, and basins paved. To reclaim them we must conceive future landscapes that move beyond "green vs gray" and into new imaginative territories of design, empathy, and empowerment.

This volume will certainly be a valuable resource for the next generation of climate-driven landscape architects as they advance strategies of intervention and that are creative, considered, systematic, and cumulative.

Contributors

Traci Birch is an Urban Planner and Assistant Professor in the School of Architecture at Louisiana State University. She also serves as the Managing Director for the LSU Coastal Sustainability Studio, a multidisciplinary center focused on designing resilient ecosystems in the Louisiana coastal zone. Dr. Birch's research focuses on the fields of ecosystem management, urban planning, community resilience, and cultural adaptation. Her work has an applied focus, working closely with stakeholders in neighborhoods, cities, and regions to develop strategies that improve quality of life and reduce risk for coastal residents.

Haley Blakeman holds the Suzanne L. Turner Professorship and serves as the undergraduate coordinator in the Robert Reich School of Landscape Architecture at Louisiana State University. Haley received her BLA from Louisiana State University and her Master of Urban and Regional Planning (MURP) from the University of New Orleans. Haley's research focuses on civic engagement and empowerment, strengthening neighborhoods, and alternative transportation networks. She is a licensed landscape architect and a certified planner, with over 20 years of professional experience.

Carla Brisotto is a Post-Doctoral Associate at the Florida Institute for the Built Environment Resilience (FIBER) at the University of Florida. She obtained a PhD in Design, Planning, and Construction (DCP) from the University of Florida and an architectural degree from the University IUAV of Venice (Italy). She has 15 years of practitioner experience in the UK and – as a licensed architect – in Italy. Her projects span the realm of commercial, residential, and historic preservation. She focuses her research agenda on identifying and developing design strategies for a resilient built environment. Her PhD dissertation was a comparative study of agrarian urbanism cases and the analysis of their design process. At FIBER, she has been researching community-based design strategies such as the Urban Living Lab, Design Thinking, and Exhibition methodologies.

Jules Bruck is Professor and Founding Director of Landscape Architecture at the University of Delaware. She also serves as the Director of the UD's Mangone Climate Science and Policy Hub and the Principal of the Delaware Sea Grant funded Coastal Resilience Design Studio. Dr. Bruck's research interests relate to coastal resilience, green infrastructure, community engagement through citizen science, and public perception of sustainable landscape practices such as designing for ecosystem services.

Jeff Carney is Associate Professor in the School of Architecture and Director of the Florida Institute for Built Environment Resilience (FIBER) at the University of Florida. He is a registered architect and certified city planner working at the interface of housing, neighborhoods, and ecosystems with a focus on climate change adaptation. Jeff's work in Florida is focused on the resilience of communities achieved through transdisciplinary and community engaged design processes. His current projects include a HUD funded effort to design post-disaster modular housing, and projects to assist the City of Port St. Joe and Jacksonville to reduce flood risk that balance health, environment, and housing needs.

Victoria Chanse is Program Director for Landscape Architecture at Te Herenga Waka – Victoria University of Wellington. She is a founding member of the Te Ātea – Spatial Justice Co-design Lab. Dr. Chanse focuses her research, teaching, and practice on solving problems associated with sea level rise, flooding, and stormwater. Her work focuses on participatory, community-based approaches to develop local responsive designs that consider community needs and landscape changes under different scenarios of sea level rise and stormwater management. Past and current projects have faced critical environmental concerns such as design and planning adaptations to sea level change, the use of green infrastructure in addressing stormwater issues, and engaging communities in addressing both equity and environmental problems. Prior to arriving in Aotearoa New Zealand, she taught at the University of Maryland and at Clemson University in the United States.

Pudtan Chantarangkul is a lecturer in the Department of Landscape Architecture at Kasetsart University. Her research experience and background cover Low Impact Development, Green Infrastructure, sustainable landscape architecture construction, soil bioengineering applied in low income housing, and green urban design guidelines to reduce urban heat island effects. Her research is primarily conducted at the microscale. In the beginning of her career, she was a part of the vernacular architecture research team known as the "Holistic Study for the Adaptability in Different Contexts of Tai-Lao in the Central Region Basin of Thailand."

Maria Debije Counts is Principal of Studio Counts, President of Landscape Skills Inc. and Adjunct Professor at Florida International University. Her urban planning, landscape architecture, and architectural research focus on advancing landscape-based solutions to sea level rise, flooding, and accessibility through topographic manipulation and planted form. She leads grant-funded research, studios, and design projects to address human experience and engagement at the scale of the site in both public and private sectors.

Alexander J. Felson is at the University of Melbourne as Elisabeth Murdoch Chair of Landscape Architecture. He was formerly at CIRCA as the Deputy Executive Director and Director of Resilience Design. He now serves as an affiliated staff on the Connecticut Connections Coastal

Resilience Plan – a US Department of Housing and Urban Development (HUD) National Disaster Resilience (NDR) grant. Dr. Felson is a senior certified ecologist and a registered landscape architect who founded the Urban Ecology and Design Lab and runs Ecopolitan Design.

Isaac Hametz is Principal and Research Director at Mahan Rykiel Associates. He collaborates with clients and strategic partners to study, imagine, and shape landscapes that enrich the human condition and support vibrant natural systems. His work emphasizes ecological integrity, economic uplift, and cultural identity. He leads the Design with Dredge program and manages the firm's design research portfolio including partnerships, projects, and publications. Prior to joining Mahan Rykiel Associates, Isaac founded and ran two non-profit organizations that utilized landscape as a vehicle for civic engagement and design activism.

Karishma Joshi works as an Associate Landscape Designer at Carducci Associates in the San Francisco – Bay Area. She is a registered Architect with the Council of Architecture in India. She earned her Bachelor's in Architecture with a merit award from the University of Pune and a Master of Landscape Architecture with a certificate in Sustainable Urbanism from Texas A&M University. She was named the LAF Olmsted Scholar for Texas A&M University in 2020. Karishma's work as a landscape designer focuses on developing innovative design solutions, based on a green infrastructure-based approach to mitigate the effects of sea level rise, storm surge-inundation, and flooding, especially in underrepresented or marginalized communities.

Tamiyo Kondo is Associate Professor in the Graduate School of Engineering at Kobe University. She engages in housing recovery and post-disaster recovery planning studies after Hurricane Katrina and the Great East Japan Earthquake. Her recent article "Maladaptation, Fragmentation, and Other Secondary Effects of Centralized Post-Disaster Urban Planning: The case of the 2011 cascading disaster in Japan" reveals urban sprawl, risks of landslides, urban fragmentation, and significant internal relocation with explanations of how and why.

Nano Langenheim teaches in both the undergraduate and graduate levels of Landscape Architecture and Urban Design at the University of Melbourne's School of Design. For the past eight years she has coordinated and taught the multidisciplinary third year core landscape architecture subject Site Tectonics course, Shaping the Landscape courses, and for the past two years, Flexible Urban Modeling. These subjects broadly bridge digital and manual design techniques and deal with critical issues for the design industry, as they grapple with the impact of climate change (flooding), aging populations (equitable access), and urban development (landscape modification).

Cleary Larkin is Acting Director of the University of Florida's Historic Preservation program and an Assistant Scholar in the Department of Urban Planning. From 2019 to 2021, Dr. Larkin was Program Coordinator for the Florida Resilient Cities (FRC) program at the Florida Institute for Built Environment Resilience (FIBER), where she was part of the project team focused on the recovery of Port St. Joe, a historic mill town in the Florida panhandle that was damaged by Hurricane Michael in 2018. Her current research focuses on the impact of climate change on heritage and preservation as a social justice practice.

Gillian Lawson is an Associate Professor and Head of the School of Landscape Architecture at Lincoln University in Christchurch, Aotearoa New Zealand, but is originally from Australia. Her research interests are in landscape pedagogy, landscape visualization, and landscape sociology in Australia, New Zealand, and other Asia-Pacific countries. Further, she conducts work on water and plants as catalysts for improving the adaptation of our cities to climate change. Her work has focused on the sociology of education, social practices in public/private open spaces, green infrastructure, and waterfront communities in landscape planning and design with her PhD students.

Dongying Li is an Assistant Professor in the Department of Landscape Architecture and Urban Planning at Texas A&M University. Her research investigates human–environment relationships, environmental health, environmental psychology, and child development, as well as GeoDesign and geovisualization.

Sani Limthongsakul currently serves as an Associate Professor of Landscape Architecture in the Department of Architecture at Kasetsart University, Thailand. Her initial interest in water sensitive planning and management has led to the current research focus in flood resilience and climate adaptation utilizing nature-based solutions within peri-urban areas.

Yi Luo is an Assistant Professor in the Department of Landscape Architecture at the University of Florida. She received her Bachelor of Architecture from Huazhong University of Science and Technology, Master of Landscape Architecture from Utah State University, and PhD in Urban and Regional Science from Texas A&M University. Her research interest includes landscape performance evaluation, evaluation metrics and methods, stormwater management/green infrastructure, and therapeutic landscapes. Before pursuing her PhD, Dr. Luo practiced architecture and landscape architecture and has been a licensed Professional Landscape Architect in the state of Utah since 2009.

Bruno Marques is Associate Dean (Academic Development) and a Senior Lecturer in Landscape Architecture at Victoria University of Wellington and a Faculty of Architecture and Design Innovation in Aotearoa – New Zealand. His main research interests relate to the integration of Indigenous methods in participatory design and place-making in landscape rehabilitation and ecosystem services.

Brett Milligan is Professor of Landscape Architecture and Environmental Design at the University of California, Davis. He is a founding member of the Dredge Research Collaborative, a nonprofit that explores the human alteration and design of sedimentary processes and landscapes through transdisciplinary design. He is director of Metamorphic Landscapes, a California-based research lab prototyping adaptation to conditions of accelerated climatic and environmental change through ethnography, fieldwork, and applied design. Recent projects include Franks Tract Futures in the CA Delta, and the Public Sediment Team's *Unlock Alameda Creek* for the Bay Area Resilient by Design Competition. Brett is also currently a designer and scholar in residence at the Exploratorium Museum.

David N. Myers is Associate Professor and Director of Landscape Architecture in the Department of Plant Science and Landscape Architecture at the University of Maryland. His research and teaching focus on the application of landscape ecological principles to the built environment including green infrastructure, community greening, and greenway planning and design. He has received funding from Chesapeake Bay Trust, National Park Service, Maryland–National Capital Park and Planning Commission: Montgomery County and Prince George's County, and the Maryland Department of Environment.

Anne Loes Nillesen is founding Director of the Dutch design office Defacto Urbanism. She specializes in urban research and design in the domain of climate adaptation and flood risk management. She founded the Climate Adaptation Lab and Delta Interventions graduate studios at Delft University of Technology Faculty of Architecture. Her PhD research explored the relation between urban design and flood risk strategies. Anne Loes worked on several complex urban adaptation projects such as the Dutch, Bangladesh, and Mekong Deltaplan, the Netherland long sea level rise strategy and river vision, and local scale adaptation strategies for Houston, Khulna, Amsterdam, The Hague, Rotterdam, and Kigali. For more information, see www.d.efac.to.

Bill O'Dell is Director of the Shimberg Center for Housing Studies at the University of Florida. The Shimberg Center conducts research into housing policy and planning, with a special focus on housing affordability for Florida residents. The Center provides data and applied research to a variety of stakeholders involved in shaping housing policy in Florida. Its current research focuses on documenting housing market conditions and affordable housing needs in Florida's counties, cities and neighborhoods; preserving Florida's affordable rental housing; supporting the development of energy efficient and healthy homes; and examining the impact of climate change on Florida's affordable housing stock and delivery system. The Center maintains the Clearinghouse COVID-19 Workforce & Housing Indicators application and the COVID-19 page with links to information about the CDC's eviction moratorium, mortgage forbearance programs, the OUR Florida rental assistance program, county and local rental assistance programs, and legal assistance providers; it is also extensively involved in eviction tracking and prevention activities. The Center also produces the Florida Housing Data Clearinghouse, which provides public access to data on housing needs and supply for Florida's cities and counties.

Kate Orff is a Professor at Columbia University where she directs the Urban Design Program at the Graduate School of Architecture Planning and Preservation. She is also co-Director of the Center for Resilient Cities and Landscapes (crcl.columbia.edu). Her teaching and practice at

SCAPE (www.scapestudio.com) integrate work across water, climate, justice, and community engagement.

Yunmi Park is an Assistant Professor at Ewha Woman's University and completed her PhD in Urban Regional Science at Texas A&M University. Several years of professional planning experience and academic research led her to focus on urban design and planning, urban shrinkage and revitalization, land use planning, and spatial analytics.

Shivani Patel works as a Landscape Architect and an Architectural Designer in New Zealand. She has a Bachelor of Architectural Studies, Master of Landscape Architecture, and is working towards a Graduate Diploma in Designed Environments from Victoria University of Wellington. As a landscape architect and an architectural designer, Shivani's focus is on designing sustainable urban built environments and public spaces. Shivani's interests include designing for urban adaptation to ambiguous sea level rise and storm surges to create new forms of public spaces and coastal environments with the application of resiliency and adaptability. Her approach envisions guidelines for architectural built-form and open space resiliency parameters for the future of New Zealand that are informed by proactive multi-interdisciplinary strategies, cultural heritage, ecology, and infrastructural design to uncertainty and change.

Maria Rodgers is a PhD candidate and teaching fellow in landscape architecture at Te Herenga Waka – Victoria University of Wellington. Her research examines the benefits of celebrating natural heritage in the urban realm in Aotearoa New Zealand. She is a member of the Te Ātea – Spatial Justice Co-design Lab. Ms. Rodgers is particularly interested in the use of plants by Indigenous people, planting design, participatory design, tactical urbanism, and cultural landscapes. Her thesis for her Master of Landscape Architecture investigated ways in which landscape architecture reveals and connects Māori and Pākehā to the land and to the past in rural Aotearoa New Zealand. She continues to teach studio and lecture courses in the landscape program at Te Herenga Waka – Victoria University of Wellington.

Emma Ruggiero is a Master student in the Department of Plant and Soil Sciences at the University of Delaware (UD). She holds a Bachelor of Science in Landscape Architecture with a minor in Biology from UD. Emma has worked on several design projects focused on coastal resilience and flood mitigation throughout Delaware as part of the Coastal Resilience Design Studio. Her research interests include nature-based infrastructure design, living shorelines for coastal protection, and regenerative landscape design. She recently completed a Master's thesis exploring feasibility of a living shoreline installment on a remote site experiencing ship wake on the Delaware River.

Jiyeon Shin is a graduate student in the Architectural & Urban Systems Engineering of Ewha Woman's University. She has done several pieces of research with Dr. Yunmi Park and her research interests are focused on spatial analysis of urban environmental problems, socioeconomic and spatial factors causing environmental inequality, and environmental planning–community development.

Zhihan Tao is a a fourth year PhD student studying in the Urban and Regional Sciences program in the Department of Landscape Architecture and Urban Planning at Texas A&M University. He has a Master degree in Landscape Architecture from Texas A&M University. His research interests include community resilience, green infrastructure performance, and resilient strategies against environmental hazards.

Nada Toueir is a Lecturer at the School of Landscape Architecture at Lincoln University in Christchurch, Aotearoa New Zealand. Her research focuses on the relationship between landscape architecture, culture, resilience, and landscape education. Her interests include fostering community resilience and drawing commonalities between cases at the national and international levels with a focus on place attachment, memory, informal social networks, and cultural identity to understand the intricate relationships that people build with their environment. Also, her interests span landscape education and how educators can shape the future of teaching while using blended learning and hybrid forms of teaching (online and face-to-face), especially in studio environments.

Michael Volk is a Florida registered Landscape Architect, partner at Volk Design Consultants, LLC, and Research Assistant Professor in the University of Florida Center for Landscape Conservation Planning, Department of Landscape Architecture. He has a Master Degree in Landscape Architecture from the University of Florida and a degree in Architecture from the Frank Lloyd Wright School of Architecture. Michael's work with the Center for Landscape Conservation Planning (http://conservation.dcp.ufl.edu/) includes applied research with conservation partners throughout Florida on land use, regional conservation planning, and urban green infrastructure; the impacts of sea level rise on natural resources and coastal communities; and climate change adaptation strategies and information needs for landscape architecture students and professionals (https://dcp.ufl.edu/landscapechange/). Michael is also a partner with Florida Resilient Cities (https://dcp.ufl.edu/frc/), an initiative which works with communities across Florida to be more prepared for and resilient to increased risk and future changes.

Amy Whitesides is Director of Resilience and Research at Stoss Landscape Urbanism where she brings her background in landscape architecture, science communication, ecology, and biology to projects across a wide range of scales. At Stoss, Amy leads waterfront planning efforts focused on resilient public open space. Recent projects include the Boston Urban Forest Plan, Climate Ready East Boston, Charlestown, Downtown and The North End, as well as design efforts at waterfront sites including Moakley Park, Suffolk Downs, and 776 Summer Street. Amy is also a design critic at the Harvard GSD where she teaches design studios centered on response to climate-based risk along the Massachusetts shoreline.

Anna Wik is a registered professional landscape architect in Delaware and Pennsylvania and an Associate Professor in the Department of Plant and Soil Sciences at the University of Delaware. She has designed, documented, and managed construction of many landscape projects in the Delaware Valley region, working with community and non-profit partners including Delaware State Parks, Delaware Historical and Cultural Affairs, Delaware Historical Society, Philadelphia Parks and Recreation, Philadelphia Water Department, the Lenape Indian Tribe of Delaware, and numerous community groups. Anna's courses investigate the relationship between the cultural practice of design and the built environment. She is passionate about equitable design and is interested in historical, social and cultural influences upon the urban and rural landscape. Other research areas include children's outdoor learning environments, coastal resilience related to cultural landscapes, and edible forest gardens. Anna earned her Master of Landscape Architecture from the Rhode Island School of Design.

Hong Wu is an Assistant Professor of Landscape Architecture at Pennsylvania State University. She is a co-chair of the Council of Educators in Landscape Architecture's Geo-spatial and Digital Analytics Track, a co-chair of Penn State's University Water Council, and Director of the Penn State Stormwater Living Lab. Wu specializes in urban sustainability, watershed stewardship, green stormwater infrastructure, and landscape performance.

Supreeya Wungpatcharapon is an Assistant Professor in the Department of Architecture at Kasetsart University based in Bangkok, Thailand. Her practice and research interests are focused on participatory design and community engagement in housing and community development, urban green infrastructure, and built environment for well-being.

KongJian Yu is a recipient of Doctor of Design at Harvard GSD, Professor and founding dean of Peking University College of Architecture and Landscape, founder and design principle of Turenscape. He is a strong advocator of "ecological security patterns" and "sponge cities" that have been adopted by the Chinese government for the nationwide ecological campaign. His projects have won numerous international design awards including 14 American Society of Landscape Architects (ASLA) Excellence and Honor Awards. He was elected member of the American Academy of Arts and Sciences, and fellow of the American Society of Landscape Architects. He has also received the 2020 IFLA Sir Geffrey Jellico Award and the 2021 John Cobb Common Good Award.

Rui Zhu is a fourth year PhD student studying in the Urban and Regional Sciences program in the Department of Landscape Architecture and Urban Planning at Texas A&M University. She has a Master and Bachelor's degree in Landscape Architecture. Her research interests include urban regeneration, community resilience, and landscape performance.

Mona zum Felde is a Master student in Urbanism at TU Delft, the Netherlands. Her research examines the largest city in Tanzania, Dar es Salaam, which faces increasing flood risk, causing frequent sickness, loss of life, and widespread damage to property. She examines fast growing cities with significant amounts of informal settlements facing high flood risk.

Part 1

Landscape Architecture and Sea Level Rise

INTRODUCTION

Galen D. Newman and Zixu Qiao

Introduction

The appropriate mixture of integrated, multi-scalar flood protection mechanisms can reduce risks associated with flood events including sea level rise. The magnitude of flood risk is a function of a site's hazard exposure, the characteristics of a particular location, and the vulnerability of an area's people and property. The measures that have been taken to mitigate the potential impact of flooding play a large role in reducing or decreasing the associated risk. It is important for those located in the floodplain or future floodplain considering sea level rise and those responsible for land use, developmental, and population-related activities within these areas to strategically implement a series of integrated constructed and green infrastructure-based flood risk reduction mechanisms to adequately protect threatened areas.

Because sea level rise is a global issue, in this book we assess and illustrate innovative and practical measures for combating sea level rise from the profession of landscape architecture. Illustrative case studies are performed in 18 unique locations worldwide (10 in the US and 8 outside of the US) using an identical framework and identifying the structural (engineered), non-structural (nature-based), and hybrid mechanisms used to combat sea level rise and increase flood resilience. The alternative flood risk reduction mechanisms are extracted and analyzed from each case study to develop and explain a set of design-based typologies to combat sea level rise which can then be applied to help proctor new and existing communities.

The book is arranged in three parts. The first part provides the rationale and background for the book while discussing many of the current landscape architecture approaches to helping solve the myriad of issues related to sea level rise. The introduction, here, will lay the foundation of the contents of the book through providing visualized scientific justification for the existence of sea level rise worldwide. Following this setup, we utilize Chapter 1 to further discuss different climate change projections and their current and future impacts and integrate these findings into design and planning solutions related to green (non-structural) and grey (structural) flood control mechanisms. Finally, at the conclusion of Part 1, in Chapter 2 the book examines different flood mitigation management portfolios utilized and applied in four differing locations globally.

DOI: 10.4324/9781003183419-2

Chapter Index

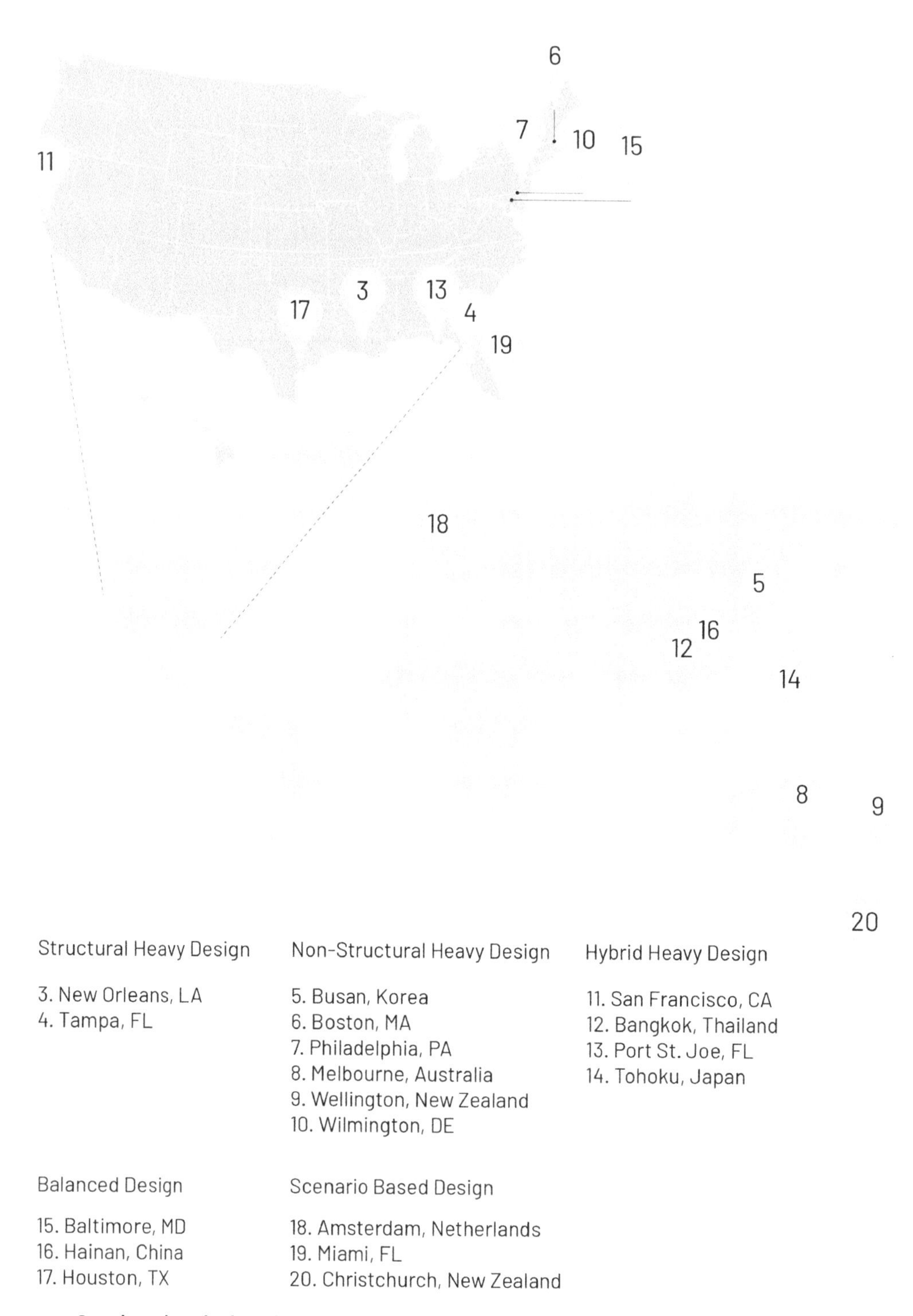

Figure 0.1 Case locations by location and chapter number.

Part 2 is a collection of 18 in-depth global case studies (see Figure 0.1) which are all organized along a similar framework and discuss existing and possible structural, non-structural, and hybrid mechanisms for combating flood risks and sea level rise. The part is sub-categorized based on the mechanisms which are favored or used most heavily. Those that did not show a clear reliance on a particular type of mechanism (e.g. structural, non-structural, or hybrid) or were based on scenario evaluation, were classified as either Balanced or Scenario-based Design categories.

The final part of the book extracts the utilized structural, non-structural, and hybrid mechanisms identified within the case studies, then defines, visualizes, and describes their characteristics. Each mechanism is evaluated and defined along an identical framework. We end this part by presenting a new term for landscape architecture: the *urban periculum* – a collection of areas that are at risk of flood hazards and sea level rise which constitute a landscape at risk in which the mechanisms showcased in this book should be integrated, mixed, and applied.

Flooding and Sea Level Rise

In the past 21 years, 2.3 billion people were affected by floods and 242,000 deaths were a result of flooding (see Figure 0.2); floods accounted for 40% of the global total for all weather-related disasters during this time period (COOPS, 2016) (see Figure 0.3). In 2017, floods caused approximately $60.7 billion worth of property and crop damage and 116 fatalities across the United States (DESAPD, 2018) (see Figure 0.4).

Figure 0.2 Number of weather-related disasters reported per country (1995–2015). Data source: United Nations, 2015.

1-25
26-69
70-163
167-472

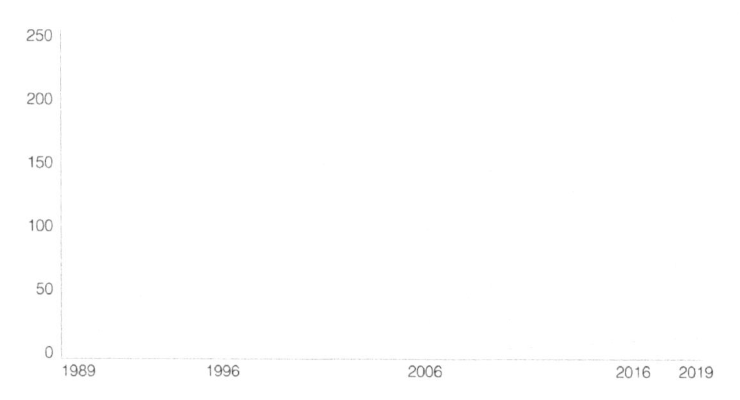

Figure 0.3 Global annual reported number of floods.
Data sources: US DOC, 2014; NASA, 2017; Statista, 2021.

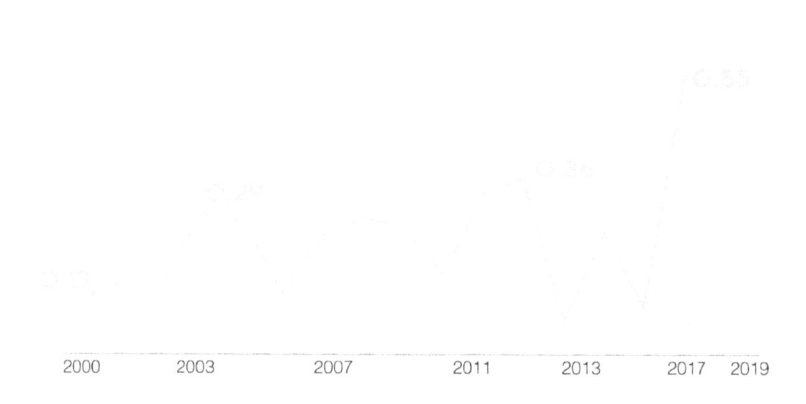

Figure 0.4 Economic damage and fatality rates caused by floods and flash floods in the US.
Data sources: US DOC, 2014; NASA, 2017.

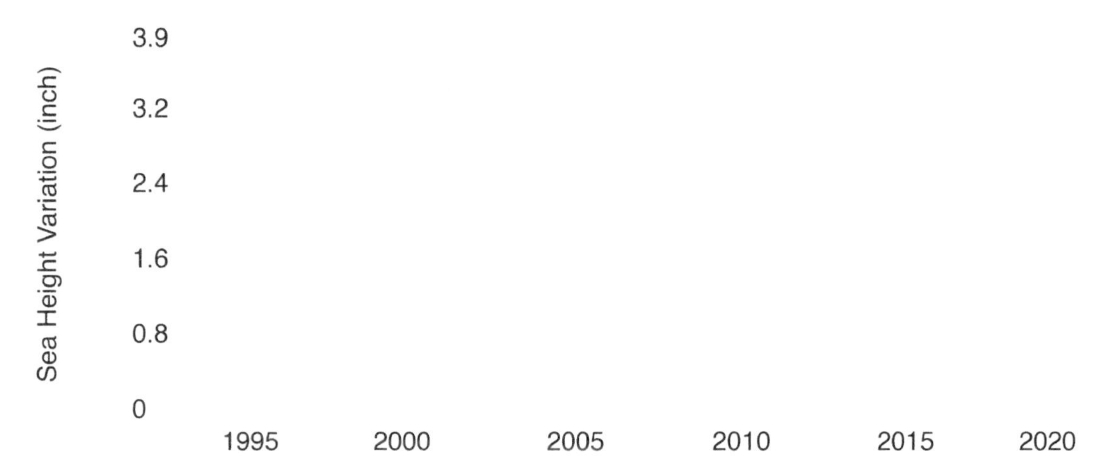

Figure 0.5 Global mean sea level since 1993 as observed by satellites.
Data source: NASA, 2021.

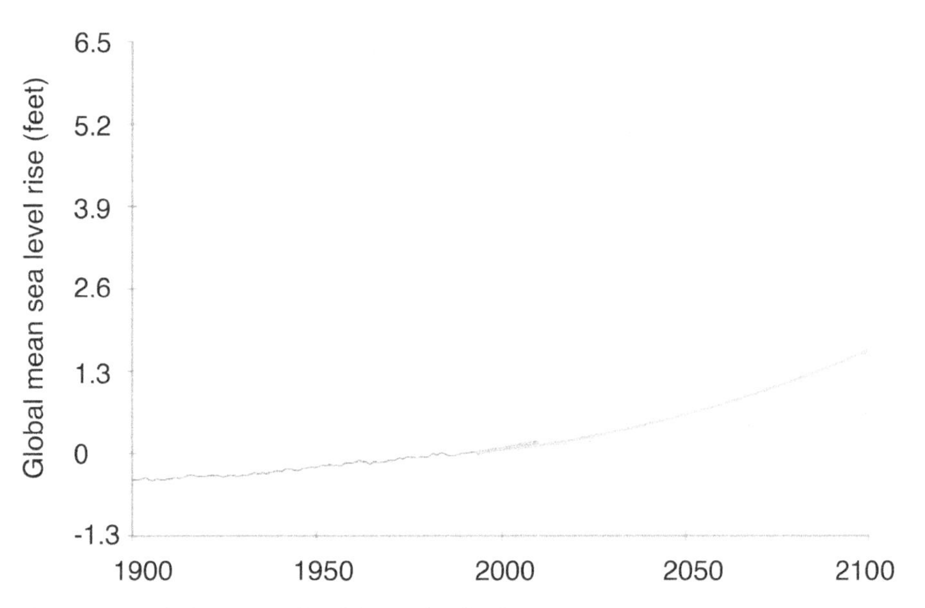

Figure 0.6 Global mean sea level rise projection by NOAA.
Data source: NOAA, 2017a.

With 4–8 inches of sea level rise expected by 2050, coastal flooding will more than double. Global mean sea level could rise up to 6.6 feet by 2100 (Parris et al., 2012) (see Figures 0.5 and 0.6).

Nuisance flooding is estimated to increase up to 900 percent more frequently within U.S. coastal communities than in the previous 50 years (NOAA, 2017b) (see Figure 0.7).

Today, 55% of the world's population lives in urban areas; this is expected to increase to 68% by 2050 (United Nations, 2015). In the US, in 1910, 46% of the population lived in urban areas and by 2010 this number

Figure 0.7 Sea level rise scenarios of 0 to 6 feet along the US Coast.
Data source: NOAA, 2020.

Figure 0.8 Ranking of United States cities by population in 2017 and the population change from 2010 to 2017.
Data source: U.S. Census Bureau, 2015.

increased to 81% (U.S. Census Bureau, 2015). Coastal areas have the highest population density in the US, with 14 of the nation's 20 largest cities and 19 of the 20 most densely populated counties along the coast (U.S. Census Bureau, 2015) (see Figure 0.8).

An estimated 6–8 million commercial and residential buildings now reside in the US 100-year floodplains, with an estimated 3 to 7 million additional flood prone buildings within the 500-year floodplains (DiVincenti, 2006) (see Figure 0.9).

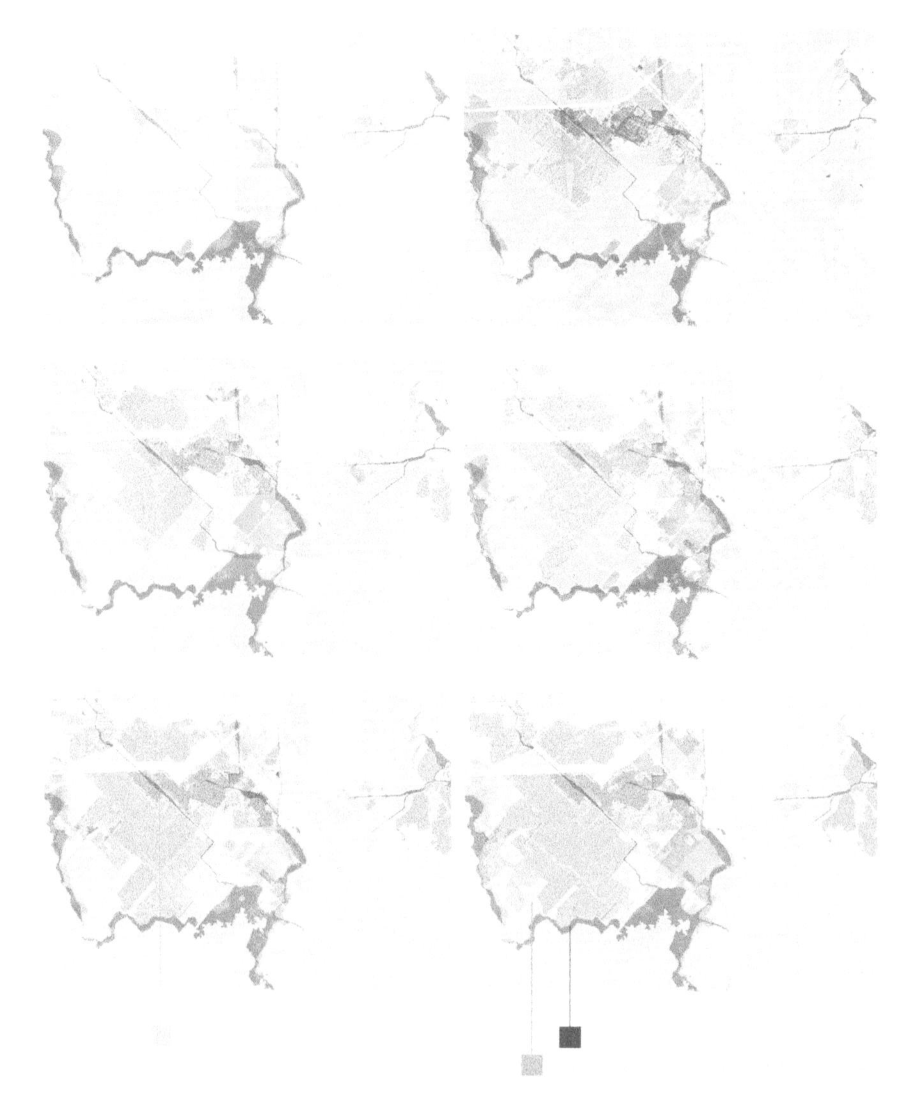

Figure 0.9 Landcover change within the 100-year and 500-year floodplain in Houston.
Data sources: Google Earth, 2020: FEMA, 2016.

References

Center for Operational Oceanographic Products and Services (COOPS). (2016). NOAA Tides and Currents. Retrieved January 28, 2021, from https://tidesandcurrents.noaa.gov/ports.html

Department of Economic and Social Affairs Population Division (DESAPD). (2018). World Urbanization Prospects: The 2018 Revision. Retrieved November 15, 2020, from https://population.un.org on

DiVincenti, C., Wetmore, F., & Bernstein, G. (2006). *The evaluation of the National Flood Insurance Program final report*. Washington D.C.: American Institutes for Research. Retrieved from https://biotech.law.lsu.edu/disasters/insurance/nfip_eval_final_report.pdf

Federal Emergency Management Agency (FEMA). (2020). FEMA Flood Map Service Center: Search by Address. Retrieved October 26, 2020, from https://msc.fema.gov/portal/search#searchresultsanchor on

Google Earth. (2020). V 6.2.2.6613, December 30, 2020. Houston, TX, USA. DigitalGlobe. Retrieved October 26, 2020, from www.earth.google.com

National Aeronautic and Space Administration (NASA) (2017). Sea Level Change, Observations from Space. Retrieved July 10, 2020, from https://sealevel.nasa.gov/

National Aeronautics and Space Administration (NASA) Goddard Space Flight Center. (2020). Global Climate Change: Vital Signs of the Planet. *Global mean sea level since 1993 as observed by satellites* [Chart]. Retrieved December 13, 2020, from https://climate.nasa.gov/vital-signs/sea-level/

National Oceanic and Atmospheric Administration (NOAA). (2017a). National Ocean Service Sea Level Rise Viewer. Retrieved January 15, 2021, from https://coast.noaa.gov/slr/#/layer/slr/0/-11581024.663779823/5095888.569004184/4/satellite/none/0.8/2050/interHigh/midAccretion

National Oceanic and Atmospheric Administration (NOAA). (2017b). In Port: *NOAA Office for Coastal Management sea level rise data: 1–10 ft sea level rise inundation* [Dataset]. Retrieved December 5, 2020 from www.fisheries.noaa.gov/inport/item/48106

Parris, A. S., Bromirski, P., Burkett, V., Cayan, D. R., Culver, M. E., Hall, J., . . . & Weiss, J. (2012). *Global sea level rise scenarios for the United States*. National Climate Assessment. Retrieved from https://repository.library.noaa.gov/view/noaa/11124

Statista. (2021). "In your view, what are the most important environmental issues that Italy faces today?" New York: Statista. Retrieved August 13, 2020, from www.statista.com/statistics/865499/top-three-most-concerning-environmental-issues-in-italy/

United Nations. (2015). *The human cost of weather-related disasters*. Centre for Research on the Epidemiology of Disasters Office for Disaster Risk Reduction. Retrieved February 25, 2021, from www.undrr.org/publication/human-cost-weather-related-disasters-1995-2015

U.S. Census Bureau. (2015). Emergency Management: *Floods*. Retrieved January 9, 2021, from www.census.gov/topics/preparedness/events/floods.html

U.S. Department of Commerce (US DOC). (2014). *Global sea level rise scenarios for the United States National Climate Assessment: Technical report*. Washington D.C.: CreateSpace Independent Publishing Platform.

Vitousek, S., Barnard, P. L., Fletcher, C. H., Frazer, N., Erikson, L., & Storlazzi, C. D. (2017). Doubling of coastal flooding frequency within decades due to sea-level rise. Scientific Reports, 7(1), 1399.

1

SEA LEVEL RISE AS A DESIGN AND PLANNING ISSUE

Galen D. Newman, Zixu Qiao, and Rui Zhu

Introduction

Hazard Exposure and Climate Change

Climate change is a global issue which has had observable negative impacts on standard development practices and has resulted in increased disaster risk for both people and communities. One of the impacts of climate change is increased flood frequency and magnitude. Floods are the most common natural disaster and the leading cause of natural disaster fatalities worldwide (Doocy et al., 2013). They can cause significant catastrophes and result in the loss of life, property, and natural resources and functions. A recent report entitled *The Human Cost of Weather-Related Disasters* by the United Nations (UN) (2015) shows that, in the past 21 years, floods account for nearly 40% of the global total for all weather-related disasters, have affected 2.3 billion people, and accounted for 242,000 deaths. Further, 89% of flood-related deaths occurred in lower-income countries, despite only experiencing 26% of all flood-related storms.

In 2017 alone, floods caused approximately $60.7 billion worth of property and crop damage, and 116 fatalities across the United States (Pen6ning-Rowsell et al., 2018). For example, Hurricane Harvey wreaked havoc on the Texas coast in 2017, causing 89 deaths and $125 billion in damage (Stone et al., 2019). More than 30 inches of rainfall fell on 6.9 million people during Harvey (see Figure 1.1), while 1.25 million people experienced over 45 inches of rainfall (Sebastian et al., 2019). This historic US rainfall event caused unprecedented amounts of floodwater which displaced over 30,000 people and damaged or destroyed over 200,000 homes and businesses (NOAA, 2018).

All coastal regions are projected to experience significant increases in frequency of both minor and major flooding over a range of future sea level rise levels. Global climate change also increases the frequency of coastal flooding. A report from the U.S. Geological Survey (Ober, 2017) suggests an expected 4–8 inches of sea level rise by 2050, causing coastal flooding probabilities to more than double. This dramatic increase in coastal flooding results from a combination of rising sea levels and increased storm-driven flooding such as rainfall and storm surge.

DOI: 10.4324/9781003183419-3

Figure 1.1 Hurricane Harvey inundated area in Houston, TX in 2017.

For these and other reasons, it is important that designers and planners seek to increase resilience in their approaches to developing interventions strategies for regions, cities, and sites. Resilience is typically characterized by levels of physical and social vulnerability. Masterson et al. (2019) define physical vulnerability as an area's sensitivity to hazard damage that is caused by the interaction between hazard exposure and the built environment. Physical characteristics can consist of structures, such as homes and businesses, and infrastructure such as roads, water/sewage systems, and critical facilities. Social vulnerability can be defined as the capacity of a person or group to anticipate, resist and recover from the impact of natural hazards (Masterson et al., 2019). The geophysical forces that adjust the physical and social vulnerabilities to hazards can include hurricanes, coastal storms, rising sea levels, climate change, earthquakes, tsunamis, drought, heat waves, wildfires, and coastal resource depletion. Physical vulnerability addresses the interaction between geophysical forces and human decisions and is related to the level of risk within the built environment (Beatley, 2011). Specifically, such vulnerability stems from human decisions to place property in precarious positions. Inversely, social vulnerability is more related to a a population's susceptibility to natural hazards and its ability to recover from them (Cutter & Finch, 2008). Individual- and household-level factors can be identified to measure social vulnerability and the influence of a community's ability to respond to natural hazards including race and ethnicity, gender, household composition, education, poverty, age, and housing tenure (Hendricks et al., 2018).

Both physical and social conditions contribute to a community's overall hazard vulnerability; vulnerability (the degree to which the human environment is at risk from flood) and hazard exposure (the frequency of disaster events) are the two major factors influencing community resilience (Walker & Salt, 2012). Resilience is an approach that assumes that people interact with and shape their environment on macro-, meso-, and micro-scales and that the environment can provide services to sustain the well-being of human societies (Berkes et al., 1998). While many different definitions of resilience exist across hazards and disasters research, resilience is typically defined as the measure of a system's capacity to obtain, withstand, and recover from a hazard event (Klein et al., 2003). It can also be interpreted in terms of the propensity of certain social units to move toward mitigation, resistance of natural hazards, recovery from impacts, and the reduction of vulnerability through adaptive strategies (Peacock et al., 2008). Resilient communities strive to build capacity to address different, largely unpredictable, changes including both current and future scenarios. Based on this definition, a combination of three characteristics can help to delineate the resilience of a system: (1) the magnitude of shock that the system can absorb and remain within a given state, (2) the degree to which the system is capable of self-organization, and (3) the degree to which the system can build capacity for learning and adaptation (Folke et al., 2002).

Sea Level Rise

Resilience can lessen over time due to climate change conditions, as climate change drives sea level rise. According to multiple scientific organizations, sea level has risen over the past century. Global sea levels rose 6.7 inches (17 cm) through the 20th century and the rate has accelerated in recent decades, averaging currently about one-eighth inch (3.2 mm) per year (Nicholls, 2011). In 2017, global mean sea level was 3 inches (77 mm) above the 1993 average – the highest annual average in the satellite record.

Multiple authorities have used differing models to predict sea level rise, each with slightly different results. For example, the National Oceanic and Atmospheric Administration (NOAA) predicts that global mean sea level will rise at least 8 inches (0.2 meters) but no more than 6.6 feet (2.0 meters) by 2100 (Parris et al., 2012). One constant variable related to these prediction models relates to how quickly land ice sheets in Greenland and Antarctica will destabilize (Kulp & Strauss, 2019). In general, there are two ways to predict sea level rise: process-based modeling and ice-sheet models. The process-based model is based on a well-understood physical understanding of the climate system established through time and patterns. A disadvantage of this method is that it projects sea level rise primarily using greenhouse gas concentrations and simulated temperature with no training on observed sea levels, which can lead to a lack of sensitivity to the uncertainty of sea level rise (Church et al., 2013). The ice-sheet model, on the other hand, is dependent on an understanding of the processes that controlled the behaviors of the Greenland and Antarctic Ice Sheets during the last glacial period to predict the ice sheet's response to external forces (Huybrechts, 2007).

According to the 2017 climate science report from the Fourth National Climate Assessment (NCA4), it is likely that the global mean sea level (GMSL) will rise by 9–18 cm by 2030, 15–38 cm by 2050, and 30–130 cm by 2100, compared to 2000. Emerging science on the stability of the Antarctic Ice Sheet indicates that, for high-emission scenarios, the GMSL may rise by more than 2.4 m by 2100 (USGCRP, 2017). In 2019, Bamber et al. (2019) projected that, relative to 2000, the GMSL is likely to rise 30 cm by 2050 and 69 cm by 2100 in the low greenhouse gas emission scenario. Under the high greenhouse gas emission scenario, the GMSL may rise 34 cm by 2050 and 11cm by 2100. It is not impossible that this increase may exceed 2 m by 2100 in a high emission scenario, which may result in the displacement of up to 187 million people. Climate Center uses a Coastal Digital Elevation Model (DEM), which takes land elevation into account, to simulate sea level rise and find that the land currently inhabited by 300 million people may be lower than the average annual coastal flood height by 2050. Further, the land currently inhabited by 200 million people could fall permanently below the high tide line (Kulp & Strauss, 2019). In addition, the Intergovernmental Panel on Climate Change (IPCC) published a 2019 special report on the ocean and cryosphere in a changing climate, discussing future sea level rise using different Representative Concentration Pathway (RCP) emission scenarios (a Representative Concentration Pathway refers to a greenhouse gas concentration trajectory adopted by the IPCC). Based on their prediction, the GMSL will could rise by 0.61–1.10 m in an RCP8.5 scenario by 2100, relative to the time frame of 1986 to 2005. They estimated that the Greenland Ice Sheet could contribute up to 27 cm and the Antarctic could contribute up to 28 cm to the GMSL between 2000 to 2100, respectively. Relatedly, because of continuous deep ocean heat absorption and mass loss of Greenland and Antarctic Ice Sheets, the sea level will continue to rise for centuries after 2100 (Oppenheimer et al., 2019). NASA's prediction results further confirm the predictions in the IPCC 2019 Ocean and Cryosphere Special Report. The Ice Sheet Model Intercomparison Project (ISMIP6) led by NASA's Goddard Space Flight Center adopted the low emissions scenario and the high emissions scenario that the IPCC set for future sea level rise. Their results showed that, by 2100, the Greenland Ice Sheet may cause global sea levels to rise another 9 cm in a high emissions scenario (see Figure 1.2); in the case of the lower emissions scenario, the loss of the ice sheet may raise the global sea level by approximately 3 cm (Ramsayer, 2020).

While the predictions for sea level rising may vastly vary, what is clear is that the sea level is certainly rising. Higher mean sea levels increase the frequency, magnitude, and duration of flooding associated with a given storm, which often have disproportionately high impacts in most coastal regions. Further, extreme weather events will continue to be

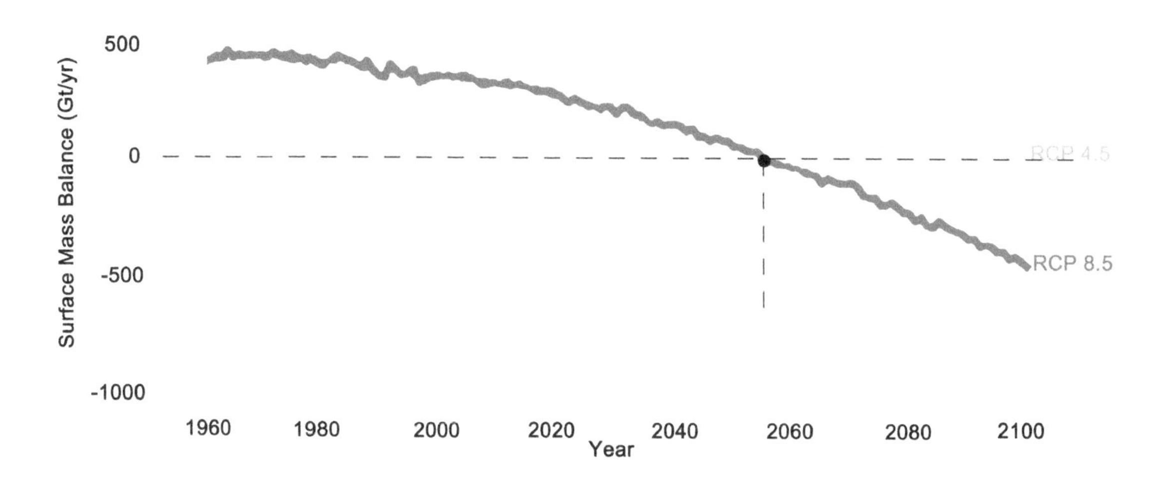

Figure 1.2 Surface mass balance from the Greenland ice sheet in under a high emissions (RCP 8.5), medium emissions (RCP 4.5), and low emissions (RCP 2.6) scenario.
Data source: Hofer et al., 2020.

the primary driver of the highest water level (Parris et al., 2012). Higher sea levels indicate more deadly and destructive storm surges which will push farther inland than they once did, also resulting in more frequent nuisance flooding. Disruptive and expensive, nuisance flooding is estimated to be from 300% to 900% more frequent within US coastal communities than it was just 50 years ago (NOAA, 2020).

Rising sea level brings a host of problems to coastal cities, including an increased severity in flooding, erosion, and infrastructure damage as well as threats to cities' culturally and economically important natural resources such as wetlands, marshes, and fresh water supplies (Kim & Newman, 2020). Globally, eight of the world's ten largest cities are near a coast, and more than 600 million people (roughly 10% of the global population) lived within 10 meters of the existing sea level in 2000 (Neumann et al., 2015). NOAA's National Coastal Population Report claims that, in the US, 40% of the nation's population are coastal residents (Ache et al., 2015). The concentration of people in low-elevation coastal zones makes millions of people's lives and property highly vulnerable to storm surges and flooding from high tides.

Flood Mitigation as a Planning and Design Issue

Land Use and Land Cover Alteration

Several studies conclude that it can be challenging to choose an appropriate spatial scale to advance master plans to manage hazards, and that greater emphasis should be placed on the local level to reduce the frequency of hazards. Local provisions, however, must be effectively integrated with community and regional scaled strategies. Adopting integrated approaches into the design process to develop land use-based solutions to mitigate hazards requires long-term strategies and forward thinking to reduce hazard vulnerability (NRC, 2012). Flood mitigation or the adoption of sustainable strategies to reduce hazard risks and impacts on people relies upon local tools such as building codes and encouragement of better communication and citizen involvement in development related decision making; it also, however, involves broader techniques involving zoning, land use plans, and green space systems. An often-overlooked element of mitigation is the capability to forecast future circumstances. Communities suffering from high hazard exposure often increase pressure on local governments to include resiliency in their decision-making processes. From a design and planning perspective, master plans can be an extremely effective tool for long-term action (Schwab, 2010). Unfortunately, most master plans do not take into account long-term impacts of climate change or utilize future scenarios to inform decision making.

The effects of sea level rise are largely related to land cover and land use configurations. Land use and land cover changes affect local, regional, and global climate processes and alter over time in response to evolving economic, social, and biophysical conditions (Loveland, 2012). As a result, land use regulations through master planning can be used to adapt to or reduce the effects of climate change. Land use and land-cover-related options for mitigating climate change can include the expansion of forests for the amplified removal of carbon, modification and reorganization of the built environment to reduce energy demands, and altering agricultural and nature-based management practices to increase stormwater sequestration. Unfortunately, humans have heavily altered coastal environments through development, changes in impervious surfaces, and overexploitation of natural resources. *The 2018 Revision of World Urbanization Prospects* produced by the United Nations (UN, 2018) states that 55% of the world's population lives in urban areas; this amount is expected to increase to 68% by 2050 (Gu, 2019). In the US, 46% of the population lived in urban areas in 1910; this number increased to 81% by 2010, according to the U.S. Census Bureau (2010). In the US, coastal areas have the highest population density and 14 of the nation's 20 largest cities and 19 of the 20 most densely populated counties lie along the coast (Newman et al., 2020).

Future climate changes will affect how and where humans live and use land for various purposes. Changes in land use and land cover affected 8.6% of the conterminous United States between 1973 and 2000 (Sleeter et al., 2013). The U.S. Census Bureau (2010) reports that the urban land uses are projected to increase in the lower 48 states by 73% to 98% by 2050. Density rate projections, however, remain unclear. Higher population density means that less land is converted from forests or grasslands, but can result in a greater extent of paved area within a concentrated area.

Pervious and Impervious Surfaces

The average cost per major flood event in the United States is estimated at about $4.3 billion (Aerts, 2018). The Federal Emergency Management Agency (FEMA) recognizes that the total number of US buildings in the 100-year floodplain has increased over time, with a current estimate of 6 to 8 million commercial and residential buildings located in the 100-year floodplain and an estimated 7 million additional flood prone buildings lying outside that area, within the 500-year floodplain

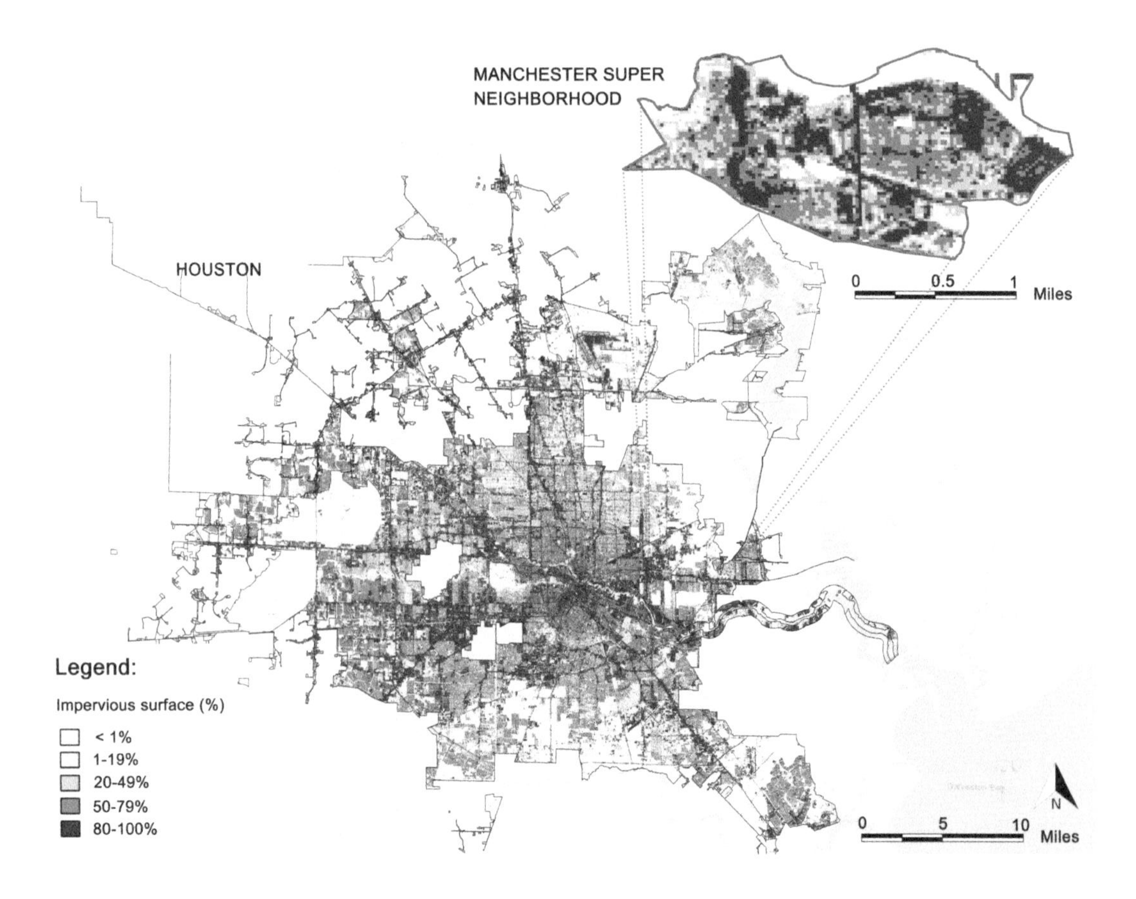

Figure 1.3 Pervious/impervious surface ratio of Houston, TX and the neighborhood of Manchester in Houston as of 2016.
Data source: Esri, 2020.

(Huang & Wang, 2020). One side effect of increased development within the flood plain is increased impervious surfaces, or artificial structures which use considerable paved areas that are covered by water-resistant materials (Kim & Newman, 2020). Inversely, a pervious surface is a surface that allows the percolation of water into the underlying soil (e.g. a vegetated area) (Newman et al., 2017). Limiting impervious surface amounts protects water quality and wildlife habitat, reduces heat island effects, and decreases stormwater runoff amounts. Impervious surfaces have been identified as an indicator of increased flood risk and vulnerability (Ebrahimian et al., 2015). As watersheds are urbanized, much of their vegetation is replaced by impervious surfaces, thus reducing the area where infiltration to groundwater can occur. Impervious surfaces also convey urban pollution to receiving streams and directly impact stream water quality. In the US, about 1.05% (20,593,021 acres) of land area is considered impervious surface, while 0.43% of the global land surface is constructed imperviously (Elvidge et al., 2007). For example, Figure 1.3 shows pervious and impervious surface ratios for Houston, Texas, one of the fastest growing cities in the US.

Low Impact Development and Beyond

The term "low impact development" (LID) refers to systems and land planning/design approaches that use or mimic natural processes for the infiltration, evapotranspiration or (re)use of stormwater in order to protect water quality and associated aquatic habitat (Berke et al., 2015). At both the site and regional scales, LID practices aim to preserve, restore, and create green space using soils, vegetation, and rainwater harvesting techniques. LID is an approach to land development (or re-development) that works with nature to manage stormwater as close to its source as possible (Newman et al., 2014). The approach seeks to balance pervious and impervious ratios through the increase of non-structural flood mitigation mechanisms over structural ones. The basic principle of LID is to use nature as a model; this is accomplished through the sequential implementation of runoff prevention strategies, runoff mitigation strategies, and treatment controls to properly store and convey stormwater while removing pollutants. Many practices have been used in LID such as bioretention facilities, rain gardens, vegetated rooftops, rain barrels, and permeable pavement.

Applied on a large scale, LID can help maintain or restore a watershed's hydrologic and ecological functions. LID practices are designed to capture and treat polluted runoff, and are scalable to various sized projects and land use types. The approach can be practiced at the community scale by connecting local scaled facilities such as rainwater harvesting facilities, rain gardens, green roofs, and infiltration basins with larger scaled mechanisms such as dikes, levees, and constructed wetlands. This approach, then, inherently requires the integration of both structural and non-structural mechanisms for maximum efficiency.

Conclusions

Both green infrastructure (nature based, or non-structural) and grey infrastructure (engineered, or structural) play an important role in flood control and water management. Green infrastructure refers to a multi-functional network of natural lands and green spaces that provide a range of ecosystem services by building with nature. Grey infrastructure, on the other hand, refers to the human-engineered infrastructure for water management such as sewers, storm drains, pipelines, dikes, sea walls, and levees. Typically, grey infrastructure requires technical engineering, continual maintenance, and regularly needs to be upgraded to meet the growing demands of urban and urbanizing areas, often at a high economic cost. Heavy rain events often exceed the capacity of non-structural systems, when used singularly. This can cause overflows resulting in the discharge of a mixture of untreated stormwater and sanitary sewage directly into receiving rivers, lakes or seas, with negative environmental and public health consequences.

Compared to grey infrastructure, green infrastructure is generally decentralized and provides increased flexibility to communities faced with the need to adapt infrastructure to a changing climate. The primary components of green infrastructure include stormwater management, climate adaptation, less heat refection (albedo), higher biodiversity, increased air quality, more sustainable energy production, cleaner water and healthier soils, as well as the more anthropocentric functions such as increased quality of life through recreation and shade provision. In addition, green infrastructure and non-structural stormwater management mechanisms can generate significant cost savings in operation and help to alleviate pressures on existing water infrastructure, potentially avoiding large investments in new or expanded grey infrastructure (Bertule et al., 2014). Green infrastructure plays an important role in climate change adaptation and mitigation through benefits such as carbon sequestration, reduced maintenance costs, and increased aquifer recharge (Newman et al., 2017). However, quantifying the benefits of green infrastructure presents challenges in terms of measuring return on investment, risk management, and effectiveness in urban areas due to modeling and statistical difficulties related to its continually dynamic nature. Because of the ability of green infrastructure solutions to deliver the anticipated water ecosystem services is governed by complex natural processes that can be affected by a number of variables. As a result, increased awareness of the various options available may help to identify the appropriate combination of green and grey infrastructure in specific areas to effectively suit site-specific requirements through integrated urban hydrological management.

References

Ache, B. W., Crossett, K. M., Pacheco, P. A., Adkins, J. E., & Wiley, P. C. (2015). "The coast" is complicated: a model to consistently describe the nation's coastal population. *Estuaries and Coasts, 38*(1), 151–155.

Aerts, J. C. (2018). A review of cost estimates for flood adaptation. *Water, 10*(11), 1646.

Bamber, J. L., Oppenheimer, M., Kopp, R. E., Aspinall, W. P., & Cooke, R. M. (2019). Ice sheet contributions to future sea-level rise from structured expert judgment. *Proceedings of the National Academy of Sciences of the United States of America, 116*(23), 11195–11200. https://doi.org/10.1073/pnas.1817205116

Beatley, T. (2011). Resiliency to disasters. In R. F. Abrams, E. Malizia, A. Wendel, J. Sallis, R. A. Millstein, J. A. Carlson, C. Cannuscio, K. Glanz, J. Samet, D. A. Sleet, & R. B. Naumann (Eds.), *Making healthy places* (pp. 244–258). Washington, DC: Island Press.

Berke, P., Newman, G., Lee, J., Combs, T., Kolosna, C., & Salvensen, D. (2015). Assessing networks of plans and vulnerability to coastal hazards and climate change. *Journal of the American Planning Association, 81*(4), 287–302.

Berkes, F., Kislalioglu, M., Folke, C., & Gadgil, M. (1998). Minireviews: exploring the basic ecological unit: Ecosystem-like concepts in traditional societies. *Ecosystems, 1*(5), 409–415.

Bertule, M., Lloyd, G. J., Korsgaard, L., Dalton, J., Welling, R., Barchiesi, S., . . . & Cole, R. (2014). *Green infrastructure guide for water management: Ecosystem-based management approaches for water-related infrastructure projects.* Nairobi: United Nations Environment Programme. Retrieved from www.unep.org/resources/publication/green-infrastructure-guide-water-management

Church, J. A., Monselesan, D., Gregory, J. M., & Marzeion, B. (2013). Evaluating the ability of process based models to project sea-level change. *Environmental Research Letters, 8*(1), 014051. https://doi.org/10.1088/1748-9326/8/1/014051

Cutter, S. L., & Finch, C. (2008). Temporal and spatial changes in social vulnerability to natural hazards. *Proceedings of the National Academy of Sciences, 105*(7), 2301–2306.

Doocy, S., Daniels, A., Packer, C., Dick, A., & Kirsch, T. D. (2013). The human impact of earthquakes: A historical review of events 1980–2009 and systematic literature review. *PLoS Currents*, 5. Retrieved from www.ncbi.nlm.nih.gov/pmc/articles/PMC3644288/

Ebrahimian, A., Gulliver, J. S., & Wilson, B. N. (2015). *Determination of effective impervious area in urban watersheds*. Dissertation, University of Minnesota. Retrieved from https://hdl.handle.net/11299/175425

Elvidge, C. D., Tuttle, B. T., Sutton, P. C., Baugh, K. E., Howard, A. T., Milesi, C., . . . & Nemani, R. (2007). Global distribution and density of constructed impervious surfaces. *Sensors*, 7(9), 1962–1979.

Esri. (2020). USA NLCD Impervious Surface Time Series. Retrieved from https://landscapeteam.maps.arcgis.com/home/item.html?id=1fdbb561c58b45c58f8f966c00c78ae6

Folke, C., Carpenter, S., Elmqvist, T., Gunderson, L., Holling, C. S., & Walker, B. (2002). Resilience and sustainable development: building adaptive capacity in a world of transformations. *AMBIO: A Journal of the Human Environment*, *31*(5), 437–440.

Gu, D. (2019). Exposure and vulnerability to natural disasters for world's cities. United Nations Department of Economic and Social Affairs, Population Division, Technical Paper, (2019/4). Retrieved from www.un.org/en/development/desa/population/publications/pdf/technical/TP2019-4.pdf

Hendricks, M., Newman, G., Yu, S., Horney, J. (2018). Leveling the landscape: landscape performance as a green infrastructure evaluation tool for service-learning products. *Landscape Journal*, *37*(2), 19–39.

Hofer, S., Lang, C., Amory, C., Kittel, C., Delhasse, A., Tedstone, A., & Fettweis, X. (2020). Greater Greenland Ice Sheet contribution to global sea level rise in CMIP6. *Nature Communications*, *11*(1), 6289. https://doi.org/10.1038/s41467-020-20011-8

Huang, X., & Wang, C. (2020). Estimates of exposure to the 100-year floods in the conterminous United States using national building footprints. *International Journal of Disaster Risk Reduction*, *50*, 101731.

Huybrechts, P. (2007). Ice sheet modeling. In B. Riffenburgh (Ed.): *Encyclopedia of the Antarctic*. New York and London: Routledge. https://epic.awi.de/id/eprint/13358/

Kim Y., & Newman, G. (2020). Advancing scenario planning through integrating urban growth prediction with future flood risk models. *Computers, Environment, and Urban Systems*, *82*, 101498.

Klein, R. J., Nicholls, R. J., & Thomalla, F. (2003). Resilience to natural hazards: How useful is this concept? *Global Environmental Change Part B: Environmental Hazards*, *5*(1), 35–45.

Kulp, S. A., & Strauss, B. H. (2019). New elevation data triple estimates of global vulnerability to sea-level rise and coastal flooding. *Nature Communications*, *10*(1), 4844. https://doi.org/10.1038/s41467-019-12808-z

Loveland, T., Mahmood, R., Patel-Weynand, T., Karstensen, K., Beckendorf, K., Bliss, N., & Carleton, A. (2012). National climate assessment technical report on the impacts of climate and land use and land cover change. *US Geological Survey Open-File Report 2012*, 1155, 1–87.

Masterson, J., Meyer, M., Ghariabeh, N., Hendricks, M., Lee, R. J., Musharrat, S., Newman, G., Sansom, G., & Van Zandt, S. (2019). Interdisciplinary citizen science for hazard and disaster education. *International Journal of Mass Emergencies and Disasters*, *37*(1), 6–24.

National Research Council (NRC) (2012). *Disaster resilience: A national imperative*. Washington, DC: National Academies Press.

Neumann, B., Vafeidis, A. T., Zimmermann, J., & Nicholls, R. J. (2015). Future coastal population growth and exposure to sea-level rise and coastal flooding-a global assessment. *PloS one*, 10(3), e0118571.

Newman, G., Brody, S., & Smith, A. (2017). Repurposing vacant land through landscape connectivity. *Landscape Journal*, *36*, 37–57.

Newman, G., Shi, T., Yao, Z., Li, D., Sansom, G., Kirsch, K., Casillas, G., Horney, J. (2020). Citizen science-informed community master planning: Land use and built environment changes to increase flood resilience and decrease contaminant exposure. *International Journal of Environmental Research and Public Health*, *17*(2), 486.

Newman, G., Sohn, W. M, & Li, M. H. (2014). Performance evaluation of low impact development: Groundwater infiltration in a drought prone landscape in Conroe, Texas. *Landscape Architecture Frontiers*, *2*(4), 122–133.

Nicholls, R. J. (2011). Planning for the impacts of sea level rise. *Oceanography*, *24*(2), 144–157.

NOAA. (2020). *Climate change: Global sea level*. Lindsey, R., author. Retrieved from www.climate.gov/news-features/understanding-climate/climate-change-global-sea-level

NOAA. (2018). *U.S. billion-dollar weather & climate disasters 1980–2017*. Retrieved January 10, 2018, from www.ncdc.noaa.gov/billions/events.pdf [Google Scholar].

Ober, J. A. (2017). *Mineral commodity summaries*. US Geological Survey. https://doi.org/10.3133/70180197

Oppenheimer, M., Glavovic, B. C., Hinkel, J., van de Wal, R., Magnan, A. K., Abd-Elgawad, A., Cai, R., Cifuentes-Jara, M., Rica, C., DeConto, R. M., Ghosh, T., Hay, J., Islands, C., Isla, F., Marzeion, B., Meyssignac, B., & Sebesvari, Z. (2019). Sea level rise and implications for low-lying islands, coasts and communities. In H.-O. Pörtner, D. C. Roberts, V. Masson-Delmotte, P. Zhai, M. Tignor, E. Poloczanska, K. Mintenbeck, A. Alegría, M. Nicolai, A. Okem, J. Petzold, B. Rama, & N. M. Weyer (Eds.), *IPCC special report on the ocean and cryosphere in a changing climate*. Cambridge, UK: Cambridge University Press.

Parris, A., Bromirski, P., Burkett, V., Cayan, D., Culver, M., Hall, J., . . . & Weiss, J. (2012). *Global sea level rise scenarios for the United States National Climate Assessment NOAA Technical Report OAR CPO-1*. Climate Program Office, Silver Springs, MD, USA [Google Scholar].

Peacock, W. G., Kunreuther, H., Hooke, W. H., Cutter, S. L., Chang, S. E., & Berke, P. R. (2008). *Toward a resiliency and vulnerability observatory network: RAVON. HRRC reports*. Retrieved from www.nehrp.gov/pdf/ravon.pdf

Penning-Rowsell, E., Priest, S., Viavattene, C., & Parker, D. (2018, April). Counting the costs of floods: Continuity and innovation in the UK. In *EGU General Assembly Conference Abstracts* (p. 1537).

Ramsayer, K. (2020, September 16). *Emissions could add 15 inches to 2100 sea level rise*. NASA. Retrieved from www.nasa.gov/feature/goddard/2020/emissions-could-add-15-inches-to-2100-sea-level-rise-nasa-led-study-finds

Schwab, J. (2010). *Hazard mitigation: Integrating best practices into planning*. Chicago, IL: American Planning Association.

Sebastian, A., Gori, A., Blessing, R. B., van der Wiel, K., & Bass, B. (2019). Disentangling the impacts of human and environmental change on catchment response during Hurricane Harvey. *Environmental Research Letters*, *14*(12), 124023.

Sleeter, B. M., Sohl, T. L., Loveland, T. R., Auch, R. F., Acevedo, W., Drummond, M. A., . . . & Stehman, S. V. (2013). Land-cover change in the conterminous United States from 1973 to 2000. *Global Environmental Change*, *23*(4), 733–748.

Stone, K., Horney, J., Newman G., Karaye, I., Casaillas, G. (2019). A spatial analysis of possible environmental exposures in recreational areas impacted by Hurricane Harvey Flooding, Harris County, Texas. *Environmental Management*, *64*(4), 381–390.

United Nations. (2015). *The human cost of weather related disasters*. Geneva: United Nations Office for Disaster Risk Reduction.

United Nations. (2018). *2018 revision of world urbanization prospects*. Department of Economic and Social Affairs. Retrieved from www.un.org/development/desa/publications/2018-revision-of-world-urbanization-prospects.html

U.S. Census Bureau. (2010). *Population report*. Retrieved from www.census.gov/topics/population.html

US Global Change Research Program (USGCRP). (2017). Climate Science Special Report. *Chapter 12: Sea level rise*. Retrieved from https://science2017.globalchange.gov/chapter/12/

Walker, B., & Salt, D. (2012). *Resilience thinking: Sustaining ecosystems and people in a changing world*. Washington D.C.: Island Press.

2

GLOBAL STRATEGIES FOR FLOOD AND SEA LEVEL RISE MITIGATION

Zhihan Tao, Rui Zhu, and Galen D. Newman

Introduction

Due to the cumulative combined effects of rapid urbanization, climate change, and sea level rise, flood events have become more frequent and intense (Filho & Pina, 2010). Floods account for nearly 40% of the total disasters globally, making them the most frequent catastrophe (Reja et al., 2017). Further, floods and associated water flow account for about 90% of the damages from natural disasters, excluding drought. The death toll from flood events is also almost twice the number of tornadoes and hurricanes combined (CXA-Arquitectura E Engenharia Ltda & Fag, 2018). Due to rising sea levels, millions more people who currently live outside of flood-prone areas will likely suffer from increased flood risk in the future (Atkinson et al., 2013). In response to increasing flood events, new flood mitigation measures integrating structural (using engineering methods), non-structural (nature-based methods), and hybrid (combination of engineered and green approaches) mechanisms should be taken.

Structural flood mitigation mechanisms typically place emphasis on physical interventions and investments in engineered infrastructure, such as constructing seawalls, dams, and levees, to reduce flood damages (Parkinson, 2003). Historically, structural flood mitigation mechanisms have been the dominant approach globally to mitigate the physical and economic losses caused by flood events as well as to create a sense of security in high flood risk communities (Birkland et al., 2003). The U.S. Army Corps of Engineers posits that such flood mitigation efforts can prevent billions of dollars in losses, showing a fixed amount of loss prevention of $709 billion from 1928 to 2020 due to structural interventions (Birkland et al., 2003). However, structural flood mitigation mechanisms do not always completely prevent flood damage and can also sometimes even bring adverse effects, particularly with regard to habitat loss. Engineered flood prevention structures built to protect a community can also sometimes result in greater flood disasters in communities outside of protected zones such as along a given river or downstream of the protected community (Birkland et al., 2003). Moreover, the physical presence of

DOI: 10.4324/9781003183419-4

a structural flood protection mechanism can potentially lead to a false sense of security, sometimes promoting excessive amounts of development within flood-prone areas and then increasing stormwater runoff to superfluous proportions. Inappropriate levels of development can significantly degrade the natural environment and increase pollution (Tyler, 2016). Also, if engineered levees fail, the loss of property is oftentimes greater than it would have been if the levee had never been built (Birkland et al., 2003).

Non-structural flood mitigation mechanisms, inversely, focus primarily on nature-based interventions, but can also include social solutions and preventative action such as flood forecasting and warning, emergency response, land use regulations, insurance programs, and subsidies integrated with green infrastructure (Abbas et al., 2015; Parkinson, 2003; Tyler, 2016). Compared to engineered works, implementing non-structural flood mitigation mechanisms is often considered more ecologically sustainable and, like structural mechanisms, can also help lessen flood risks (Tyler, 2016). In the US, the National Flood Insurance Program (NFIP) was implemented to provide insurance to people who live in flood vulnerable regions (Brody et al., 2010). Land use regulations are responsible for discouraging inappropriate land uses (such as intensive commercial, industrial, and residential developments) in the floodplain to reduce impermeable surfaces, thereby reducing the risk of flooding and protecting natural habitats and water quality (Birkland et al., 2003). Increased green space or recreational land uses can also limit the amount of impervious land uses, thereby limiting flood impacts. Subsidies to the NFIP can include holding a referendum to fund disaster reduction plans or acquiring lands that have high flood risk and converting them to open space (e.g. buyouts) (Brody et al., 2010). Non-structural mechanisms also have some imperfections, including rising property values due to restrictions on the development of high flood risk areas (which can result in gentrification), increased maintenance costs, and an inability to fully mitigate infrequent or unprecedented/large events (Petry, 2002).

The global structural and non-structural flood mitigation mechanisms utilized and applied vary across countries, especially with regard to reactions against different issues caused by sea level rise and common flooding. This chapter introduces some of these global differences by examining some of the broad approaches and mechanisms applied by Houston, Texas, New Orleans, Louisiana, Japan, and the Netherlands. Through this discussion we offer a wide glimpse into some of the differing strategies, both structurally and non-structurally. Such strategies are then explored, detailed, and visualized much more thoroughly in subsequent case study chapters later in the book.

Houston

Background

The Houston, Texas landscape is characterized by low topographical relief, large floodplains, and low soil permeability, all of which can contribute to frequent flooding, making Houston one of the most flood-prone cities in the US (Kim & Newman, 2019; Loughran et al., 2019). In addition, with most planning goals targeted primarily on growth and development, provisions for public services, such as parks and sewers, can sometimes be suppressed in Houston (Kim & Newman, 2019; Qian, 2010), undoubtedly exacerbating many existing problems related to or causing flooding. Since 1937, about 30 devastating floods have occurred in Houston (Sebastian et al., 2017) including Tropical Storm Claudette (1979), Tropical Storm Allison (2001), and Hurricane Ike (2008), the Memorial Day Flood (2015), the Tax Day Flood (2016), and Hurricane Harvey (2017) (Holmes et al., 2018; Sebastian et al., 2017).

Approaches to Flood and Sea Level Rise Protection

Due to multiple major floods in the early 20th century, two detention reservoirs, Addicks and Barker located in the upper watershed of Buffalo Bayou, were created as part of a federal project to alleviate flood risk along Buffalo Bayou downstream of the reservoirs and within downtown Houston. The lengths of Addicks and Barker are 11.7 miles and 13.6 miles, respectively (Borenstein & Bajak, 2017; HCFCD, n.d.). These two reservoirs worked well initially, but were encompassed by urbanization in recent decades; approximately 14,000 houses have been developed in close proximity to them, increasing runoff volume into their current storage capacity. Surprisingly, both reservoirs were actually mostly dry prior to Hurricane Harvey, but because the impervious surfaces surrounding them have elevated stormwater runoff amounts to the point where it exceeds the reservoirs' storage limits, the U.S. Army Corps of Engineers had to drain them during Harvey to minimize their risk of collapse. As a result, 5,138 homes were flooded during Harvey (Satija et al., 2017).

Moreover, compared with other US cities, Houston has the least amount of drainage through pipe systems; these current systems can hold only up to 1.5 inches of rain at maximum capacity (Borenstein & Bajak, 2017). The city's detention and drainage infrastructure are also quite old, mostly dating back to the 1940s and 1950s. Due to inadequate drainage systems, some areas, especially those built before 1985, were prone to flooding (see Figure 2.1). It is estimated that more than $650 million is needed each year for the reconstruction and maintenance of the existing drainage infrastructure in Houston (Kathleen, 2018). Further, due to lack of maintenance, silt and debris can accumulate in the system, further reducing its capacity (ASCE, 2012).

Houston has implemented several non-structural mechanisms to assist its existing structural mechanisms in preventing future flood damages. Somewhat due to a lack of zoning, many residential areas have been built in Houston's high flood risk areas. The Home Buyout Program conducted by the Harris County Flood Control District (HCFD) can help such homeowners prevent future flood damages by acquiring developments located in high flood risk areas and demolishing and relocating households from said acquired properties (HCFCD, 2021). Further, the Flood Mitigation Assistance (FMA) Grant Program

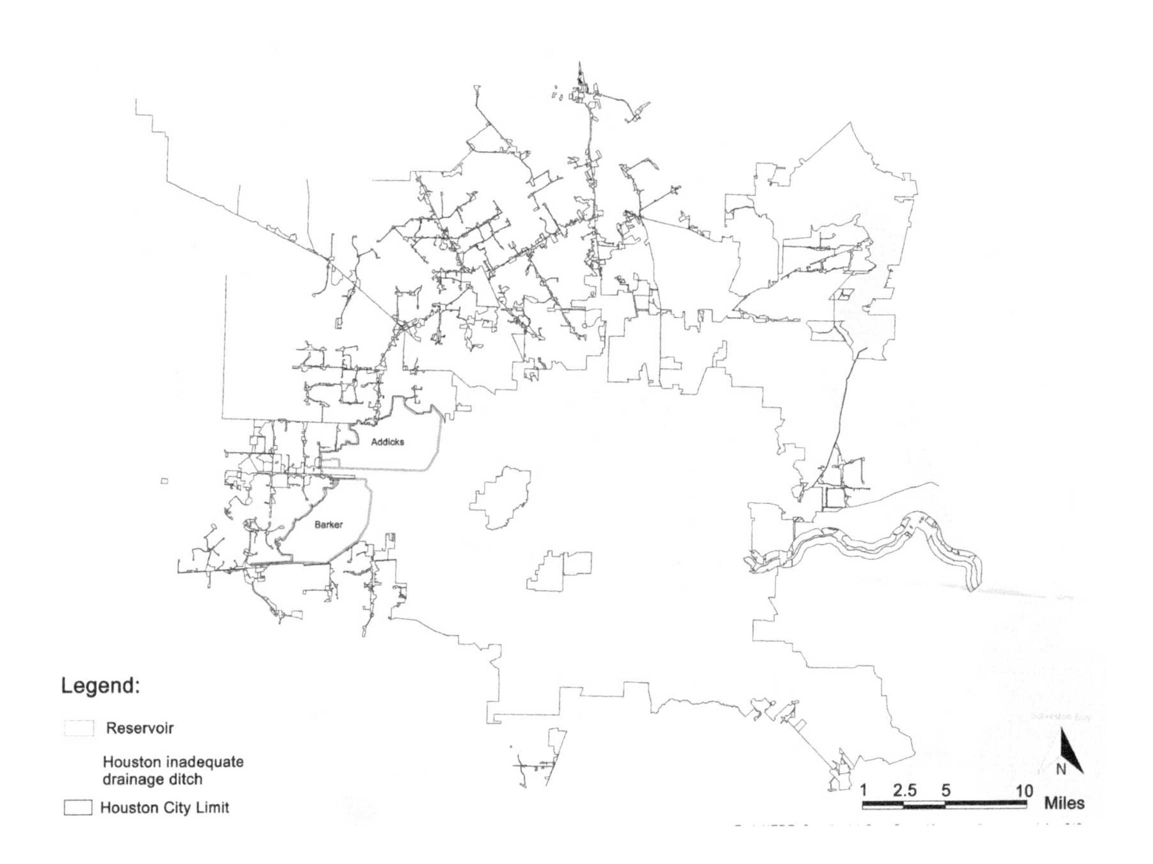

Figure 2.1 Flood reservoirs and inadequate drainage ditches in Houston, TX.

implemented by the Texas Water Development Board (TWDB) and the Federal Emergency Management Agency (FEMA) offer federal funding assistance to reduce the risk of flood damage to buildings insured by the NFIP (City of Houston Disaster Recovery Information, 2020). The City of Houston has also put much effort into developing educational and outreach programs to help residents protect themselves from flooding. The Program of Public Information (PPI) is one such outreach project that seeks to fulfill the City's goal of increasing CRS (Community Rating System) points, thereby providing Houston's NFIP policyholders with additional discounts on their annual flood insurance premiums (City of Houston, 2021a). In addition to the PPI, Flood Insurance Assessment (FIA) and Coverage Improvement Plans (CIPs) can also serve as further outreach methods to improve flood insurance coverage by identifying areas that need coverage improvement (City of Houston, 2021b).

New Orleans

Background

Low geographical elevation, intense precipitation, and the excessive amounts of impervious surfaces in New Orleans, Louisiana help determine the city's rate of flood occurrence and related effects. New Orleans is located within one meter above sea level on the eastern edge of the

Mississippi river deltaic plain and is surrounded by levees, basically creating a shallow bowl which houses the city (Ready for Rain – NOLA Ready, n.d.). Moreover, due to land subsidence, many parts of the city are also sinking (Ready for Rain – NOLA Ready, n.d.). New Orleans is also one of the rainiest cities in the US, thanks to a combination of high Gulf of Mexico-related temperatures and excessive moisture (Cigler, 2007). Compounding these circumstances, category 3–5 hurricanes are more likely to occur on the Gulf Coast than other place in the US, placing New Orleans at high risk for severe hurricanes (Cigler, 2007). In the past decade, New Orleans has experienced several major flood events, including Hurricane Katrina in 2005 (Ready for Rain – NOLA Ready, n.d.). Like most large cities, New Orleans has a significant number of impervious surfaces, such as parking lots, buildings, and streets, resulting in excess rainwater unable to be absorbed into the ground.

Approaches to Flood and Sea Level Rise Protection

Levees, floodwalls, pumps, and canals are the primary structural storm and flood damage reduction mechanisms used in New Orleans (see Figure 2.2). Levees and floodwalls were designed to protect coastal storms and flooding threats, while pumps and canals were built to deal with urban waterlogging. Federal projects, such as Lake Pontchartrain, the Vicinity Hurricane Protection Project, the West Bank, and the Southeast Louisiana Urban Flood Control Project are primarily responsible for the construction of much of the structural infrastructure in New Orleans (Carter, 2005). Two levee systems in New Orleans, the East Bank System, and the West Bank System occupy a total of 192

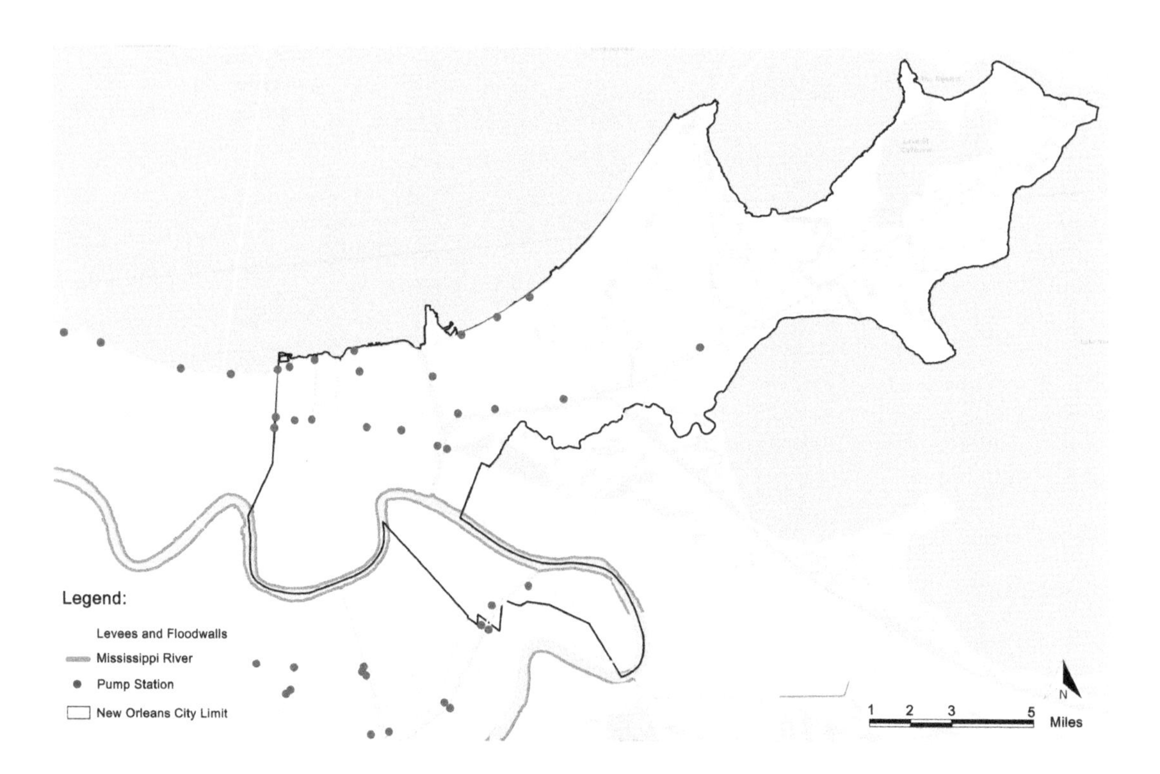

Figure 2.2 Structural mechanisms in New Orleans including levees, floodwalls, and pump stations.

miles of levees and 99 miles of floodwalls. While artificial levees and floodwalls help keep out rising rivers, they can also result in adverse effects if they fail or collapse (McFall-Johnsen, 2019). For example, in 2005, the New Orleans coastal levee collapsed and many pumps also stopped working during Hurricane Katrina. It is estimated that the total interior flooding during Hurricane Katrina was nearly 105,000 acre-ft, of which 21% was from rainfall, 66% from the broken levee, and 13% from overtopping and failure of pumps (Sills et al., 2008). The busted levees released vast amounts of water, resulting in approximately 1,000 deaths and leading to a $15 billion investment to repair the levee system around New Orleans (McFall-Johnsen, 2019).

After Hurricanes Katrina and Rita impacted New Orleans, the Coastal Protection and Restoration Authority (CPRA) was established by the state Legislature to protect the coastal population and environment. In 2007, the CPRA released Louisiana's Coastal Master Plan to supplement the structural flood mitigation mechanisms. This plan is updated every five years, and its latest update was completed in 2017. The 2017 Coastal Master Plan emphasizes the integration of environmental, social, and economic factors to reduce losses caused by disasters (State of Louisiana, 2017). One of the important programs of CPRA is the Flood Risk and Resilience Program. This program targets the implementation of non-structural policies such as conducting a detailed coastal flood risk vulnerability analysis, defining non-structural project areas, determining project priorities, promoting project implementation, and raising public awareness to reduce future floods. Fifty-four candidate non-structural project areas were identified through the Flood Risk and Resilience Program, including many in the City of New Orleans (Coastal Protection and Restoration Authority, 2017). There are three main types of non-structural risk reduction projects in the Flood Risk and Resilience Plan: flood prevention, ground level elevation, and voluntary acquisition of high-risk properties. Further, the New Orleans Hazard Mitigation Plan is based on the Disaster Mitigation Act of 2000 and establishes a strategy to understand and reduce the risks and vulnerabilities of the city. Various stakeholders, such as non-profit organizations, community organizations, environmental groups and regional government agencies are included in the plan. Like the Coastal Master Plan, the Hazard Mitigation Plan is also updated every five years.

Japan

Background

The steep and volcanic mountains covering most of the land in Japan make its landmass largely geographically unstable. Simultaneously, Japan is frequently confronted with seasonal rain and typhoons (Takeuchi, 2002). In the summer, precipitation in the Pacific coastal areas can be immense, often comprising more than half of its annual rainfall amounts (Ikeda et al., 2005). In the winter, coastal areas around the Sea of Japan also face extreme snow due to the northwestern winds (Takeuchi, 2002). These circumstances, combined with climate change, have created a situation where the rivers in Japan are quickly rising, showing significant differences in water volume throughout the year and massive fluctuations in sediment transport (Takeuchi, 2002). Demographically, about half of the national population and three-fourths of national assets are located on the 10% of the nation's land in alluvial plains (Takeuchi, 2001). This concentration of population and assets in high flood risk zones causes many homes and offices to be exposed to potential devastating losses, if flooded. Rapid urbanization within the last decades also aggregates challenges of flood mitigation in Japan (Fan & Huang, 2020).

Approaches to Flood and Sea Level Rise Protection

Many river relocation projects have been undertaken to mitigate flooding and sea level rise in Japan. For instance, the Ara River Floodway project, which begun after the great flood of 1910, was implemented to help protect downtown Tokyo from flood events. This project included a 13.67 mile long and 1,640 ft wide constructed floodway, which was completed in 1930. In addition, super levees (see Figure 2.3), which are high standard embankments with 300 m to 500 m in width, have been implemented adjacent to six rivers running through metropolitan areas such as Tokyo and Osaka (Takeuchi, 2002). These super levees were built to minimize the damage from extreme floods and sea level rise and have shown optimal performance for attenuating water overtopping, water seepage, and stability from being harmed by earthquakes (Zhang et al., 2021). Multiple features are included in the Super Levees Construction Project such as no need of land acquisition, efficient utilization of land, integration with urban planning goals, providing green space for communities, and providing higher elevation evacuation areas for flood impacted neighborhoods (Takeuchi, 2002; Nakamura et al., 2020).

To strengthen flood mitigation capabilities in metropolitan areas where it can be difficult to widen rivers or build new discharge channels, underground control reservoirs have also been implemented (Takeuchi, 2002). After the disastrous event of the 2011 tsunami in Fukushima, Japan updated its laws and engineering guidelines for flood mitigation structures, requiring sea defense structure design to recognize return periods, protect from lower-level hazard events, and provide a degree of protection for high-level hazard events (Raby et al., 2015). In addition, the 2015 Flood Control Act promoted evacuation and use of underground space such as underground malls to be implemented with mechanisms such as flood stops and other facilities (Niira et al., 2016). Since Japan has a long history of combating floods and earthquakes, many Japanese traditional architectural structures are already equipped with flood and shake resistant elements (Okubo, 2016).

To raise public awareness and inform urban planning guidelines, flood hazard maps were created with anticipated inundation zones to advance preparation and reduce future damage (Takeuchi, 2002; Nakamura & Llasat, 2017). A river information system has also been developed and linked to high speed and capacity networks, sensors, and

Figure 2.3 A conceptualization of a super levee built in Tokyo, Japan.

Geographic Information Systems coordinates to monitor and gather data for advancing land use planning and constructing flood information networks (Takeuchi, 2002). Policy-wise, to mitigate the increasingly frequent occurrence of floods, Japan has developed several flood mitigation acts and laws. Comprehensive Flood Risk Management Measures (CFRMMs), aimed to improve river flood control works and manage urban runoff, were developed in 1980 (Fan & Huang, 2020). To increase cooperation between different governmental agencies, the government enacted the Act on Countermeasures Against Flood Damage of Specified Rivers Running across Cities. In addition, it promoted cooperation between the public and private sectors (Fan & Huang, 2020). In 2018, the Act on Special Measures concerning Urban Reconstruction permitted local governments' the right to designate disaster vulnerable areas and prohibit residential construction in disaster risk zones (Fan & Huang, 2020). Finally, green infrastructure also contributes to the flood mitigation portfolio (as in the super levees) and functions to maintain a healthy ecosystem and provide recreational spaces for local residents (Nakamura et al. 2020).

The Netherlands

Background

The Netherlands houses the deltas of the Rhine, Meuse, and Scheldt rivers as well as the North Sea. It has a mostly below sea level elevation and an extremely flat topography, with one-third of the land below sea level and half of the land below or less than 1 meter above sea level. Other than threats from sea level rise, periodic sea flooding has also disturbed the Netherlands for centuries. Further, research suggests that annual flood risk could intensify up to 185% by 2030, compared to 2000, due to land use and climate changes (Poussin et al., 2012). In addition, the Netherlands is a densely populated country. More than 10 million people as well as a multitude of large industries which account for 70% of the total GDP are located in heavily flood-prone area (Vis et al., 2003).

Due to its historical battle with floods, the Netherlands has a tradition of water management, which includes strict safety standards, dedicated forms of governance (including taxation), regular safety assessments, and sound, advanced engineering. Flood prone areas are safeguarded from flooding by approximately 3,800 kilometers of flood protection structures. About 90% of these structures are managed by regional water authorities; the remaining structures are managed by the national water authority (Rijkswaterstaat, part of the Ministry of Infrastructure and Environment) (Jorissen & Kraaij, 2016).

Approaches to Flood and Sea Level Rise Protection

The major large-scale flood protection structures in the Netherlands are found along its large-scale rivers, lakes, estuaries, and the coast. The most extensive flood protection structures are the country's renowned dikes. The total length of the dikes exceeds 22,500 kilometers and they are supplemented by large-scale sluice and sector gates. Besides the traditional structural mechanisms (such as the dikes), the Netherlands also utilizes dunes and small-scaled green infrastructure facilities to add natural protection to coastal areas from flooding.

The most iconic and well-known structural flood protection projects in the Netherlands are the Zuiderzee Works and the Delta Works (Deltawerken). The Zuiderzee Works are a system of water drainage infrastructure, land reclamation, and dams triggered by the floods of 1916. They began from a large shallow inlet of the North Sea known as the Zuiderzee. This project reclaimed 220,000 hectares of land, 120,000 hectares of fresh water reservoir, and shortened the coastline by 300 km. The Afsluitdijh dam, built in 1932–33, separated the Zuiderzee from the North Sea (Bergsma, 2019; VanKoningsveld et al., 2008). Delta Works also constructed a series of dams, storm surge barriers, locks, dikes, levees, and sluices from 1954 to 1997 in the provinces of South Holland and Zeeland to shorten the coastline. The project protects a large area around the Rhine-Meuse-Scheldt delta from coastal flood events (VanKoningsveld et al. 2008).

As the coastline in the Netherlands began to retreat due to erosion and sea level rise, sand nourishments have since been used to maintain foreshores, create dunes for flood protection, and increase local ecosystem services (Stronkhorst et al., 2018). The Sand Engine (see Figure 2.4), or the Sand Motor, is an experimental project which utilizes concentrated mega-nourishments along coastal Holland (Van Slobbe et al., 2013). It uses coastal currents to deposit sediment along the shoreline naturally, as sediment is provided from other locations. The Sand Engine is expected to be a more efficient, economical, and ecological alternative for beach nourishment and elongation compared to the traditional shoreface nourishments (Stive et al., 2013).

Since flood risk and flood intensity are increasing, traditional strategies against flood control require endless improvements. As a result, the concept of promoting how to "live with floods" rather than "fight the flooding," has been adopted by the Netherlands. Compartmentalized water detention and green infrastructure are the county's most elaborate local strategies, interacting with the larger-scaled dikes and dams (Vis et al., 2003). Detention in compartments reduces the limit of flooded areas and minimizes flood damage by dividing large areas surrounded by dikes and providing temporary water storage. Polders are subdivided into cells in order to prevent flooding to an entire land surface (Egli, 2002). Green river edges and living shorelines act as floodwater discharge compartments in normally high-risk flood zones, decreasing economic loss when flooded. Such riverine edges

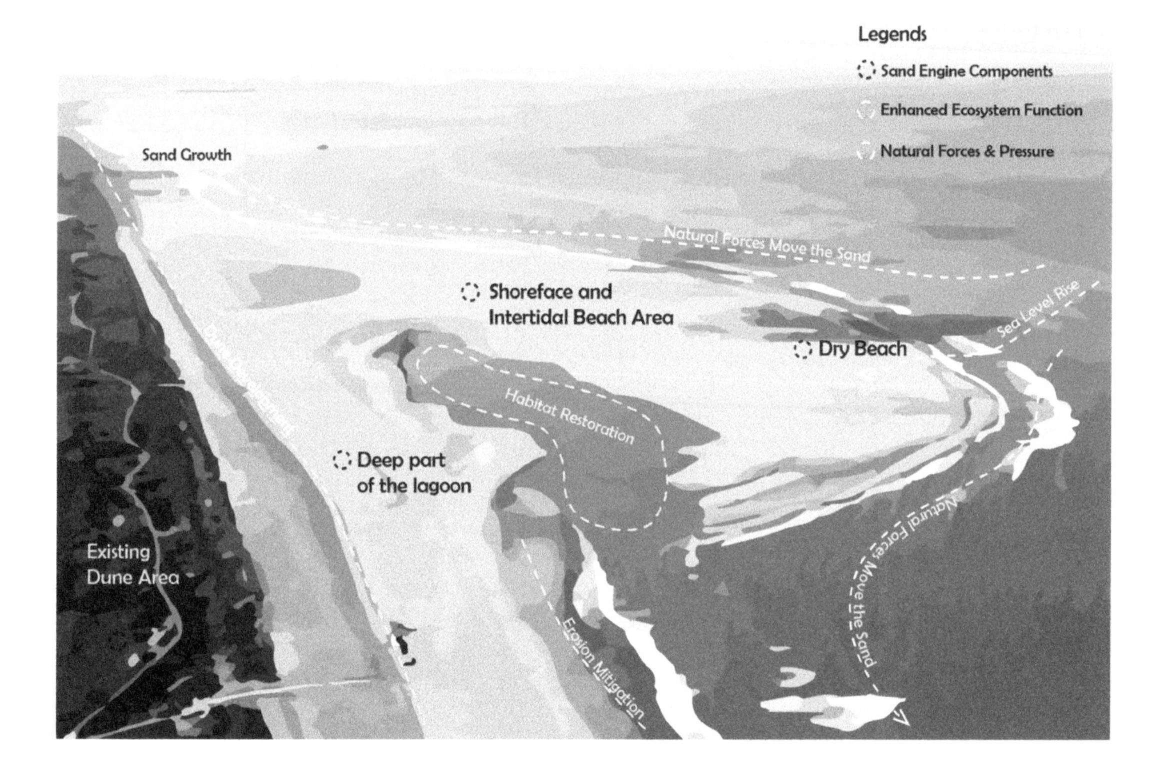

Figure 2.4 Composition and ecological benefits of the Sand Engine.

also improve discharge capacity and reduce peak flow of stormwater (Vis et al., 2003). Emergency spillways are also part of the Netherland's approach to living with floods, but are only reserved for emergency situations such as extreme flood events (Egli, 2002).

Conclusion

Flood risk management worldwide is not static, but is constantly in a state of flux. To counteract this conundrum, there is a growing trend towards more integrated flood risk management. The primary differences in mitigation approaches are a direct result of the initial situations faced by each individual region or locality. The pace and direction of change also varies across countries. While this chapter presented a series of flood mitigation portfolios across four different locations, it also explained why these places opted for their different flood risk management approaches. Each framework presented tended to utilize insights from a range of policy science while also considering other factors such as geographical characteristics, historical experiences with flood disasters, and social/behavioral aspects.

References

Abbas, A., Amjath-Babu, T. S., Kächele, H., & Müller, K. (2015). Non-structural flood risk mitigation under developing country conditions: An analysis on the determinants of willingness to pay for flood insurance in rural Pakistan. *Natural Hazards*, *75*(3), 2119–2135. https://doi.org/10.1007/s11069-014-1415-x

ASCE. (2012). *2012 Report Card for Houston Area Infrastructure*. Retrieved from www.hcfcd.org/About/Flooding-and-Floodplains/Drainage-Network

Atkinson, J., McKee Smith, J., & Bender, C. (2013). Sea-level rise effects on storm surge and nearshore waves on the Texas coast: Influence of landscape and storm characteristics. *Journal of Waterway, Port, Coastal, and Ocean Engineering*, *139*(2), 98–117. https://doi.org/10.1061/(ASCE)WW.1943-5460.0000187

Bergsma, E. (2019). *From flood safety to spatial management: Expert–policy interactions in Dutch and US flood governance*. Berlin: Springer.

Birkland, T. A., Burby, R. J., Conrad, D., Cortner, H., & Michener, W. K. (2003). River ecology and flood hazard mitigation. *Natural Hazards Review*, *4*(1), 46–54. https://doi.org/10.1061/(ASCE)1527-6988(2003)4:1(46)

Borenstein, S., & Bajak, F. (2017). Houston drainage grid "so obsolete it's just unbelievable." *Chicago Tribune*. Retrieved from www.chicagotribune.com/nation-world/ct-houston-drainage-grid-obsolete-20170829-story.html

Brody, S. D., Kang, J. E., & Bernhardt, S. (2010). Identifying factors influencing flood mitigation at the local level in Texas and Florida: The role of organizational capacity. *Natural Hazards*, *52*(1), 167–184. https://doi.org/10.1007/s11069-009-9364-5

Carter, N. T. (2005). *New Orleans levees and floodwalls: Hurricane damage protection*. CRS Report for Congress, Order Code RS2238. Retrieved from https://sgp.fas.org/crs/misc/RS22238.pdf

Cigler, B. A. (2007). The "big questions" of Katrina and the 2005 Great Flood of New Orleans. *Public Administration Review*, *67*(s1), 64–76. https://doi.org/10.1111/j.1540-6210.2007.00814.x

City of Houston. (2021a). *City of Houston, Texas, Community Rating System (CRS) Program for Public Information (PPI)*. Retrieved from www.houstonpermittingcenter.org/office-city-engineer/floodplain-management-office

City of Houston. (2021b). *Houston Flood Insurance Assessment (FIA) and Coverage Improvement Plan (CP) Narrative Summary for Level of Coverage*. Retrieved from https://crsresources.org/files/300/preparing_a_flood_insurance_assessment.pdf

City of Houston Disaster Recovery Information. (2020). *Flood risk reduction*. HoustonRecovers.Org. Retrieved from https://houstonrecovers.org/risk reduction/

Coastal Protection and Restoration Authority. (2017). 2017 Coastal Master Plan Attachment E3: Nonstructural Model Results. Retrieved from http://coastal.la.gov/wp-content/uploads/2017/04/Attachment-E3_FINAL_04.24.2017.pdf

CXA- Arquitectura E Engenharia Ltda, & Fag, A. (2018). Flood control and its management. *Journal of Atmospheric & Earth Science*, *2*(1), 1–13. https://doi.org/10.24966/AES-8780/100005

Egli, T. (2002). *Non structural flood plain management: Measures and their effectiveness*. Sankt Augustin, Germany: International Commission for the Protection of the Rhine (ICPR).

Fan, J., and Huang, G. (2020). Evaluation of flood risk management in Japan through a recent case. *Sustainability*, *12*(13), 5357.

Filho, A. C. D. P., & Pina, A. C. D. (2010). *Methods and techniques in urban engineering*. Books on Demand (BoD). London: Intechopen.

HCFCD. (n.d.). *Flooding impacts in connection with the reservoirs*. Retrieved February 20, 2021, from www.hcfcd.org/About/Harris-Countys-Flooding-History/Hurricane-Harvey/Countywide-Impacts/Flooding-Impacts-in-Connection-with-the-Reservoirs

HCFCD. (2021). *Home buyout program*. Retrieved from www.hcfcd.org/Activity/Additional-Programs/Home-Buyout-Program

Holmes, C., Shao, M., Zhao, G., & Gao, H. (2018). Evaluating the impacts of urbanization on hydrological processes that contribute to flooding in Brays Bayou, Houston, Texas. *AGU Fall Meeting Abstracts*, *33*. http://adsabs.harvard.edu/abs/2018AGUFM.H33S2313H

Ikeda, T., Yoshitani, J., & Terakawa, A. (2005). Flood management under climatic variability and its future perspective in Japan. *Water Science and Technology*, *51*(5), 133–140.

Jorissen, R., & Kraaij, E. (2016). *Dutch flood protection policy and measures based on risk assessment*. E3S Web of Conferences, EDP Sciences. Retrieved from www.e3s-conferences.org/articles/e3sconf/pdf/2016/02/e3sconf_flood 2016_20016.pdf

Kathleen, M. (2018). *Post-Harvey policy landscape*. Retrieved from www.lincolninst.edu/sites/default/files/pubfiles/houston-post-harvey-lla180404.pdf

Kim, Y., & Newman, G. (2019). Climate change preparedness: comparing future urban growth and flood risk in Amsterdam and Houston. *Sustainability*, *11*(4), 1048. https://doi.org/10.3390/su11041048

Loughran, K., Elliott, J. R., & Kennedy, S. W. (2019). Urban ecology in the time of climate change: Houston, flooding, and the case of federal buyouts. *Social Currents*, *6*(2), 121–140. https://doi.org/10.1177/2329496518797851

McFall-Johnsen, M. (2019). Hurricane Barry could breach New Orleans' river levees. Here's how the levee system works and how much it can withstand. *Business Insider*. Retrieved from www.businessinsider.com/tropical-storm-barry-heres-how-new-orleans-river-levees-work-2019-7

Nakamura, F., Ishiyama, N., Yamanaka, S., Higa, M., Akasaka, T., Kobayashi, Y., Ono, S., Fuke, N., Kitazawa, M., Morimoto, J., & Shoji, Y. (2020). Adaptation to climate change and conservation of biodiversity using green infrastructure. *River Research and Applications*, *36*(6), 921–933.

Nakamura, I., & Llasat, M. C. (2017). Policy and systems of flood risk management: A comparative study between Japan and Spain. *Natural Hazards*, *87*(2), 919–943.

Niira, K., Shigeno, K., Kikuchi, M., & Inoue, T. (2016). Disaster-prevention measures for underground space to deal with large-scale earthquakes and intensified flood disasters in Japan. *Procedia Engineering*, *165*, 224–232.

Okubo, T. (2016). Traditional wisdom for disaster mitigation in history of Japanese architectures and historic cities. *Journal of Cultural Heritage*, *20*, 715–724.

Parkinson, J. (2003). Drainage and stormwater management strategies for low-income urban communities. *Environment and Urbanization*, *15*(2), 115–126. https://doi.org/10.1177/095624780301500203

Petry, B. (2002). Keynote lecture: Coping with floods: Complementarity of structural and non-structural measures. *Flood Defense*, 60–70.

Poussin, J., Bubeck, P., Aerts, J. C. J. H., & Ward, P. J. (2012). Potential of semi-structural and non-structural adaptation strategies to reduce future flood risk: Case study for the Meuse. *Natural Hazards and Earth System Sciences*, *12*(11), 3455–3471.

Qian, Z. (2010). Without zoning: Urban development and land use controls in Houston. *Cities*, *27*(1), 31–41. https://doi.org/10.1016/j.cities.2009.11.006

Raby, A., Macabuag, J., Pomonis, A., Wilkinson, S., & Rossetto, T. (2015). Implications of the 2011 Great East Japan Tsunami on sea defense design. *International Journal of Disaster Risk Reduction*, *14*, 332–346.

Ready for Rain – NOLA Ready. (n.d.). Retrieved February 18, 2021, from https://ready.nola.gov/rain/

Reja, M. Y., Brody, S. D., Highfield, W. E., & Newman, G. D. (2017). Hurricane recovery and ecological resilience: Measuring the impacts of wetland alteration post Hurricane Ike on the upper TX coast. *Environmental Management*, *60*(6), 1116–1126. https://doi.org/10.1007/s00267-017-0943-z

Satija, N., Tribune, T. T., Reveal, Collier, K., Tribune, T. T., & Shaw, A. (2017). Everyone knew Houston's reservoirs would flood – except for the people who bought homes inside them. *ProPublica*. Retrieved from https://projects.propublica.org/graphics/harvey-reservoirs

Sebastian, A., Lendering, K. T., Kothuis, B. L. M., Brand, A. D., Jonkman, S. N., van Gelder, P. H. a. J. M., Godfroij, M., Kolen, B., Comes, M., Lhermitte, S. L. M., Meesters, K., van de Walle, B. A., Ebrahimi Fard, A., Cunningham, S., Khakzad, N., & Nespeca, V. (2017). *Hurricane Harvey Report: A fact-finding effort in the direct aftermath of Hurricane Harvey in the Greater Houston Region*. Retrieved from https://repository.tudelft.nl/islandora/object/uuid%3A54c24519-c366-4f2f-a3b9-0807db26f69c

Sills, G. L., Vroman, N. D., Wahl, R. E., & Schwanz, N. T. (2008). Overview of New Orleans levee failures: lessons learned and their impact on national levee design and assessment. *Journal of Geotechnical and Geoenvironmental Engineering*, *134*(5), 556–565. https://doi.org/10.1061/(ASCE)1090-0241(2008)134:5(556)

State of Louisiana. (2017). *Louisiana's comprehensive master plan for a sustainable coast – effective June 2, 2017*. 184. Retrieved from http://coastal.la.gov/wp-content/uploads/2017/04/2017-Coastal-Master-Plan_Web-Book_CFinal-with-Effective-Date-06092017.pdf

Stive, M. J., De Schipper, M. A., Luijendijk, A. P., Aarninkhof, S. G. J., van Gelder-Maas, C., Van Thiel de Vries, J. S. M., De Vries, S., Henriquez, M., Marx, S., & Ranasinghe, R. (2013). A new alternative to saving our beaches from sea-level rise: The sand engine. *Journal of Coastal Research*, 29(5), 1001–1008.

Stronkhorst, J., Huisman, B., Giardini, A., Santinelli, G., & Duarte Santos, F. (2018). Sand nourishment strategies to mitigate coastal erosion and sea level rise at the coasts of Holland (The Netherlands) and Aveiro (Portugal) in the 21st century. *Ocean & Coastal Management*, *156*, 266–276.

Takeuchi, K. (2001). Increasing vulnerability to extreme floods and societal needs of hydrological forecasting. *Hydrological Sciences Journal*, *46*(6), 869–881.

Takeuchi, K. (2002). Flood management in Japan – from rivers to basins. *Water International*, *27*(1), 20–26.

Tyler, J. (2016). Sustainable hazard mitigation: Exploring the importance of green infrastructure in building disaster resilient communities. *Consilience*, 15(1), 134–145. https://doi.org/10.7916/D8HD7VG3

Van Slobbe, E., de Vriend, H. J., Aarninkhof, S., Lulofs, K., de Vries, M., & Dircke, P. et al. (2013). Building with nature: In search of resilient storm surge protection strategies. *Natural Hazards*, *66*(3), 1461–1480.

VanKoningsveld, M., Mulder, J. P., Stive, M. J., Van Der Valk, L., & Van Der Weck, A. W. (2008). Living with sea-level rise and climate change: A case study of the Netherlands. *Journal of Coastal Research*, *24*(2), 367–379.

Vis, M., Klijn, F., de Bruijn, K. M., & Van Buuren, M. (2003). Resilience strategies for flood risk management in the Netherlands. *International Journal of River Basin Management*, *1*(1): 33–40.

Zhang, Y., Shen, Z., & Lin, Y. (2021). *The construction of water-sensitive urban design in the context of Japan*. IOP Conference Series: Earth and Environmental Science, IOP Publishing.

Part 2

Global Design for Sea Level Rise

Structural Heavy Design

3

JEFFERSON PARISH, NEW ORLEANS REGION, LOUISIANA

Traci Birch and Haley Blakeman

Site: Jefferson Parish, Louisiana: 23.5 acres

Introduction/Rationale

Climate change poses significant risks to both coastal and inland communities. This is particularly true in Louisiana, where coastal processes continue to move inland toward heavily populated areas. The State has lost approximately 1,900 square miles of coastal wetlands since 1930, and another 1,750 square miles are at risk over the next 50 years (Couvillion et al., 2017). Coastal Louisiana is a relatively young landscape which was built over the last 5,000 years through regular Mississippi River floods which left rich sediment behind as the waters receded (Keddy et al., 2007). Land loss in the region is a result of several complex factors, but the primary related issues include the construction of levees separating the delta from the Mississippi River, hydrologic alteration from oil and gas exploration, and accelerating eustatic sea level rise (Day et al., 2007). Episodic events, like hurricanes, drastically affect coastal wetland loss, further exacerbating the area's vulnerability to sea level rise. New Orleans is often considered a harbinger for climate flood risk in the US. In fact, many scientists view the region as both a predictor of coastal ecosystem stress worldwide (Kent, 2012; Wang et al., 2011), and a laboratory for coastal restoration and climate adaptation efforts (Birch & Carney, 2019; Gotham & Faust, 2019).

Prior to Hurricanes Katrina and Rita, Louisiana's coastal planning and restoration was conducted with a typical divided governance model, with natural resources being managed across multiple state agencies. Further, coastal resource management happened separately from flood and hurricane protection (Colten, 2017). After 2005, the State (a) consolidated coastal management under the Coastal Protection and Restoration Authority (CPRA), and (b) adopted a "multiple lines of defense" (MLOD) strategy employing natural and man-made landscape features (lines of defense) to directly impede storm surge or reduce storm damage (Lopez, 2009). MLOD recognized the decades-old "levees-only" strategy did not provide adequate flood protection. The following case study outlines how the Lake Pontchartrain shoreline in Jefferson Parish is being redesigned to adopt MLOD.

DOI: 10.4324/9781003183419-6

Study Area

Jefferson is the most populous parish (or county) in metropolitan New Orleans, which, as a whole, contains more than a quarter of Louisiana's population. The Parish is bordered to the north by Lake Pontchartrain (a brackish estuary), the Gulf of Mexico to the south, and bisected by the Mississippi River. Flooding may occur during any season of the year from rainfall ponding in low lying areas or levee overtopping due to hurricane storm surge. Regional levee protection systems take two distinct forms: protection against river flooding and protection against storm surge. The Parish is drained by a system of man-made canals that outflow to pumping stations. This system has historically been inadequate in capacity to handle floodwater volume and has often operated below capacity during storms (Waggonner & Ball, 2013). As a result, Jefferson Parish has over 5,500 National Flood Insurance Program repetitive loss structures, which, along with Orleans, puts it at the top of the list for repetitive losses in the country (FEMA, 2021).

In 2010, Louisiana's Office of Community Development funded a range of resilience planning processes. The largest of these was the Greater New Orleans Water Plan (2013), which addressed issues of regional infrastructure, storm and groundwater management. The effort, led by Waggonner & Ball Architects, engaged local and international designers and water management experts to develop a framework for integrating natural processes with mechanical systems to enhance water storage, natural habitats, and community resilience (ibid.). This process spurred a re-evaluation of regional water management and flood protection systems. Within Jefferson Parish, the lakefront shoreline was of particular concern due to high rates of relative sea level rise, lack of MLOD along the northern boundary, and a desire to reconnect residents to the lake. In 2018, the Parish completed an ambitious lakefront renewal plan with the overarching goal of using restored marsh and bio-engineered features to increase levee system resilience and community protections. Beginning with Bucktown Harbor, Parish staff, urban and environmental planners, and the community collaboratively developed a 23.5-acre vision for living shorelines and marina facilities outside the hurricane protection levee (see Figures 3.3 and 3.4) (Jefferson Parish, 2018). Upon completion, this will be one of the largest living shoreline projects in the US. In partnership with CPRA, the Louisiana Department of Natural Resources, the U.S. Army Corps of Engineers (USACE), and other state and federal agencies, Jefferson Parish's long-term goal is to extend living shorelines from Bucktown Harbor to the western extent of the Parish, a total of nearly 10 miles of protected lakefront (ibid.).

Sea Level Rise Projections

Southeast Louisiana (where the New Orleans metropolitan region is located) has an average elevation of 3 feet above sea level and has long been considered one of the landscapes most threatened by climate change. Much like other deltaic systems, the city's land is sinking faster than waters are rising. Historically, settlements developed

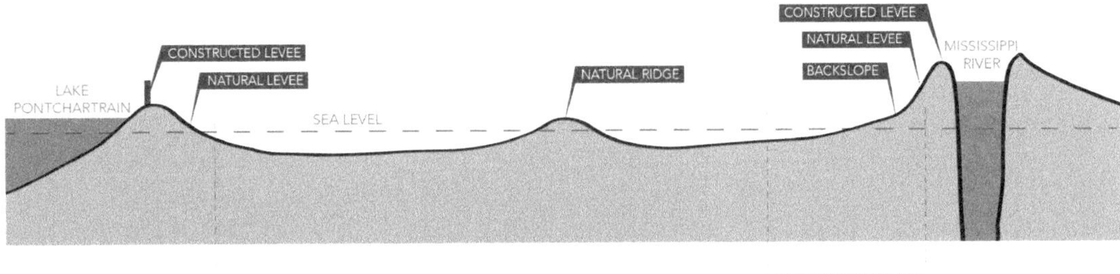

Figure 3.1 Section of metropolitan New Orleans showing levees, Mississippi River, and bowl-like depression.

along natural ridges formed as the Mississippi River meandered and receded across the landscape. As New Orleans' population grew, levees were constructed, and swamps and marshes were drained to make room for development. Dredged peat and mud were used to elevate the region for habitation, and a canal and pump system was implemented to reduce flooding. This combination of weak organic soils and hydrologic disruption resulted in persistent regional subsidence (Kolker et al., 2011), particularly within the levee protection system. This subsidence, estimated at between 0.59 and 0.73 inches/year (Tornqvist et al., 2020), combined with a slow rise in sea level (about one foot/century) has caused much of the area to drop 10 or more feet relative to sea level, creating a bowl-like depression in the center. Sea level in this area is projected to rise 1.8–3.5 inches by 2073 and 3.0–6.2 inches by 2100 (CPRA, 2017) (Figure 3.1).

Examples of Previous Floods and Damage Caused

Since 1855, 70 hurricanes have made landfall within 65-miles of metropolitan New Orleans (USACE, 2019). Nine of these storms caused storm surge flooding within the Lake Pontchartrain basin (ibid.). Despite contradictions in the research (e.g. Bengtsson et al., 2007; Dailey et al., 2008; Emanuel, 2013), most experts project that the Gulf of Mexico tropical storm frequencies will remain essentially unchanged or slightly decrease by 2100. Although tropical storms may become fewer, the frequency of major hurricanes (Category 3–5) with more intense wind speed, rainfall, and storm surge is expected to increase.

The levees protecting metropolitan New Orleans were not built to prevent flooding during the most severe hurricanes, but rather during a standard project hurricane equivalent to a Category 2 on the Saffir-Simpson Scale. It was a well-known fact that a severe hurricane could lead to overtopping or breaching of the levees. In Jefferson Parish, Katrina's storm surge overtopped the 15' hurricane protection levees by several feet causing significant flooding along the northern portion of the Parish (ibid.). An estimated 30,000 homes flooded as a result. The following project(s) will not prevent levee overtopping during severe storms. However, it will provide additional protection to levee foundations to reduce the risk of catastrophic failure and can prevent or reduce overtopping during less severe events.

Design Synopsis

Structural and Non-Structural Mechanisms

Lake Pontchartrain's southern shoreline is fortified with clay core levees, foreshore protection, t-wall levees, and pump stations. The Bucktown Harbor Vision Plan, and subsequent feasibility studies, recommended and developed a series of structural and non-structural measures to protect the levees and pump stations, so they work together as MLOD to reduce flooding (see Table 3.1). Structural interventions include 1.2 miles of 2.0′–3.5′-high offshore segmented curvilinear breakwaters used for wave attenuation (see Figure 3.2). These are aligned to the 5-to-6-ft contours (approximately 150 to 350 ft offshore) and are composed of a combination of recycled concrete and quarry-run materials (M&N, 2020a). Non-structural measures include 23+ acres of intertidal marsh on the leeward side of the breakwaters, constructed using offshore dredged material. Proposed marsh includes scrub–shrub habitat (1.5 acres), intertidal marsh (22 acres), and tidal creeks, all of which will further protect the shoreline, reduce tropical weather impacts, provide recreational amenities, and enhance ecosystem services such as water filtration and wildlife habitat. Upon completion, the 1.2-mile living shoreline will be one of the largest projects of its kind in the US (ibid.). The site increases lakefront access by incorporating a 20-ft-wide protected blueway for kayaks, kayak launch, improved marina facilities, public open space, educational boardwalk, and a multi-purpose pavilion.

Table 3.1 Bucktown Harbor structural and non-structural mechanisms

Program elements	*Structural*	*Non-structural*	*Hybrid*
Clay core levee	X		
T-wall levee	X		
Floodgate	X		
Pump station	X		
Dredged areas		X	
Constructed wetlands		X	
Edging			X
Segmented breakwaters			X

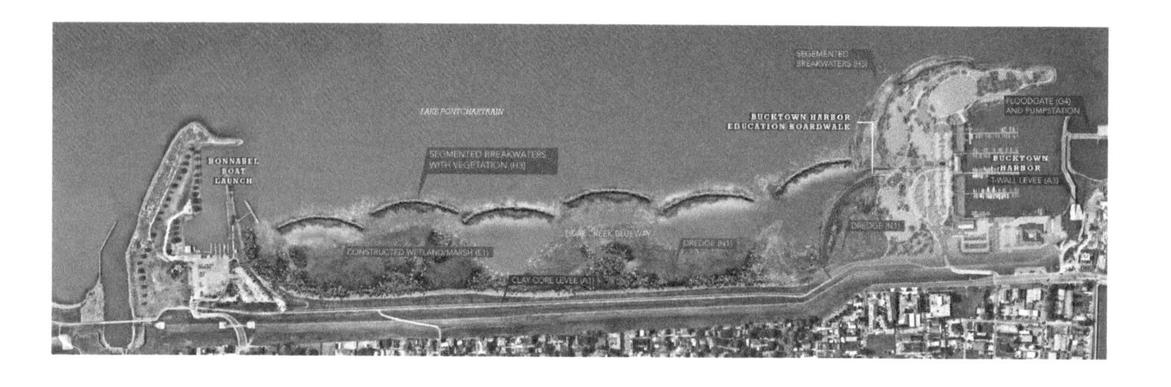

Figure 3.2 Bucktown Harbor structural and non-structural mechanisms.
Source: Moffitt & Nichol, 2020a.

Design Impact

The south shore of Lake Pontchartrain was primarily estuarine marsh and forested wetland prior to the formation of the levee system. Following Hurricane Katrina, the USACE recommended system upgrades as part of the Lake Pontchartrain and Vicinity Project. Today, the Eastbank of Jefferson Parish is completely surrounded by levees and floodwalls (L. Avrill, personal interview, 2/17/2021). Upgrades included reconstructed clay core and T-wall levees, protective segmented breakwaters, new floodgates, and foreshore riprap protection at levee toes (USACE, 2019). What was lost were the few remaining naturalized shorelines supporting ecosystem services such as fisheries habitat, water filtration, wave attenuation, and reduced erosion. Subsequent embrace of MLOD has prioritized projects like the Bucktown Living Shoreline to provide multiple benefits and enhanced protection to coastal residents and systems (Hillman et al., 2019; Temmerman & Kirwan, 2015).

Daily wave action and storm surge are erosive and leave adjacent levees, coastal communities, and supporting infrastructure vulnerable. Marsh vegetation has been shown to have a significant positive effect on wave attenuation and shoreline stabilization (Shepard et al., 2011). Fifteen feet of healthy marsh acts as a natural barrier, absorbing 50% of incoming wave energy (NOAA, 2021). Living shorelines also trap sediments from tidal waters, allowing them to accrete as sea levels rise (ibid.). The Bucktown Living Shoreline will provide MLOD against Lake Pontchartrain wave activity and delineate between open water and the hurricane protection levee. Protective breakwaters provide the first barrier from waves eroding or degrading the marsh. The wetland behind the breakwater protection provides a second buffer to the storm energy, further reducing its strength. The levee acts as the third barrier against storm surge flooding. This investment increases levee system resilience, directly protecting 1,350 homes, critical infrastructure, and evacuation routes in the Bucktown neighborhood (M&N, 2020a). Additional levee fortification increases protection of over 50,000 households in the northern portion of the Parish, many of which flooded in Hurricane Katrina (ibid.).

NOAA (2021) predicts that 33% of US shorelines will be hardened by 2100, greatly impacting fisheries habitats and biodiversity. Starting in the mid-19th century, commercial fishing launched from Bucktown and other lakefront communities fed local residents. While shrimp, crab, and other seafood landings are far from their previous historic highs, commercial fishing remains an important activity in the area. As noted in the Bucktown Harbor Vision Plan (2018: 9), by the late 1960s Bucktown and the Jefferson Lakefront "started to feel less like a small town and more like an engineered safe zone, part of the growing suburban sprawl emanating from Orleans and Jefferson Parish communities." In 2006, the US Coast Guard established a station in the harbor. Development of this facility included a partially reclaimed stretch of 30 acres of lake bottom and the construction of 3.5 acres of intertidal marsh to support commercial fishing and recreational boating. The establishment of 23 acres of heterogenous marsh, submerged aquatic, and

Figure 3.3 Scrub–shrub wetland and boardwalk with Bucktown Harbor behind.
Source: Moffitt & Nichol 2020b.

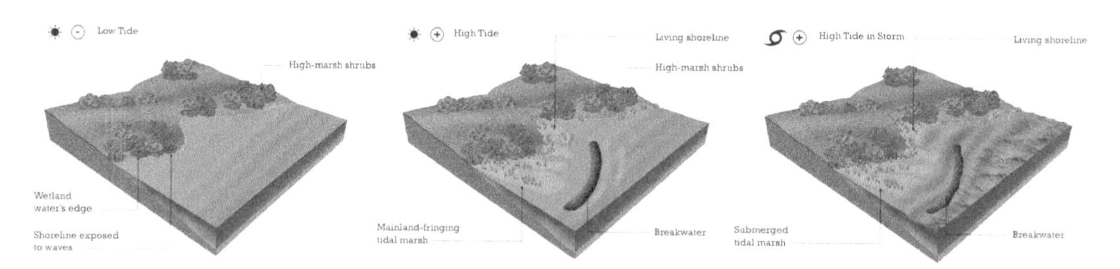

Figure 3.4 Wetland, tidal marsh, and breakwaters in low and high tide.
Source: Moffitt & Nichol 2020a.

tidal creek habitat will serve as a nursery and refuge for commercially and recreationally important species. In addition, this project will facilitate a stronger relationship between residents and surrounding native habitats (M&N 2020b: 10). Enhancement of the shoreline will increase environmental education and research opportunities, and on-shore and in-water recreation through activities such as birdwatching, kayaking, and stand-up paddle boarding.

Conclusions

Design Innovations and Global Applicability

Damage from flooding is a significant and growing problem in the United States despite decades of investment in flood protection, hazard mitigation, and campaigns to educate the public about risk. From 2005 to 2014, total flood insurance claims averaged more than $3.5 billion per year, and since 2010, all 50 states have experienced damaging floods (Cannon et al., 2020). To protect against hurricanes and heavy rainfall, Jefferson Parish built levees to keep water out, canals to drain stormwater, and pumps to get rid of water quickly. However, these measures have caused additional problems by accelerating subsidence, disrupting hydrology, hastening wetland loss, and reducing biodiversity. While the combination of extreme land loss and frequent flooding may be unique to Louisiana, rapid growth in vulnerable coastal areas worldwide combined with increased hazard intensity necessitates new structural and non-structural approaches to flood risk reduction (IPCC, 2014). This case study shows how large-scale naturalized shorelines can be used to reduce flood risk and support a myriad of ecosystem services. The ultimate goal of this approach is to naturalize the entire Jefferson Parish shoreline to increase infrastructure and community resilience, and to reconnect people to their waterfront. By supplementing levee protections, this project explores new methods of integrated engineered and natural edges that will in turn influence future levee development, flood control, and similar coastal protection features around the Gulf Coast, the US, and the world.

References

Bengtsson, L., Hodges, K., Esch, M., Keenlyside, N., Kornblueh, L., Luo, J., & Yamagata, T. (2007). How may tropical cyclones change in a warmer climate? *Tellus A*, *59*(4).

Birch, T., & Carney, J. (2019). Regional resilience: Building adaptive capacity and community well-being across Louisiana's dynamic coastal–inland continuum. In S. Laska (Ed.), *Louisiana's response to extreme weather: A test case for coastal resilience*. Springer.

Bucktown Harbor Vision Book. (2018). Prepared by Councilwoman Jennifer Van Vrancken, Moffat & Nichol, and BBEC. Retrieved from www.bucktownharbor.com/wp-content/uploads/BucktownHarborVisionPlan_opt.pdf

Cannon, C., Gotham, K. F., Lauve-Moon, K., & Powers, B. (2020). The climate change double whammy: Flood damage and the determinants of flood insurance coverage, the case of post-Katrina New Orleans. *Climate Risk Management*, *27*. https://doi.org/10.1016/j.crm.2019.100210

Colten, C. E. (2017). Environmental management in coastal Louisiana: A historical review. *Journal of Coastal Research*, *33*(3), 699–711.

Couvillion, B. R., Barras, J. A., Steyer, G. D., Sleavin, W., Fischer, M., Beck, H., Trahan, N., Griffin, B., & Heckman, D. (2011). *Land area change in coastal Louisiana from 1932 to 2010: USGS Scientific Investigations Map 3164, scale 1:265,000*. Baton Rouge. Retrieved from https://pubs.usgs.gov/sim/3164/

CPRA. (2017). *Louisiana's comprehensive master plan for a sustainable coast*. Retrieved from https://coastal.la.gov/our-plan/2017-coastal-master-plan/

Dailey, P., Zuba, G., Ljung, G., Dima, I., & Guin, J. (2008). On the relationship between North Atlantic sea surface temperatures and U.S. hurricane landfall risk. *Journal of Applied Meteorology and Climatology*, *48*(1), 111–129.

Day, J. W., Boesch, D. F., Clairain, E. J., Kemp, G. P., Laska, S. B., Mitsch, W. J., Orth, K., Mashriqui, H., Reed, D. J., Shabman, L., & Simenstad, C. A. (2007). Restoration of the Mississippi Delta: Lessons from hurricanes Katrina and Rita. *Science*, *315*(5819), 1679–1684.

Emanuel, K. (2013). Downscaling CMIP5 climate models shows increased tropical cyclone activity over the 21st century. *Proceedings of the National Academy of Sciences of the United States of America*, *110*(30). Retrieved from www.pnas.org/content/110/30/12219.short

FEMA. (February 11, 2021). *Promoting mitigation: FEMA and the State of Louisiana*. Retrieved March 3, 2021, from www.fema.gov/case-study/promoting-mitigation-fema-and-state-louisiana

Gotham, K. F., & Faust, M. (2019). Antagonisms of adaptation: Climate change adaptation strategies in New Orleans and New York. In S. Laska (Ed.), *Louisiana's response to extreme weather: A test case for coastal resilience*. Springer.

Hillman, E., Baker, D., Butcher, K., Henkel, T., Krolopp, T., Songy, A., & Lopez, J. (2019). Bucktown Marsh and Park Monitoring 2018. Lake Pontchartrain Basin Foundation. Prepared for Jefferson Parish Coastal Division.

IPCC. (2014). *Climate change 2014: Synthesis report*. Geneva. Retrieved from www.ipcc.ch/report/ar5/syr/

Jefferson Parish (2018). *Bucktown Harbor Vision Book*. https://www.bucktown harbor.com/

Keddy, P. A., Campbell, D., McFalls, T., Shaffer, G. P., Moreau, R., Dranguet, C., & Heleniak, R. (2007). The wetlands of Lakes Pontchartrain and Maurepas: Past, present and future. *Environmental Reviews*, *15*.

Kent, J.D. (2012). *Assessing the long-term impact of subsidence and global climate change on emergency evacuation routes in coastal Louisiana: A report of findings for the Gulf Coast Center for Evacuation and Transportation Resiliency*. LSU Center for Geoinformatics. Retrieved from www.evaccenter.lsu.edu/pub/11-09.pdf

Kolker, A. S., Allison, M. A., & Hameed, S. (2011). An evaluation of subsidence rates and sea-level variability in the northern Gulf of Mexico. *Geophysical Research Letters*, *38*(21). Retrieved November 26, 2021, from https://agupubs.onlinelibrary.wiley.com/doi/pdf/10.1029/2011GL049458

Lopez, J. A. (2009). The multiple lines of defense strategy to sustain coastal Louisiana. *Journal of Coastal Research*, *54*, 186–197.

M&N (Moffatt & Nichol). (2020a). *Bucktown Living Shoreline Feasibility Study Report*. New Orleans. Retrieved from http://trnerr.org/wp-content/uploads/2017/06/Final-Feasibility-Study-with-attachments.pdf

M&N (Moffatt & Nichol). (2020b). *Bucktown Living Shoreline Value Engineering Report*. New Orleans. Retrieved from www.portsanluis.com/DocumentCenter/View/4851/Discussion-Ab-Attachment-2-Moffatt-Nichol-Proposal

NOAA. (2021). *What is a living shoreline?* National Ocean Service website. Retrieved 26 February, 2021, from https://oceanservice.noaa.gov/facts/living-shoreline.html

Shepard, C. C., Crain, C. M., & Beck, M. W. (2011). The protective role of coastal marshes: A systematic review and meta-analysis. *PloS One*, *6*(11), e27374. https://doi.org/10.1371/journal.pone.0027374

Temmerman, S., & Kirwan, M. L. (2015). Building land with a rising sea. *Science*, *349*(6248), 588–589.

Tornqvist, T., Jankowski, K., Li, Y. X., & Gonzalez, J. (2020). Tipping points of Mississippi Delta marshes due to accelerated sea-level rise. *Science Advances*, *6*(21), p.eaaz5512.

USACE. (2019). *Lake Pontchartrain & Vicinity, Louisiana General Re-Evaluation Report*. United States Army Corps of Engineers, New Orleans. Retrieved from www.mvn.usace.army.mil/Portals/56/00_LPV%20Main%20Report.pdf

Waggonner & Ball Architects. (2013). *Greater New Orleans urban water plan*. Retrieved from www.livingwithwater.com

Wang, F., Xu, Y. J., & Dean, T. J. (2011). Projecting climate change effects on forest net primary productivity in subtropical Louisiana, USA. *Ambio*, *405*, 506–520.

4

TAMPA, FLORIDA

Karishma Joshi and Galen D. Newman

Site: Tampa, FL: 2273 acres

Introduction/Rationale

Project Overview

Tampa, Florida is one of the top five US cities most vulnerable to flooding and is expected to grow by over 100,000 people by 2040 (Chen et al., 2015). Compounding this, sea level rise makes coastal populations more susceptible to flood risks, especially in marginalized or underserved neighborhoods (Hendricks et al., 2018). When open space land uses within high flood-risk areas (e.g. the 100-year flood plain) are converted to urban land uses, flood risk can increase (Du et al., 2015). The capability to accurately predict both future flood plain changes and future urban growth allows for the better protection of coastal communities from the effects of climate change while helping support flood risk mitigation.

In this project, we integrate sea level rise and urban growth prediction modelling to help inform resilient design solutions for an urban design master plan in Tampa, Florida for a heavily industrialized and marginalized neighborhood. The design integrates urban analytics with performance modeling, linking in-depth analysis and urban growth predictions using GIS with structural and non-structural design solutions aimed at safeguarding local ecosystems and protecting vulnerable local communities. We use the Land Transformation Model (LTM) (Kim & Newman, 2019) to predict for future urban growth, restricting any future growth within the 100 year flood plain; we use these projections to inform where built environment features are to occur within the design, then reconstitute green infrastructure provisions within the undeveloped areas within the floodplain and other non-developed areas to increase resilience. Through this approach, we compare how effective the design is in adapting urban growth to decreasing flood risk and pollutant load. The project both develops and operationalizes measures to evaluate the performance of the built environment, using baseline data to compare the new urban growth scheme against existing conditions to determine design benefits. We then offer comparisons of the design projections to existing circumstances as well as solutions to offset any of its shortcomings.

DOI: 10.4324/9781003183419-7

Rationale

According to Newman et al. (2020a), floods are the costliest natural hazard worldwide. Flood vulnerability can be compounded by land use conversion from natural to developed and increased impervious surfaces, amplifying the harmful social and economic impacts of recent and future floods. Given the far-reaching impacts of recent major US storms, such as Hurricanes Katrina (2008), Ike (2005), Sandy (2012), and Harvey (2017), it is clear that the increased frequency and damage costs of flooding is not an issue solved through only engineering solutions (Chakraborty et al., 2019). The way humans settle and build upon the physical landscape is a major factor contributing to flood risk.

Since flood disasters are largely a human-induced phenomenon; changing the way we shape communities through their development patterns may be the most effective way to mitigate repetitive and costly flood events. Urbanization and the proliferation of impervious surfaces across watershed units have long been considered a major contributor to adverse impacts associated with flood events (Berke et al., 2015). Conversion of natural landscapes to urban or suburban developments can reduce the functionality of hydrological systems, leading to reduced soil infiltration and increased surface runoff and peak discharge into nearby streams (Bhaduri et al., 2000). More recent research indicates that flood impacts are not driven solely by the amount of impervious surface, but by its pattern and intensity across a given landscape (Brody et al., 2011). In this sense, the form of the built environment is an important trigger for flood losses over time. For example, neighborhoods with large amounts of high-intensity development have been shown to experience, on average, lower amounts of property damage from floods when development is located properly prior to development or supported by green infrastructure (Newman et al., 2020b). Socio-economic characteristics and household composition can also be significant factors predicting the likelihood and extent of flood disasters (Cutter et al., 2003).

Design Synopsis

Study Area

The site is located within the southeast of Tampa, along the Palm River, where the river meets the McKay Bay (which feeds into Tampa Bay). It is both heavily affected by flooding and characterized by high amounts of industrial land uses, landfill, brownfields, and toxic release sites, resulting in severe pollution and related effects from runoff containing industrial by-products. This creates a direct impact on the aquatic life, local biodiversity, and indirectly affects human health due to polluted groundwater and air particulates. Tampa's existing growth patterns project intense growth patterns within coastal areas and are negligent towards these environmental problems. The site is in need of a design which properly applies both structural and nonstructural mechanisms to create a neighborhood resilient to both floods and contamination (see Figure 4.1). The severe pollution and related effects from runoff containing industrial

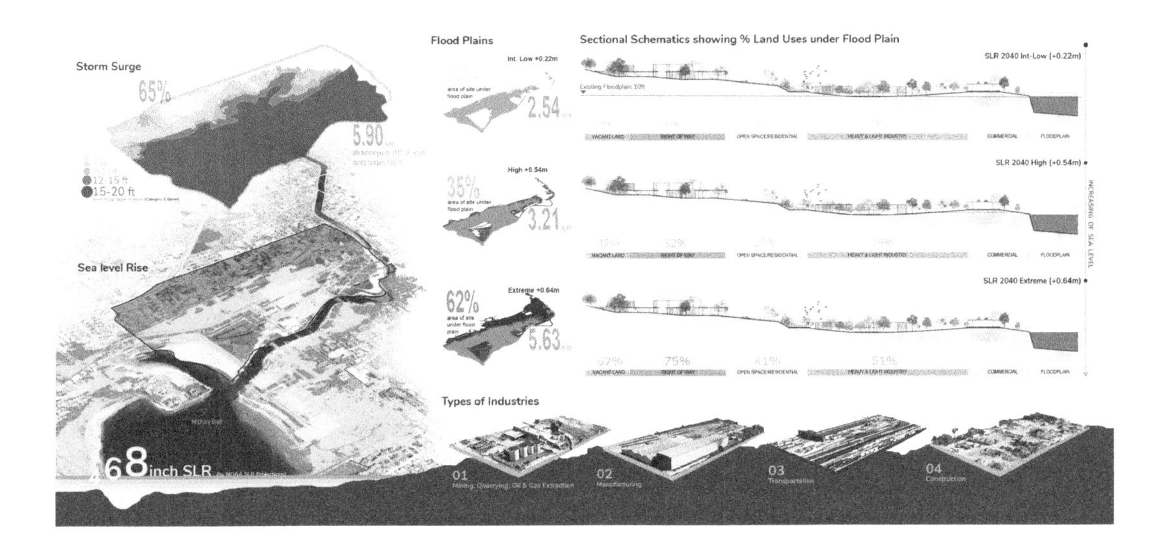

Figure 4.1 Sea level rise and storm surge projections on site and corresponding land uses impacted.

by-products can result in mixtures of hazardous substances during flood events, worsening contamination levels and effects, and intensifying negative public health outcomes (Newman et al., 2020b).

Land Transformation Modeling

Scenario-based design typically links technology into the management of uncertain futures through the creation of alternative forms of growth (Ringland & Schwartz, 1998). To create our design concept, we used a series of tools on multi-scalar spatial datasets in an effort to increase resiliency for future urban development within the site. To achieve this, LTM, a GIS-based neural network used to predict land uses and examine relationships between spatial driving factors and land use changes (Kim et al., 2020), was applied. The LTM uses machine learning to calculate complex patterns through an artificial neural network. In this project, the LTM was used to predict potential future urban growth of Tampa according to a resilient developmental scenario. The design scenario utilized was labeled as a "Resilient Growth" scenario in that all predicted urban growth is based on all future development occurring outside of the floodplain.

After urban prediction outputs were outputted, flood exposure was calculated by overlapping existing urban and projected future urban growth with the delineated future flood risk zones. Following the previous land use change ratio (calculated by the LTM), there was a change of 8,917 pixels between 2001 and 2011, projecting a population increase of 32,600 people. The future urban growth projects a change of 48,395 pixels corresponding to a 176,928 population change between 2001 and 2040. The predicted development pixel and its location is based on different exclusionary layers in the design scenario. In its full extent, the resilient growth prediction model excludes urban growth in existing urban areas, rivers and lakes, highways, airports, and parks from future development areas; it also excludes environmentally sensitive areas from the future land use (according to the comprehensive plan's policy). Finally, as noted, it also excludes development within future flood risk zones (the 100-year floodplain).

Design Schematics

The design used the relative locations and amounts of the LTM prediction output to inform future development locations and land use arrangement (see Figure 4.2). Within the site only 5% of the development would be in flood plain (all existing). The master plan was built on a framework of design strategies categorized under four major categories of promoting economy, reducing pollutant transfer, flood mitigation, and conserving ecology. The design strategies aimed to restore the riparian corridor along the river by planting wetland species, conserving existing mangroves, promoting a forest patch corridor mechanism to act as a natural sponge for flood events, and conserving biodiversity (see Table 4.1).

Structural and Nonstructural Mechanisms

The resilient master plan for the site focused on regeneration of the under-utilized industrialized neighborhood and promoted a holistic developmental approach in tune with the ecological needs. The urban design master plan was comprised of programming elements fostering economic development like creating recreational infrastructure and boardwalks along the Palm River, strengthening the connectivity between different land uses by planning bike loops and pedestrians' walkways and circulation. Newer development will ensure elevated buildings and infrastructure with proper stormwater management strategies. The master plan ensured the integration of community facilities

Figure 4.2 Prediction outputs translated into land use percentages for master planning.

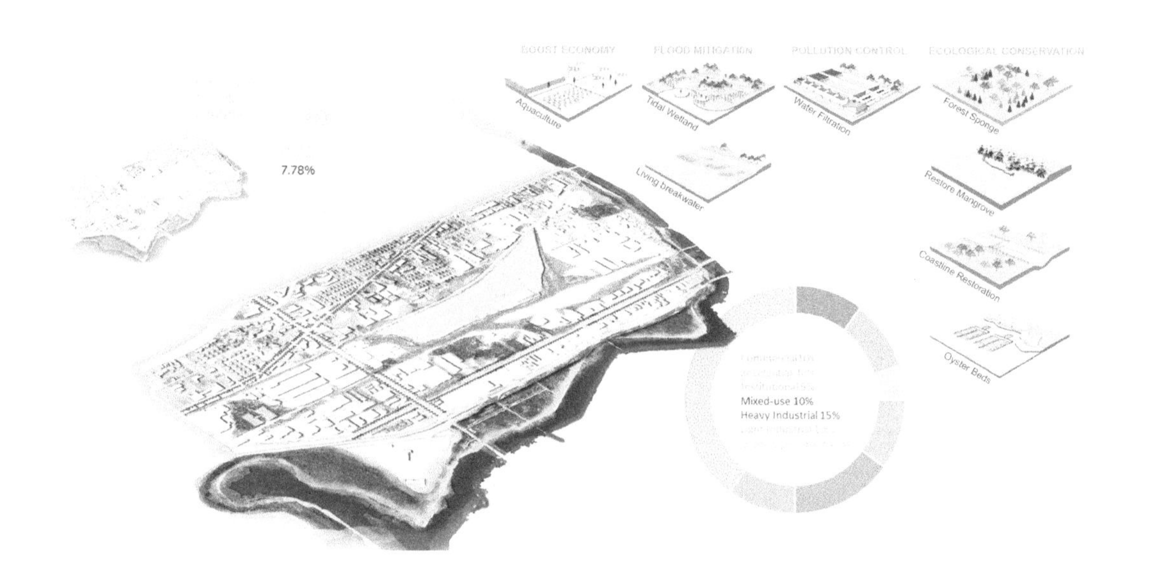

Table 4.1 Strategies and mechanisms utilized within the design for Tampa, FL

Program elements for economic development:	*Structural*	*Non-structural*	*Hybrid*
Residential development	X		
Commercial and office space	X		
Industrial parks			X
Museums	X		
Community centers and community facilities	X		
Rowing/boating infrastructure			X
Recreational boardwalks			X
Program elements for flood mitigation:			
Stormwater run-off storage cells		X	
Community & pocket gardens		X	
Urban forests		X	
Railway peripheral improvements			X
Pervious materials			X
Program elements for reducing pollutant load:			
Riparian buffers around waterbodies		X	
Natural habitat improvement	X		
Plant species promoting phytoremediation	X		
Soil amendments	X		
Material reuse and recycling			X
Program elements for ecological conservation:			
Eco-bike loops			X
Mangrove restoration	X		
Public parks & green infrastructure	X		
Bikeways & walking promenades			X
No development in floodplain	X		
Living shoreline	X		
Improved water quality & aquatic life	X		

such as urban parks and pocket gardens and building onto the existing forest sponges to increase the overall perviousness of the site. The new parking spaces are designed with pervious paving materials and suggest significantly increasing canopy coverage to assist in the mitigation of flooding on a broader scale. Flood mitigation was achieved by ensuring an increase in pervious surfaces. Creation of landscape berms (see Figure 4.3) along the river banks ensured that low lying areas were free of water-logging and accumulation during flood events. These innovative design strategies complement the approach towards strengthening local habitats and restoring a riparian corridor and living shoreline along the river banks. Use of passive landscape design strategies such

Figure 4.3 Low impact development and design strategies to mitigate pollutant transfer and flooding.

as the creation of buffers along the point source of pollutants helped reduce pollutant transfer to local water resources while natural phytoremediation processes help reduce pollutant load. Finally, the master plan promotes the conservation of local ecosystems and mangroves to ensure ecological conservation while simultaneously passively contributing to flood prevention and mitigation.

Design Impact

The performance model outputs were based on the L-THIA low impact development spreadsheet. The L-THIA is a landscape performance tool that uses land-use configuration inputs to calculate and project probable runoff and pollutant loads for cities and neighborhoods (Hendricks et al., 2018). It uses internal algorithms to test differing land use scenarios, tallying up results on stormwater runoff amounts (acre-ft) and 14 different pollutants (lbs) per scenario. In this project, we use the current land-use layout and the land-use configuration of the design as comparative scenarios. Using the L-THIA outcomes, we compare the current conditions to the design's projected performance. Overall, results suggest that the resilient design decreases impervious surfaces, increases green infrastructure area, decreases developed area within high flood risk, and decreases public exposure to contaminants/pollutants in surface runoff. The current surface water runoff on site is 4647.42 acre-ft. But after implementing the design strategies, the surface water run-off decreases to 3966.8 acre-ft, a reduction of 17%. A similar trend was found when examining average run-off depth, with resilient growth decreasing the amount by nearly by three-quarters when compared to current conditions. Further, all 14 pollutants decrease significantly based on the master plan. This reduction is nearly 12% lower than the current situation (see Figure 4.4). While the design appears to be an optimal approach to future development, it is

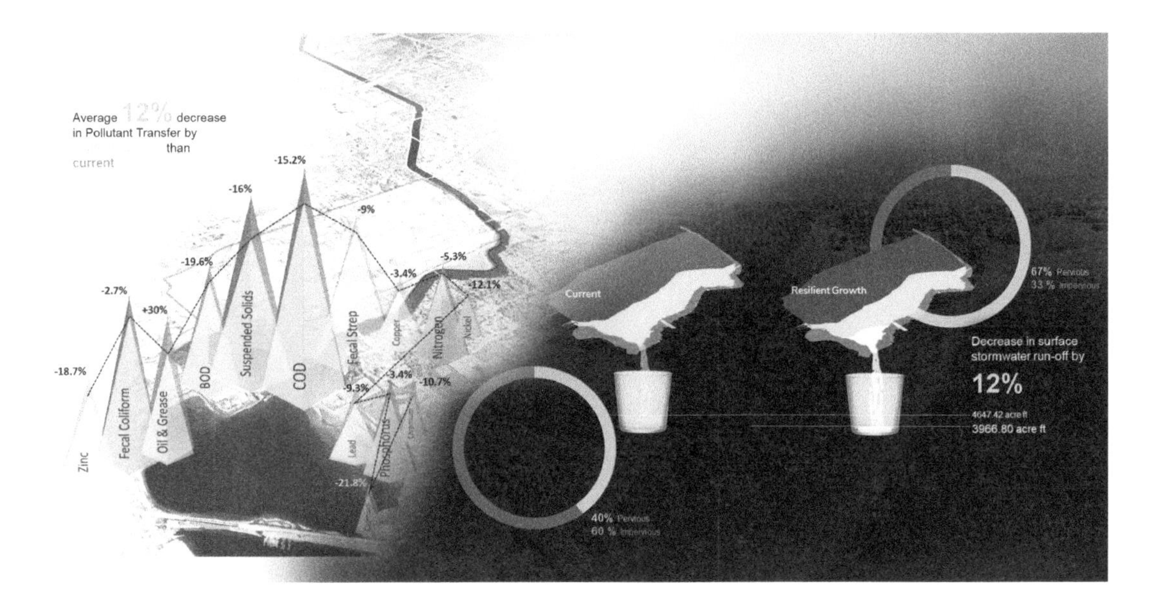

important to note that construction/maintenance costs for low impact facilities and the increased densities to achieve the desired land use regulations can increase upfront costs. These costs are, however, lessened over time due to indirect benefits such as increased groundwater, increased carbon sequestration, decreased runoff, and decreased energy costs.

Figure 4.4 Impact of the Master plan to compared to existing conditions in mitigating pollutant transfer and flooding.

Conclusion

Innovations and Applicability

The project examined future urbanization using prediction modeling coupled with scenario planning to advance conditions for uncertain future climate change. Through our approach, we set an example to demonstrate a comparison-based matrix using urban growth and flood risk with sea level rise scenarios and impact analysis with scenario evaluation. Analytical findings showed that the current future land-use plan for Tampa may not be the best approach for dealing with climate change, in terms of urban flood exposure, stormwater run-off increase, and pollutant discharge, and can be made more suitable with the application of innovative design solutions and urban design and planning guidelines incorporated through a more resilient growth approach. This project also suggests that the design creates a more resilient community compared to conventional development practices. The reduction of the area of the 100-year flood plain due to an appropriate combination and placement of structural and non-structural flood attenuation mechanisms as well as the pollutant load reduction due to increased green infrastructure show that resilience is also increased. The approach not only allows for increases in current resiliency, but can also better prepare neighborhoods for the future impacts of sea level rise. This project is unique in that most modeling and projections for climate change only occur at the regional scale or larger. As demonstrated, community scaled conditions can be used to proactively inform community layout, resulting in longer-term stability, reductions to future flood risks, and decreased contamination.

References

Berke, P., Newman, G., Lee, J., Combs, T., Kolosna, C., & Salvensen, D. (2015). Assessing networks of plans and vulnerability to coastal hazards and climate change. *Journal of the American Planning Association*, *81*(4), 287–302.

Bhaduri, B., Harbor, J. O. N., Engel, B., & Grove, M. (2000). Assessing watershed-scale, long-term hydrologic impacts of land-use change using a GIS-NPS model. *Environmental management*, *26*(6), 643–658.

Brody, S. D., Gunn, J., Peacock, W., & Highfield, W. E. (2011). Examining the influence of development patterns on flood damages along the Gulf of Mexico. *Journal of Planning Education and Research*, *31*(4), 438–448.

Chakraborty, J., Collins, T. W., & Grineski, S. E. (2019). Exploring the environmental justice implications of Hurricane Harvey flooding in Greater Houston, Texas. *American journal of public health*, *109*(2), 244–250.

Chen, X. Z., Lu, Q. C., Peng, Z. R., & Ash, J. E. (2015). Analysis of transportation network vulnerability under flooding disasters. *Transportation research record*, *2532*(1), 37–44.

Cutter, S. L., Boruff, B. J., & Shirley, W. L. (2003). Social vulnerability to environmental hazards. *Social Science Quarterly*, *84*(2), 242–261.

Du, S., Shi, P., Van Rompaey, A., & Wen, J. (2015). Quantifying the impact of impervious surface location on flood peak discharge in urban areas. *Natural Hazards*, *76*(3), 1457–1471.

Hendricks, M. D., Newman, G., Yu, S., & Horney, J. (2018). Leveling the landscape: Landscape performance as a green infrastructure evaluation tool for service-learning products. *Landscape Journal*, *37*(2), 19–39.

Kim, Y., Newman, G., & Güneralp, B. (2020). A review of driving factors, scenarios, and topics in urban land change models. *Land*, *9*(8), 246.

Kim, Y., & Newman, G. (2019). Climate change preparedness: Comparing future urban growth and flood risk in Amsterdam and Houston. *Sustainability*, *11*(4), 1048.

Newman, G., Malecha, M., Yu, S., Qiao, Z., Horney, J. A., Lee, J., . . . & Berke, P. (2020a). Integrating a resilience scorecard and landscape performance tools into a Geodesign process. *Landscape research*, *45*(1), 63–80.

Newman, G., Shi, T., Yao, Z., Li, D., Sansom, G., Kirsch, K., . . . & Horney, J. (2020b). Citizen science-informed community master planning: Land use and built environment changes to increase flood resilience and decrease contaminant exposure. *International Journal of Environmental Research and Public Health*, *17*(2), 486.

Ringland, G., & Schwartz, P. P. (1998). *Scenario planning: Managing for the future*. John Wiley & Sons.

Non-structural Heavy Design

5 BUSAN, SOUTH KOREA

Yunmi Park and Jiyeon Shin

Site: Eco-Delta Smart City, Busan, S. Korea

Introduction/Rationale

Located at the southeastern end of the Korean peninsula, Busan is the second-most populous city in South Korea with 3.5 million residents. Ten out of its 16 neighborhood districts touch the seashores, and two districts are on the border of the Nakdong River, which flows into the South Sea. The total length of the coastline reaches nearly 380 km, and most of the coastal areas are occupied by ports, port facilities, roads, or open space (H. J. Kim et al., 2019). However, recent intensified developments (including cafés, hotels, and high-rise apartments) that benefit from beautiful, elongated seascapes have induced more concerns. Coastal land reclamation and sea level rise have rapidly deepened the coastal erosion, and the reduced beach areas can no longer absorb sufficient amounts of wave energy as they were once able to (Zhang et al., 2004). Additionally, these areas are frequently hit by typhoons because they tend to be closely situated on lower slopes and facing high waves.

One such example of new development near the seashore is Haeundae Beach, which is stricken by typhoons and heavy rains on a regular basis, especially during the summer monsoon season. The storm surge, combined with high tides, frequently overtops the existing breakwaters, causing flooding and damage to roads, vehicles, and buildings (The City of Busan, 2019). Since typhoons that land on the Korean Peninsula are becoming stronger and more frequent due to climate change, flood damage around the coastal area has also increased (Choi et al., 2012). As shown in Figure 5.1, the 2003 Typhoon Maemi caused $2.6 billion in property damage, killed 17, and left 7,791 in Busan as flood victims (J.-M. Kim et al., 2019). The City of Busan (2016) projected a rise in total precipitation by 38.5% (1,532 mm to 2,122 mm) and a sea level rise of up to 70.6 cm by 2100. Song and Lee (2015) also anticipate that many beaches, ports, coastal residential areas, and commercial areas of Busan would be flooded due to a sea level rise by one meter and a simultaneous peak tide of between 1.57–1.74 meters. Greenpeace (2020) expects that 134,288 people and 19% of the area (144.09 km^2) in Busan will be affected by flooding by 2070 if no climate actions are taken. The responses to climate change and sea level rise have been

DOI: 10.4324/9781003183419-9

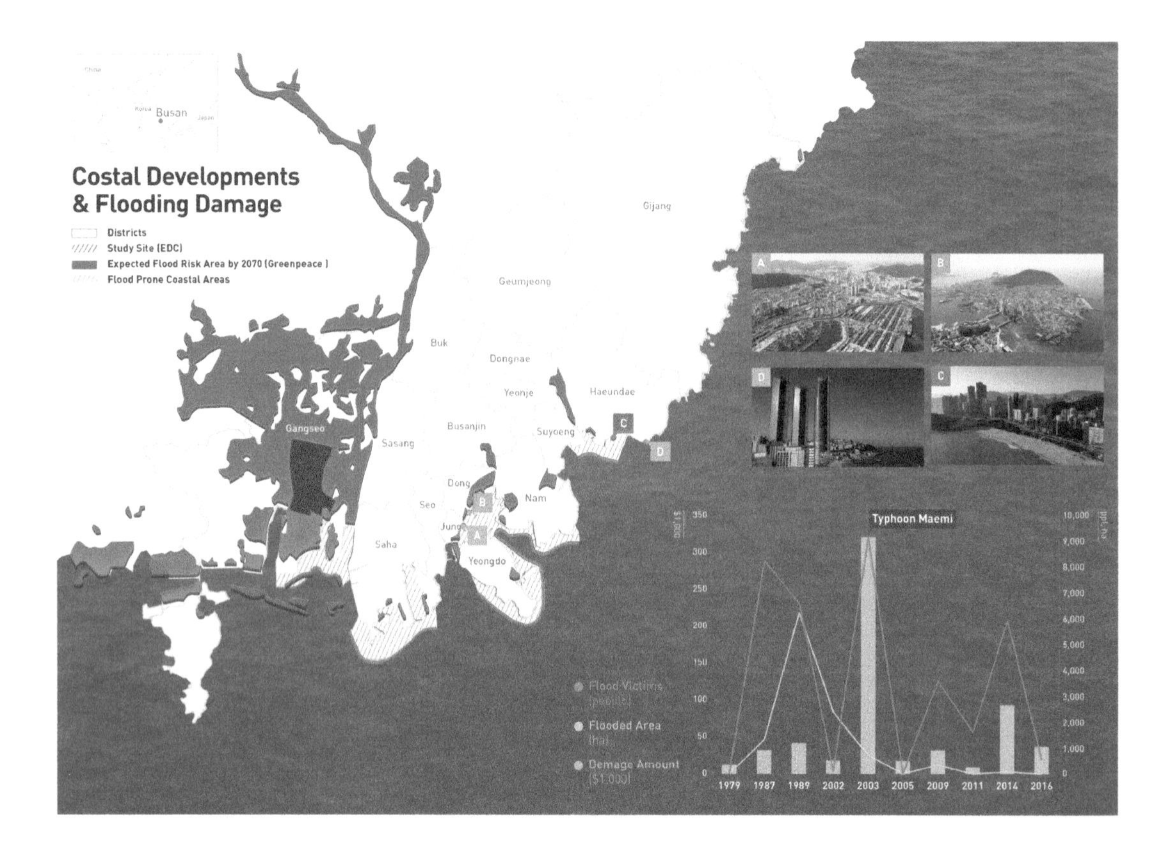

Figure 5.1 Coastal developments in Busan and flooding damages.

relatively slow but are speeding up because people have witnessed its unpredictable and detrimental consequences. The central and local governments have begun developing "Plans for Climate Change Adaptation" every five years since 2011. Flood risk maps derived for 50, 80, 100, 200, and 500-year return periods were first opened to the public in 2021. Still, in its early planning and construction stages, the new town development project, "Eco-Delta City" (EDC), was also encouraged to actively embrace different sorts of flooding prevention, mitigation, and monitoring mechanisms. This chapter raises concerns about flooding that could occur in sites adjacent to the sea and riverfronts at the same time, and introduces the new adoption of smart technologies and mitigation strategies.

Design Synopsis

Study Area

A river delta that borders various sorts of water bodies both inside and outside its boundaries, the EDC will serve 76,000 people on 11.77 km^2 of land. It is surrounded by the Macdo and West Nakdong Rivers that coalesce into the South Sea. Three tributaries of the Pyeonggang Stream gather at the center of the EDC, an area full of great scenery and waterfronts. The site has been designated as a green belt since the 1970s, but a new development plan was proposed in 2010 to meet increasing housing and industrial needs due to the growth of the western part of Busan and Busan New Port. The specific locations and functions of the design strategies introduced were retrieved from several EDC plans so that the content could be modified during the actual construction.

Projection

The current elevation of the EDC ranges from 0.4–4.0 meters, and the difference between the land and any river or stream is less than 1.0 meter. The area is protected by breakwaters completed in 1936 to transform this wetland into agricultural land since there has been frequent flood damage caused by inundation of the Nakdong River as well as saltwater damage from the eastern and western mudflats (Heo et al., 2016). Despite the breakwaters and seawalls around the site, this area has always been flood-prone due to its flat topography and close adjacency to rivers and the sea (Figure 5.2). If one were to take a 100-year frequency of a tidal wave that is 2.74 meters and combine it with the highest tide by 0.50 meters around this area, the flooding level would be more than 3.24 meters. Flood levels can reach up to 4.0 meters when taking into account a sea level rise of between 0.76–1.0 meters (B.-R. Kim et al., 2019). Song and Lee (2015) predicted that the flood level of the EDC area could experience 6.42 meters of storm surge when a super typhoon arrives. Even though different scenarios reported different results under various assumptions, it is clear that 1.6–3.0 meters of ground-level elevation increase alone may not be enough to deal with

Figure 5.2 The formation and location of Eco-Delta area and flood projection scenarios.

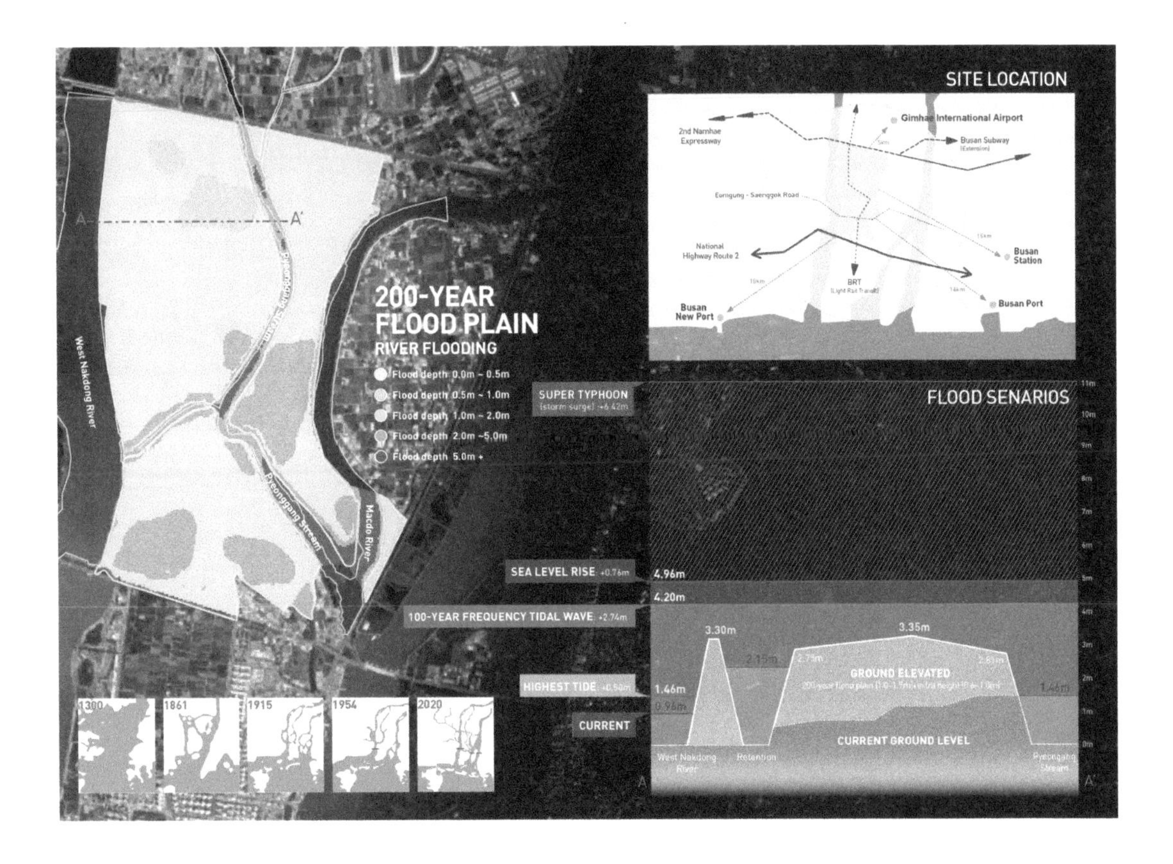

future sea level rise. Additionally, increases in impervious cover – after the conversion of cropland to urban developed land – would increase surface runoff volumes and decrease the infiltration of precipitation. As a result, the peak discharge, frequency, and volume of floods may increase in nearby streams and rivers.

Structural and Non-structural Mechanisms and Design Impact

As shown in Figure 5.3 and Table 5.1, the master plan of the EDC introduced structural, non-structural, and hybrid mechanisms to help mitigate flooding. Because of the topographical and geographical features of the delta region, the master plan proposed to elevate the ground level by 1.6–3.0 meters, which took into account the 200-year flood plain (expected to reach 1.0–1.7 meters high) and allowed for an additional height buffer (0.6–1.0 meters). The plan also proposed

Table 5.1 Structural, non-structural, and hybrid program elements

Program elements	*Structural*	*Non-structural*	*Hybrid*
Flood mitigation:			
Elevated ground level (200-year flood plain+extra height)		X	
Rainwater storage & drainage facility	X		
Land use: building height and density controls	X		
Riparian buffer zone & wet land		X	
Green levee		X	
Bio retention, detention, rain garden		X	
Vegetated filter strip		X	
Green roof		X	
Infiltration trench			X
Infiltration ditch		X	
Infiltration chamber, infiltration ditch culvert	X		
Porous pavement			X
Monitoring:			
Intelligent flood monitoring system with IoT			X
digital twin	X		
Smart urban safety control	X		
K-water Hydro Intelligent Toolkit for flood simulation			X

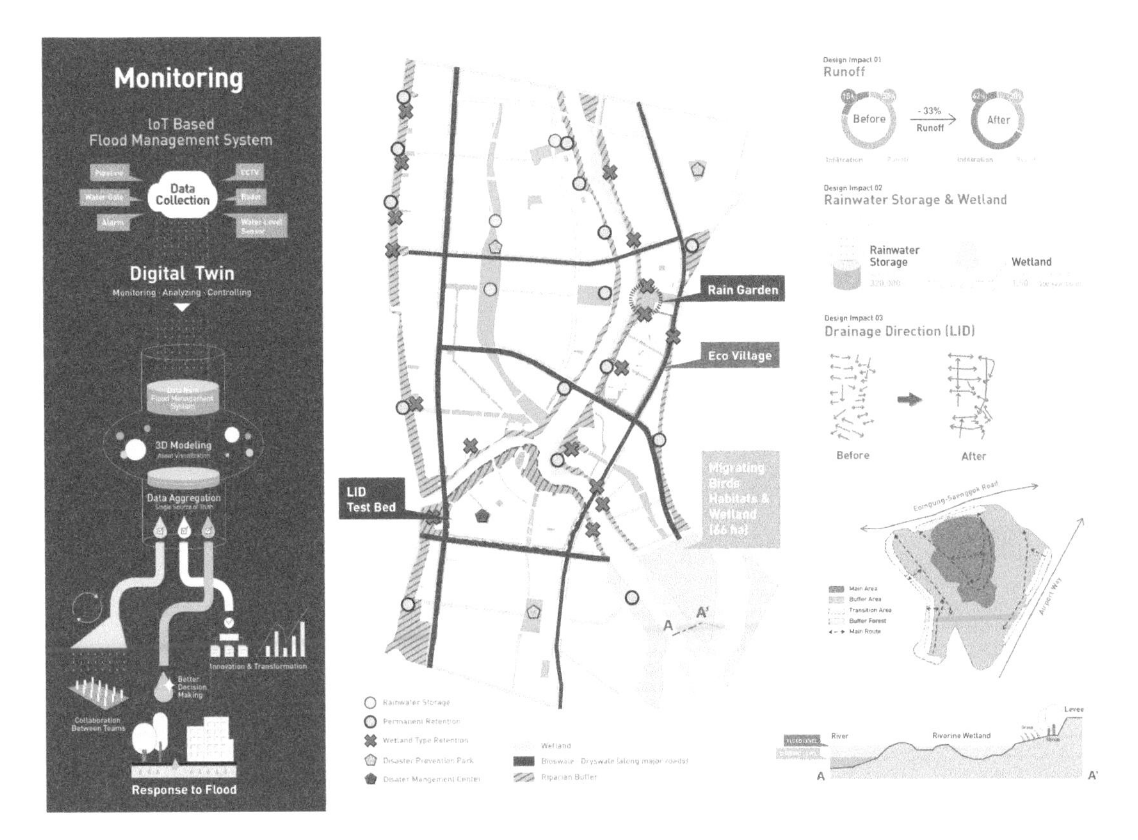

Figure 5.3 Applied mechanisms and major design impacts on EDC.

0.5 meter high green mounding from the coast where necessary. Rainwater storage and drainage facilities were also installed, which could handle 100 mm of precipitation per hour and hold up to 320,000 m^3 of water, as the national flooding guideline suggests that measures be implemented to respond to a 90 mm/hour rainfall intensity. Rainwater storage will hold the rainwater during heavy rains to slowly reduce the peak flood volume by draining away water when weather conditions allow.

Ecologically well-designed threefold shields (breakwaters, retentions, and riparian zones) were also implemented around the area. A 100-meter-wide ecological riparian buffer zone (approximately 6.6 ha) called the "Delta Esplanade" was planned along the West Nakdong River to serve as a habitat for migratory birds and a recreation area for residents. Retention and detention ponds, rain gardens, migratory habitats, and constructed wetlands (approximately 66 ha) were also planned along the major stream and riverfronts. The riparian buffer and wetland systems are the first natural defense against flooding when water overflows past the breakwaters. It will also provide added benefits such as habitat provision, ecosystem processes, recreation, and scenic beauty during the dry season when water infiltration is enhanced

Figure 5.4 Detention park at the riparian buffer: dry season (left) – flooding (right).

and water runoff during flooding slows (Figure 5.4). The constructed wetland also has the ability to reduce the flood stage up to 1.5 meters, considering a 200-year flood (Jung et al., 2020). Three central parks in each district, divided by the Pyeonggang Stream, are designed with disaster prevention functions such as evacuation, education, and relief goods storage.

Building height controls were applied. The town center and riverside will be developed with lower density and low-rise buildings, while high-rise residential complexes will be placed away from the river and streams to mitigate the damage from flooding and maintain the scenic view toward the waterfronts. One of the other primary non-structural mechanisms is the implementation of several facilities related to low-impact development (LID). Different types of vegetation and infiltration tools were established to slow the path of runoff and retain rainfall on-site. Bioswales, dry swales, trenches, and open ditches comprise an effective rainwater drainage system for the site's low and below sea level elevations. The porous pavement was designed with a target of seeping 42% of precipitation and 20% of runoff; if not applied, ground filtration would be only 15% and surface runoff would be 55%. LID components are also expected to change the direction of the drainage flow toward the retention ponds and water storage facilities installed along riverfronts.

Similar projects should take inspiration from the EDC's refreshing key strategy of adopting digital twin sensors within its different intelligent monitoring systems. With the EDC being described as exemplifying the concept of a "smart city" of the future, it was hoped that the site will serve as a model to encourage the adoption of the digital twin platform and new technologies. Digital twin and virtual reality (VR) models were used to carry out a design review of the first development of a residential neighborhood with 56 households in 2021. VR allowed review committees to realistically anticipate the color, the layout, and other aesthetics that might not be found in two-dimensional site plans or bird's eye view drawings. Further, the technology allows for a high-precision small rain radar that analyzes the amount of rain and predicts flooding in real-time by using Internet of

Things (IoT) sensors that are positioned at streets, reservoirs, retentions, floodgates, and drainage facilities. These sensors can be monitored, and real-time data can be transferred to the flooding management system. The digital twin platform can synchronize the data from the flooding management system, predict flood areas, and issue a timely alarm to residents. The flooding management system that was designed to respond to disasters in the EDC consists of a modified K-water Hydro Intelligent Toolkit (K-HIT) composed of different simulation models; for example, a real-time hydrological data acquisition and processing system, a precipitation forecasting system, a distributed rainfall-runoff model, a reservoir water supply system, and a generation-integrated operational system.

Conclusions

Innovation and Applicability

The EDC is a naturally flood-prone area due to its low-lying topography, surrounding rivers and seas, and climate with heavy summer rains. The proposed master plan acknowledges the flood risk from rainwater and rivers and actively adopts different layers of prevention and mitigation strategies. The major developer, K-water, is a public corporation that has made huge investments in water management and flood prevention possible. The EDC adopted the ground level elevation rise approach based on the 200-year flood plain. Additionally, it made allowances for extra heights and was equipped with high-volume rainwater containers and drainage facilities. From there, large amounts of land around the riversides were assigned to riparian zones, wetlands, and retention and detention ponds to hold overflow from seawalls and breakwaters. As part of a third protection strategy, different types of LID facilities were applied, along with planned surface water flows. Low-density developments were assigned away from the riverfronts to minimize damage after disasters. While a digital twin and IoT-based flood management system and digital twin may not directly protect the area from flood damage, the systems will help people evacuate promptly and safely.

Despite the merits of planned tool kits to alleviate flood risks, several points require further consideration. In addition to flood risks from topographical and geographical conditions, other events such as intensified localized rainfall, storm surges and water waves induced by super typhoons, sea level rises, and the highest tide from climate change should be more actively taken into consideration to improve the efficiency of future flood risk responses. Emergency response preparedness actions to address possible scenarios arising from climate change should be introduced into future master plans. This is especially important in the eventuality that climate change causes seawater flooding to exceed the typical prevention design criteria. Therefore, long-term strategies associated with shelters, evacuation routes, and recovery require more detailed inclusion in future plans. Another risk posed is the possibility of infiltration and discharging facilities being planned along riverfronts, increasing the already elevated groundwater level and worsening flood damage. Also, while digital twin technology and smart warning systems may sound attractive, smart devices are not foolproof. IoT sensors and related devices may not work properly under all conditions. Therefore, flood depths and the functional capabilities of these devices should be considered when deciding on the location and placement of these tools. Threefold shields (breakwaters, retentions, and riparian zones) from rivers to residential and commercial areas will diminish flood risks to residential zones, but the width of the riparian buffer zone/strip and vegetation techniques need further detailing. As suggested by Semlitsch and Bodie (2003), the width should reach at least 30 meters to ensure water quality and up to 180 meters for wildlife habitat; less than 20 meters of width does not hold water for a sufficient period. The combination and amount of grass, shrubs, and trees for the vegetation can be different based on the purpose of the riparian buffer, but flood protection trees would be the most effective means of helping to minimize flood risk. Trees should also be planted away from the flood zone because taller plants could entrap debris and divert rushing water. Lastly, the master plan and the government should provide detailed information about flood-prone areas, sea level rise projections, and the probable impacts of climate change to individual developers so that people can better prepare for hazardous events. Building codes should also require buildings in flood-prone areas to install flooding prevention provisions. Examples of these include the installation of mechanical equipment on top of buildings to minimize the risk of damage from flooding and the design of a ground floor to sit above the inundation level.

References

Choi, K.-S., Cha, Y.-M., & Kim, T.-R. (2012). Decadal change of frequency in Korea landfalling tropical cyclone activity. *Journal of the Korean Regional Development Association*, *33*(1), 49–58.

Greenpeace. (2020). *2030 flood simulation on the Korean Peninsula*. Retrieved from www.climate.or.kr/

Heo, M., Son, I., & Tak, H. (2016). A study on the landscape change in Nakdong River delta: The case of Myeongjidong. *Journal of the Korean Geographical Society*, *51*(4), 491–508.

Jung, J., Bae, Y., Lee, H. N., Kim, S., & Kim, H. S. (2020). A study on the benefit estimation by artificial wetland construction. *Journal of Wetlands Research*, *22*(1), 39–48.

Kim, B.-R., O, G.-Y., & Sim, U.-B. (2019). Development of urban planning flood management techniques to create safe smart cities around rivers. *Water for Future*, *52*(11), 53–61.

Kim, H. J., Kim, J. S., & Lee, S. H. (2019). Spatial classification and inventory of adaptive strategy considering disaster vulnerabilities in the coastal area: Focused on Busan. *Journal of the Korean Regional Development Association*, *31*(3), 231–251.

Kim, J.-M., Kim, T., Son, K., Yum, S.-G., & Ahn, S. (2019). Measuring vulnerability of typhoon in residential facilities: Focusing on typhoon Maemi in South Korea. *Sustainability*, *11*(10), 2768.

Semlitsch, R. D., & Bodie, J. R. (2003). Biological criteria for buffer zones around wetlands and riparian habitats for amphibians and reptiles. *Conservation Biology*, *17*(5), 1219–1228.

Song, G.-W., & Lee, C. (2015). *Climate change adaptation measures in Busan coastal areas* (Policy Research 2015-08-06). Retrieved from www.bdi.re.kr/03station/04_01.asp?SType=ReR_Title&SString=&dept=D4101&year=&cate=&cate1=f4&idx=1013&page=12

The City of Busan. (2016). *2nd Action plan for climate change adaptation measures in Busan Metropolitan City (2017–2021)*. The City of Busan (Publication Registration Number 52-6260000-000407-13). Retrieved from http://book.busan.go.kr/Viewer/IKFPQF6CIDOH

The City of Busan. (2019). *Action plan for climate change adaptation measures in Haeundae District, Busan (2020–2024)*. The City of Busan. (Publication Number 11-136000-001213-01). Retrieved from www.climate.go.kr/home/cc_data/scenario_web_report/Busan_Haeundae.pdf

Zhang, K., Douglas, B. C., & Leatherman, S. P. (2004). Global warming and coastal erosion. *Climatic change*, *64*(1), 41–58.

6

MOAKLEY PARK, BOSTON, MASSACHUSETTS

Amy Whitesides

Site: Boston, MA, Moakley Park: 60 acres

Introduction/Rationale

Boston, Massachusetts, USA is subject to multiple climate-based risk factors including coastal flooding due to sea level rise, increasing storms, increased precipitation and stormwater flooding, and increasing heat and incidence of extreme temperatures (BRAG, 2016; City of Boston, 2016). To date, Boston has been relatively fortunate and missed significant impacts from major coastal storms in the Northeastern United States including Hurricane Irene (2011) and Superstorm Sandy (2012). However, it has not been immune. Regular king tides bring waters up and over the seawall at historic Long Wharf in Downtown and along Lewis Street in East Boston (Figure 6.1). In 2018, two 100-year storms, Greyson and Riley, hit within one month of each other causing flood damage in many areas, most notably the South Boston, East Boston, and Downtown neighborhoods.

These impacts, fortunately, did not come as a surprise. The City of Boston recognized the threat of climate change early and has pursued a multifaceted and integrated approach to address it. In 2000, Boston joined the Cities for Climate Protection Campaign of Local Governments for Sustainability. Since this time, the City of Boston has led multiple efforts to reduce emissions citywide with the goal of slowing the pace of climate change. In 2007, the City initiated its Climate Action Plan (updated in 2011, 2014 and 2019) (City of Boston, 2019), which outlined a strategy of integrating climate preparedness into all aspects of city planning and regulation. Climate Ready Boston, a multi-plan initiative that is still under way, began in 2016 as an effort to build on the Climate Action Plan and guide Boston's adaptation efforts.

The 2016 Climate Ready Boston Report (CRB) features four main components: climate projections, vulnerability assessments, identification of focus areas for future study and specific action, and climate resilience initiatives. The climate projections include four factors: extreme temperatures, extreme precipitation, relative sea level rise, and coastal storms. Vulnerability assessments follow from these projections and

DOI: 10.4324/9781003183419-10

Figure 6.1 A king tide comes up over Long Wharf in Downtown Boston. Once or twice a year, visitors get their feet wet exploring these indicators of future conditions at more and more locations along Boston's waterfront.

identify stormwater flooding, extreme heat and coastal flooding as anticipated future chronic hazards. Coastal flooding has been the focus of an ongoing series of neighborhood-based plans and the catalyst for a series of open space projects that serve as the basis for the discussions within this chapter. Stormwater management actions as well as city-wide urban heat and urban forest plans, now under way, will be critical components of climate adaptation and development of social resilience throughout the region.

Since the completion of the CRB report, a series of neighborhood-level plans have been undertaken, beginning with Phase 1 of East Boston and Charlestown in 2017 (City of Boston, 2017), followed by South Boston, Downtown, Dorchester, and Phase II of both East Boston and Charlestown. These plans build on the city-wide effort with both further specific analysis of coastal risks and a focus on planning and design solutions that reduce risk through adaptations that promote quality public open space, access to the waterfront, and other social and environmental benefits.

In each of the plans, neighborhood specific roadmaps guide the implementation of near-term actions (prior to 2030) and long-term actions (through 2050 and beyond). They include high-level phasing plans based on key milestones, cost estimates, and benefit–cost analysis as well as identification of responsible parties and prerequisite measures. The most immediate near-term actions are then further described with design recommendations, key policy changes or partnerships required, and opportunities for funding.

Social vulnerability, defined by Martin (2015) as the disproportionate susceptibility of some social groups to the impacts of hazards including death, injury, loss or disruption of livelihood, and ability to recover from the impacts of risk, has been a significant additional qualitative consideration in Boston's planning efforts.

Seven groups were identified by the 2016 Climate Ready Boston report as particularly susceptible to future climate risks. These include adults over the age of 65, children, people of color, and people with limited English proficiency, low to no income, disabilities, or chronic and acute medical illness. Each of these factors creates additional challenges to the ability to adapt to climate risks. Many of these co-occur among Boston's diverse population.

Social vulnerability was an important deciding factor in where to begin focused study. East Boston was chosen first due to its high incidence of many factors for social vulnerability. These include a large immigrant population with low levels of English proficiency, low incomes, and high numbers of children and seniors living in an area with variable, but overall low levels of tree canopy as well as areas subject to flooding today and increasingly widespread flooding with as little as 9" of sea level rise. For similar reasons, Moakley Park, a 60-acre waterfront park along the flood pathways in South Boston was chosen as a site of early investment by the city due in part to its proximity to many lower income neighborhoods, with significant racial diversity and social vulnerability.

Design Synopsis

Study Area

With 47 miles of shoreline, Boston has an extensive waterfront. This waterfront and the Harbor Islands just beyond it are one of its greatest public resources. Boston was historically a set of islands and peninsulas connected by the harbor, extensive salt marshes, and mud flats. Over time, these marshes were filled in to create the distinct neighborhoods that define the city today (Seasholes, 2013). The distinct shorelines of each neighborhood have been in flux since their formation, with wharves and piers removed, redeveloped, or abandoned. This historic geography is both relevant to predicted patterns of coastal flooding and to the study methodology outlined in the CRB report.

Plans for adaptation to sea level rise and coastal storms in Boston have highlighted the need for continued and even improved access to the resource of the harbor and advocated for the creation of improved ecological and social value along the waterfront as benefits that can and should coincide with investment in coastal infrastructure.

First among the many near-term projects initiated by the City through its Climate Ready program in partnership with Boston Parks and Recreation are a number of waterfront parks and open spaces. Langone and Puopolo Park, recently constructed in the North End, is the first of these to be completed. Lewis Mall and Carlton Wharf in East Boston are just getting under way, as is Ryan Playground in Charlestown. Moakley Park, in South Boston, is the largest and most complex project undertaken to date. At 60 acres, Moakley Park is one of the City's largest parks and the largest along the waterfront. The park is a 'missing link' in Frederick Law Olmsted's original Emerald Necklace vision. Early Olmsted drawings show Moakley Park connected to Franklin Park via a parkway along Columbia Road. The Columbia Road parkway was never completed, leaving Moakley disconnected and an under-appreciated gem in the Boston Parks and Recreation Department collection of parks and open spaces.

Current projections for sea level rise and storm impacts indicate that with approximately 21 inches of sea level rise and a 1% storm, Moakley Park becomes the third arm in a triad of flood pathways that, over time, flood large portions of Boston including South Boston, the South End, Dorchester, and Roxbury (BRAG, 2016). Of critical importance within this flood pathway are two of Boston Housing Authority's oldest properties, Mary Ellen McCormack Housing and Old Colony Houses (Figure 6.2). Compounding these risks are a series of infrastructural challenges, both buried, and on the surface, including numerous underground utilities, high groundwater, and difficult geotechnical conditions. The Moakley Park Resilience Plan, a multi-year design and planning process begun in 2017 as the "Moakley Park Vision Plan" (City of Boston, 2018), tackles these challenging conditions and transforms this single-use recreational facility into a resilient, inclusive and multifaceted community park. Through this plan, Moakley Park is poised to address the city's most pressing climate resilience, social justice, and community health and welfare priorities.

Figure 6.2 Projected flood pathways, Moakley Park (at center), Morrissey Boulevard (South), and Fort Point Channel (North).

Sea Level Rise Projections

Projections for sea level rise and their impacts in Boston have utilized a means of assessment that provides complete probability distributions of flood risk under changing climate conditions. These physics-based models utilize both site-specific data and national data that are adjusted down to the specific conditions and dynamics of the landscape in Boston. The work of Kirk Bosma and his team at Woods Hole Group, which has been a basis for the Climate Ready Boston regional and district-level plans, takes the science and site-specific sea level rise predictions and applies them to high-resolution climate and hydrodynamic modeling that accurately represents physical processes causing coastal flooding. Modeled processes include dynamic assessment of tide, wind, surge, and waves that are used for mapping the extent of inundation in a probabilistic manner. The result of this type of modeling is site-specific information, which can be used to develop design parameters and provide direction for planning and design, and far exceeds that of traditional, more simplistic, 'bathtub' type modeling (Bosma et al., 2015). The 'bathtub' approach simply compares the predicted water surface elevation against existing topography to generate an anticipated area of future inundation. This does not account for coastal dynamics, land cover, or anticipated length of time over which flooding may occur. The danger of this method is that it results in the possibility of over-prediction of flooding in some areas and under-prediction of other areas which would likely be inundated (Bosma, 2015).

Boston, with its highly variable, densely populated, and lengthy coastline should benefit greatly from this advanced approach to understanding coastal dynamics and developing risk assessments. With these models as a basis, the City of Boston (through the Climate Ready Boston reports) selected three sea level rise markers (9 inches, 21 inches, and 40 inches above sea levels measured in 2000) that are likely to occur within the century as a basis for planning. These levels are generally assumed to relate to dates of 2030, 2050, and 2070–2100. However, the actual sea level rise Boston experiences will be driven by many factors, including the degree of reduction in global carbon emissions achieved over the coming years. Regardless, climate models show that near-term sea level rise of at least 9 inches should be assumed even if there is a major reduction in emissions due to carbon emissions that have already occurred (City of Boston, 2016). Patterns of large storms such as hurricanes and nor'easters that regularly impact Boston's shores are also of significance. According to the BRAG report, there remains uncertainty regarding the response of these storms to changing environmental conditions (e.g. predictions for future increase in intensity or number). Continued assessment will be informative to the City's understanding of risk.

An important feature of Boston's approach is the general embrace of these models as themselves being dynamic and constantly undergoing a process of re-evaluation and evolution as more information is gained. Since the development of the Boston Harbor Flood Risk Model

(BHFRM), which much of the Climate Ready Boston work used as a basis, the state has been developing the Massachusetts Coastal Flood Risk Model (MCFRM) which expands the BHFRM to the entire coast of Massachusetts. This model suggests new design elevations for most locations in Boston and is quickly becoming the standard for assessing coastal assets. At the same time, a new assessment project, called the Greater Boston Research Advisory Group (GBRAG) is under way and intended to update and expand upon the original BRAG report assessments. This project is being conducted by the School for the Environment and the Urban Harbors Institute at the University of Massachusetts Boston and the Metropolitan Area Planning Council (MAPC) (UMass, 2019). Boston, and the region, has thus far taken an approach of support for the evolution of the data and continues to seek means for integrating recommendations into planning and design in as coordinated a way as possible, given the shifting environment of coastal assessments.

These evolving projections have been taken into account in the planning and design for Moakley Park. The design has also been informed by highly site-specific hydrologic models completed by Woods Hole Group. Based on these models, the core wall which acts as the primary mechanism for flood risk reduction has been designed to an elevation of 22′ using the Boston City Base datum. This is roughly equivalent to 15.5′ using the NAVD88 datum discussed in many of the references provided.

Design Synopsis

Structural and Non-Structural Mechanisms

Once a salt marsh and mudflat, Moakley Park has been unofficially used for recreation since 1909 when it served as first a garbage dump and then a playground. Filled in 1919 with harbor-dredged clay, the site's flat profile and impermeable soil cause flooding after even mild rain events, often leaving recreational amenities unusable.

The coastal flood management strategy developed in the Moakley Park Resilience Plan is deeply informed by this historical context and is designed to provide both environmental and social benefits. An engineered flood-protection wall runs the length of the park embedded into the topography, and creates new nodes for play, exploration, year-round recreation, and improved biodiversity. Early plans envisioned this wall as a landscaped berm. Geotechnical findings completed after the initial vision revealed remarkably varied subgrade conditions including soils prone to subsidence. This, in combination with the presence of large, below grade utilities indicated that an engineered wall with lightweight fill where feasible was the preferred strategy. The integration of the wall both lightens the footprint and overall weight of the berm, and, most importantly, allows for the planting of shade trees much closer to the top of the berm, allowing for cooler conditions on hot summer days.

A series of coastal hydrologic studies were completed to determine the required height of the wall. Through these studies, it was found that a regular program of beach nourishment and dune restoration on the adjacent Carson Beach and the coastal landscape within the park could reduce the required height of the core wall, allowing for a reduced overall soil load. These measures, if implemented, will also add important areas of public recreation and biodiversity at the waterfront.

The coastal protection at Moakley is only fully effective if it ties into efforts taking place on adjacent properties. Designing and implementing a contiguous line of protection to block the full flood pathway will require continued conversation with property owners, private developers, City and State utilities, the Massachusetts Department of Conservation and Recreation, the Massachusetts Department of Transportation,

Table 6.1 Moakley Park proposed ecological and social resilience strategies

Moakley Park proposed program elements:	*Structural*	*Non-structural*	*Hybrid*
Program elements for coastal & stormwater flood mitigation:			
Core wall	X		
Coastal dunes		X	
Stormwater meadows		X	
Elevated landscape		X	
Subgrade stormwater tanks	X		
Tree trenches	X		
Bioswales		X	
Pervious materials		X	
Program elements for heat mitigation:			
Increased tree canopy		X	
Light colored pavements		X	
Splash pad/fountains		X	
Misting stations		X	
Drinking fountains		X	
Program elements for social & ecological benefit:			
Gardens		X	
Increased vegetative diversity		X	
Community center/resilience hub			X
Bikeways & walking promenades		X	
Community plazas		X	
Playgrounds		X	
Improved active recreation amenities		X	

as well as numerous community members and advocacy groups who utilize and value this important coastal asset.

Under current conditions, the athletic fields are often unusable after rains due to stormwater flooding, a condition that is anticipated to worsen with increased precipitation. Green infrastructure strategies are therefore planned across the site, including stormwater meadows, bioswales, subgrade storage tanks, tree trenches, and porous pavement. These strategies, in addition to the introduction of hundreds of new trees and a mix of native plants including coastal marsh species, maritime shrublands, and woodland communities, are envisioned to help reduce heat and increase biodiversity. A full list of resiliency strategies planned for is shown in Table 6.1.

Design Impact

While addressing resilience and infrastructural challenges, the design seeks to address multiple known community risks including sea level rise, extreme heat, ecological degradation, obesity, safety, and social injustice. It additionally champions multi-modal transportation and safe access to adjacent spaces like Carson Beach and the HarborWalk, a 43-mile linear park along Boston's shoreline. Community input alongside engineering discovery were the major forces guiding critical design decisions – always filtered through a lens of equity and inclusion. Open houses, on-site events, community meetings, and surveys were valuable tools of community engagement that continue to allow for diverse voices to guide the design and planning process.

The design programmatically divides the park into three zones – the coastal park, the core and crest, and the city edge. These zones are largely defined by the location of the coastal flood protection (the core wall) running north to south. Along the "city edge" adjacent to the Mary Ellen McCormack community to the west, the focus is on critical issues of access and connectivity, promoting rich opportunities for social interaction. A tree-lined community path, running trail, and raised cycle track create an edge that is designed to draw people into the park. Connections outward into the neighborhood promote safe access for pedestrians, cyclists, people arriving from buses and The T, Boston's mass transit system. Healthy play amenities such as street hockey, a skate plaza, basketball, and table games combine with spaces for community gathering to activate the park (Figure 6.3).

The "crest and core," the interior zone, is defined by the location of the "core wall." The wall is woven through the landscape and layered into park programming to act as flood risk reduction without disconnecting the city from the waterfront. Sports fields are placed behind the wall and provided with improved drainage to reduce stormwater flooding. Spaces between fields become new destinations. For example, a large nature play area situated on the inland side of the core wall encourages exploration for people of all ages and abilities.

Figure 6.3 Moakley Park Resilience Plan at top with City Edge along the adjacent community, coastal park along the waterfront, and core and crest between. The City Edge activates the park immediately adjacent to the neighborhood with recreational program, bikeways, and shaded pedestrian walkways. Stormwater management through green infrastructure and underground storage is embedded throughout.

From the top of the flood barrier eastward, the "coastal park" provides a critical connection between the park and the waterfront at Carson beach. The design accepts future coastal flooding allowing water to inundate the landscape. In addition to coastal dunes and marshes, this area features a central waterfront plaza and amphitheater designed for year-round use from festival events and food trucks to water-play in the fountain in summer, and ice skating in winter (Figure 6.4).

Throughout the park, measures are anticipated to promote social and ecological resilience. A Community Resilience hub with access to critical

Figure 6.4 Moakley Park Resilience Plan. The coastal park creates areas of diverse habitat that help to reduce risk of coastal flooding. The Core wall, shown in a white dashed line (above) separating the coastal park from the sports fields and community amenities, is the primary flood risk reduction measure. The waterfront plaza and amphitheater act as community event space on sunny days while providing risk reduction for the park and the neighborhood during storms up to the 1% annual storm risk with 40" of sea level rise.

services during emergencies such as high heat days or flood events is envisioned in the Community Center building at the Northwest corner of the park. Plazas provide locations for farmers markets, food trucks or community events. Increased canopy and improved vegetative diversity both generate shade and improve ecological conditions. Gardens and other activities to connect people to nature provide opportunity for education and community building.

Together these features create a modern, 21st-century community park that addresses pressing climate change needs while also prioritizing social, cultural, economic, and environmental equity through the creation of an unparalleled amenity for the City of Boston.

Conclusions

Innovation and Applicability

This case study demonstrates the application of multi-scalar planning and design from city-wide planning to district/neighborhood level planning and site-specific design. These varied scales are assessed interdependently but inform one another. District-wide studies are critical to the development of planning timelines and processes that guide resources toward site-specific projects. In the city-wide context, no single project can be the solution to the many issues posed by a changing climate. Instead, a series of well-timed and coordinated projects, each of which addresses a section of the anticipated flood pathways and/or different climate-based risks (heat, stormwater, coastal flooding) will allow for full district level risk reduction.

Boston and the State of Massachusetts' approach to flood risk modeling sets an example for cities and regions worldwide. Highly specific hydrologic models that incorporate the dynamics of Boston's coastal environment provide targeted and site-specific recommendations for planning and design that are anticipated to reduce both over- and under-prediction of risks. Development of planning and design across scales and through multiple State and City entities has continued to develop these models and encouraged ongoing evaluation and adaptation of data that inform design decisions, ensuring that both the data analysis and the design are adaptable as future conditions are better understood.

Moakley Park, when coupled with projects on adjacent properties and nearby flood pathways, will reduce the risk of coastal flooding for a significant area of Boston over the next 50 years, and possibly beyond. The coordinated effort between properties, and the vision for the site emerged directly from the district-level planning that set the goals and vision for Boston. Completing these risk reduction measures through renovation of an underutilized waterfront park is a recognition of the social and ecological value of public waterfronts and the opportunity for multiple ecological and community benefits to be integrated into climate-adaptive infrastructure. The placement of social and environmental justice at the core of this work provides a framework from which other cities can begin to evaluate their own historic patterns, both social and environmental, to envision a resilient future for all.

References

Bosma, K., Douglas, E., Kirshen, P., McArthur, K., Miller, S., & Watson, C. (2015). *Climate change and extreme weather vulnerability assessments and adaptation options for the central artery*. Boston, MA: MassDOT.

Boston Research Advisory Group (BRAG). (2016). *Climate change and sea level rise projections for Boston: Boston Research Advisory Group report*. City of Boston. Retrieved from www.boston.gov/sites/default/files/document-file-12-2016/brag_report_-_final.pdf

City of Boston. (2019). *2019 Climate action plan*. Retrieved from www.boston.gov/departments/environment/boston-climate-action

City of Boston. (2016). *Climate ready Boston*. Retrieved from www.boston.gov/sites/default/files/embed/2/20161207_climate_ready_boston_digital2.pdf

City of Boston. (2017). *Coastal resilience solutions for East Boston and Charlestown. Final report October 2017*. Retrieved from www.boston.gov/sites/default/files/embed/c/climatereadyeastbostoncharlestown_finalreport_web.pdf

City of Boston. (2018). *Moakley Park Vision Plan, 2018* (and ongoing). Retrieved from www.boston.gov/moakley-park-vision-plan

Martin, S. A. (2015). A framework to understand the relationship between social factors that reduce resilience in cities: Application to the City of Boston. *International Journal of Disaster Risk Reduction*, 12, 53–80.

Seasholes, N. S. (2003). *Gaining ground: A history of landmaking in Boston*. Cambridge, MA: MIT Press.

UMass Boston. (2019). Updated climate change projections for Greater Boston communities. Retrieved from www.umb.edu/gbrag/about

7

PHILADELPHIA, PENNSYLVANIA

Hong Wu

Site: Philadelphia, PA; multi-scalar

Introduction/Rationale

Low-lying coastal cities face combined threats from sea level rise, storm surges, and riverine/tidal flooding, which will likely be significantly exacerbated with unmitigated climate change impacts (Spanger-Siegfried et al., 2014). Due to rising sea levels, higher baseline river levels in and around coastal cities would not only permanently inundate larger parts of the cities, but also increase the frequency and severity of flooding brought by storm surges and high tides. Further, increases in both the magnitude and frequency of coastal storms and tides are already becoming a reality (Li et al., 2021), making flooding the costliest of all natural hazards in coastal cities.

This chapter showcases multi-scalar climate planning and design efforts in Philadelphia, PA, USA, an early adapter city threatened by the multiple sources of flooding mentioned above due to its location 90 miles inland from the mouth of the Delaware Bay (Uittenbroek et al., 2016). As the second-most populous city on the US East Coast and a historical urban treasure, Philadelphia is endeavoring to adapt to the changing climate while facing challenges from aging infrastructure and meeting the demands of a growing, diverse population. The city is anticipating a warmer and wetter future climate, primarily in the form of heatwaves and heavy rain or snow events. In addition, there is a projected potential sea level rise of up to 2 feet by 2050 and 4 feet by 2100, under a moderate carbon emissions scenario along the Philadelphia coast; this projection reaches up to 6 feet by 2100 under a high emissions scenario (ICF International, 2014). Extreme events, such as heavy rain or snowstorms, tropical storms, and hurricanes, will likely become more frequent and severe (ICF International, 2014). Rising water levels in the Delaware and Schuylkill rivers surrounding the city, combined with larger storm surges and high and more extensive tides, will increase both the magnitude and frequency of flooding (see Figure 7.1a and b).

Specifically, floods within the Delaware Estuary will likely exceed 4 feet above the local high tide line – a level never experienced before 1900 – by 2040, under a mid-range sea level rise scenario. Under a high-range scenario, however, the probability of floods exceeding 4 feet may increase their chance of occurrence by 75% by 2040, and floods exceeding 9 feet

DOI: 10.4324/9781003183419-11

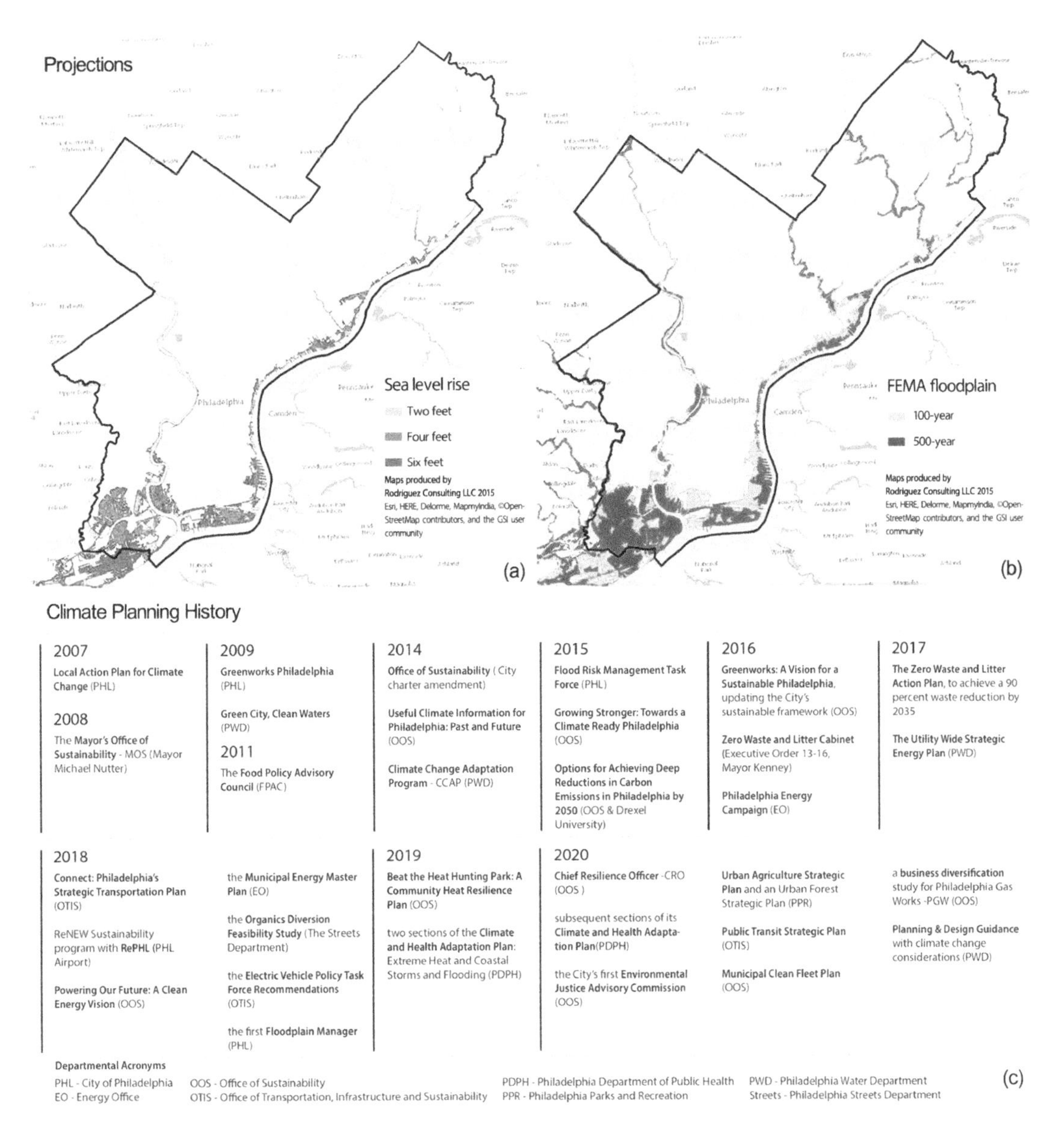

Figure 7.1 Projections of potential inundation and Philadelphia's climate planning history: (a) areas at risk of inundation by a Category 1 storm (the most severe historical hurricane in the region) on top of 2/4/6 feet of sea level rise; (b) areas at risk of inundation under 100-year/500-year flood (Office of Sustainability and ICF International, 2015); (c) Philadelphia's climate planning history (Office of Sustainability, 2021).

may increase by 80% by 2100 (see Figure 7.1a and b) (Strauss et al., 2016). Regarding the frequency of flooding, Philadelphia will likely face over 200 tidal floods per year by 2045, compared to 19 events per year currently (Spanger-Siegfried et al., 2014). Under these projections, over 30 city-owned facilities, including the Philadelphia International Airport, will be highly or moderately vulnerable to flooding. Around 3,640 acres of land lie below the 4 feet above high tide line level, 75% of which are not protected by any engineered or natural flood control features. This circumstance also indicates that roughly 1,700 housing units, 3,220 people (73% of whom are people of color), 38 miles of roads, and a total of $524 million in property value will be unprotected from the 4-foot flood level (Climate Central, 2016).

Design Synopsis

City-scale

Named a Global Climate Leader on the 2020 "A List" by CDP (Office of Sustainability, 2020), a non-profit organization known for corporate and city environmental impacts disclosure, Philadelphia demonstrated early awareness of climate change risks and initiated its climate action efforts as early as 2007 (see Figure 7.1c). The city has since implemented many plans and measures to reduce energy use and greenhouse gas emissions, transition to renewable energy resources, reduce and manage waste, and mitigate flood impacts (Office of Sustainability and ICF International, 2015). Notable plans and guidelines include the *Greenworks Philadelphia* plan (Office of Sustainability, n.d.), the *Green City, Clean Waters* Program (PWD, n.d.), both released in 2009, as well as the *Powering Our Future: A Clean Energy Vision* released in 2018 (Office of Sustainability, 2018).

The renowned *Green City, Clean Waters* Program, established in 2011, is the first EPA-approved, comprehensive, city-scale plan that leverages primarily green infrastructure to address stormwater quantity and quality issues. It is also part of the city's climate action efforts, with benefits beyond stormwater management. The extensive network of over 2,800 green infrastructure installed to date has kept more than 2.7 billion gallons of polluted stormwater runoff out of the Schuylkill and Delaware Rivers (PWD, n.d.). They are also estimated to help clean and cool the air, reduce asthma and heat-related illnesses, avoid approximately 1.5 billion pounds of CO_2 annually, and increase property values by $390 million over 45 years (PWD, n.d.).

Besides the *Green City, Clean Waters* Program, the master plan for the Central Delaware completed in 2011 (DRWC, 2014) represents the city's large-scale waterfront planning efforts to transform its fragmented post-industrial riverfront into vibrant urban assets adaptive to future river conditions. Efforts are being made to enable new and existing riverfront parks to serve as buffers that protect the city from the encroaching sea (DRWC, 2014). This park network will also allow public access at half-mile intervals along the 6-mile shoreline. Besides, the plan carefully chose locations where bulkhead edges will be replaced to restore wetlands and enhance habitat continuity among mudflats, low marsh, high marsh, and upland habitat (OLIN, n.d.).

Franklin Delano Roosevelt (FDR) Park Showcase

Because the FDR Park master plan represents Philadelphia's state-of-the-art large-scale site planning efforts, hereafter, we elaborate on the specific design mechanisms proposed for FDR (see Figure 7.2) to provide adaptive design implications for large-scale urban parks. Historically a freshwater tidal marsh, the 348-acre FDR Park is located by the Delaware River in the southernmost point of South Philadelphia and was initially designed by the Olmsted Brothers as the district's only large urban oasis. FDR Park currently consists of lakes, lagoons, the American Swedish Historical Museum, a golf course, and other sports facilities (see Figure 7.2c). Heavily used by the public since 1921, aging infrastructure and degraded environment have compromised the park's ability to provide essential ecosystem services. Because most of the park lies below sea level, flooding has been a persistent challenge for FDR, and this condition will be exacerbated by the effects of climate change (See Figure 7.2a). In 2017, the Fairmount Park Conservancy, along with Philadelphia Parks and Recreation and Friends of FDR Park, launched a master planning process to restore FDR to its original intent as a "green treasure" while adapting to the needs of a changing city and environment.

The persistent flooding issues at FDR, which have rendered many of the park's primary recreation facilities inaccessible, can be primarily attributed to its semi-functional tide gate, excessive and untreated stormwater, high groundwater table, and poor site drainage. The tide gate, currently located in the Navy Yard Reserve Basin, can no longer

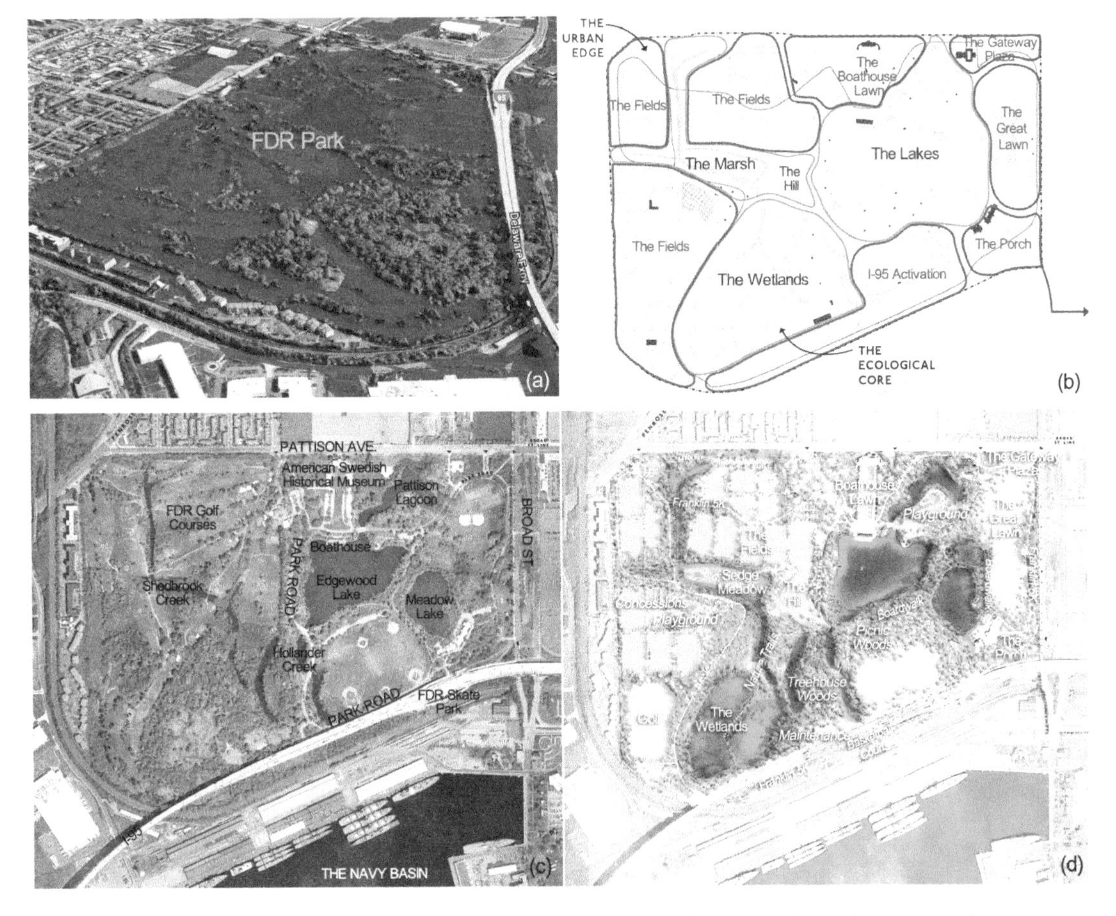

Figure 7.2 The Master Plan shows a two-part structure (Ecological Core + Urban Edge) responsive to current and future inundations: (a) Rendering by the Surging Seas tool, showing FDR inundation under an extreme sea-level rise scenario in 2100 (Credit: Climate Central); (b) The proposed Ecological Core and Urban Edge structure; (c) Aerial image of the park today (ca. 2020); (d) Master Plan in Spring 2021.
Source: b, c, d: adapted from The Fairmount Park Conservancy et al. (2021).

properly close at high tide and open at low tide, and is therefore unable to sufficiently drain the park during storms. Moreover, the park receives a massive amount of untreated stormwater from surrounding areas, especially around roadway I-95, leading to water quality impairment. Under climate change, the expected 2-foot sea level rise by 2050, along with more severe and frequent storms and tides, will impact the drainage capacity and prolong the time it takes to drain the park.

Structural and Non-structural Mechanisms

The master plan for FDR employed three primary strategies integrating various structural, non-structural, and hybrid mechanisms to create resilience to current and future climatic impacts (see Figure 7.3 and Table 7.1). They include: (1) rebuilding the tide gate and improving flow connections among the lagoon, lakes, and creeks to increase flood storage; (2) recontouring the land by creating and expanding water bodies and using the excavated material to raise critical park programming out of the existing floodplain; and (3) creating a large number of rain gardens and bioswales to increase the park's capacity to store and fully treat internal and external stormwater. These strategies were proposed to be implemented with a two-part spatial structure that involves the "ecological core" and "urban edge" (see Figure 7.2b). The former consists of the Wetlands, Marsh, Lakes, and Hill, whereas the latter includes the Gateway Plaza, Great Lawn, Boathouse Lawn, Porch, Fields, and I-95 activation. Next, we elaborate on specific strategies in the core and edge that work together to facilitate water circulation, filtration, and storage.

The Tide Gate (Structural)

The primary structural mechanism proposed is to relocate and rebuild the tide gate to facilitate water circulation and more sufficiently drain the park after flood events to enhance accessibility. The tide gate, currently in the Navy Basin, will be moved inside to be maintained by the park's own staff. The twin arch culvert will be repaired, clogged debris removed, with a new grate at the Navy Basin mouth to prevent river debris from entering the park.

The Wetlands, Marsh, and Lakes (Primarily Non-structural)

The Wetlands, Marsh, and Lakes will be the major water bodies of the Ecological Core (see Figure 7.2b). First, the master plan proposed to create a new system of tidal and non-tidal wetlands on a 45-acre site in the southwest corner of FDR. Historically a natural backwater retention reservoir providing emergency flood storage, the site for the Wetlands has become a derelict land filled with debris, construction waste, and invasive vegetation. The wetland creation was not only the single most significant water body addition to drain the park faster after a rain event, but it was also part of a regional strategy to create a permanent wetland mitigation bank to attenuate future development impacts at the Philadelphia International Airport. The approximately 270,000 m^3 of earth to be excavated will become the primary source of fill to raise active programming areas out of the existing floodplain. Besides, the wetlands will perform critical water quality treatment functions intercepting and cleansing stormwater runoff via natural processes. Flow control devices, such as a sluice gate (structural) and a high-hanging valley channel (hybrid), will be installed to connect the upstream Shedbrook Creek with the Wetlands for the latter to provide additional stormwater storage during high flows.

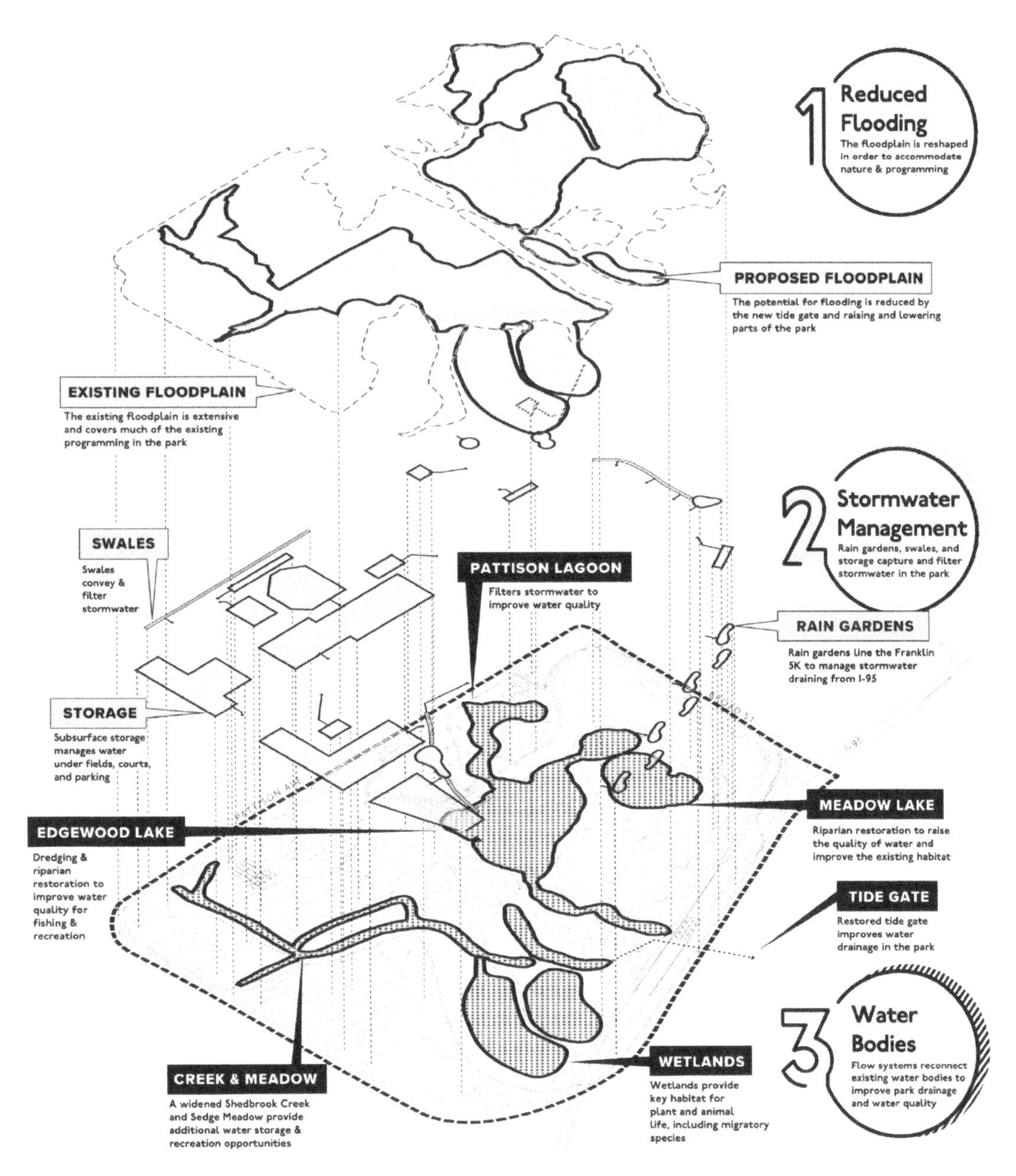

Figure 7.3 The master plan employs three strategies of floodplain modification, stormwater management, and water body creation to address flooding and improve water quality.
Credit: The Fairmount Park Conservancy.

Table 7.1 FDR Park program elements and structural, non-structural, and hybrid mechanisms

Program elements	*Structural*	*Non-structural*	*Hybrid*
Program elements for flood mitigation:			
Sluice gate	X		
Natural weir			X
High-hanging valley channel			X
Widened/deepened channel		X	
Dredged areas		X	
Wetland creation		X	
Underground stormwater storage	X		
Bioswales		X	
Rain gardens		X	
Program elements for reducing pollutant load:			
Riparian buffers around waterbodies		X	
Select dredging		X	
Plant species promoting phytoremediation	X		
Material reuse and recycling			X
Wetland forebay		X	
Floating wetlands		X	
Bioswales		X	
Rain gardens		X	
Program elements for ecological restoration:			
Wetland creation		X	
Sedge meadow restoration		X	
Urban forest		X	
Program elements for enhancing recreation:			
Earthen mounds		X	
Recreational boardwalks			X
Multipurpose recreation fields and courts	X		
Playground			X
Treehouse woods		X	
Picnic woods		X	
5 km multipurpose trail			X
Event lawns		X	
Concessions			X

Second, the proposed Marsh area includes an expansion to Shedbrook Creek – the key waterway within the Ecological Core – and a restored 4-acre Sedge Meadow. The wider and deeper Shedbrook Creek, now also with a raised boardwalk trail, will increase stormwater capacity while offering visitors new recreational opportunities to immerse themselves in nature. The Sedge Meadow not only helps to increase flood storage and balance overall cut-and-fill, but also reclaims some of the park's original freshwater tide marsh eco-type.

Third, various stormwater management and water quality treatment strategies were proposed for the Lakes, including the Pattison Lagoon, Edgewood Lake, and Meadow Lake. The Pattison Lagoon, which used to receive two of the largest external stormwater sources, will be restored with a wetland forebay with pre-treatment filtration to reduce pollutant discharges into the park's water system. The existing, small bioswale east of the lagoon, which filters the piped stormwater inflow from Broad Street, will be transformed into an enhanced rain garden infiltrating larger volumes of runoff, meanwhile providing natural habitat and enhancing the park aesthetics. A new, lower natural weir (hybrid) will replace the overly high concrete dam spillway that currently connects the two lakes, enabling the Meadow Lake to serve as a flood storage reserve. Moreover, other measures, including select dredging of the lagoon and Edgewood Lake, floating islands in the Meadow Lake, and riparian reforestation along all lake edges, will be undertaken to increase storage, remove legacy pollution, improve water quality, and enhance habitat.

Stormwater Management throughout (Primarily Non-structural)

A system of new and enhanced rain gardens, swales, and subsurface storage will retain, cleanse, and store stormwater before releasing it into the central water bodies mentioned above. Specifically, all new sports fields, courts, and certain parking lots will be designed with subsurface storage (structural) with overflow connections to the Lakes or Shedbrook Creek. A large number of periphery rain gardens will manage stormwater from adjacent roads, including I-95 and Pattison Avenue. Swales and rain gardens will also manage internal runoff from the Great Lawn, park road, the Porch, and the Gateway Plaza.

Design Impacts

The restored park will offer a wide range of environmental, social, and economic benefits to the residents and visitors of Philadelphia (see Figure 7.4). The reconfigured water system will help mitigate flooding impacts and filter polluted stormwater for both the park itself and surrounding areas. Ecosystem preservation and restoration will protect and enhance the last remnants of natural habitat in the Atlantic Coastal Plain in Pennsylvania. Improved park access and recreational programming will connect people from across the city and beyond, nurture social interaction and community cohesion, provide nature experiences, and improve physical and mental health. The transformation of the historical park into a city icon and tourist destination will enable the park to self-sustain its long-term operations and maintenance.

Figure 7.4 (a) Birds-eye of the future Park; (b) View towards the proposed Marsh from the Hill to be constructed with excavated material from the creation of new water bodies; (c) Nature experience along the trail weaving through the proposed new Wetlands.
Credit: The Fairmount Park Conservancy.

Conclusions

Innovations and Applicability

The cross-scale climate planning and design efforts in Philadelphia offer many transferable lessons to cities facing similar future challenges. Perhaps the most critical take-home message would be that comprehensive, multi-scalar, long-term, and ambitious actions will be required to combat our current climate crisis. Broad applications of nature-based solutions, such as the Green City, Clean Water Program, are powerful tools that offer diverse environmental, social, and economic benefits.

The large-scale site planning at FDR Park, specifically, offers inspiration to urban public parks in derelict conditions but is uniquely positioned to help cities rebuild environmental and social resilience. The most critical lesson of FDR's master plan lies in its community-driven approach that integrates the needs of protecting the city from climate change, preserving critical natural habitats, and providing health and well-being benefits to the residents. Besides, FDR holds promise to become a national model for climate resilience design, showcasing the capabilities of combining innovative structural and non-structural water management mechanisms. Parks are often referred to as agents of social, environmental, and economic transformations. The next decade of reshaping FDR will demonstrate the power of reinvesting in public spaces to transform cities into more livable places, meanwhile resilient to future challenges.

References

Climate Central. (2016). *Sea level rise and coastal flood exposure: Summary for Philadelphia, PA*. Surging Seas Risk Finder file created July 21, 2016. Retrieved from http://ssrf.climatecentral.org.s3-website-us-east-1.amazonaws.com/Buffer2/states/PA/downloads/pdf_reports/Town/PA_Philadelphiareport.pdf

Delaware River Waterfront Corporation (DRWC). (2011). *Master plan for the central Delaware: Transforming Philadelphia's waterfront*. Retrieved from www.delawareriverwaterfront.com/planning/masterplan-for-the-central-delaware

ICF International. (2014). *Useful climate science for Philadelphia: Past and future* (p. 28). Retrieved from www.phila.gov/media/20160505145605/Useful-Climate-Science-for-Philadelphia.pdf

Li, S., Wahl, T., Talke, S. A., Jay, D. A., Orton, P. M., Liang, X., Wang, G., & Liu, L. (2021). Evolving tides aggravate nuisance flooding along the U.S. coastline. *Science Advances*, *7*(10), eabe2412.

Office of Sustainability, The City of Philadelphia. (2018). *Powering our future: A clean energy vision for Philadelphia*. Retrieved from www.phila.gov/media/20180821150658/Powering-Our-Future-Full-Report.pdf

Office of Sustainability, The City of Philadelphia. (2020). *Philadelphia named as a global climate leader on CDP 2020 "A List" for cities*. Retrieved February 17, 2021, from www.phila.gov/2020-11-23-philadelphia-named-as-a-global-climate-leader-on-cdp-2020-a-list-for-cities/

Office of Sustainability, The City of Philadelphia. (2021). *Philadelphia Climate Action Playbook*. Retrieved from www.phila.gov/media/20210113125627/Philadelphia-Climate-Action-Playbook.pdf

Office of Sustainability, The City of Philadelphia. (n.d.). *Greenworks*. Retrieved February 17, 2021, from www.phila.gov/programs/greenworks/

Office of Sustainability, & ICF International. (2015). *Growing stronger: Toward a climate-ready Philadelphia* (p. 82). Retrieved from www.phila.gov/media/20160504162056/Growing-Stronger-Toward-a-Climate-Ready-Philadelphia.pdf

OLIN. (n.d.). *Master plan for the Central Delaware*. Retrieved June 17, 2021, from www.theolinstudio.com/master-plan-for-the-central-delaware

Philadelphia Water Department (PWD). (n.d.). *Green city clean waters*. Retrieved June 17, 2021, from https://water.phila.gov/green-city/

Spanger-Siegfried, E., Fitzpatrick, M., & Dahl, K. (2014). *Encroaching tides: How sea level rise and tidal flooding threaten U.S. East and Gulf Coast communities over the next 30 years*. Union of Concerned Scientists.

Strauss, B., Tebaldi, C., Kulp, S., Cutter, S., Emrich, C., Rizza, D., & Yawitz, D. (2016). Pennsylvania and the surging sea: A vulnerability assessment with projections for sea level rise and coastal flood risk (p. 31). *Climate Central*. Retrieved from https://sealevel.climatecentral.org/uploads/ssrf/PA-Report.pdf

The Fairmount Park Conservancy, Philadelphia Parks & Recreation, & WRT, LLC. (2021). *FDR Park Master Plan*. Retrieved from https://myphillypark.org/what-we-do/capital-projects/fdr-park/

Uittenbroek, C. J., Janssen-Jansen, L. B., & Runhaar, H. A. C. (2016). Stimuli for climate adaptation in cities: Insights from Philadelphia – an early adapter. *International Journal of Climate Change Strategies and Management*, *8*(1), 38–56.

8

FISHERMAN'S BEND, VICTORIA, AUSTRALIA

Alexander J. Felson and Nano Langenheim

Site Size and Location

Fisherman's Bend was originally a tidal estuary with coastal salt marsh, swamp scrub, brackish estuarine wetlands and herb-rich woodlands located at the mouth of the Yarra River facing Port Phillip Bay (PPB). The aboriginal language groups called the Wurundjeri Woi-Wurrung and Boonwurrung peoples of the Kulin nation used the site as a fishing and meeting ground. The site has undergone indelible, irrevocable, and intensive change since European settlement, including widening and re-alignment of the shallow winding river bed and construction of the Coode Canal in 1887 to facilitate ship docking (Travers et al., 2017).

Introduction and Rationale

Fisherman's Bend (FB) is the largest urban renewal site in Australia and one of the largest brownfield redevelopments in the southern hemisphere. This former lowland swamp has an extensive industrial past including 80 years of occupation by the Department of Defence Science and Technology Group and General Motor's Holden (GMH). The latter, located on the site's highest ground, is where a new University of Melbourne campus is proposed (see Figure 8.1). The renewal and redevelopment of this large low-lying post-industrial site follows a calculated effort initiated in the 1970s to counteract sprawl, densifying near Melbourne's central business district (CBD). Between 2012 and 2016, the FB site, rezoned from industrial to commercial, business, and residential, is 2.5 times the size of the existing CBD. At completion in 2050, it is expected to house 80,000 new residents and a corresponding number of employment opportunities.

Despite its size and strategic proximity to Melbourne's CBD, the site has persistent overlapping problems. Flooding from storms, rainfall, river, and predicted sea level rise (SLR) of .82 to 1.2m, will complicate on-site water management, green infrastructure and building development options (Nicholls & Cazenave, 2010). The highwater table (groundwater), limited infiltration and soil storage capacity exacerbate and compound development risks. Undersized drainage infrastructure and

DOI: 10.4324/9781003183419-12

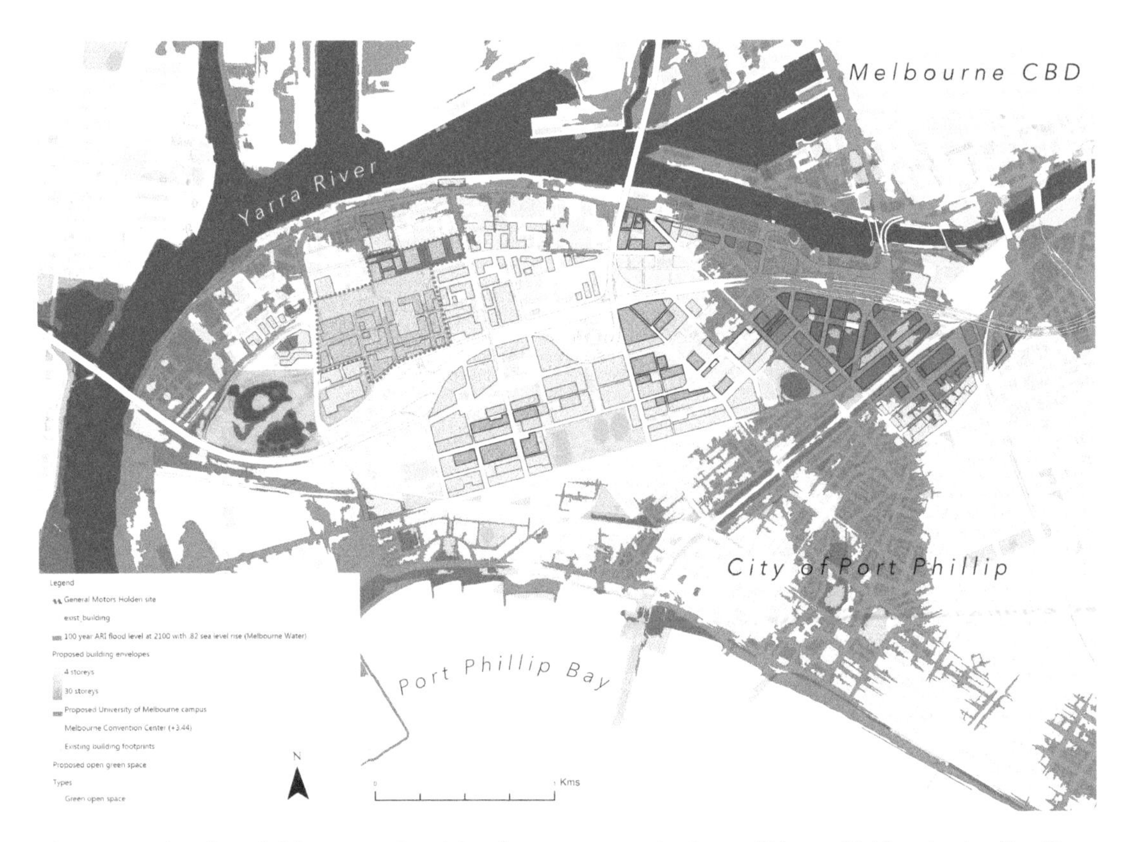

Figure 8.1 Site plan of Fisherman's Bend development area, the General Motors Holden site (outlined in red), within which lies the proposed University of Melbourne campus. The flood overlay shows a modelled 2100 extent at storm tide with a projected sea level rise of 82 cm and an increase in storm surge of 19% (Melbourne Water Corporation 2014). The existing Melbourne Convention Centre (integrated levee building) is shown in yellow.

geotechnical issues require large public utility investments and deep piling for structures over eight storeys. Extensive soil and ground water contamination demand heavy investment and cannot be fully remediated. In the long term, predicted widespread inundation of coastal terrestrial areas due to SLR will raise groundwater levels and exacerbate sub-surface contamination impacts. The groundwater hazards threaten the health and resilience of residential neighbourhoods, infrastructure, and ecosystems (Befus et al., 2020).

Given this complexity, the committed transportation and infrastructure investments, and the remediation requirements due to earlier industrial practices, repercussions based on land development decisions are unavoidable and critical to consider. Efforts of the range of stakeholders at FB, including two local governments, water, transport, road and port authorities, and multiple communities, to establish viable adaptation planning will face challenges around how to manage, finance, implement and stage the flood defences and to what level of service. In addition, high rates of private ownership may compete with other uses such as open space provision and accessibility (AECOM, 2018).

In this chapter we explore three flood infrastructure and urban design response scenarios at FB, principally focusing on the three primary, interdependent facets of development: buildings, streetscapes and levees.

Projections and Effects of Sea Level at Fisherman's Bend

Compound flooding from four sources impact FB: storm surge, rainfall, riverine, and tidal, each requiring targeted management strategies, and all exacerbated by SLR.

1. **Fluvial or riverine flooding** impact FB, due to its location at the base of four adjacent catchments that discharge into the Yarra River and Port Phillip Bay.
2. **Flooding from storm surge** can raise the sea level for days to weeks as strong westerly winds trap water within PPB. Officially released modelling for storm surge impact by 2100 anticipates an increase of 19%, responding to the Intergovernmental Panel on Climate Change (IPCC) 2007 projections of SLR of .8m (Meehl et al., 2007, p. 751). Modelling is not yet available for the revised IPCC for an SLR of 1.2m released in 2020 that takes into account projected melting of the Greenland and Antarctic glaciers and ice sheets (Millar, 2021).
3. **Tidal flooding** is also likely to impact the site with increasing sea levels, caused by astronomical tides known as sunny day flooding. The combined implications of storm surge and tidal flooding (**storm tide flooding**) represents the most dramatic flood condition for the site and has potential to increase salinity and water table heights through sea water intrusion processes into the contaminated groundwater.
4. **Rainfall patterns** in Australia also display an evolving long-term increase in intensity alongside decreased annual quantity and prolonged periods of drought. At FB, intense storm events will increase occurrence of pluvial flooding, overwhelming the existing pit and pipe system, designed to cater for low rise industry. Extended drought and water restrictions can increase tree mortality, restrict green infrastructure maintenance, increase ground movement, alter the water table and increase soil salinity. Such alterations can lower the life expectancy of transportation infrastructure and increase maintenance costs (AECOM, 2018).

While there are multiple options for managing floods at FB including upgrading the pipe and pit network, adding pumping stations, and raising ground levels across the entire site, the costs of these interventions are substantial to prohibitive. To support any built infrastructural upgrades, innovative, surface drainage strategies that are integrated with planning and urban design are required. In the following section we describe the advantages and disadvantages of three primary yet divergent options for structuring integrated flood and redevelopment proposals. We describe each of these three strategies in isolation, though they will likely be used in conjunction on site (see Figure 8.2).

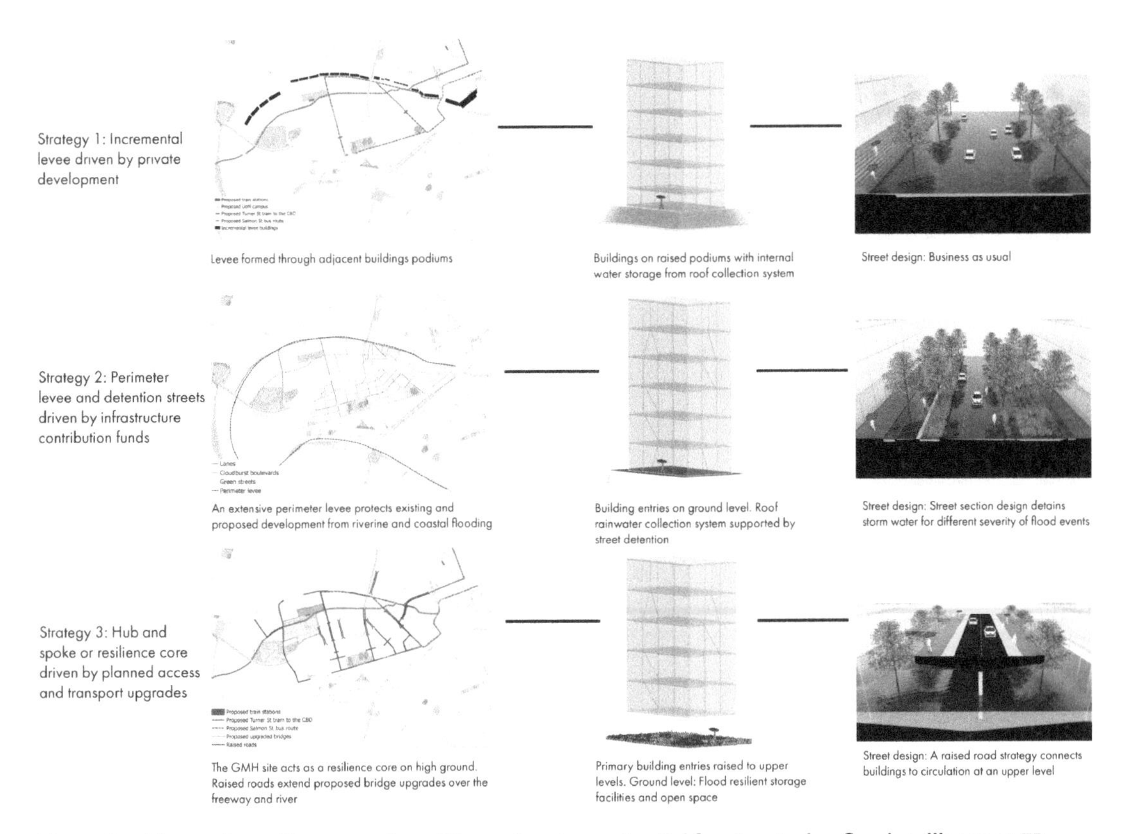

Figure 8.2 Three alternative scenarios with overlapping potential for structuring flood resilience at FB.

1. **Incremental flood mitigation** or base level of service scenario: buildings on podium as an integrated levee with conventional streets. The Melbourne Water current development trajectory.
2. **Perimeter levee and detention streetscapes** or flood level of service scenario: buildings on ground with an extensive perimeter levee, integrated active transport infrastructure and streets performing storm water detention. The Ramboll development proposal (Ramboll Environ, 2018).
3. **Alternative hub and spoke** or core resilience node and connectors scenario: buildings on pilotis (or piers) with a minimal internal or zero levee and selected raised streets that work with extensive bridging proposals.

Design Strategies: Structural and Non-structural Mechanisms

Option 1: Base Level of Service with Perimeter Buildings Built as Levees

Overview

Climate change and SLR impacts will require a regional approach and structural mechanisms such as levees and dykes. Until recently, no holistic approach to manage SLR and flooding has occurred for the regional area of FB. Instead, the current approach is to consider riverine and coastal flooding issues in a decoupled manner, with small-scale projects considered in isolation from other local proposals. This approach to development is considered as 'base level of service strategy', in which adaptation and management are incrementally implemented as needed (GHD, 2017) (see Table 8.1).

Buildings as an Incrementally Implemented Levee

Future flood levels are expected to impact land under elevation +2.4 Australian Height Datum (AHD). Proposed sustainable buildings (K) below this level will be elevated to the base level of flood and include integrated water storage and a levee. Building floor levels are raised

Table 8.1 Structural, non-structural, and hybrid mechanisms utilized

Program elements for economic development:	*Structural*	*Non-structural*	*Hybrid*
Residential development	X		
Commercial and office space	X		
Industrial parks	X		
Metro station	X		
University campus	X		
Connector-raised pathway	X		
Program elements for flood mitigation:			
Stormwater run-off storage cells		X	
Community & pocket gardens		X	
Campus			X
Rain garden			X
Detention/Retention			X
Greenbuilding:			
Green roof			X
Green wall			X
Rainwater harvesting			X
Permeable paving		X	
Soil amendments		X	
Roadways and parks:			
Sidewalk swales			X
Check dam swale	X		
Public parks & green infrastructure	X		
Bikeways & walking promenades			X
Detention	X		
Oversized pipes	X		
Subsurface infiltration	X		

to between +2.5 and +3.5 AHD, on podiums. These are also a form of adaptive housing (E). Rooftop rainwater collectors direct water to indoor building tanks. One example is the Convention Centre (built 2009) positioned at a low-lying hinge point (shown in yellow in Figure 6.1). The Convention Centre's finished flood level (+3.44 AHD), sits 1–2 meters above the adjacent ground, interfacing the street on one side with stairs and the river on the other side aligned with a continuous concrete wall.

The Streets

Most streets remain conventional and largely unchanged from their industrial past. Changes to streets will be tied to building levee development and coordinated to distinct levee components for optimizing flood mitigation.

Advantages and Disadvantages of This Strategy

This may be the most applicable development pathway in this 90% privately owned site. Flood infrastructure is contained within private holdings, meaning the infrastructural costs are largely borne by private developers. Working carefully using a series of interconnected buildings as levees, the approach can be built over time, matching pace with development as it evolves, providing critical flood mitigation alongside building functions. A focus on low-lying hinge points is essential for ensuring long-term functions, where the system is only as effective as its weakest link. This approach could allow for the establishment of a low public cost smart district.

This option has advantages and drawbacks associated with development costs and urban design outcomes. Planning and regulating the location, quality, and integration of discrete levee buildings, incrementally constructed on private land overtime will be challenging and may produce a disjointed urban morphology. The elevational relationship between the raised buildings and the streetscape create accessibility challenges for vehicles and people, while the 'blank wall' street interface negatively impacts retail visibility. In a precinct with steep private investment costs due to site fill volumes and requirements for internal flood resistant infrastructure, these issues impact both incentives and investment returns.

Option 2: Flood Level of Service: Streets as Detention, Buildings on Ground, a Perimeter Levee

Overview

Ramboll Environmental (2018) provided an alternative method for managing stormwater and tidal flooding based on the Copenhagen Cloudburst Management Plan of 2012. In this scenario a perimeter levee blocks riverine and tidal flooding. The precinct's streets and parks are the primary method for controlling stormwater flooding.

Lowered open spaces and parks accommodate excess stormwater beyond the street detention system.

The Buildings and Streets

In this scenario, new buildings have a highly desirable 'on ground' interface with streets. Reflecting urban design fashions of the 20th century and the site's industrial past, the existing streets are at times excessively wide. Harnessing this as a strength, in this scenario streets are retrofitted with terrace swales to act as part of a distributed surface-based storage system. In this scenario the streets act as elongated water squares to briefly detain stormwater above ground while avoiding infiltration into the contaminated soil and groundwater below. These roadside ditches and curbless swales (Chapter 25) and sidewalk bioswales (O), alongside the water squares including parking lot and terrace rain gardens (R) operate as detentions zones during storms and as open space when not flooding. Narrower streets and lanes with roadside terraces provide smaller interconnected supporting detention pockets (see Figure 8.3). Level changes and roadway slope or cross falls on these hybrid water storage streets enable ongoing roadway functions depending on flood levels. The lowered median and curbside open spaces can contain a 1% annual exceedance probability (AEP) flood. The 5% AEP flood fills the entire carriageway, leaving only pedestrian footpaths and raised crosswalks (Joyce et al., 2019).

The Levee

A perimeter levee (A) is proposed around FB encompassing Port Melbourne, Albert Park, South Wharf and South Melbourne. The levee seeks to manage northern riverine flooding and southern tidal flooding. A sustainable transportation proposal includes a 'liveable' road levee for walking and cycling and active transport. The levee height is substantial (+3.00 AHD) to enable buildings to interface with the street at ground level. The 0.4m predicted increase in SLR (IPCC 2020) will likely raise the levee height.

Advantages and Disadvantages of This Strategy

While the levee construction challenges on the Yarra River edge are surmountable, the southern edge levee through the City of Port Phillip will likely be contentious and complicated to negotiate with the multiple homeowners.

Compared to the base level, this scenario is costly but includes key advantages. Allowing buildings to interface with the street at ground level decreases blank facades and inaccessible stairs in the public realm. This scenario works elegantly to repurpose redundant street space as hybrid detention and open spaces. On the other hand, the water management zones on streets create accessibility issues such as constricting crossing points, and limits space for public transportation which would then require elevation. The extensive length of the

Figure 8.3 Above: a perimeter levee with streets reconfigured to be a hybrid transport detention network, to manage stormwater whilst still allowing critical pedestrian movement. Below: typical detail of a 'Green Street' showing stormwater for a 100-year ARI flood contained within a terraced side detention pond and the street carriageway. Buildings interface the street at ground level.

levee infrastructure situated largely within public land is costly and requires well planned designs plus incentives and shared cost schemes to ensure their delivery. The levee should be readily raised in the future as required. Furthermore, walling in the entire FB creates serious internal flooding issues or a bathtub effect if the wall is breached and during large storm events.

Option 3: Hub and Spoke: Raised Streets, Buildings as Urban Gills and a Minimal Levee

Overview

The third development scenario requires less investment and connects the employment and residential precincts to the existing Westgate Freeway transportation infrastructure. New development on high ground serves as a hub for the precinct with raised roads connected to lower lying zones and the freeway off ramps. This scenario proposes a lower internal berm creating a resilient core (Places Victoria, 2013), and avoids extensive levee and pump maintenance costs. Most of the site floods and drains naturally.

The Buildings

New sustainable buildings (K) outside the resilient hub are raised on piloti, piles, or cores, to become urban gills that extend into the dynamic and altered floodplain, with connected raised pedestrian corridors (see Figure 8.4). Existing buildings below the 1% AEP flood line would utilize local building cluster flood mitigation. The University of Melbourne Campus, within the GMH site, could potentially serve as a resilience hub (in collaboration with Development Victoria). This near-term development can set the trend for raised pedestrian corridors and raised roads supporting a floodplain development. The raised roadways at both Salmon and Turner streets can provide the building blocks for resiliency where they intersect with the campus.

The Streets

Streets should be selected sparingly and should capitalize on connections to the freeway and high ground. Roads that connect the hub(s) to development zones across the precinct should become primary egress routes with bundled utilities. Selected roads would be raised and connected to distributed parking structures. Bike lanes and pedestrian walkways should be extensive. Public transport should create a major spine and function during flooding. Walkways and corridors can access buildings at the second level and open spaces and parks can be raised or at the ground plane and work across these elevations. This decouples the vehicular from other transport modes.

The Levee

In this scenario, the levee is internal. Therefore, it will not have to be as high or as robust since wave action will be diminished across FB before

Figure 8.4 Above: the hub and spoke scenario working with existing ground conditions and natural flooding. Below: shows a detail of a typical raised road, as it extends over the flood plane from the proposed bridges between the employment and housing precincts over the freeway.

it reaches the internal levee. The lower levee can be integrated into buildings, streets, and open spaces.

Advantages and Disadvantages of This Strategy

While raised roads can be costly, they may work well at FB where flooding into large industrial parcels could be managed internally with raised road berms. It encourages parkland within the floodplain across the precinct. The plan is an efficient option and avoids the need for extensive pumping and infrastructure investment. However, while it does provide more parkland as floodplains, it also reduces the developable area and may increase building costs. Additionally, shrinking the levee may reduce the time frame and approach for negotiating flood defences for the new precinct. It avoids having to focus on the household scale negotiations required for the Port Phillip side. From a social equity perspective, however, using the investment for the precinct to fund flood defences for Port Phillip may be the only way to harness an investment for the scale of adaptation required in the region. Otherwise, an entire population gets left out (GHD, 2017).

Conclusions

Design Innovations and Global Applicability

In this chapter we explored critical choices around post-industrial floodplain redevelopment using Melbourne as a case study. Like other floodplain redevelopments, FB's flood risks are complex, interactive, mutable and compounding. Three divergent flood resilience scenarios for FB illustrated the heavy investments, including hidden costs, and interacting and conflicting risks and opportunities. The costly drainage infrastructure and buildings reduce development profit margins and reduce incentives to provide public amenities and social infrastructure.

FB's large highly influential and heavily studied floodplain redevelopment options expose critical considerations for future floodplain development. How can the planning regulations be improved to enable developers to effectively incorporate climate resilience? How can we encourage green infrastructure and build projects that establish long-term resiliency while avoiding short-sighted developments and cutting corners that can incentivize poor investment patterns or introduce new challenges for existing and future owners? Site scale development within FB, such as the campus, should be coordinated with the broader precinct plan to ensure efficiency and functionality of the precinct as a whole.

Fostering cross-disciplinary communication, collaboration, and coordination is essential. People cannot afford to waste smart adaptation options when redeveloping floodplains. Working in silos and holding out on shared negotiations can squander real opportunities. Coordinating infrastructure, transportation and other investments as seeking smart compromises and 'win–wins' or, at a minimum, neutral impacts that avoid encouraging poor future choices, is necessary. Especially with contamination, shallow groundwater and flood risks, there are multiple shared risks crossing boundaries. Given the flooding potential, all of the water management on site and storage capacity options should be studied holistically as well as locally. The need for public transportation, egress routes and associated utilities to connect to low areas requires careful considerations of tie-backs, road elevations and infrastructure. Investments in transportation and public infrastructure should ensure that everything designed and built increases resiliency and is failsafe during flooding.

Floodplain redevelopment requires a holistic and systemic approach to address the complex multi-layered challenges of flooding and SLR. Building and road design as well as infrastructure and parkland development all require strategic phasing and careful planning. Development approvals that embed unresolved issues are at risk of catalysing poor development patterns. With FB, the university is moving into schematic design in advance of critical stakeholders who remain at earlier planning stages. Moving forward and establishing plans puts the university in a strategic role to broker the resilient design of the larger precinct. The university can set the bar high in terms of creating a foundation for smart developments around vehicular traffic, water management, building elevations, infrastructure, open space, and pedestrian connectors to ensure a healthy precinct redevelopment. Given its location on the highest ground, the university can choose to move forward with its own planning regardless of how the precinct develops. However, this would ignore the critical nature of floodplain redevelopment as a holistic approach. Without a resilient precinct, the campus and the overall FB redevelopment will likely face flood issues over time and require periodic retrofits. The university has the opportunity to serve as a resilient hub for the precinct and ensure the creation of an innovative floodplain redevelopment.

Image credit: all images are the original work of the authors.

References

AECOM. (2018). *Fishermans Bend Climate Readiness Strategy: Organising framework stage 1*. Department of Environment Land Water and Planning. Retrieved from https://s3.ap-southeast-2.amazonaws.com/hdp.au.prod.app.vic-engage.files/2615/2383/4342/Document_199_-_Fishermans_Bend_Climate_Readiness_Strategy_-_organising_framework_stage_1.pdf

Befus, K. M., Barnard, P. L., Hoover, D. J., Finzi Hart, J. A., & Voss, C. I. (2020). Increasing threat of coastal groundwater hazards from sea-level rise in California. *Nature Climate Change*, *10*(10), 946–952. https://doi.org/10.1038/s41558-020-0874-1

GHD. (2017). *FB Document 78c Annexure 7 Baseline Drainage Plan Options pt1.pdf*. Retrieved from https://s3.ap-southeast-2.amazonaws.com/hdp.au.prod.app.vic-engage.files/4215/2055/1778/Document_78c_-_Annexure_7_-_Baseline_Drainage_Plan_Options_pt1.pdf

Joyce, P., Innes, S., GHD, & City of Port Phillip. (2019). Water sensitive drainage and flood management strategy for Fishermans Bend. *Stormwater Victoria Conference Proceedings 2019*. Retrieved from www.stormwatervictoria.com.au/images/2019_Events/2019_Conference_Proceedings/Phillip_Joyce_and_Sam_Innes_-_Water_Sensitive_Drainage_and_Flood_Management_Strategy_for_Fishermans_Bend.pdf

Meehl, G. A., Stocker, T. F., Collins, W. D., Friedlingstein, P., Gaye, A. T., Gregory, J. M., Kitoh, A., Knutti, R., Murphy, J. M., Noda, A., Raper, S. C. B., Watterson, I. G., Weaver, A. J., Zhao, Z.-C., Alley, R. B., Annan, J., Arblaster, J., Bitz, C., Brockmann, P., . . . Pant, G. B. (2007). Global climate projections. In S. Soloman, M. Manning, M. Marquis, & D. Quin (Eds.), *Climate change 2007: The physical science basis: Contribution of Working Group I to the Fourth Assessment Report of the Intergovernmental Panel on Climate Change* (p. 100). Cambridge University Press.

Millar, R. (2021, January 23). *Victoria gets trillion-dollar bad news: Sea level rises will swamp parts of the state*. The Age. Retrieved from www.theage.com.au/politics/victoria/victoria-gets-trillion-dollar-bad-news-sea-level-rises-will-swamp-parts-of-the-state-20210122-p56w8h.html

Nicholls, R. J., & Cazenave, A. (2010). Sea-level rise and its impact on coastal zones. *Science*, *328*(5985), 1517–1520. https://doi.org/10.1126/science.1185782

Places Victoria. (2013). *Fishermans Bend draft vision*. Retrieved from www.fishermansbend.vic.gov.au/__data/assets/pdf_file/0020/30359/Draft_2013_Vision.pdf

Ramboll Environ. (2018). *FB Document 78b Annexure 4 Integrated and Innovative Water Management Report part_1*. Retrieved from https://s3.ap-southeast-2.amazonaws.com/hdp.au.prod.app.vic-engage.files/9715/2055/2135/Document_78b_-_Annexure_4_-_Integrated_and_Innovative_Water_Management_Report_-_part_1.pdf

Travers, I., Welsh, L., & Wheeler, J. (2017). *Aboriginal Cultural Values Interpretation Strategy* (p. 46) [Heritage report]. Fishermans Bend Taskforce.

9

ISLAND BAY, GREATER WELLINGTON REGION OF AOTEAROA – NEW ZEALAND

Victoria Chanse, Maria Rodgers,
Shivani Patel, and Bruno Marques

Site: Island Bay, New Zealand: 12.77 acres

Introduction/Rationale

The capital city of Te Whanganui-a-Tara, Wellington, is located on the southern tip of the North Island of Aotearoa, New Zealand. Wellington's population is expected to grow by approximately 23–37% by 2053 (Mitchell Daysh, 2019; WCC et al., 2019; Beca, 2019), despite facing a housing shortage. This coastal city – many parts of which are low-lying – is vulnerable to sea-level rise, nuisance flooding, and natural hazards like earthquakes and tsunamis.

Climate change impacts in Aotearoa have resulted in increases in rare and extreme rainfall events. Both of these events are likely to have impacts on landslides, saturated soil, and adverse impacts on urban stormwater systems and transportation infrastructure. Some of the largest and increasing risks to Wellington from climate change include increased rainfall intensity, coastal inundation, coastal flooding, and increased wave impacts (Cameron & Wood, 2018; NIWA, 2017, 2019). Both tropical cyclone intensity and extreme storm events with higher levels of rainfall intensity are predicted to increase (NIWA, 2017). This will lead to increased stormwater, coastal erosion, and potential for landslides, with subsequent negative impacts on the city's aging stormwater, sewer, and transport infrastructure (NIWA, 2019). Further, small increases in sea level rise will lead to significant increases in nuisance flooding, depending on tidal conditions (NIWA, 2020).

The National Institute of Water and Atmospheric (NIWA) Research (2019) estimates that, in Wellington, approximately 22.5 miles of roads and 4,084 buildings are exposed to a 1% annual exceedance probability (AEP). With an approximate 3.2 ft rise in sea level, 107.5 miles of roads and 14,336 buildings will be exposed to a 1% AEP. Wellington's southern coast, in particular, is highly vulnerable to sea-level rise and extreme high tide storm events (NIWA, 2019). NIWA (2020) notes that the south coast of Wellington is already facing increasing levels of nuisance

DOI: 10.4324/9781003183419-13

flooding with an increased frequency of greater flooding projected in the future. High tides and storms with heavy swells and high winds have led to highways, local roads, and seawalls being washed away or damaged (Thomas & Dooney, 2016). In 2021, 21-foot waves smashed into the city's south coast, closing coastal road access, damaging property, and leading to many evacuations and power cuts (Campbell, 2021).

Estimates to upgrade the stormwater and sewer infrastructure range from approximately USD 1.54 billion to 3.15 billion, just to cover population growth (Hunt, 2020). With nuisance flooding likely to increase due to climate change, upgrading the aging infrastructure could become even more expensive. Projected costs for homeowner insurance are estimated to become prohibitively expensive. One recent study estimates that, by 2030, Wellington will face a partial insurance retreat (Climate Sigma, 2020). This same report estimates that, by 2050, approximately 10,000 homes in New Zealand will have become uninsurable (Climate Sigma, 2020).

Design Synopsis

Study Area

The suburb of Island Bay is situated on the south coast of Wellington and faces the island of Taputeranga. Māori valued the setting of Island Bay by siting *kāinga*, villages or settlements, on the flats and *pā*, fortified villages, on the headlands. In the 1880s, farmland at Island Bay was subdivided for housing and Italian fishermen settlements as the island created safe anchorage. The suburb has long been appreciated for having a family focus, village-like shopping area, and coastal location. The Taputeranga Marine Reserve extends out from the island's coast. The beach and bay are popular areas for recreation and approximately 558 residents live in the low-lying portions of the suburb (Patel, 2020).

In 1906, a roadway was constructed along the crest of the foredune, which was later fortified as a seawall in the 1930s (Tonkin & Taylor, 2014). The seawall included a sloped concrete revetment and a recurved upstand wall to protect the road from erosion, wind-blown sand, and waves (Tonkin & Taylor 2014). The existing, highly modified urban beach is narrow, with the seawall, road, and footpath running alongside the beach. Shorland Park sits opposite the beach and seawall. When a storm damaged the seawall in 2013, alternative seawall options were rejected in place of simply retaining the wall in the same alignment basis (McConnell, 2016; Tonkin & Taylor, 2014). Before the final repairs were approved, another storm in 2015 further damaged the Island Bay Seawall (Forbes, 2015); more than USD 700K was spent on repairs and reconstruction (McConnell, 2016).

Island Bay is vulnerable to the combined impacts of sea level rise, storm surge, and nuisance flooding. Sea-level rise scenarios of roughly 2 feet, 4 feet, and 10 feet for the site found that several assets, properties, community sites, recreational amenities, and culturally significant sites are at risk (see Figure 9.1). Corollary, an approximate 4 ft storm surge would damage a substantial portion of the low-lying areas of Island Bay.

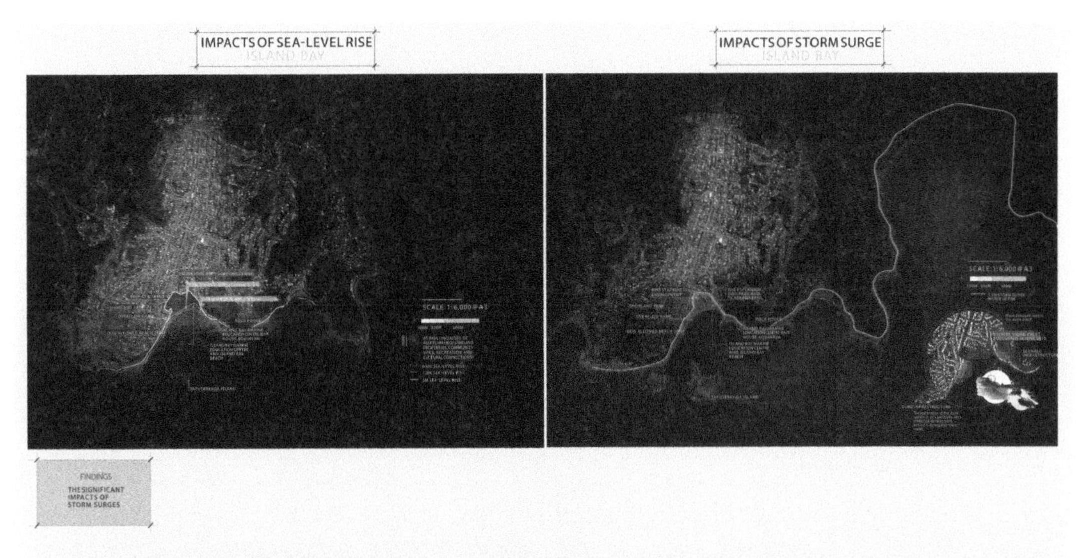

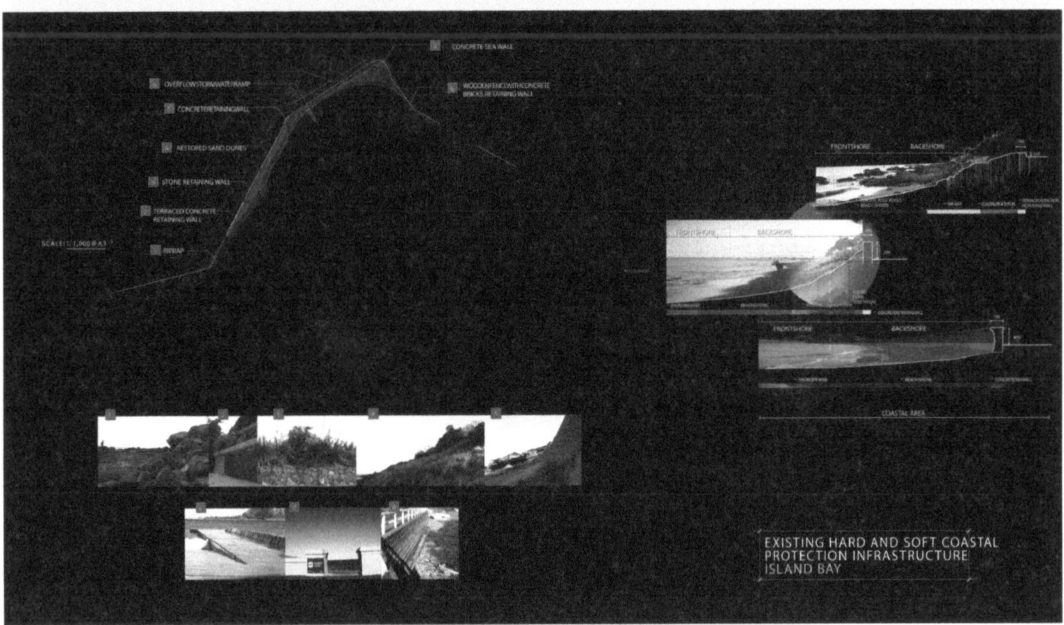

Figure 9.1 Existing coastal protection and project impacts of sea level rise and storm surge.
Image courtesy of Shivani Patel.

Structural and Non-structural Mechanisms

This project proposes a re-design of an existing residential neighborhood that includes the beach, Shorland Park, and a low-lying residential neighborhood into a floodable zone with an amphibious component. Together, the design integrates proactive flood and coastal multi-layered management systems, hybrid infrastructure, and land use planning. The design includes an adaptive capacity to mitigate coastal inundation and storm surges, and accommodates 3.94 ft sea-level rise projections. The master plan proposes a series of structural, non-structural, and hybrid mechanisms that, in combination, increase the adaptive capacity of the coastal, low-lying neighborhood (see Table 9.1).

The design consists of three distinct zones (see Figure 9.2). The Island Bay Beach and Marine Reserve zone include hybrid, multiple layers of protection for the coastal zone from Trent Street to the Island Bay Beach. The Shorland Park recreational zone consists of coastal protection and flood management systems with wetland retention ponds. Slightly further inland is the low-lying residential zone which was designed for flood adaptation.

The adaptive mechanisms applied in the final master plan serve three functions: (1) a protective edge consisting of multiple layers of non-structural and structural defense, including dunes and levees/embankments; (2) adaptation by creating a flood zone for managing stormwater via hybrid structures (constructed wetlands, detention ponds, bio-retention infiltration ponds, and riparian buffers; and (3) living with water via amphibious buildings and adaptive, elevated houses (See Table 9.1 and Figure 9.3).

Design Phasing

The phasing for this project is a threefold approach to protect, accommodate, and manage retreat, while focusing on public space and managing stormwater. The Island Bay project was designed around three lines of defense with two final phases anticipating the inundation of the Island Bay low-lying neighborhood and establishing a managed retreat to higher ground. The phasing of the tiered coastal defense that

Figure 9.2 Master plan and the three zones.
Image courtesy of Shivani Patel.

Table 9.1 Strategies and mechanisms for Island Bay design, Wellington, New Zealand

Program elements	*Structural*	*Non-structural*	*Hybrid*
The Island Bay Beach and Marine Reserve zone mechanisms:		X	
Regenerated dune system			
Beach nourishment		X	
Constructed wetland		X	
Riparian buffers		X	
Amphibious building – Island Bay Marine Education building, dry, flood-proof	X		
Levees as promenade + hybrid levee berm	X		
Terraced amphitheatre			X
Pervious paving			X
Rain gardens		X	
Floodable basin plaza and sportsfield		X	
Underground detention/cistern	X		
Shorland Park recreational zone-mechanisms/ strategies:			
Wetland retention pond system		X	
Energy-efficient pumps and stormwater treatment stormwater	X		
Stormwater flow control devices	X		
Stormwater outlet	X		
Infiltration planter		X	
Pervious paving			
Low-lying residential zone:			
Adaptive housing – elevated houses	X		
Green building – green roof			X
Rainwater harvesting			X
Bioswale		X	
Rain garden + tree box filter		X	
Wetland retention		X	
Stream daylighted		X	
Riparian plantings		X	

establishes a floodable zone and increases adaptive capacity is characterized by strategies around protection, accommodation, and managed retreat (see Figure 9.4).

Phase 1 (Protection: Current)

The first, immediate line of coastal defense is via two non-structural mechanisms comprised of dunes and native plantings. This first line is

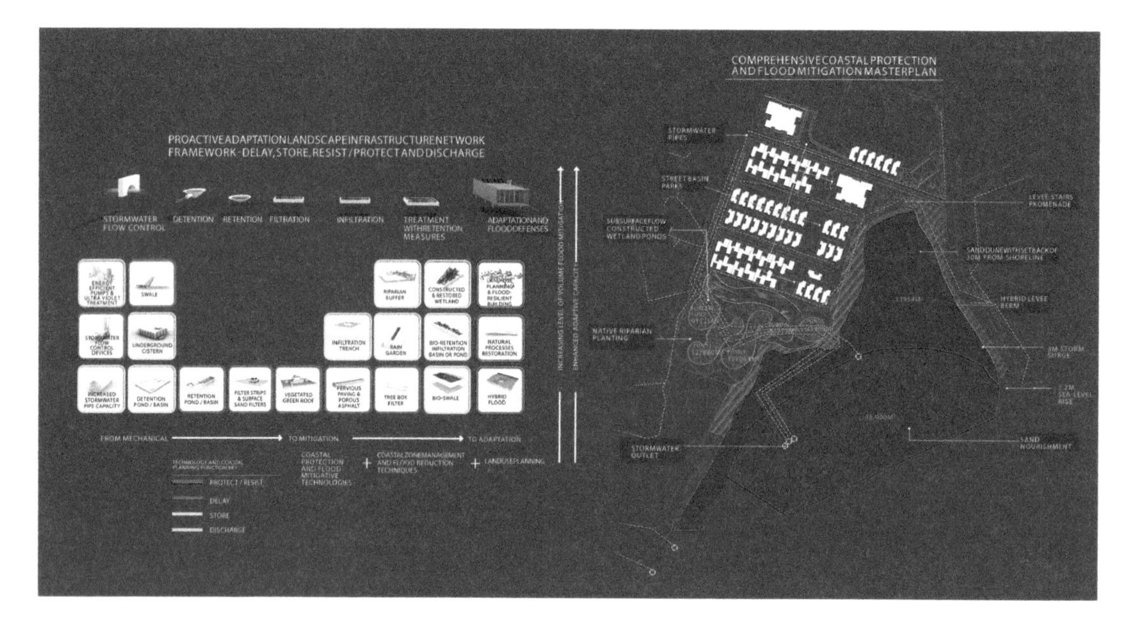

Figure 9.3 Adaptation framework.
Image courtesy of Shivani Patel.

characterized by the protection and regeneration of the coastal dune system, including removing part of the coastal access road and re-routing circulation via the other existing streets. This includes strengthening the foredune and the backdune with coastal plantings and beach nourishment created by the implementation of the foredune. This phase comprises protecting the dune system via a boardwalk/pier, kayak launch, and lookout platform into the Taputeranga Marine Reserve.

Phase 2 (Protection: 2030)

The second line of defense proposes raising the dune system to continue increased flood protection as sea levels rise. This second phase includes non-structural and structural mechanisms such as constructed wetlands, dunes, and levee/berms. The wetland is established to buffer against flooding and wave action. A boardwalk and educational trails through the wetland are also added for educational purposes.

Phase 3 (Protection: 2050)

This phase marks the third line of defense which is to protect most of the low-lying coastal area via continuing to elevate the coastal areas while emphasizing access and education around public space. The strategies during this phase are structural, establishing foundations for planted embankments as well as a levee system, and non-structural such as building up the dunes to make them higher.

Phase 4 (Creating a Floodable Zone: 2070)

This phase is quite different from the previous three given the inevitability of sea level rise and increased coastal storm events. By strategizing

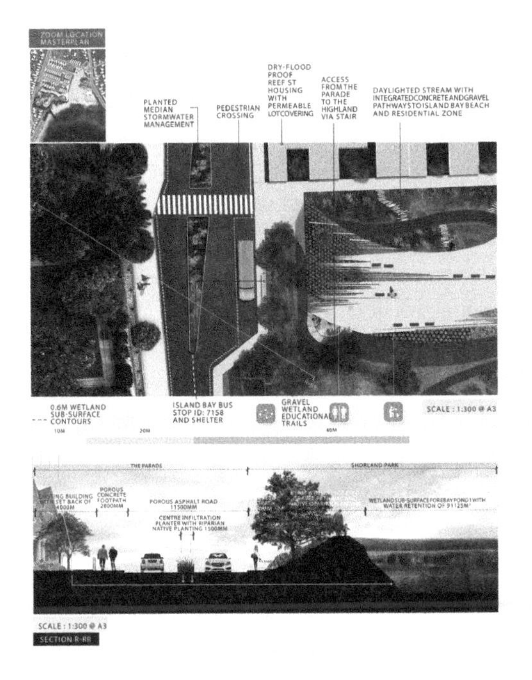

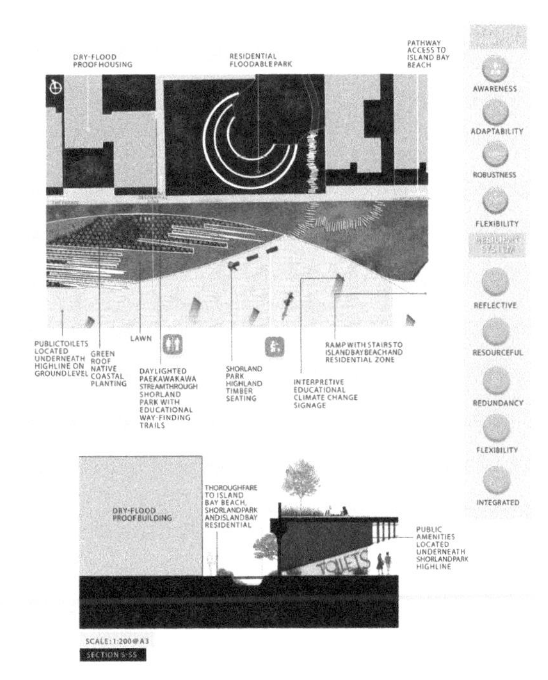

Figure 9.4 Detailed designs of The Parade.
Image courtesy of Shivani Patel.

how best to allow the water to move into the low-lying areas, Phase 4 is characterized by retrofitting the low-lying residential neighborhood by raising selected residential and commercial buildings that are adjacent to the backdunes. This phase includes several multifunctional structures that allow for flooding and increasing water storage via cisterns, green streets, swales, and rain gardens. This phase includes transforming the planted embankments into multifunctional structures with access along the spines of the embankments. Ongoing fortification of the dunes and their raising will also continue during this phase.

Phase 5 (Managed Retreat: 2100)

This phase focuses on a managed retreat onto higher ground for low-lying community residents. Wet and dry flood-proofing of buildings is proposed, with additional residential and commercial buildings raised. Walkways through the neighborhood are added and elevated to allow for access through the site. Multifunctional sports ground plaza/basins that would enable flooding are proposed.

Design Impact

As noted, residents and the coastal access road are vulnerable to increased flooding from a number of sources. Given the combined impacts of stormwater surface flooding with sea level rise and wave action, the projected design impact of this project incorporates different mechanisms to increase the adaptive capacity of flooding and stormwater management (see Figure 9.4). The design offers multiple lines of defense for coastal protection with increased adaptive capacity for flooding via the floodable, multifunctional spaces that perform during wet and dry periods.

From an accessibility standpoint, this design changes accessibility throughout the site as one part of the multiple lines of defense. The design firstly changes the circulation from the coastal access road as it meanders through Island Bay within some neighborhood streets. As flooding becomes more of a permanent feature of the neighborhood, accessibility for residents is provided via raised embankments and a re-design of public spaces that allow for flooding. Finally, the multiple lines of defense proposed offer residents more time to continue living there while providing important opportunities for managed retreat and adapting to living with water.

Conclusions

Innovation and Applicability

Increasingly, coastal areas are vulnerable to flooding from a combination of increased rainfall intensity leading to more stormwater runoff, storm surge, sea level rise, and extreme wave action (Sutrisno et al., 2020). This project's innovations are due to how the design interventions simultaneously address these combinations of flooding issues via a mixture of stormwater management techniques designed to increase adaptive capacity while offering multiple lines of defense through a phasing of raising dunes and raised embankments for accessibility.

Examinations of recent floodplain management approaches in New Zealand suggest a tiered approach around wave attenuation, protection, and planning to inform novel approaches to coastal resilience (Nordenson et al., 2018: 75). Nordensen et al. (2018) observe the need to combine a series of mitigation approaches into layers as a way to expand and thicken the coastal edge. The Island Bay design proposal of a floodable zone with a neighborhood designed to increase floodable storage capacity offers a modified approach to managed retreat while increasing adaptive flood capacity, and elevates portions of the site for protection and accommodation.

Manning et al. (2015) note the need for methods to accommodate the continuing changing uncertainties associated with climate change in Aotearoa. One essential part of the solution is working closely with Indigenous communities and their relationships with water and land (Manning et al., 2015). In Oceania, a growing need for nature-based solutions and traditional environmental knowledge is needed to respond to the urgency of climate resiliency (Zari et al., 2019; Kiddle, 2020). Mātauranga Māori (Māori knowledge) provides important implications for design responses to environmental challenges (Kiddle, 2020). When considering the future of the landscapes of Aotearoa, strategies involve an inclusive "whole of landscape" approach known as "ki uta ki tai" (from the mountains to the sea). Kiddle (2020) observes the imperative for designers to work collaboratively with Indigenous communities to enable meaningful design responses (208). Design approaches that embrace co-design and participatory processes offer ways to collaborate with Indigenous communities so as to holistically address issues of coastal resiliency (Marques et al., 2021; Rodgers et al., 2020; Chanse, 2016, 2017).

References

Beca. (2019). *Wellington City – planning for future growth: preliminary baseline scenario development – results and methodology* (February 8, 2019). Retrieved June 4, 2021, from https://planningforgrowth.wellington.govt.nz/__data/assets/pdf_file/0011/2351/wcc-preliminary-baseline-growth-scenarios-update-final-report-february2019.pdf

Cameron, C., & Wood, N. (2018). *Responding to sea level rise in Wellington*. Institute of Public Works Engineering, Australia. May 27, 2018. Retrieved April 7, 2021, from www.ipwea.org/HigherLogic/System/DownloadDocumentFile.ashx?DocumentFileKey=2b0a5556-c0dd-7643-2ba3-90713070f804

Campbell, G. (2021). Wild weather: Waves as high as 6.5m hit Wellington coastal homes; authorities to meet at 7am. *New Zealand Herald* (June 30, 2021). Retrieved July 2, 2021, from www.nzherald.co.nz/nz/wild-weather-waves-as-high-as-65m-hit-wellington-coastal-homes-authorities-to-meet-at-7am/B2HKDDKLBJ75TBPKYE5TUYCRMU/

Chanse, V. (2016). Engaging stakeholders in the sea level rise design process: A pilot project on Maryland's eastern shore. *International Journal of Climate Change: Impacts & Responses*, *8*(3), 81–88.

Chanse, V. (2017). Raise your own sea level. In D. de la Peña, D. J. Allen, R. T. Hester, J. Hou, L. L. Lawson, & M. C. McNally (Eds.), *Design as democracy: Techniques for Collective creativity* (pp. 239–244). Washington, DC: Island Press.

Climate Sigma. (2020). *Insurance retreat: Sea level rise and the withdrawal of residential insurance in Aotearoa New Zealand*. Report for the Deep South Challenge (December 2020). Retrieved May 8, 2021, from https://deepsouthchallenge.co.nz/wp-content/uploads/2021/01/Insurance-Retreat-December-2020-Final-Report.pdf

Forbes, M. (2015). Seawall in Wellington's Island repair bill climbs to $1.3M after is takes further damage. *Dominion Post* (September 17, 2015). Retrieved May 16, 2021, from www.stuff.co.nz/dominion-post/news/71159404/seawall-in-wellingtons-island-repair-bill-climbs-to-13m-after-it-takes-further-damage

Hunt, T. (2020). Wellington needs to spend more than $5 billion on pipes, council estimates. *Stuff* (October 13, 2020). Retrieved June 18, 2021, from www.stuff.co.nz/dominion-post/news/wellington/123055811/wellington-needs-to-spend-more-than-5-billion-on-pipes-council-estimates

Kiddle, R. (2020). Indigenous ecological design. In *Ecologies Design* (pp. 204–211). Routledge.

Manning, M., Lawrence, J., King, D. N., & Chapman, R. (2015). Dealing with changing risks: a New Zealand perspective on climate change adaptation. *Regional Environmental Change*, 15(4), 581–594.

Marques, B., Grabasch, G., & McIntosh, J. (2021). Fostering landscape identity through participatory design with indigenous cultures of Australia and Aotearoa/New Zealand. *Space and culture*, 24(1), 37–52.

McConnell, G. (2016). It's almost finished: Three years on, the Island Bay seawall is nearly rebuilt. *Dominion Post* (June 17, 2016). Retrieved May 16, 2021, from www.stuff.co.nz/dominion-post/news/80842276/its-almost-finished-three-years-on-the-island-bay-seawall-is-nearly-rebuilt

Mitchell Daysh. (2019). *Greater Wellington: Preparing coastal communities for climate change: Assessing coastal vulnerability to climate change, sea level rise and natural hazards* (June 2019). Retrieved May 8, 2021, from www.gw.govt.nz/assets/Uploads/Wellington-Regional-Coastal-Vulnerability-AssessmentJune-2019Final.pdf

National Institute of Water & Atmospheric Research Ltd. (2017). *Intensity of cyclones projected to increase* (October 5, 2017). Retrieved June 16, 2021, from https://niwa.co.nz/news/intensity-of-cyclones-predicted-to-increase

National Institute of Water & Atmospheric Research Ltd. (2019). *Wellington regional climate change extremes and implications. Prepared for Greater Wellington regional council*. Retrieved March 30, 2021 from www.gw.govt.nz/assets/Climate-change/GWRC-NIWA-climate-extremes-FINAL3.pdf

National Institute of Water & Atmospheric Research Ltd. (2020). *Small sea-level rises to drive more intense flooding, say scientists* (April 14, 2020). Retrieved June 18, 2021, from https://niwa.co.nz/news/small-sea-level-rises-to-drive-more-intense-flooding-say-scientists

Nordenson, C., Nordenson, G., & Chapman, J. (2018). *Structures of coastal resilience*. Washington, DC: Island Press.

Patel, S. (2020). Rising seas: Coastal adaptation to climate change. Victoria University of Wellington. Thesis. Master's in Landscape Architecture.

Rodgers, M., Marques, B., & McIntosh, J. (2020). Connecting Māori youth and landscape architecture students through participatory design. *Architecture and Culture*, *8*(2), 309–327.

Sutrisno, D., Rahadiati, A., Rudiastuti, A. W., & Dewi, R. S. (2020). Urban coastal flood-prone mapping under the combined impact of tidal wave and heavy rainfall: A proposal to the existing national standard. *ISPRS International Journal of Geo-Information*, *9*(9), 525.

Thomas, R., & Dooney, L. (2016). Massive waves close roads and destroy seawall amid weather chaos in Wellington. *Stuff*. Retrieved May 10, 2021, from www.stuff.co.nz/national/82417188/police-shut-porirua-roads-due-to-waves?rm=m

Tonkin & Taylor Ltd. (2014). *Island Bay seawall alternatives analysis: Coastal processes assessment*. Report prepared for Wellington City Council (May 2014). T&T Ref: 29595. Retrieved May 8, 2021, from https://wellington.govt.nz/~/media/your-council/projects/files/island-bay-seawall/coastal-processes-assessment-report.pdf?la=en

Wellington City Council, Hutt City Council, Poirirua City Council, Kapiti Coast District Council and Upper Hutt District Council. (2019). *Housing and business capacity assessment*. (November 8, 1029). Retrieved June 4, 2021, from https://planningforgrowth.wellington.govt.nz/__data/assets/pdf_file/0020/3287/Wellington-Regional-HBA-Chpt-1-Regional-Summary.pdf

Zari, M. P., Kiddle, G. L., Blaschke, P., Gawler, S., & Loubser, D. (2019). Utilising nature-based solutions to increase resilience in Pacific Ocean Cities. *Ecosystem Services*, *38*, 100968.

10

WILMINGTON, DELAWARE

Jules Bruck, Emma Ruggiero, and Anna Wik

Site Size and Location: Northeast Wilmington, DE: approximately 720 acres

Introduction/Rationale

Delaware has an extremely flat elevation profile, with the lowest overall mean elevation in the United States at 20 meters, and experiences recurring inundation from coastal storms that routinely produce heavy rainfall and associated storm surge (Callahan, 2017). The region is also impacted by land subsidence which causes the relative rate of sea level rise (SLR) to occur at twice the global average (Piecuch et al., 2018; Miller et. al, 2013). SLR occurred more substantially off the US mid-Atlantic coast compared to the global average during the 20th century (Piecuch et al., 2018). The mid-Atlantic SLR rate ranged between 2.4 and 4.4 millimeters per year, versus less than 1–2 millimeters per year globally (Gornitz, 1990), representing a regional rise of about 1 foot during the 20th century (Titus et al., 2009). This increased rate in the region is due to the low coastal relief, an erodible substrate, land subsidence, extensive shoreline retreat, and high wave tide energies (Gornitz, 1990). Regionally, episodic events include hurricanes and Nor'easters which impact coastlines through dramatic surge events; however, chronic events including shoreline erosion, coastal flooding, storm surge, and inundation have equally detrimental impacts over time on properties, agriculture, roadways, utilities, and cultural resources (Callahan, 2017).

Projections of severe SLR impacts in Delaware include both coastal and inland communities. For example, a 1.5-meter SLR increase would inundate 11.9% of Delaware's northern-most county's land and impact over 25 miles of roadways. Overall, 0.5 meters of SLR could inundate 8% of the state's land area, including wetlands (DE Coastal Programs, 2012).

Wilmington, DE, due to its overall low elevation at an average of 92′, is vulnerable to flood events and other issues related to SLR. The Northeast neighborhood (NE) of Wilmington, Delaware is situated along the north side of the Brandywine Creek, at its confluence with the Christina River. A large percentage of the NE is covered with impervious surface and 30% is located within the FEMA floodplain (see Figure 10.1). Compounding issues, the NE has the largest combined sewer overflow (CSO) on the Brandywine in the city of Wilmington (Whitman, Requardt, & Associates (WRA), 2019). Legacy industrial facilities sited along the

DOI: 10.4324/9781003183419-14

Figure 10.1 Sea level rise and flood risk in the NE.

river in various stages of remediation also raise concern about water quality (WRA, 2019). Several recent plans developed collaboratively with the community recognize that addressing flooding and remediating brownfields along the Brandywine would contribute to overall community revitalization (Crawl-Bey et al., 2017).

While historic floods, such as Hurricane Agnes in 1972, inundated this neighborhood and forced evacuation of over 100 homes (Federal Emergency Management Agency (FEMA), 2015), stormwater management problems in the recent past have been those typically found in older cities with aging CSO infrastructure including discharges that raise concerns about the impact on public health and the environment (Tibbetts, 2005). The Wilmington Comprehensive Plan (WRA, 2019) urges property owners to manage stormwater on-site through the use of low impact development (LID) practices and for city agencies to provide technical assistance; however, an overall vision is needed to provide the residents and policymakers with an understanding of what benefit the combination of these efforts can provide, both visually and through quantitative assessments.

Design Synopsis

Study Area

Wilmington is Delaware's largest and most populous city. Located in the northern part of the state along the Delaware River, the city's population is approximately 70,000. The area is the ancestral home of the

Lenni Lenape, and the first colonial settlement was established in this region in 1638 by Swedish colonists at Fort Christina at the confluence of the Christina River and Brandywine Creek. In other areas of the city, residents enjoy these tidal waterways through a series of river walks and parks that provide access and recreational opportunities.

The project site is located in Northeast Wilmington (NE) on the north bank of the Brandywine Creek. Access to the NE from center city Wilmington is provided by several bridges that cross the Brandywine. The neighborhood has approximately 9,300 residents, 36% of whom live in poverty, and a vacancy rate of 14% (Crawl-Bey et al., 2017). Residents face multiple environmental vulnerabilities, but the most pressing issues stem from flooding. The updated City of Wilmington Comprehensive Plan (CP) acknowledges climate change and discusses impacts of concern including rising seas, hotter temperatures, and increased frequency of extreme weather events, noting that these issues will have the most severe impact on minority and low-income neighborhoods (Schwartz, 2019). To protect against flooding and SLR, Wilmington's CP promotes planning efforts that increase the absorptive capacity of land surrounding key transportation infrastructure with landscaping and bioretention facilities and work has begun in several neighborhoods to integrate green stormwater infrastructure into Wilmington's street design (Schwartz, 2019).

Design Schematics

The master green infrastructure (GI) plan showing three treatments for the NE (Figure 10.2) was developed as a collaborative effort between the University of Delaware (UD) and Collaborate NE, a loose coalition of nonprofits, state agencies, and academic partners with a mission to advance place-based redevelopment to improve the quality of life of residents in the NE. A National Fish and Wildlife Grant provided funding for two universities, UD and Texas A&M, to develop a multi-pronged approach to community engagement and design visioning to mitigate flooding. Graduate students from Texas A&M analyzed the project area, presenting their findings to Collaborate NE and a UD urban design studio course for undergraduate landscape architecture students. UD students evaluated the information provided by Texas A&M, took site tours, and conducted interviews with community members to enhance their understanding of the issues impacting local residents and develop their own comprehensive ideas about the site. These students prepared conceptual plans describing attainable GI interventions for the design study area. These concepts, along with the final conceptual plan from Texas A&M, allow Collaborate NE to promote their goals of community greening and ecological enhancement to city officials, as well as develop grant strategies in efforts to pursue implementation.

Sea Level Rise Projections

While the Delaware Geological Survey shows SLR impacts in the NE study area with as little as 4′ of SLR, much of the vulnerability of the specific study area relates to the amount of impervious surface and impacts from regional storms, as the Brandywine Creek drains an area

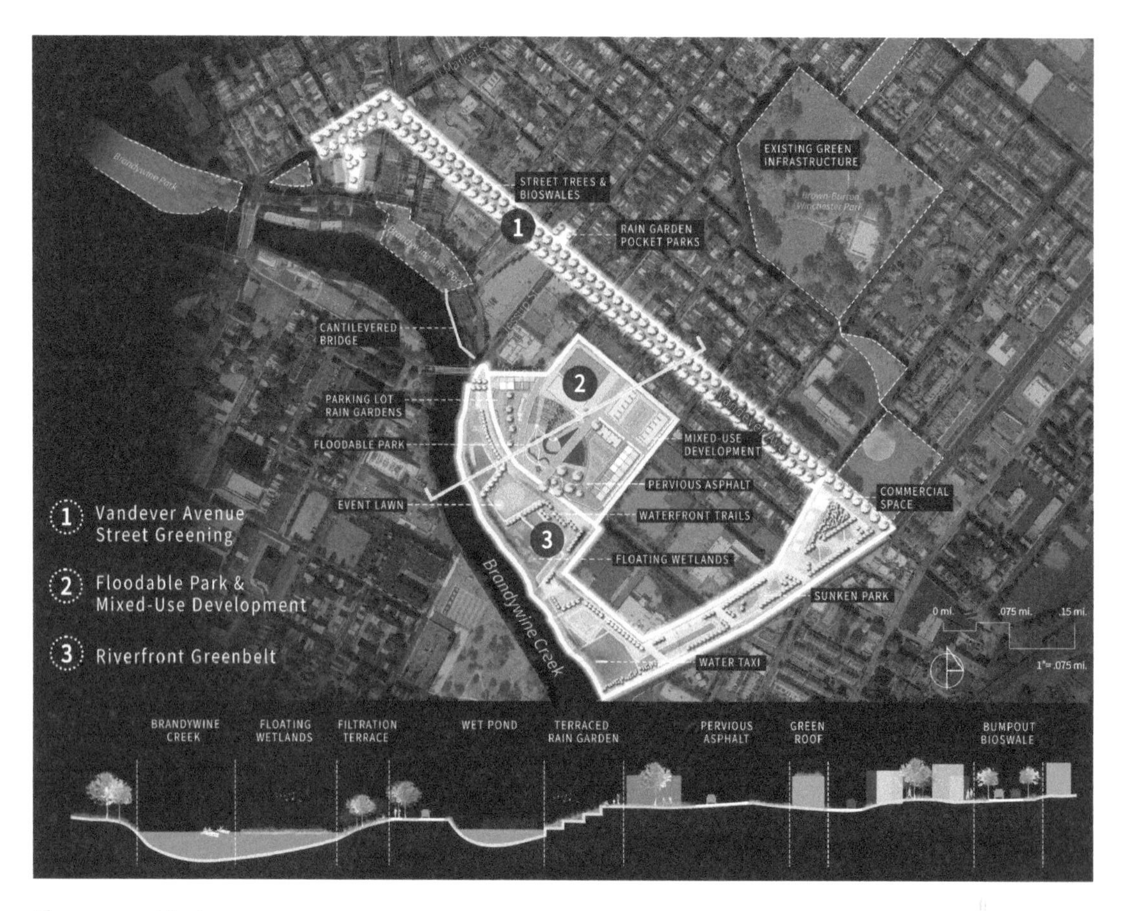

Figure 10.2 Master green infrastructure plan showing three treatments in the NE.

of 314 square miles at its confluence with the Christina River in the city of Wilmington (FEMA, 2015). Sea level rise projections were determined using the Delaware SLR Inundation Mapping methodology (Bates & Callahan, 2016). Flood impact data and elevations were determined by mapping 1% and 0.2% annual chance floodplain boundaries, determined at cross-section transects as recorded in the FEMA Flood Insurance Study (2015), to the base site area, and comparing the percent of inundation based on pervious vs impervious surfaces. FEMA flood maps indicate that roughly 25% of the site has a 1% annual rate of flooding and requires homeowners to purchase flood insurance and build above the 15.5′ elevation in the lower Brandywine. Additionally, the Social Vulnerability Index (SoVI) rates the NE as highly vulnerable to environmental hazards (NOAA, 2021). The Delaware Flood Planning Tool provided visualization and cross-referencing of the site areas impacted by flood and SLR (Delaware Department of Natural Resources, n.d.).

Structural and Non-Structural Mechanisms

The master plan incorporates a series of adaptable, structural, and non-structural mechanisms that address the aesthetic and environmental goals of the community and Comprehensive Plan (see Figure 10.3 and Table 10.1). The design includes small-scale hybrid systems, including rain gardens, bioswales, and terracing, as well as medium-scale hybrid and non-structural elements, such as detention systems and green roofs. Non-structural mechanisms are emphasized because these elements serve multiple community goals, such as flood mitigation, provision of ecosystem services, enhanced air quality and

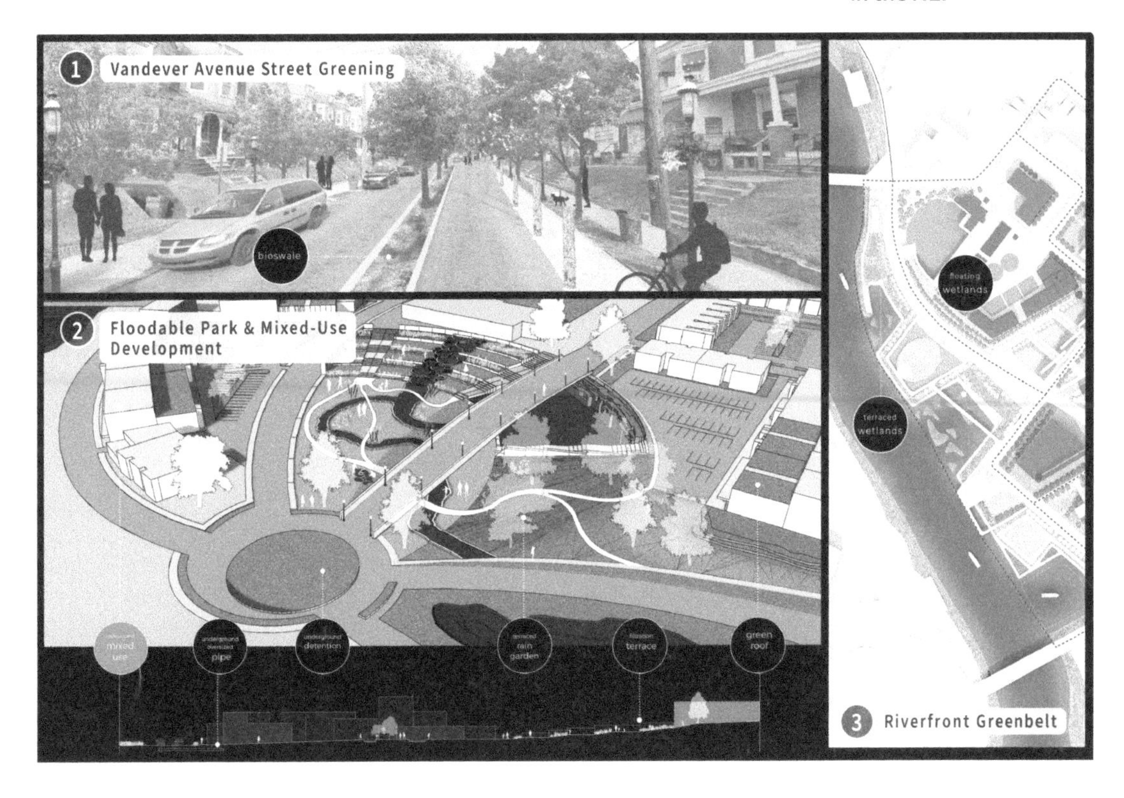

Figure 10.3 Structural and non-structural mechanisms for three treatment areas in the NE.

Table 10.3 Structural and non-structural mechanisms applied to the site's program

Program elements	*Structural*	*Non-structural*	*Hybrid*
Underground oversized pipe	X		
Underground detention	X		
Terraced rain garden		X	
Residential rain garden		X	
Parking lot rain garden		X	
Bump-out bioswale		X	
Sidewalk bioswale		X	
Floating wetlands		X	
Wet pond		X	
Green roof			X
Filtration terrace			X
Pervious asphalt			X

increased aesthetics in the post-industrial landscape. Low-cost, natural GI systems reduce flooding and absorb or store stormwater and are strategically used throughout the NE as community amenities.

Design Impact

Three areas were prioritized for LID design based on their vulnerability or contribution to flooding. The sites were evaluated independently using the EPA National Stormwater Calculator to determine how LID affects stormwater runoff in a phased approach. The three treatments work together to enhance overall resilience to flooding, while having calculable benefit for runoff reduction individually. The desire for a phased approach has been voiced by Collaborate NE as a way to garner support for multiple funding opportunities. Each treatment contributes to reductions in average annual runoff and days per year with runoff, while increasing the percent of wet days retained, as determined by calculation. The GI treatments proposed reduce flood hazards and impacts, while encouraging overall social and economic sustainability in the NE.

Treatment (1) Vandever Avenue Street Greening

A complete street redesign establishes bioswale and rain garden stormwater management features along a prominent thoroughfare, Vandever Avenue, to capture runoff from the heavily polluted impervious surface. In addition to reducing flow volumes, green streets improve safety of pedestrian and cyclist users and aesthetics along the roadway (Rodriguez-Valencia & Ortiz-Ramirez, 2021). Green street segments connect two new pocket parks, replacing impervious asphalt lots with residential rain gardens and lawn. This treatment reduces impervious surface by 29%, average annual runoff by 34%, and days per year with runoff by 9 days. Percent of wet days retained increases by 11 days and maximum rainfall retained increases by 494%.

Treatment (2) Floodable Park and Mixed-Use Development

This treatment incorporates resilient mixed-use development alongside stormwater management in the form of a floodable park system. Runoff is channeled from the surrounding region into a floodable wet pond, filling a series of pools that slowly release stormwater to the creek, rerouting a portion of flow that currently contributes to combined sewer overflow. The system is hydrologically connected to the Brandywine Creek by an underground oversized pipe, providing a designated space for floodwaters to pool when water levels rise, reducing impacts to homes, streets, and other infrastructure during storm events. Twenty new mixed-use four-plexes, ten new single-family homes, and five new separate commercial buildings surround the park amenity. Located on a partially remediated brownfield, the proposal provides housing (60 residential units) and economic opportunity (20 businesses units) on currently underutilized space. This treatment increases the total amount of impervious surface by 36%. However, the other LID techniques and GI treatments, including green roofs on 50% of new development, pervious asphalt on all new roads and parking areas, rain gardens in new parking lots and along the park terrace, rain harvesting along a pedestrian bridge stored in underground detention, and the wet pond, reduce the average annual runoff overall by 35% and the days per year with runoff by 19 days. Increases are shown in the number of wet days retained (24%), the largest rainfall the site can receive without producing runoff (73%), and the maximum rainfall retained (15%).

Treatment (3) Riverfront Greenbelt

The third treatment celebrates a hydrological and community connection to the Brandywine Creek as part of a riverfront greenbelt. Filtration terracing and floating wetlands take the place of a vacant industrial waterfront to buffer flood volumes and provide habitat, while highlighting the beauty of the creek. Waterfront amenities including trails, commercial space, a bridge, an event lawn, a water taxi, and a sunken park amend the natural landscape features and strengthen the community connection to the river once inhibited by industrial land use. Here, the total impervious surface is reduced by 38%, annual runoff is reduced by 70%, and days per year with runoff are reduced by 38 days. The percent of wet days retained increases by 47% and the maximum rainfall retained increases by 78%.

Once implemented, the three treatments overall increase average wet days retained to 28%, increase the largest rainfall amount without runoff by 129%, reduce the days per year with runoff by 22, and reduce annual runoff by 35.86 inches (see Figure 10.4).

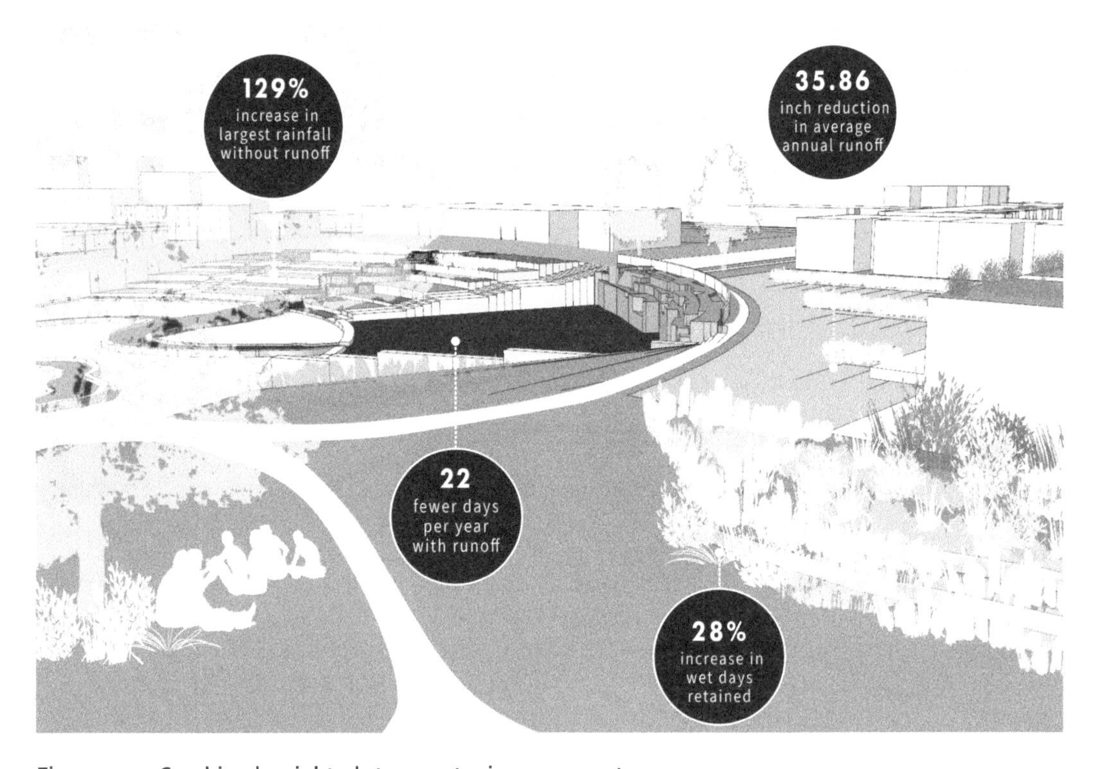

Figure 10.4 Combined weighted stormwater improvements.

Conclusions

Innovation and Applicability

This case described the use of collaborative academic exercises that further the needs of a community to develop resilient solutions. The efforts by the students and collaborative partners, which over time lead to aggregate community and policymaker awareness of community concerns, draw attention to the impacts of flooding and SLR on these vulnerable, yet vital, communities and magnify understanding of new methods, both structural and non-structural, of increasing resiliency. A limitation of this strategy is that students are regularly engaged with the project for a period of only one academic semester, and more time and in-depth study of the proposed strategies are warranted to (a) determine quantifiable data and (b) ascertain community opinion. Some of the often-criticized aspects of community engagement are the lack of long-term investment by the University, and lack of return on tangible results for the community (Weerts & Sandmann, 2010).

By applying the EPA's National Stormwater Calculator, the proposed solutions have demonstrated the capacity to engender real change and mitigate environmental challenges. The calculator can assist municipalities and other entities in assessing design performance related to SLR for evaluating design alternatives.

Globally, many impoverished urban neighborhoods face challenges related to stormwater and SLR. Universities are well positioned to partner with disadvantaged communities to study land use patterns and make recommendations. Community engagement allows for an accurate determination of the existing problems and what additional impacts (economic, health, and safety) the community members are facing. Once planning is complete, a strategy that prioritizes a variety of lower cost, small scale, non-structural interventions allows for implementation of small treatments to catalyze communities and bring attention to the greater needs of economic development. Leveraging smaller successful implementations, large-scale structural changes can be tackled. Continued university involvement ensures project continuity and additional advocacy to drive future changes.

References

Bates, N., & Callahan, J. (2016). *Delaware sea-level rise inundation mapping methodology*. Delaware Geological Survey. Retrieved from www.dgs.udel.edu/sites/default/files/projects-docs/Coastal_Inundation_Mapping_Methodology_2017.pdf

Callahan, J. (2017). *Recommendation of sea-level rise planning scenarios for Delaware: Technical report*. Delaware Geological Survey. Retrieved from www.dgs.udel.edu/sites/default/files/projects-docs/Delaware%20SLR%20Technical%20Report%202017.pdf

Crawl-Bey, T., Dobson, W., et al. (2017). *Northeast Wilmington community revitalization plan*. Northeast BluePrint Team. Collaborate Northeast. Retrieved from http://northeastwilmington.com/wp-content/uploads/2017/08/NE-Wilmington-Community-Revitalization-Plan.pdf

Delaware Department of Natural Resources. (n.d.). *Flood planning tool* [Interactive Viewer]. Retrieved April 1, 2021, from https://floodplanning.dnrec.delaware.gov/

Delaware Coastal Programs of the Department of Natural Resources and Environmental Control (DNREC). (2012). *Preparing for tomorrow's high tide: Sea level rise vulnerability assessment for the State of Delaware*. Retrieved from www.dnrec.delaware.gov/coastal/Documents/SeaLevelRise/AssesmentForWeb.pdf

Federal Emergency Management Agency (FEMA). (2015). US Department of Homeland Security. *Flood insurance study New Castle County and incorporated areas*. Retrieved from https://evogov.s3.amazonaws.com/media/126/media/48965.pdf

Gornitz, V. (1990). Vulnerability of the East Coast, U.S.A. to future sea level rise. *Journal of Coastal Research*, 201–237. Retrieved March 30, 2021, from www.jstor.org/stable/44868636

Miller, K. G., Kopp, R. E., Horton, B.P., Browning, J. V., & Kemp, A. C. (2013), A geological perspective on sea-level rise and its impacts along the U.S. mid-Atlantic coast. Earth's Future, *AGU Publications*, doi:10.1002/2013EF000135.

NOAA Office for Coastal Management. (n.d). *Sea level rise viewer.* Retrieved April 1, 2021, from https://coast.noaa.gov/slr/#/layer/vul-soc/4/-8409221.871557243/4829324.388195096/14/satellite/none/0.8/2050/interHigh/midAccretion

Piecuch, C. G., Huybers, P., Hay, C. C., Kemp, A. C., Little, C. M., Mitrovica, J. X., Ponte, R. M., & Tingley, M. P. (2018). Origin of spatial variation in US East Coast sea-level trends during 1900–2017. *Nature*, *564*, 400–404. https://doi.org/10.1038/s41586-018-0787-6

Rodriguez-Valencia, A., & Ortiz-Ramirez, H. A. (2021). Understanding green street design: Evidence from three cases in the U.S. *Sustainability*, *13*, 1916. https://doi.org/10.3390/su13041916.

Schwartz, S. (2019). *Wilmington 2028: A comprehensive plan for our city and communities.* Interface Studios, Econsult Solutions. Retrieved from www.wilmingtonde.gov/home/showpublisheddocument?id=8490

Tibbetts J. (2005). Combined sewer systems: Down, dirty, and out of date. *Environmental Health Perspectives*, *113*(7), 464–467. https://doi.org/10.1289/ehp.113-a464

Titus, J. G., Hudgens, D. E., Trescott, D. L., Craghan, M., Nuckols, W. H., Hershner, C. H., Kassakian, J. M., Linn, C. J., Merritt, P. G., McCue, T. M., & O'Connell, J. F. (2009). State and local governments plan for development of most land vulnerable to rising sea level along the US Atlantic coast. *Environmental Research Letters*. Retrieved from https://iopscience.iop.org/article/10.1088/1748-9326/4/4/044008

Weerts, D., & Sandmann, L. (2010). Community engagement and boundary-spanning roles at research universities. *The Journal of Higher Education*, *81*(6), 632–657. https://doi.org/10.1080/00221546.2010.11779075

Whitman, Requardt, & Associates [WRA], LLP (2019). *Northeast Wilmington implementation plan.* BluePrint Communities, Collaborate Northeast. Retrieved from http://northeastwilmington.com/wp-content/uploads/2020/02/201910_NE-Wilmington-Implementation-Report.pdf

Hybrid Heavy Design

11

FRANKS TRACT FUTURES, SACRAMENTO: SAN JOAQUIN DELTA, CALIFORNIA

Brett Milligan

Site Size and Location: Franks Tract State Recreation Area: 3,523 acres (1,426 ha)

Introduction/Rationale

Franks Tract is a shallow tidal lake in the heart of California's Sacramento–San Joaquin Delta. The lake formed in the 1930s when levees protecting reclaimed farmland failed, and the tract filled with water. As a place where broken levees were left unrepaired and farming practices have been abandoned, the Tract eventually found a use as a Navy bombing practice site, and later, as a unique State Recreational Area. Today, Franks Tract is a contemporary park mired in ecological and socio-political contestation. The Tract is at the center of California's "water wars," and is the primary source of tidal salinity intrusion from the San Francisco Bay, which threatens Delta water exports to the southern half of the state (see Figure 11.1). The Western Delta, which includes Franks Tract, is a polder landscape, meaning that, like the Netherlands, it is fully engineered, reclaimed land. Wherever there is dry land, it is protected by a large network of dikes (or levees), since such lands are far below sea level due to subsidence of their peat soils (with some as low as 25 feet below mean sea level). The still-functioning levees of the many polders surrounding Franks Tract are subject to potential liquefaction due to earthquakes, and increasingly subject to overtopping due to sea level rise and storm surges (see Figure 11.1). If these levees fail, they will further exacerbate salinity intrusion into the Delta. As droughts recur more frequently or lengthen in California and sea level continues to rise, attenuating saltwater intrusion from the ocean will require expensive and disruptive management measures, such as the emergency drought barrier constructed in 2015 on the False River (next to the Tract) that was highly unpopular with local stakeholders (Kimmerer et al., 2019).

As a radically altered and novel ecosystem, this tidal lake has also become the home of expanding numbers of aquatic introduced plant species (or weeds) that blanket its surface and fill the water column, making boat navigation increasingly difficult. Even with the extensive and costly application of herbicides, the weeds continue to expand with

DOI: 10.4324/9781003183419-16

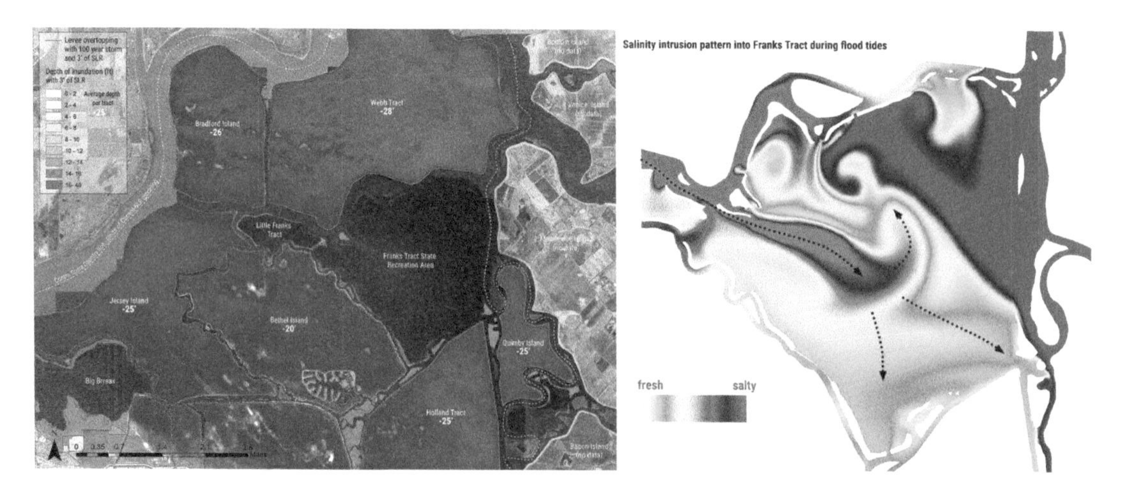

Figure 11.1 Sea level rise and salinity intrusion. (Left) map of levee overtopping projections for Contra Costa county during a 100-year storm event with 3 feet of sea level rise. The color ramp shows the depth of water inundation that would occur in the subsided tracts of land surrounding Franks Tract, if breached, with most of them at least 25 feet underwater. Data provided by Bay Conservation and Development Commission; (right) hydrodynamic model of tidal-based salinity intrusion into Franks Tract, which increases with sea level rise, threatening the state's water export infrastructure. Model image by California Department of Water Resources (arrows added by author).

each drought. Franks Tract is also dominated by introduced predatory fish species that thrive in these altered conditions, such as black bass. While such species support economically significant fishing tournaments, they reduce the habitat value for critically endangered species such as Delta smelt and Chinook salmon. There are year-round fishing tournaments here and, from March through May, there is a tournament every weekend, the largest of which can generate up to a half a million dollars in economic activity (EPS, 2020). Overall, 98% of the tidal marshes that made up the Delta (which Franks Tract formerly was) have been eradicated (SFEI, 2014). Yet, despite these concerns, the Tract persists as a world-class bass fishing area, a primary boating interchange, and the site of highly valued regional recreational activities.

Several past planning efforts have attempted to address Franks Tract's salinity problem with engineered solutions. The Franks Tract Futures project was the first that sought to integrate ecological and other community-based concerns into design and planning objectives, primarily because past efforts had failed for this very reason (CDFW, 2020). Working on behalf of multiple state agencies, the interdisciplinary planning team collaborated with a variety of experts and public stakeholders to determine whether the Tract could be redesigned to adapt to rapidly changing conditions and diversifying needs. Specifically, the goals of the Franks Tract Futures feasibility study were to (1) benefit threatened native and desirable species by re-establishing natural ecological processes and habitats, (2) provide enhanced recreational opportunities and other community benefits, and (3) improve water quality and reliability as a critical logistical hub in the state's massive water infrastructure (ibid.). Overall, the project sought to find synergies within the benefits across all objectives that will be sustainable over time.

Design Synopsis

Scenario Development and Co-Design Processes

The project team used a transdisciplinary co-design process that included participatory mapping, scenario planning, structured decision making, and multiple design workshops to create design scenarios that were preferable to the "do nothing" status quo. Several research methods were key to this outcome. The first was thoroughly understanding how diverse stakeholders and publics use the tract, what they value, their concerns, and what could be improved. The team came to understand these questions through public meetings, interviews, and geospatial surveys that allowed participants to author their own user maps, such as their key boating routes, where and how they recreate, where tidal marsh could be best located, and where improvements were needed (see Figure 11.2). We took this stakeholder information and combined it with projective science of how the tract is likely to continue to change without design intervention. This "no action" scenario, as it was referred to, made it tangible to stakeholders that a "leave it as is" approach was untenable within an already rapidly changing Delta. This understanding increased public support for proactive design strategies that could sustain and improve what they value in the tract. Lastly, we used an iterative, research-by-design approach, refining design concepts through stakeholder-responsive landscape modeling, consultation with experts, a series of participatory design workshops, and service-learning-based design studios to generate three viable design scenarios.

All of the project's design scenarios entail a volumetric reworking of the tract through extensive cut and fill dredging operations. These earthworks would significantly deepen some areas, while raising others back to sea level to reclaim large expanses of tidal wetland habitat and to create new recreational features. The form and distribution of the earthworks had to be parametrically sculpted in such a way as

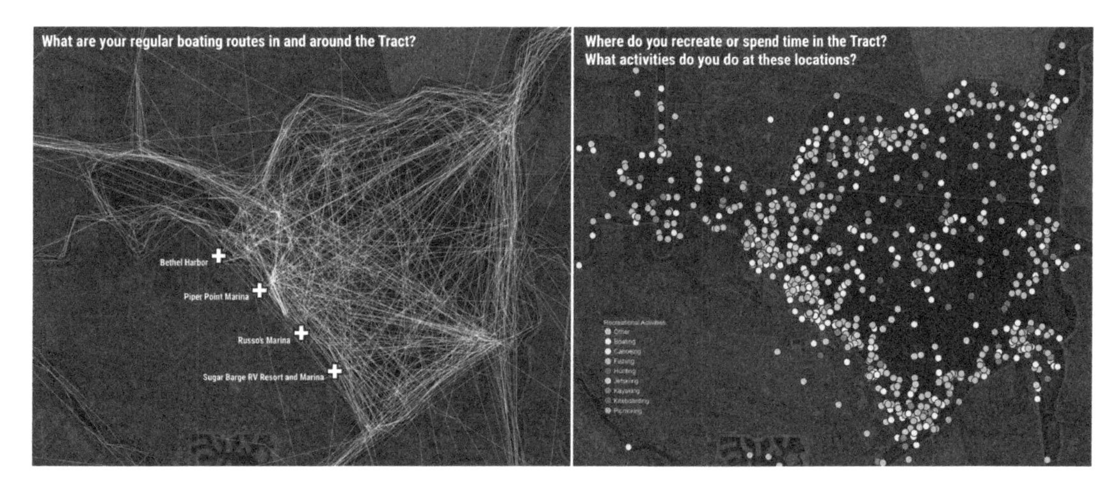

Figure 11.2 Selection of results from the Franks Tract Futures map-based online public user survey, showing preferred boating routes and location and type of recreational uses.

to meet the seeming incompatible parameters of salinity reduction, recreational needs, and effective ecological restoration. Thus, an iterative design research process was the essential foundation for scenario development.

Participatory scenario planning techniques were combined with structured decision making to facilitate collective learning and building of adaptive capacity. Scenario planning allowed for participants to explore a variety of potential futures, rather than one. The structured decision-making process allowed all participant concerns and interests to be evaluated through criteria developed in facilitated conversations between technical experts and affected stakeholders. This allowed for project goals and criteria to be established transparently, and for place-based values to be given the same weight as scientific data and mandates. Once established, planning and design options were repeatedly evaluated and refined based on these criteria.

Collective investment in the project was facilitated by starting broadly with six design scenarios for stakeholders to review and from which to choose. These were reduced to three preferred designs (and the "no action" alternative) that were tested and refined through stakeholder-responsive hydro-dynamic modeling, consultation with experts, and a series of participatory design workshops. Hydrodynamic modeling was a key tool for integrating environmental data and ecological performance metrics into co-design efforts. Using the Semi-implicit Cross-scale Hydroscience Integrated System Model (SCHISM), team engineers were able to test for variances in water salinity and velocity under various design schemes and sea-level rise scenarios across time and space. These model results were communicated to stakeholders through maps and time lapse visualizations (Ateljevich and Nam, 2020). Working with local communities and the project team, two service-based undergraduate landscape architecture design studios explored a wide range of options for the siting and design of recreational features within the reshaped terrain, including beach design, detailed landform sculpting, and design of mooring and camping areas, docks, and hunting ponds (see Table 11.1).

Hybrid Mechanisms

The Central Landmass design (see Figure 11.3) was the top-rated scenario across the project's advisory and steering committee members and by members of the broader public that participated in a final online project design survey (Milligan et al., 2020). Overall, the design diversifies the landscape by creating new deep-water areas, vast tidal marshes, navigation channels, beaches, and other amenities. Its benefits include improvements to water quality, salinity reduction, increased flood safety, large-scale creation and improvements in ecological habitats and functions, improved boating navigation, provision of new recreational opportunities, and preservation and improved adaptive capacity for local communities and economies (see Figure 11.4) (CAFW, 2020). Each of these performance benefits is detailed below.

Table 11.1 Structural, non-structural, and hybrid mechanisms applied to the Franks Tract

Program elements	*Structural*	*Non-structural*	*Hybrid*
Existing Levee system (adjacent reclaimed tracts):			
Earthen levees with riprap	X		
Horizontal habitat levees:			
Aquatic-upland			X
Riparian			X
Living breakwaters (segmented):			
Aquatic-upland			X
Riparian			X
Dredging and mounding to create:			
Salinity intrusion barrier			X
Deep water pools and channels			X
Tidal wetlands			X
Upland riparian habitats			X
Recreational beaches			X
Sheltered coves and other recreational features			X

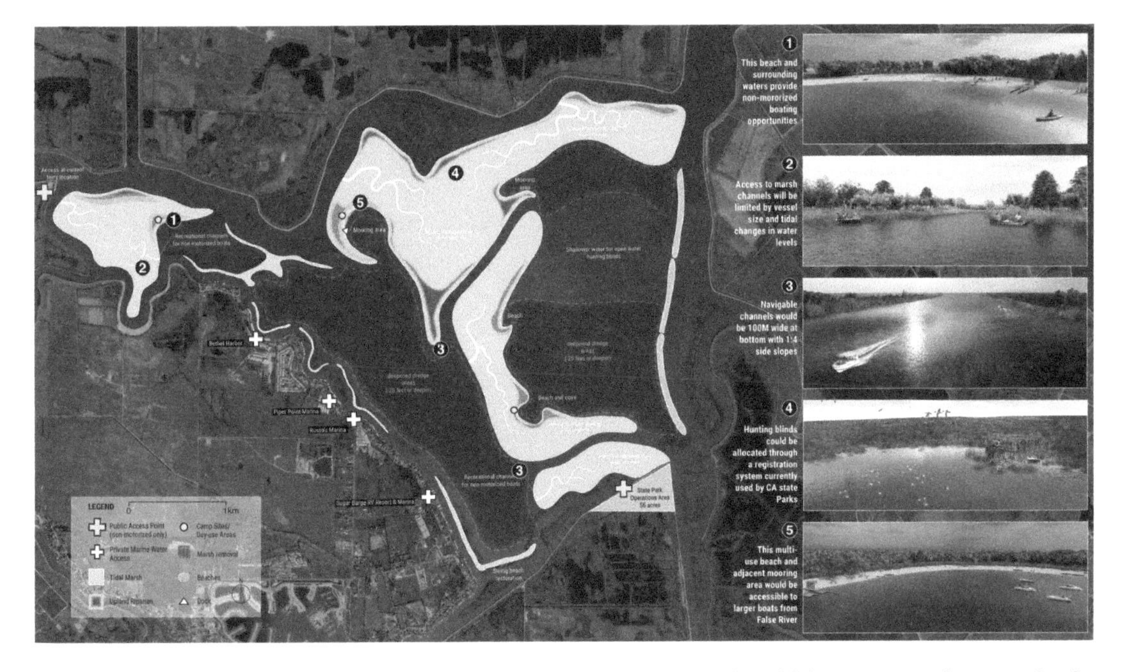

Figure 11.3 Site plan of the Central Landmass preferred design scenario, which creates two large pools of water separated by wetlands.

Figure 11.4 Renderings of project features common to all design scenarios, including (clockwise from top left) improved navigable channels, public beaches and no wake non-motorized boating areas, tidal marsh channels (section and perspective).

Design Impact

Navigation

Faster water navigation routes through and across the Tract were identified as a top concern by boaters, recreational users, and all local communities. The project, therefore, includes extensive, deepened open-water areas and navigable channels that would reduce the growth of shallow water weeds that are an expanding nuisance for boaters. The project also includes measures to improve boating safety, such as removing existing underwater snags and hazards, and sheltering the wave-exposed eastern entrances to the Tract. Provision of fast and safe boating navigation through Franks Tract while meeting water quality objectives was a key parametric challenge in the project. Channel widths that were too wide would reduce the project's ability to perform as a salinity barrier, and, if too narrow, they would compromise navigability. Thus, channel widths were hydrodynamically modeled to quantify the effects of different channel sizes and configurations on water quality and velocity impacts. The final 100-meter bottom width of the channels was the optimal size to balance these two objectives (see Figure 11.4).

Water Quality and Salinity Reduction

Based on hydrodynamic modeling, the overall configuration of tidal wetlands in all final landscape redesign concepts would reduce salinity transport through Franks Tract, with significant improvements to water quality for drinking, irrigation supply, and other uses. The preferred central landmass concept improves water quality in the central Delta under a variety of flow conditions and reduces potential fish entrainment (in the export pumps), which currently limits in-Delta diversions and the reliability of water operations. The project also provides significant drought protection, reducing the frequency with which an emergency salinity control structure would be needed, which is a major benefit for local communities. Moreover, the relative efficacy and need for the project increases as sea level rises.

Flood Protection

Remnant levees around Franks Tract (the ones that formerly reclaimed the Tract itself) shelter adjacent flood protection levees from overtopping and erosion from waves. Local reclamation districts are highly supportive of project features that enhance the remnant levees that would reduce required flood protection levee maintenance activities and associated costs. The preferred project design would raise and widen levees with dredged or other material, while retaining key openings used by boaters. Flood simulation modeling results also found that the preferred concept (with its introduction of large-scale earth formations) does not significantly affect flood conveyance or increase water levels in the Tract, adjacent channels, or other areas.

Recreation

Recreational planning and design efforts focused on maintaining open water areas for boating and creating new types of recreational features and opportunities (see Figure 11.4). Slow-water channels and pools, such as Little Franks Tract, would allow for safe non-motorized boating. Well-designed and strategically located beaches and upland areas would offer day use, sunbathing, and swimming, as well as proximity to the water for water skiing and wakeboarding. Mooring coves also provide sheltered destinations for boaters. Opportunities to maintain or enhance sport fishing were integrated into the design of habitat enhancements, such as the creation of new edge habitats and water velocity gradients.

Local Economy

The social and economic well-being of Bethel Island is dependent on the popularity of outdoor recreation in the region, and maintaining the landscape's aesthetic values. Project research found that approximately half the employment on Bethel Island is directly tied to recreation, and increasing degradation of environmental conditions is a known business risk (EPS, 2020). The local economy has the best chance for success and sustainability if boating and fishing conditions are of high quality, and navigation and access are maintained or improved. Project designs sought to provide for a broad and adaptive range of recreation uses, while maintaining and benefiting the local economy, and preserving key landscape qualities tied to resident property values. The project's design meets these objectives by providing new economic opportunities through interventions to reduce weeds, restore native ecology, maintain and improve navigation, maintain open water areas adjacent to homes and businesses, and enhance recreation.

Ecology

In all design scenarios, extensive new tidal wetlands, riparian edges, and upland areas would provide enhanced habitats and food production for a variety of fish and wildlife. Tidal marshes with narrow channels along the north of Franks Tract would provide refuge and a corridor for out-migrating juvenile Chinook salmon. Tidal marshes in Little Franks Tract and the western part of Franks Tract would provide rearing and foraging habitat and food web support in the areas endangered Delta smelt is most likely to occur. Hydrodynamic particle tracking indicates that fisheries should benefit from the project due to reduced risk of entrainment into Old River and the water export supply pumps. Project design would maintain, and likely improve, areas of sportfish habitat. The additional edge habitat along tidal marshes and remaining open water would be desirable for largemouth bass and striped bass fishing, respectively. Upland habitats provide benefits and refugia for many species, including waterfowl, which use them as rearing habitats.

Conclusions

Findings

Sea level rise has many effects and implications beyond a vertical rise in oceanic waters, such as salinity intrusion into urbanized estuaries and deltas around the world. Rising sea levels also combine, in both known and indeterminate ways, with a multitude of other accelerated climate change effects. These include increased storm intensity and flood risk, more intense droughts, increased air and water temperatures, and the bio-geophysical forcing of undesirable ecological transformations. Further complicating these co-evolutionary situations – and equally, if not more important – is the equitable integration of local and place-based values in adaptation planning and design, particularly in vulnerable and politically contested landscapes such as the Sacramento–San Joaquin Delta. Without buy-in and support from local stakeholders, purely technical and soloed solutions are bound to fail or never be realized (Milligan & Kraus Polk, 2017).

Innovation and Applicability

Using an integrative co-design research process, the Franks Tract Futures project was able to reconcile state goals of water quality and ecological improvements with regional stakeholder values and needs. It did this by taking multi-benefit adaptation projects to a new level in the Delta, creating a salinity barrier made of vast, ecologically restorative tidal marshes, all while creating new, world class recreational opportunities befitting of the Delta's new designation as a National Heritage Area (Delta Protection Commission, 2020). The exploration of landscape as a dynamic, responsive, and pluralistic medium was central to the project's design process. By rigorously testing a range of strategies for diversifying the landscape, both above and below water and across a broad range of agreed-upon goals, new adaptive design scenarios for the future came into being.

Acknowledgments

The author wishes to acknowledge all members of the Franks Tract Futures team, and the two UC Davis PhD students who worked on this project: Yiwei Huang and Alejo Kraus-Polk. The author would also like to thank all others who participated and contributed to the Franks Tract Futures project.

References

Ateljevich, E., & Nam, K. (2020). *Hydrodynamic modeling in support of Franks Tract Futures restoration project design and stakeholder outreach*. California Department of Water Resources. Retrieved from https://ucdavis.app.box.com/s/vb7pm6h523mdqjtoxwimeysbg7pqnjfp

California Department of Fish and Wildlife (CDFW). (2020). *Franks Tract Futures reimagined: Options for enhancing navigation, recreation, ecology, and water quality in the central Delta*. CDFW. Retrieved March 12, 2021, from https://franks-tract-futures-ucdavis.hub.arcgis.com/

Delta Protection Commission. (2020). *Sacramento–San Joaquin Delta national heritage area*. Retrieved March 12, 2021, from http://delta.ca.gov/wp-content/uploads/2020/05/NHA-Factsheet-2020-508.pdf

Economic Planning Systems (EPS). (2020). *Franks Tract Futures: public and user survey of design concepts; economic assessment; economic planning systems*. EPS. Retrieved March 12, 2021, from https://ucdavis.box.com/s/1q2stlkilwzqg17hoomj69uvskmvepsu

Kimmerer, W., Wilkerson, F., Downing, B., Dugdale, R., Gross, E. S., Kayfetz, K., . . . & Thompson, J. (2019). Effects of drought and the emergency drought barrier on the ecosystem of the California Delta. *San Francisco Estuary and Watershed Science*, *17*(3), 1–18. Retrieved from https://escholarship.org/uc/item/0b3731ph

Milligan, B., Kraus-Polk, A., & Huang, Y. (2020). Park, fish, salt and marshes: Participatory mapping and design in a watery uncommons. *Land*, *9*(11), 454.

Milligan, B., & Kraus-Polk, A. (2017). Evolving the evolving: Infrastructure, place and rewilding in the California Delta. *Urban Planning*, *2*(4), 93–115.

San Francisco Estuary Institute (SFEI). (2014). A delta transformed: Ecological functions, spatial metrics, and landscape change in the Sacramento-San Joaquin Delta. SFEI. Retrieved from www.sfei.org/documents/delta-transformed-ecological-functions-spatial-metrics-and-landscape-change-sacramento-san

12

SAMUT SAKHON, BANGKOK METROPOLITAN REGION, THAILAND

Sani Limthongsakul, Pudtan Chantarangkul, and Supreeya Wungpatcharapon

Site: Samut Sakhon, Bangkok Metropolitan Region, Thailand: 237.2 acres

Introduction/Rationale

Projections and Effects of Sea Level Rise

The coastline in the Upper Gulf of Thailand covers three provinces in the Bangkok Metropolitan Areas, including this chapter's case site, Samut Sakhorn province. These areas are considered important for local-based tourism, as well as for agriculture and aquaculture activities in central Thailand. A study by Saengsupavanich (2017) found that tidal stations along the upper Gulf of Thailand indicated an increasing trend of the seawater level. The study estimated that the highest seawater level along the upper gulf of Thailand in the next 100 years, specifically at Ta Chen station (the closest station to Ao Mahachai Mangrove Forest Natural Education Center (AMFC) at Samut Sakhon province) were expected to be +2.30m mean sea level. These coastal areas have experienced serious erosion problems for decades. Along its 34.45 kilometers shoreline, the coast has been severely eroding by 1 to 5 meters annually (DMCR, 2018). Recent studies inform that, while natural factors such as waves, coastal currents, tides, or monsoons have resulted in the coastal erosion in the area, human activities have also played a major role, especially in the invasion of mangrove forests by shrimp farming (Yaowasooth, 2019). Further, the expansion of industrial zones in the Samut Sakhon province and its excess pumping of groundwater have exaggerated soil liquefaction. It is speculated that an average of 20–40 millimeters of land subsidence per year could consequently result in coastal erosion of 13–26 meters annually (Jarupongsakul, 2006).

Examples of Previous Floods and Damage Caused

The case site in Samut Sakhon has been a homeland of fishery villages for generations. The communities are commonly composed of

DOI: 10.4324/9781003183419-17

lower-income families. Coastal erosion has had a serious impact on the quality of life within those coastal communities in various ways. Thammaapipon (2012) categorizes those impacts into three aspects: economic, social, and environmental. Economic impacts contain: (1) decreasing land values, (2) loss of households' income, (3) retraction of houses, and (4) high costs of coastal defense structures. Social impacts include: (1) population migrations and (2) changing lifestyles. Environmental impacts include: (1) land loss, (2) mangrove deterioration, (3) marine animal reduction, and (4) loss of coastal scenery. Further, if the external erosion continues, in the next 20 years the economic risk projects to increase by $5 million and could rise up to $12.27 million in the next 50 years (Paphawasit, 2011).

It could be said that coastal erosion protection in Thailand follows three primary methods. "White measures" focus on drawing setback zones and the control of land use, while "Green measures" emphasize mangrove afforestation. The last method, "Grey measures," are heavily concerned with engineered systems and structural mechanisms. Grey measures have been widely implemented across many coastlines, yet have also garnered much criticism. Ineffective coastal protections such as sea walls, breakwaters, and groins can accelerate erosion rates (Siripong, 2010). Further, their implementation has never been required by Environmental Impact Assessments. On the other hand, Paphawasit (2011) argues that the restoration of coastal areas through the participation of the local communities has decelerated coastal erosion in the region and strengthened coastal ecosystem restoration efficiency. She insists that public participation is required throughout the process and should be conducted alongside adaptive management. Stakeholders engage early in the adaptive management cycle to help assess problems, develop design activities, implement, and monitor those activities, and participate in the evaluation of their results.

Design Synopsis

Study Area

Ao Mahachai Mangrove Forest Natural Education Center (AMFC), located at the mouth of the Tha Chin River in the western gulf of Mahachai National Reserved Forest, Bang Ya Phraek subdistrict in Samut Sakhon province, is under supervision of the Department of Marine and Coastal Resources This area is considered the most abundant mangrove forest of Mahachai gulf. It is, however, threatened by urban sprawl, shrimp farming, industrial land use, coastal erosion, coastal flooding, and sea level rise. The coastal erosion rate recorded by the Department of Marine and Coastal Resources is more than 5 meters per year (DMCR, 2018), which is considered a severe condition. Figure 1 displays these issues as well as sea level rise projections for the study site. The AMFC's major task is to preserve and restore the mangrove forest as a part of the national forest along Mahachai bay area in Samut Sakhon.

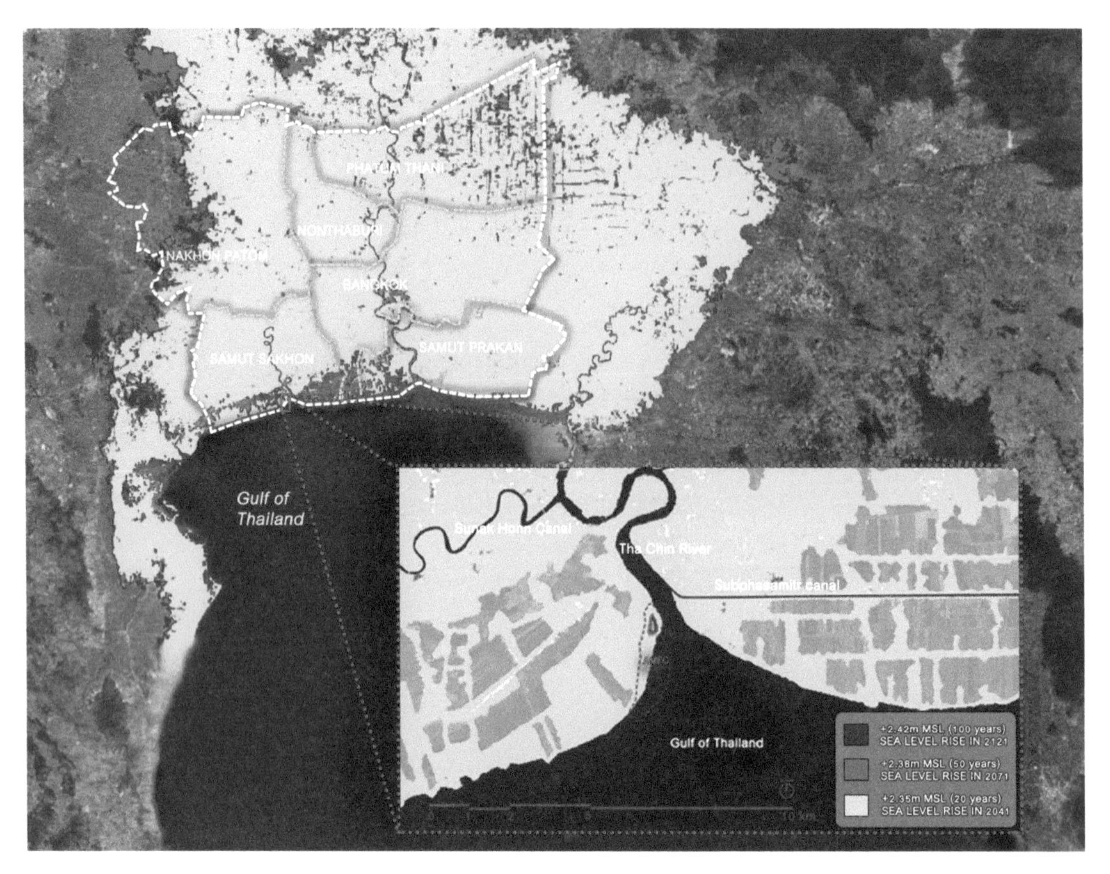

Figure 12.1 Ao Mahachai Mangrove Forest Natural Education Center (AMFC) and the sea level rise projection.
Illustration by Lakanapohn Sinparu.

Design Strategies

The restoration program of the AMFC focuses on climate change adaptation, aiming to minimize the risks of sea level rise and increase local adaptive capacity. In this project, we first identify three sensitivity aspects of the local climate. Physical sensitivity includes coastal erosion, coastal flooding, wastewater and solid waste problems, and mangrove forest deterioration and losses. Socio-economic sensitivity can be observed through food insecurity and depleted resources associated with diminishing mangrove forest area. Finally, degraded shorelines and mangrove ecosystem and habitat loss for marine lives and birds account for environmental sensitivity. With an intention to increase the local adaptive capacity, both physical and socio-economic vulnerabilities should also be minimized. To reduce physical vulnerability, we apply the IPCC techniques of coastal adaptation: protect–accommodate–retreat–avoid (IPCC CZMS, 1992). To lessen the socio-economic vulnerabilities, we increase engagement through implementing more local community participation into the existing activities of the AMFC by initiating the local livelihood enhancement programs. With this proposal, the new AMFC will not only perform as an ecotourism, education, and research center but will also serve the local communities by initiating local fisheries and aquaculture farming activities to sustain the local livelihoods.

Design Programs

The new AMFC redevelopment program integrates socio-economic aspects into the existing functions of mangrove forest preservation and restoration by offering more inclusive activities to enhance local community resilience. The final master plan of AMFC enhances local adaptive capacity and offers various types of programs such as mangrove conservation and restoration areas, research and laboratory fields, shoreline restoration and rehabilitation areas, nature trails, bird-watching areas, small-scale aquatic farming, and community co-ops for local fishery products and small tourist accommodations (see Figure 12.2).

Structural and Non-structural Mechanisms

The process of establishing the new AMFC master plan firstly creates site suitability analysis by mapping hazard and flood prone areas with projected sea level rise. Landward, mid-ward and seaward zones are identified and mapped in accordance with the existing master plan. This zonation is one of the crucial factors that influence

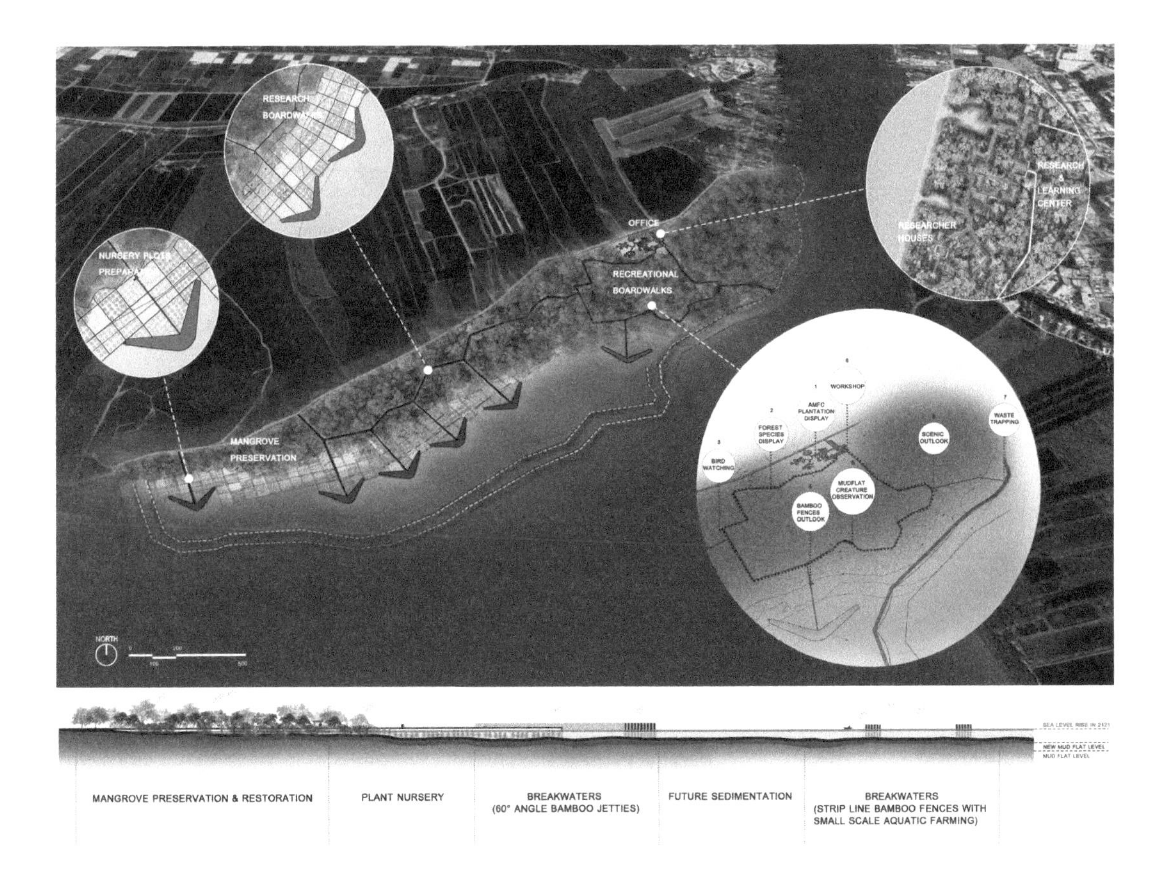

Figure 12.2 AMFC master plan and section designed by Lakanapohn Sinparu

the land use suitability analysis of the existing AMFC area. The existing land use characteristics within the AMFC are categorized as: full grown and healthy mangrove area, inland flooded area, established shoreline, mudflat area, and severely eroded shoreline. With respect to the land use suitability analysis, the new land use of the AMFC is proposed following the activities described earlier in the design program section.

The project utilizes mostly non-structural and hybrid mechanisms for flood mitigation (ranging from both medium to large scale) to mitigate sea level rise impacts (see Table 12.1). Non-structural mechanisms used within this project include building relocation, adaptive housing, and wetland restoration and rehabilitation. Within the projected flood prone area, the existing buildings with high-quality structural condition are proposed to be relocated onto higher elevated ground. Since most areas within the site are susceptible to flooding, any proposed building or structure for the AMFC master plan are required to follow the adaptive building strategies by applying elevated and floating structure techniques. As described earlier, AMFC areas are the only remnant healthy mangrove forest corridor along Samut Sakhon's coastal line. Therefore, wetland restoration and rehabilitation measures are a primary focus. This approach also, however, integrates many hybrid mechanisms into the process. To ensure the successful replanting of mangroves where the rates of coastal erosion are high, bamboo fences are introduced to perform as a living breakwater. The bamboo fences lessen current strengths, allow for sedimentary deposits to occur behind them, and allow the new resultant seedlings to survive. We also propose different bamboo fence arrangements along the eroded shoreline, particularly within the outdoor laboratory plantation to monitor long-term performance. The proposed bamboo fence techniques are strip line pyramid bamboo fences (60° angle zigzagging bamboo or 60° angle bamboo jetty) and perform as the segmented breakwaters mechanism (see Figure 12.3).

Insecurity of livelihoods and economic status significantly contribute to socio-economic sensitivity of many coastal cities in developing countries (Le, 2019). We therefore also propose another non-structural measure to enhance local adaptive capacity through local livelihood enhancement programs. The programs integrate small-scale aquatic farming into the open water along the eroded shoreline behind the bamboo breakwater fences. We suggest the practices of fish aggregating devices, shrimp cage farming, mussel and Meder's mangrove crab farming to be operated by local community members. This small-scale aquatic farming can ensure the local community's food security and engage the local community into the AMFC restoration program. Since the AMFC constantly needs seedlings for mangrove reforestation programs, local community members can earn extra income by becoming seedling suppliers through working in the center's nursery area or in their own plots. The AMFC tasks of building local resilience can be integrated into the eco-tourism activities of the project. Visitors, tourists, and volunteers will be invited to participate in the mangrove forest planting activities, bamboo breakwaters components preparation and

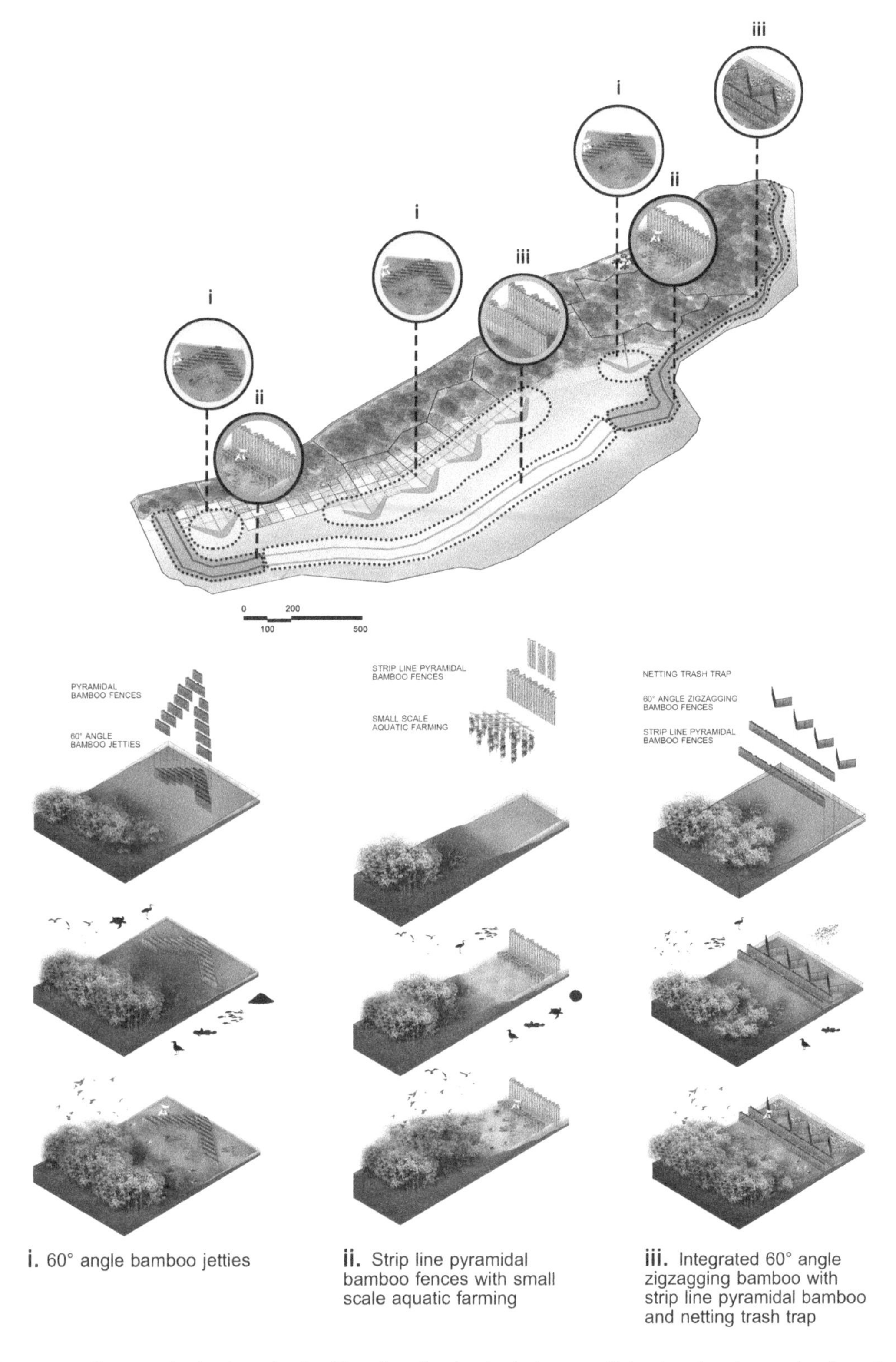

Figure 12.3 Proposed mixed methods of bamboo fencing techniques as living breakwater mechanism at AMFC's coastline.
Illustration by Lakanapohn Sinparu.

installation, fish aggregating devices or aquatic cage preparation, and are made aware of the mangrove forest's ecosystem services.

Design Impact

Mangrove afforestation and reforestation on the case site are not only are beneficial to environmental sustainability, socio-economy, and the villager's livelihood, but are also crucial to coastal protection and land accumulation behind the bamboo fence. It is well known that mangrove forests are resilient to rising sea level by keeping their surface elevations in pace with the sea level rise through the sedimentation process (McIvor et al., 2013). A study by the Department of Marine and Coastal Resources (Henocque & Tandavanitj, 2021) showing a successful coastal protection project implemented in 41 sites within 13 provinces, indicates that over 13 years the project of 83,515 meters of bamboo fence has accumulated in the public coastal area more than 632.41 acres of

Table 12.1 Structural and non-structural mechanisms

Sensitivities	*Problems*	*Adaptation strategies*	*Structural*	*Non-structural*	*Hybrid*
Physical sensitivity	Coastal erosion	Breakwaters (bamboo fences)			X
		Mangrove restoration		X	
	Coastal flooding	Building relocation	X		
		Adaptive buildings and infrastructure design	X		
		Floating boardwalks & recreational boardwalks			X
	Solid waste and wastewater	Litter trap underneath boardwalks			X
	Mangrove ecosystem losses	Mangrove forest plantation		X	
		Plants nursery		X	
Socio-economic sensitivity	Food insecurity	Small-scale aquatic farming		X	
	Loss of incomes from depleted resources	Community co-op for local fisheries products		X	
		Working in nursery plots preparation			X
		Seedling plantations			X
Environmental sensitivity	Degraded shoreline/mangrove ecosystem services	Mangrove preservation & restoration	X		
	Habitat loss for marine lives and birds	Fish aggregating device, mussel and crab larvae cages			X
		Living breakwaters			X
		Learning center	X		

mud sedimentation, and 124.5 acres of that are the mangrove forests. The installation of one meter of bamboo fencing has increased the average mud sedimentation at 0.0006 acres and 0.0001 acres of mangrove forest per year. Further, the practice shows that it can also increase species richness and diversity within the mangrove forests with regard to marine lives. The new installation of bamboo fences will decelerate coastal erosion and increase sedimentation by distributing three layers of pioneer species of mangrove from offshore toward the mainland including: (1) gray mangrove (*Avicennia officinalis L.*), (2) red mangrove (*Rhizophora mucronata*), (3) mixtures of Tall-stilt mangrove (*Rhizophora apiculata*) and gray mangrove (*Avicennia alba*), respectively, behind the bamboo fences to withstand the tidal wave velocity.

Based on a study by Montonphetch et al. (2013), by calculating direct and indirect use values including carbon dioxide sequestration, preventive coastal erosion, hatchery, and mineral storage, it is estimated that the overall value of the mangrove forest is $10,550.00 per acre. By maintaining the mangrove forest, local households directly earn $1,018.00 per household per year. Therefore, the redesign of the AMFC masterplan with an implementation of hybrid mechanisms along the 2,500 meters coastline (bamboo fencing in different types of assembly and small-scale aquatic farming) potentially increases sedimentation at 1.5 acres and 0.25 acres of mangrove forest per year. Following Montonphetch's model, the overall value of restoring the mangrove forest in the case site will earn $2,497 per year[1] (see Figure 12.4).

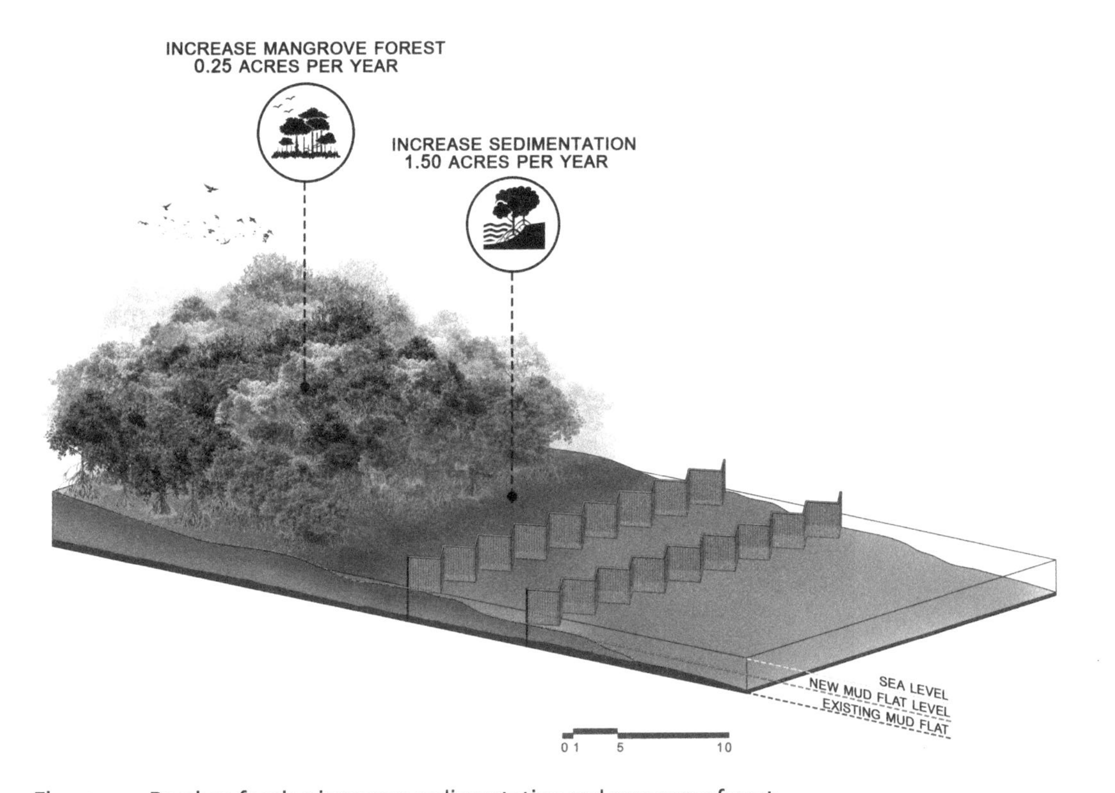

Figure 12.4 Bamboo fencing increases sedimentation and mangrove forest.
Illustration by Lakanapohn Sinparu.

There is an argument on the drawback of bamboo fencing techniques regarding their short lifespan as they begin to decompose within less than seven years. The floating debris from deteriorated bamboo structures can damage the stems of the trees as sea-level rises, especially the ones adjacent to the fence (Pranchai et al., 2019). Therefore, it is recommended that the process of constructing the coastal bamboo structures should incorporate an environmental impact assessment as well as a long-term maintenance plan. In a successful case site, the villagers regularly collect the floating bamboos to overcome the floating debris problems, and recycle them as firewood; hence creating a circular economy locally (Yaowasooth, 2021). The AMFC programs should engage the local community in long-term monitoring and maintenance activities. The sustainability of the AMFC restoration and preservation programs will also sustain the local livelihoods and minimize local vulnerabilities in the long term.

Conclusions

Innovation and Applicability

To mitigate the impacts of sea level rise and preserve the last abundant mangrove forest corridor along Samut Sakhon's coastal line, the proposal of a new AMFC master plan aims to minimize the physical, ecological, and socio-economic sensitivities through an array of programs offering support for public education, recreation, research, and local livelihoods. The planning frameworks start from identifying local climate sensitivities and risks. The data obtained from site visits and open access from websites were transferred into spatial information via digital mapping processes. The area susceptible to coastal floods and severe erosion were delineated along with the existing land use before the overlay method was applied to illustrate land use suitability for the new design programs. The new master plan is arranged under the framework of building local community resilience by increasing local adaptive capacity and minimizing vulnerability. Sustaining local livelihoods is also one of the prominent strategic programs of the new AMFC land use.

In developing countries like Thailand, the local community always plays an important role in mangrove forest restoration and preservation, as the local governments and associate agencies always have limited budgets and do not have the effective administration systems to pursue the tasks alone. Therefore, appropriate technologies are the key concept for choosing the adaptation strategies to encourage the collective methods from the local community. Since the site case is a national forest, there are rigid rules and regulations that may hinder the public and local participation. The local governance is, therefore, one of the major factors contributing to the long-term success of the AMFC new master plan.

Note

1 Exchange rate of one dollar equal 30.86 Thai baht.

References

Department of Marine and Coastal Resources (DMCR). (2018). *Marine and coastal resources in Samut Sakhon, Bangkok*. Information Center of Marine and Coastal Resources. Retrieved from www.iyor2018.org/organization/department-marine-coastal-resources-thailand/

Henocque, Y., & Tandavanitj, S. (2008). Towards sustainable coastal development in Thailand marine and coastal resources policy Green Paper. *Fish for the People*, *6*(1), 34–39.

IPCC CZMS. (1992). A common methodology for assessing vulnerability to sea level rise, 2nd revision, in IPCC CZMS, Global Climate Change and the Rising Challenge of the Sea, Report of the Coastal Zone Management Subgroup, Response Strategies Working Group of the Intergovernmental Panel on Climate Change, Ministry of Transport, Public Works and Water Management, The Hague, Appendix C.

Jarupongsakul, T. (2006). Coastal erosion in Thailand: Causes and management. Research Paper, Department of Geology, Chulalongkorn University.

Le, T. D. N. (2019). Climate change adaptation in coastal cities of developing countries: Characterizing types of vulnerability and adaptation options. *Mitigation and Adaptation Strategies for Global Change*, *25*(5), 739–761. doi:10.1007/s11027-019-09888-z

McIvor, A. L., Spencer, T., Möller, I., & Spalding, M. (2013). The response of mangrove soil surface elevation to sea level rise. *Natural Coastal Protection Series: Report 3. Cambridge Coastal Research Unit Working Paper 42. ISSN 2050-7941.*

Montonphetch, S., Sunthornhao, P., & Hoamuangkaew, W. (2013). Valuation of deforestation in mangrove forest area, Samut Sakhon province. *Thai Journal of Forestry (Thailand)*. Retrieved from https://agris.fao.org/agris-search/search.do?recordID=TH2016003737

Paphawasit, N. (2011). *Monitoring and evaluation of coastal ecosystem restoration by bamboo planting: A case study of Samut Songkhram, Samut Sakhon, Samut Prakan and Chachoengsao Province*. Coastal Resource Conservation Division. Bangkok: Prasukchai Printing.

Pranchai, A., Jenke, M., & Berger, U. (2019). Well-intentioned, but poorly implemented: Debris from coastal bamboo fences triggered mangrove decline in Thailand. *Marine Pollution Bulletin*, *146*, 900–907.

Saengsupavanich, C. (2017). The highest seawater level along the Upper Gulf of Thailand in 100 years. *Oceanography & Fisheries Open Access Journal*, 4(10) https://doi.org/19080/OFOAJ.2017.04.555650

Siripong, A. (2010). Detect the coastline changes in Thailand by remote sensing. *International Archives of the Photogrammetry, Remote Sensing and Spatial Information Science*, *38*(8), 992–996. Retrieved from www.tric.u-tokai.ac.jp/isprscom8/tc8/TC8_CD/headline/%EF%BC%B4%EF%BC%B3-10/W09O24_20100226133356.pdf

Thammaapipon, S. (2012). The study of coastal erosion problem effect on coastal communities. Research Paper, Faculty of Management Science, Silpakorn University Varawut triam martrakarn kae pan ha gud-sau choeng puenti Mob ti-prueksa lui truad naewmaipai gun cluen. [Varawut prepared a coastal erosion preventive area-based measure and assigned counselors to monitor bamboo breakwaters wall]. (2021, February 5). *Matichon Online*. Retrieved from www.matichon.co.th/local/quality-life/news_2565047

Yaowasooth, P. (2019). Analysis of factors related to bamboo structure for preventing erosion and restoration of coastal area on the Upper Gulf of Thailand. *Proceedings of International Conference on Biodiversity*: IBD2019 (2019), 148–155.

Yaowasooth, P. Marine Biologist, Department of Marine and Coastal Resources. (2021, April 29). Interview.

13

PORT ST. JOE, FLORIDA

Jeff Carney, Cleary Larkin, Michael Volk, Yi Luo, Bill O'Dell, and Carla Brisotto

Site: Port St. Joe, FL: 3,488 population (2019)

Gulf County, along St. Joseph Bay, on the eastern side of the Florida panhandle

Introduction/Rationale

In October 2018, Hurricane Michael cut a path of destruction through the central Florida panhandle as the first Category 5 hurricane to come ashore in the state since 2004. The storm devastated small coastal communities including the town of Mexico Beach, 15 miles to the west of Port St. Joe, where a highwater mark of 20.6′ was recorded on a wall in one of the few remaining houses (Masters, 2018). Port St. Joe (Figure 13.1) was on the east side of the hurricane eye and suffered severe flooding from a 9′–11′ storm surge as well as substantial wind damage.

As the impacts of climate change and sea level rise grow, Port St. Joe and similar rural coastal communities will have to grapple with the immediate needs of storm recovery, while also leveraging reconstruction efforts to adapt to future storm risk. These combined efforts – parallel desires for fast recovery and future adaptation – are embedded in definitions of resilience. The concept of resilience starts with the ability of a system to return to a stable state after a disturbance (Davoudi et al., 2012). This "bounce back" characteristic is often further defined as engineering resilience, or the return to a singular stable state (Zampieri, 2021). However, resilience also refers to the ability of a system to respond to disturbance through adaptation to a new stable condition. This is a more ecological definition of resilience that incorporates the ability of a system to absorb a shock through robustness and simultaneous adaptation to a new stable state which emerges in the aftermath of a disturbance (Brand & Jax, 2007). Communities able to successfully recover from flood-related disturbances while also adapting to sea level rise will necessarily incorporate both engineered (structural) and ecological (non-structural) resilience mechanisms.

High profile attention directed towards increasing community resilience has become a substantial part of the United State's national dialogue around coastal development and sea level rise (Al Rifat & Liu, 2020; Houston, 2015) as shown by the proliferation of design challenges

DOI: 10.4324/9781003183419-18

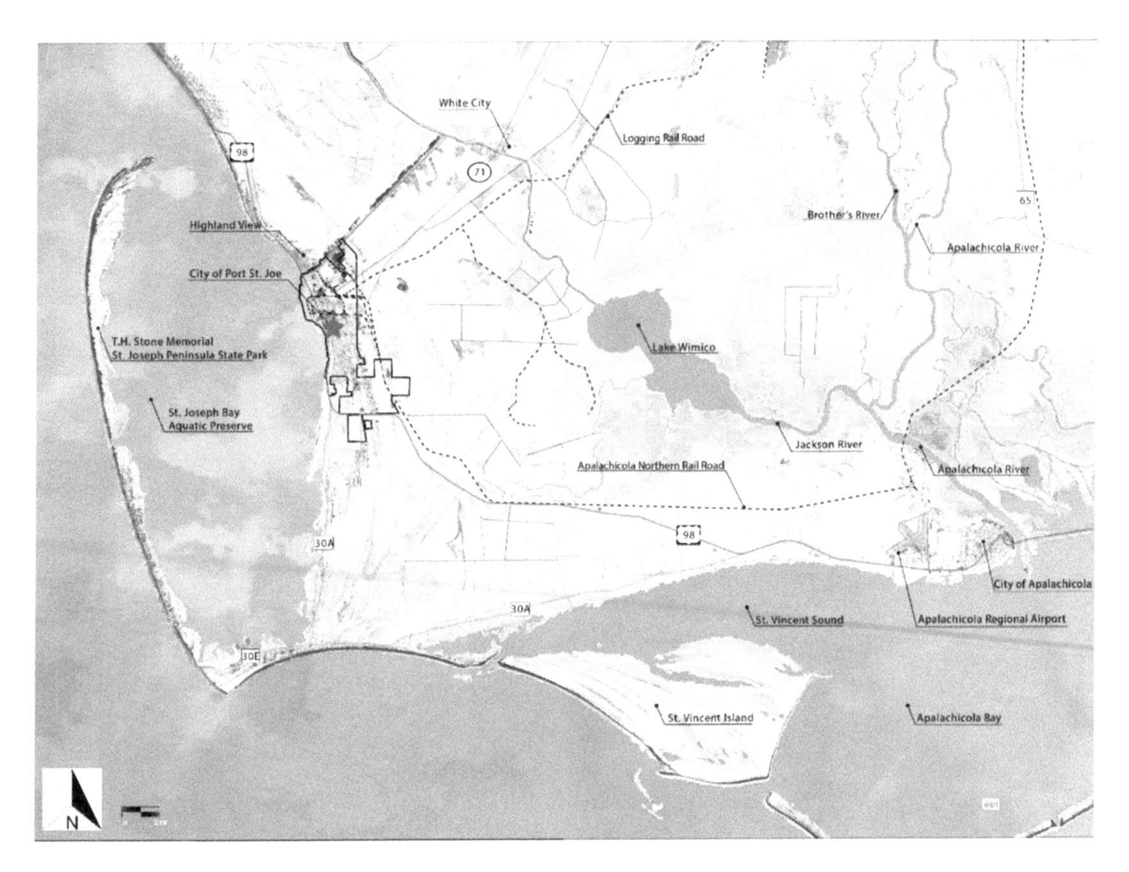

Figure 13.1 City of Port St. Joe along the "Forgotten Coast" of Florida's panhandle.

such as Rebuild by Design (Hurricane Sandy impacted areas – 2013) and Resiliency by Design (San Francisco Bay Area – 2018). These high-profile events have produced a substantial record of ambitious ideas, while programs such as the Rockefeller Resilient Cities ambitiously set out to achieve these visions by embedding staff (e.g. Chief Resilience Officers) into local governments (Rockefeller Foundation, 2018). This movement has had a substantial impact in large and medium sized cities across the country.

However, a lingering challenge facing communities recovering from disasters is a "state of exception" (Agamben, 2003) where the development of policies aimed at managing the impact of catastrophes overshadows the underlying vulnerabilities. This can leave a community striving to recover yet unable to adapt and prepare effectively for the inevitable next storm (Droege, 2010). A cycle begins following the initial disruptions where investment in recovery can compound disinvestment (a root cause of vulnerability), thus expanding social inequity and hindering attempts at adaptation towards greater resilience (Droege, 2010: 31). Increased vulnerability persists until underlying social and institutional mechanisms are resolved.

In Florida, where over 80% of municipalities have less than 50,000 people (BEBR, 2010), the capacity to plan, design, and implement robust future visions presents a daunting challenge. In small rural communities in Florida, outdated policies and regulations, a dominant focus on tourism, often extreme racial and social inequities, and limited government staff and capacity can derail more ambitious goals, leaving community leaders disillusioned and ambitious resilience efforts out of reach. Especially following a disaster, the process of building the groundwork for long-term transformation is often out of reach for rural communities.

The City of Port St. Joe faces substantial social, infrastructural, and organizational challenges to transformation. For many decades, heavy industry and a railroad divided North Port St. Joe, the historic African American community, from the downtown. The division worsened following desegregation and the closure of the area's schools in 1970. The segregation and inequity seen in North Port St. Joe has also been exacerbated by the closing of the major economic resource of the city, the St. Joe paper mill, in 1998. The closure weakened the economy and led to an unemployment rate of 14%, compared to the US rate of 3.9% at the time (U.S. Census Bureau, 2019). The city's economic decline intensified with the Deepwater Horizon oil spill in 2010. The mill buildings have since been demolished, leaving an open site for development on the city bordering scenic St. Joseph Bay. However, contrary to this narrative of decline, Port St. Joe forecasts as much as a threefold population increase over the next decade to as many as 10,000 residents. The city's coastal risks from sea level rise coupled with systemic and historic challenges stand in the way of effectively managing this growth to lead to a more resilient, equitable, and prosperous community.

Design Synopsis

Study Area

Beginning Fall 2019 and continuing through Fall 2021, the University of Florida's Florida Resilient Cities (FRC) program has been engaged with the City of Port St. Joe to assist the community to be more prepared for, and more resilient to increased risk from sea level rise and storms. The FRC program bridges community needs with design research through the College of Design, Construction, and Planning (DCP), in partnership with faculty from across the University of Florida. Design projects developed through the program focus data collection and research around the production of spaces and places through design.

The engagement with the city highlights a path to overcome exceptionalism spawned by disaster, in favor of a wholistic approach to adaptation that addresses deep and systemic challenges facing the community. This effort has not resulted in a plan or singular vision for resilience in Port St. Joe. Instead, the effort has built a strong foundation for community-based interaction, design, trust, and change. In this short time, a series of ten small research interventions established a network of collaborations between the city of Port St. Joe, regional agencies such as the Regional Planning Council, federal agencies such as the U.S. Department of Housing and Urban Development (HUD) and the Federal Emergency Management Agency (FEMA), neighborhood groups like the North Port St. Joe Project Area Coalition, and other academic institutions, including Florida A&M University (FAMU).

Design Process

The FRC program engages city officials and stakeholder through a four-part process that includes: Needs assessment, Partnership building, Project operation, and Implementation. The Port St. Joe initiative was sponsored by the Jessie Ball DuPont Fund (JBDF) for the fiscal years 2019–2021, which allowed the latitude for researchers to iteratively define and redefine research objectives as the project progressed. The following highlights elements of the ongoing process of design research in Port St. Joe.

In a kickoff workshop, held in Fall 2019, roughly 30 community stakeholders identified substantial challenges and needs resulting directly and indirectly from Hurricane Michael which struck in October of 2018. Stakeholders included community leaders, residents, business owners, neighborhood organizations, faith-based institutions, and non-profits, as well as representatives from local, county, and state government and organizations. Conversations about community concerns, goals, and values articulated the need to mitigate flood risk in the low-lying downtown: the need for affordable, workforce housing; and the need for the development of a civic center complex away from the increasingly at-risk area where these essential services currently sit.

Following the needs assessment, the FRC team developed a "Community Snapshot," a document that described the history, statistics, and current economic and environmental challenges of Port St. Joe. We distributed the Snapshot and a Request for Proposals to UF faculty, encouraging submission of research and coursework proposals to be developed into small projects for the Spring 2020 semester. Following a competitive review process, the FRC team directed funds to support seven research projects and academic courses paired with local "project champions," representing Port St. Joe's interests.

Selected projects included:

- A Cultural Resource Survey of North Port St. Joe
- Building Trust Through Stories in Port St. Joe
- Advanced Modular Multi-family Housing Design Studio
- Planning for a Resilient Community: Rural Tourism and Home-sharing in Port St. Joe
- An IoT-enabled Critical Infrastructure Information Network for a Future Resilient City
- Fieldcourse: Florida Resilient Cities: The Panhandle after Hurricane Michael – Port St. Joe
- Building a Resilient Urban Park System in Port St. Joe.

Structural and Non-Structural Mechanisms

The seven selected projects for Spring 2020 focused on two main themes of Community Narratives and Built/Natural Landscapes. Small projects were encouraged to leave the immediate confines of resilience-based problem solving and explore a broader set of methods and objectives that arose from partnerships with historic preservation, psychology, tourism, and law.

In our initial interactions with stakeholders, our team learned more about the community's history, its industrial and maritime past, its lingering segregation and racial inequities. Without this inquiry, efforts to rebuild after Hurricane Michael would have continued to cover over this largely invisible history. The following projects were selected as representative of the FRC approach not because of a finalized design or resilience solution that they propose, but for the community understanding that they garnered through active and dynamic engagement with residents.

Port St. Joe has a substantial park and open space network that runs through the city (Figure 13.2). Following Hurricane Michael, the city received state and federal funding to transform the park system to enhance flood retention and stormwater capacity. Urban parks have the capacity to provide significant green-infrastructure based stormwater benefits, in addition to enhancing social interaction and community bonds (Coley et al., 1997; Huang, 2006; Kazmierczak, 2013; Völker & Flap, 2007), providing opportunities for sharing local history and culture, and improving public health and quality of life (Bedimo-Rung et al., 2005; Groenewegen et al., 2006; Mennis et al., 2018; Ulrich et al., 1991).

Port St. Joe has two different types of parks: coastal parks and inland community parks. A preliminary survey of 97 Port St. Joe residents and visitors showed that the most-visited parks in the city are the coastal

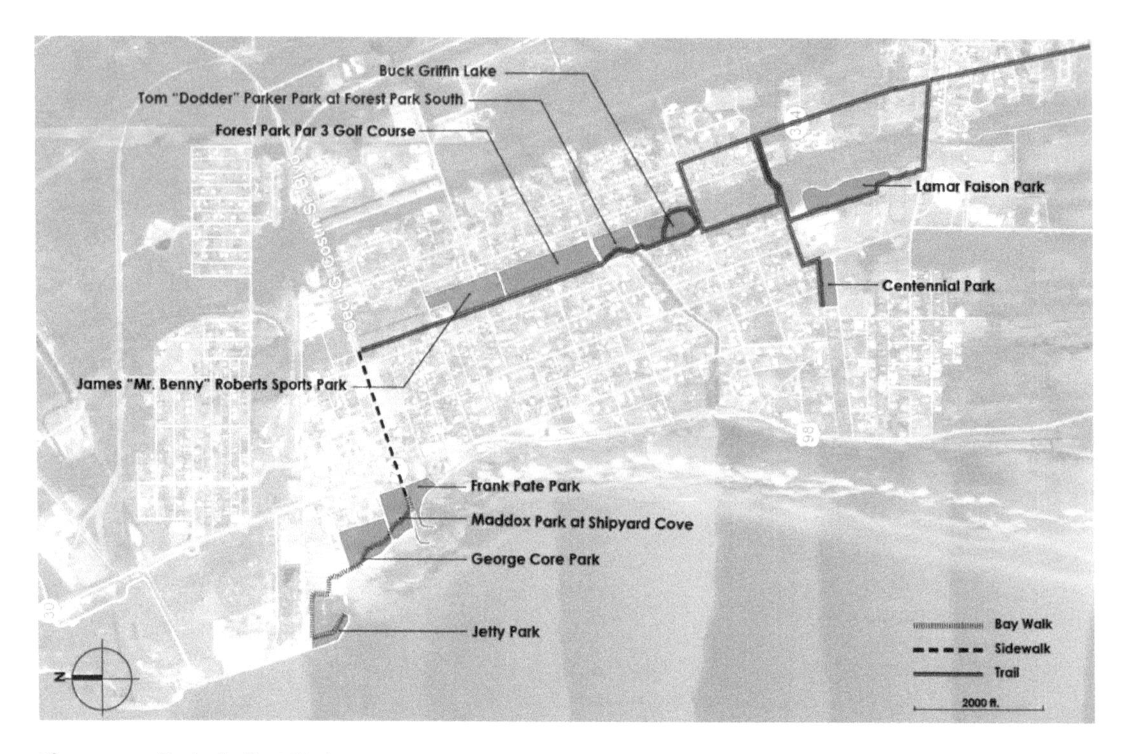

Figure 13.2 Parks in Port St. Joe.

parks including George Core Park, Frank Pate Park, and the Port City Trail (Figure 13.2). However, the use of inland Forest Park, a large linear "central park" within the city, is much rarer. Primary suggestions for improvement from the surveyed residents included adding more amenities, repairing/improving facilities, and adding public activities. Work completed in this project was focused primarily on Forest Park and a park developed on the site of the George Washington High School in North Port St. Joe (shown in red in Figure 13.2).

Located within the 100-year floodplain, Forest Park was identified by city staff as one of the key locations in the city that helped mitigate storm surge flooding during Hurricane Michael. This was due to its hydrologic connection to the coast and a central green space surrounded by residential homes that provides capacity for stormwater retention and recharge. A landscape architecture design studio was

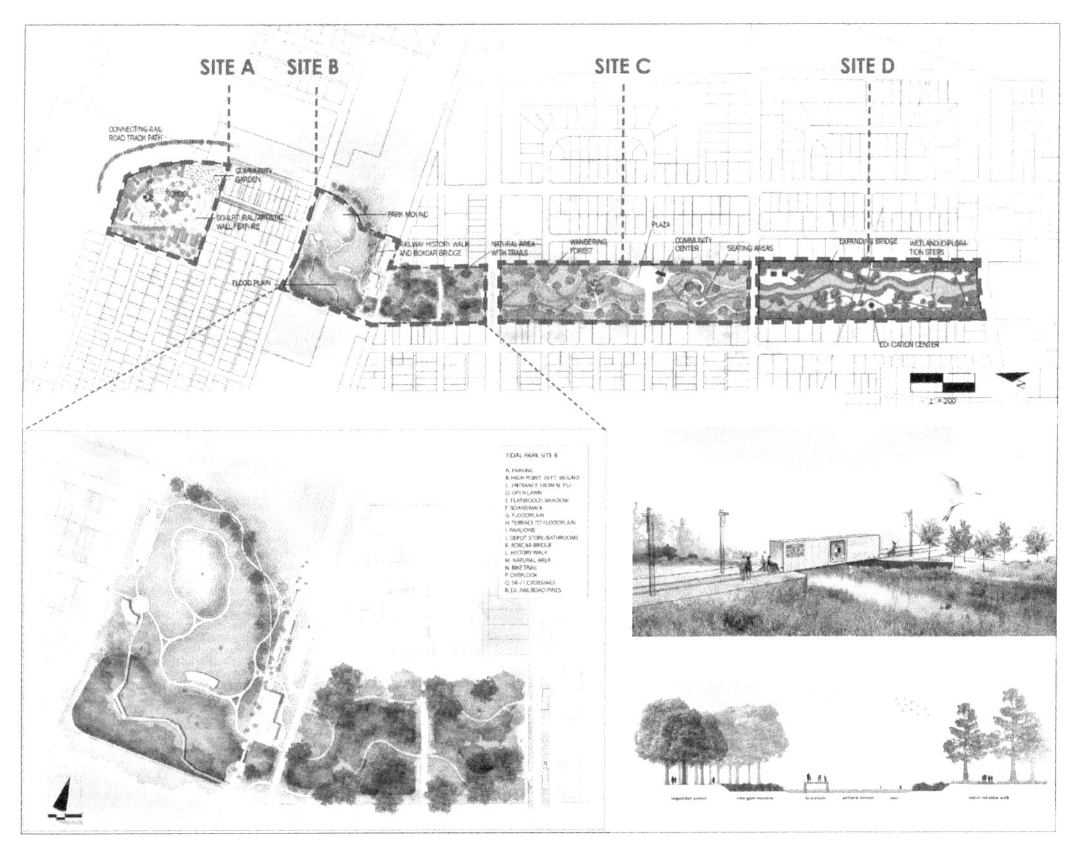

Figure 13.3 Forest Park redevelopment and stormwater improvement designs by University of Florida students showing one student team's results as an example, where existing wetlands in Site B were enhanced to increase storage capacity and restore wildlife habitat. In addition, the pedestrian trail system that runs throughout the site utilizes permeable pavement to reduce additional stormwater runoff. Similarly, the existing canal running through the park was widened and redesigned to have a more meandering form, aiming to reduce soil erosion, retain more runoff, and engage the public with stormwater management solutions. Riparian buffers comprised of native grass, shrubs, and flowers were also added to protect the canal from pollutants and prevent erosion The detailed program elements and their functions are summarized in Table 13.1.

used as the primary method for investigating design strategies for further increasing stormwater capacity within Forest Park (see Table 13.1), while addressing pedestrian connectivity between North Port St. Joe and the rest of the city and providing additional open space amenities. A simple performance assessment was completed to compare pre- and post-design stormwater capacity, finding that the post-design capacity was increased by 1.5 to 20 times, depending on the green infrastructure techniques applied by the five student design teams.

Design Impact

In the middle of the Spring 2020 semester, the world entered COVID-19 lockdown. Instead of placing the project on hold, JBDF renewed the grant for an additional year, with the intention of channeling the community-partnerships that emerged in Year 1 forward through three specific focal areas. The Year 2 goals align community-based design processes around the themes of:

- Urban connection: public and civic amenity spaces shared by all residents
- Environment: robust ecosystem services and water management for flood prevention and recreation
- Shelter: affordable housing and neighborhoods that respond to economic stress, disasters, and climate change.

These themes translated to three specific areas of social, ecological, and spatial concern and design opportunity for Port St. Joe. First, the proposed civic center, on newly acquired property along the Apalachicola Northern Railroad, presents an opportunity to repair the historic fracture between North Port St. Joe and the downtown core of the city. This project will bridge divides between people, restore ecological connectivity, and reshape the industrial corridor while providing for essential city services. At the same time, the neighborhood is concerned that the project will expose North Port St. Joe to increased risk of gentrification compounded by the relatively high elevation that the community has compared to the downtown. Second, the open space and parks network presents an opportunity for creating and expanding resilient open space to provide equitable access, strengthened social connectivity, improved public health, and enhanced stormwater

Table 13.1 Structural, non-structural, and hybrid mechanisms

Program elements	*Structural*	*Non-structural*	*Hybrid*
Bio-retention ponds		X	
Preserve and enhance existing wetlands		X	
Canal widening	X		
Meandering redesign of canal			X
Permeable pavement			X
Riparian buffers			X

management in the low-lying coastal community. Specific project objectives include additional stakeholder outreach and data collection related to community priorities and preferences, community surveys regarding the role of open spaces in providing therapeutic and mental health benefits, and documentation of stormwater vulnerabilities and green infrastructure-based opportunities to address flood risks within North Port St Joe. Third, a focus on resilient housing policy and design addresses a growing lack of affordable housing in Coastal Florida, accelerated by Hurricane Michael. This housing crisis disproportionately burdens poor and working-class families, depressing economic growth, and driving investment to other areas. This project will focus on both the planning for and rapid provision of affordable and resilient housing in Port St. Joe, integrating public policy and design.

Conclusions

Innovation and Applicability

The culmination of seven projects conducted in Year 1 and three projects conducted in Year 2 was a three-week online workshop co-sponsored by The North Port St. Joe Project Area Coalition (PAC) partnering with faculty from UF's DCP and the FAMU Architecture program. The workshop, conducted in May 2021, leveraged ongoing university research and outreach efforts sponsored by the JBDF, the U.S. Economic Development Administration (EDA), HUD, and partnered with additional expert and community stakeholders to provide innovative housing, landscape, and public policy solutions to residents of North Port St. Joe. The workshop investigated and proposed solutions to community challenges across a range of four main themes:

- Land tenure, policy, regulation, and finance
- Modular housing design options for new construction
- Stormwater, drainage, and ecological challenges
- Mixed-use development on Martin Luther King Boulevard.

The workshop took on challenges around equity, housing, and environment that have been exacerbated by the effects of sea level rise in North Port St. Joe. Importantly, adaptation to sea level rise requires robust data, visionary design, and bold leadership but efforts trained on storm recovery and climate risks including sea level rise often avoid or conceal the underlying factors that contribute to vulnerability and inequity in a community. Structural racism, poor infrastructure, health inequity, and a range of other factors are intensified by disasters and without concentrated effort will continue to get worse through the recovery and adaptation process. The engagement process, research, and measurable action of FRC in Port St. Joe demonstrates the need for relationships, community leadership, and trust as communities, especially small and rural ones, take on the challenged of sea level rise adaptation.

The outcomes of our two years of work in Port St. Joe are the ongoing need for strengthening relationships with the community, continued listening sessions as future projects evolve into the phases of design and costing, and building collaborative partnerships with regional and state organizations who can provide assistance with capacity building and funding applications. Specific projects from both years will move forward, with separate funders, while remaining part of the FRC holistic program for continued partnership with the community. In addition to the four workshop projects, the Cultural Resources Survey has evolved into a grant-funded documentation of the historic George Washington High School in North Port St. Joe. The Building Trust through Stories project will likely continue as a phase of a larger, statewide project exploring narratives of resilience and community–identity. Lastly, a month-long exhibit this Fall will provide further opportunities for community input and feedback, as the FRC team continues to assist with future funding identification and movement towards implementation. While we are still actively working on this project, two conclusions have already been determined: (1) much like the cycle of resilience, community-based design and research must be a cycle of building trust and reassessment of community goals and proposals in order to make continuous progress, and (2) working at multiple scales requires an interdisciplinary approach to fully develop a holistic perspective of a community's values and needs for long-term resilience.

References

Agamben, G. (2003) *Lo stato di eccezione*. Torino: Bollati Boringhieri.

Al Rifat, S. A., & Liu, W. (2020). Measuring community disaster resilience in the conterminous coastal United States. *International Journal of Geo-Information* 9 (8), 469–491. https://doi.org/10.3390/ijgi9080469.

Bedimo-Rung, A. L., Mowen, A. J., & Cohen, D. A. (2005). The significance of parks to physical activity and public health: A conceptual model. *American Journal of Preventive Medicine*, *28*(2), 159–168.

Brand, F. S., & Jax, K. (2007). Focusing the meaning(s) of resilience: Resilience as a descriptive concept and a boundary object. *Ecology and Society*, *12*(1), 23. Retrieved from www.ecologyandsociety.org/vol12/iss1/art23/

Bureau of Economic and Business Research (BEBR). (2010). *Florida population: Census summary*. University of Florida. Retrieved June 8, 2021, from www.bebr.ufl.edu/population/population-data/florida-population-census-summary-2010

Coley, R. L., Kuo, F. E., & Sullivan, W. C. (1997). Where does community grow? The social context created by nature in urban public housing. *Environment and Behavior*, *29*(4), 468–494.

Davoudi, S., Shaw, K., Haider, L. J., Quinlan, A. E., Peterson, G. D., Wilkinson, C., Fünfgeld, H., McEvoy, D., Porter, L. (2012). Resilience: A bridging concept or a dead end?, *Planning Theory and Practice*, 13(2), 299–333. Retrieved from https://doi.org/10.1080/14649357.2012.677124

Droege, P. (2010). *Climate design: Design and planning for the age of climate change*. Pt. Reyes Station, CA: ORO Editions.

Groenewegen, P. P., Van den Berg, A. E., De Vries, S., & Verheij, R. A. (2006). Vitamin G: Effects of green space on health, well-being, and social safety. *BMC Public Health*, *6*(1), 149.

Houston, J. B. 2015. Bouncing forward: Assessing advances in community resilience assessment, intervention, and theory to guide future work. *American Behavioral Scientist*, *59*(2), 175–180.

Huang, S.-C. L. (2006). A study in outdoor international spaces in high-rise housing. *Landscape and Urban Planning*, *78*, 193–204.

Kazmierczak, A. (2013). The contribution of local parks to neighbourhood social ties. *Landscape and Urban Planning*, *109* (1), 31–44.
Masters, J. (2018). Hurricane Michael brought water levels over 20′ high to the coast. Blog. Retrieved from www.wunderground.com/cat6/Hurricane-Michael-Brought-Water-Levels-Over-20-High-Coast
Mennis, J., Mason, M., & Ambrus, A. (2018). Urban greenspace is associated with reduced psychological stress among adolescents: A Geographic Ecological Momentary Assessment (GEMA) analysis of activity space. *Landscape and Urban Planning*, *174*, 1–9.
Rockefeller Foundation. (2018). *Resilient cities*. Retrieved from www.rockefellerfoundation.org/our-work/topics/resilientcities/
Ulrich, R. S., Simons, R. F., Losito, B. D., Fiorito, E., Miles, M. A., & Zelson, M. (1991). Stress recovery during exposure to natural and urban environments. *Journal of Environmental Psychology*, *11*(3), 201–230.
U.S. Census Bureau. (2019). *Quick facts: United States*. Retrieved June 8, 2021, from www.census.gov/quickfacts/fact/table/US/PST045219
Völker, B., & Flap, H. (2007). Sixteen million neighbors: A multilevel study of the role of neighbors in the personal networks of the Dutch. *Urban Affairs Review*, *43*(2), 256–284.
Zampieri, M. (2021). Reconciling the ecological and engineering definitions of resilience. *Ecosphere*, *12*(2), 1–8. https://doi.org/10.1002/ecs2.3375

14

MIYAGI PREFECTURE, SENDAI, JAPAN

Tamiyo Kondo

Site: Miyagino and Wakabayashi-Ward, Sendai City, Miyagi: 109 km^2

Introduction/Rationale

In Japan, floods, storm surges, and landslides caused by typhoons and torrential rains have become more frequent and amplified in scale. Although the population of Japan has continued to decline since 2008, the number of households within the estimated flood inundation area has steadily increased since 1995 (Hada & Maeda, 2020). The Intergovernmental Panel on Climate Change's Assessment Report estimates that sea levels may rise by up to 0.82 meters by 2100 (IPCC, 2013). Future beach losses in Japan are predicted to be greater than 90% due to a 1 meter sea level rise by 2100 (Ministry of the Environment, 2001). Moreover, urban areas lying at sea level within the three major cities in Japan including Osaka, Nagoya, and Tokyo will increase by approximately 60%, and the additional population left exposed will increase by approximately 40%, if sea level rises 80 cm as projected (MLIT, 2007). Given these circumstances, specialized committees have been established by national ministries to design flood control measures (both structural and non-structural) and coastal conservation strategies, and develop climate change adaptation plans for sea level rise.

Spurred by the 2011 Tohoku Earthquake that occurred off the Pacific Coast, the role of green infrastructure in mitigation has attracted increased attention (Ichinose, 2017). This chapter examines the coastal areas of Sendai City in Miyagi Prefecture which were severely damaged by the 2011 tsunami and analyzes the impacts of the multi-layered tsunami risk reduction system implemented along the Sendai coast. Then, challenges related to the resilient design are explored in the context of sea level rise.

Study Area

Eastern Japan, where Sendai is located, is hit with fewer typhoons compared to the Kyushu and Kansai regions of Western Japan. Climate change is not only causing larger typhoons but also causing changes in their routes. According to Kossin et al. (2016), the annual mean latitude where tropical cyclones reach their lifetime maximum intensity over the western North Pacific basin has shifted northward since the early 1980s.

DOI: 10.4324/9781003183419-19

For example, typhoon Hagibis directly hit the Tohoku region in 2019 and devastated Japan, killing 91 people and damaging 85,000 homes. The damage exceeded 1.8 trillion yen, a record for a water-caused natural disaster that was not related to a tsunami (Margolis, 2021).

The 2011 Japan tsunami traveled approximately 5 km inland from the coasts and had a maximum depth of 19.5 m (Mori et al., 2011). The main hazards that have historically caused great damage to coastal areas of Sendai are tsunami and earthquakes. For instance, the tsunami created in the aftermath of the 1611 Sanriku earthquake reportedly reached as far as the Namiwake (literally Wave Split) Shrine, 5.5 km from the coast (see Figure 14.1).

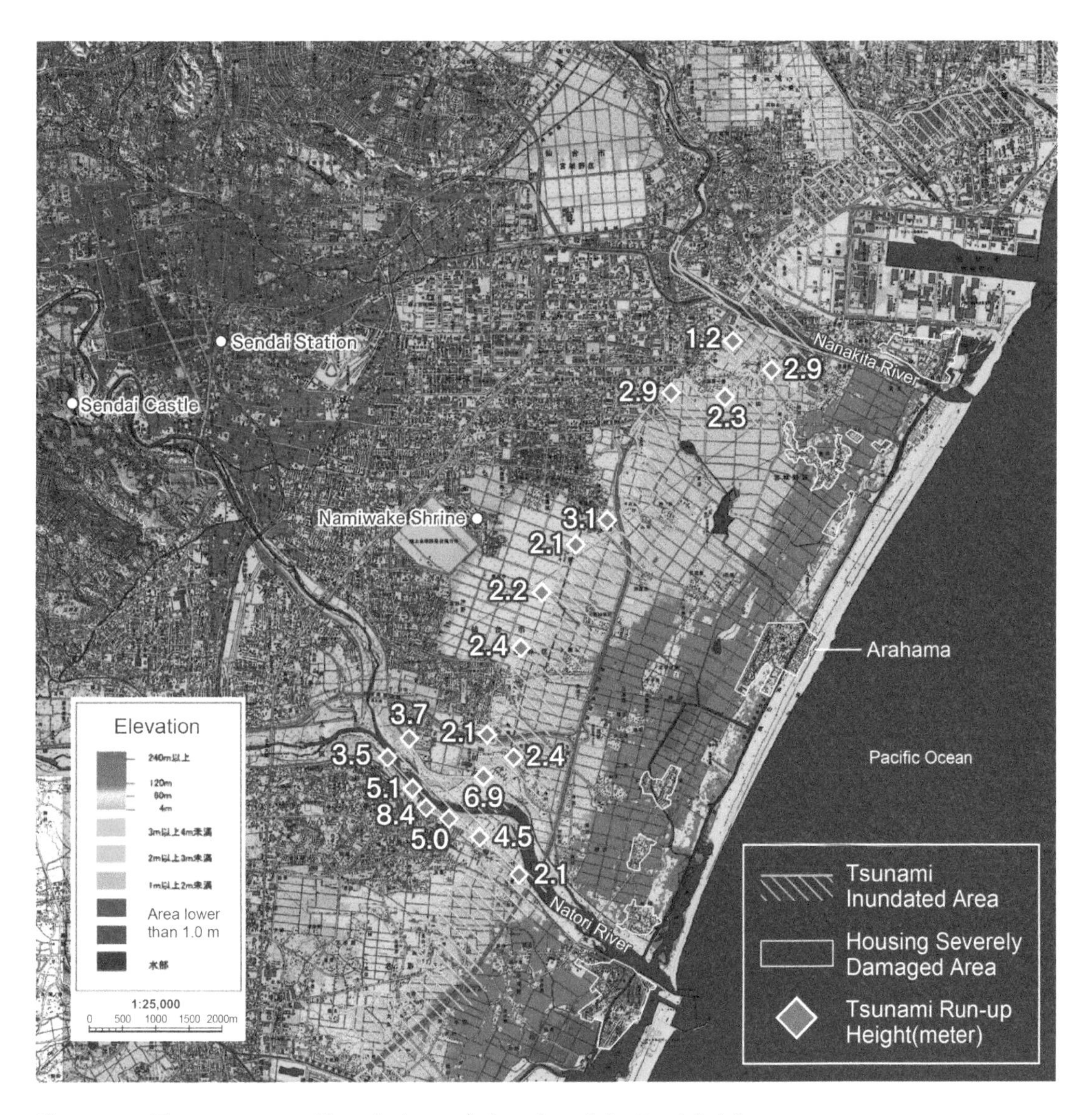

Figure 14.1 The 2011 tsunami inundation and elevation of the Sendai plain.
By author. The basemap is the digital elevation map published by Geospatial Information Authority. Tsunami inundation area and run-up height from the Association of Japanese Geographers, http://133.6.118.74/map/map/?mid=10&cid=2&gid=0.

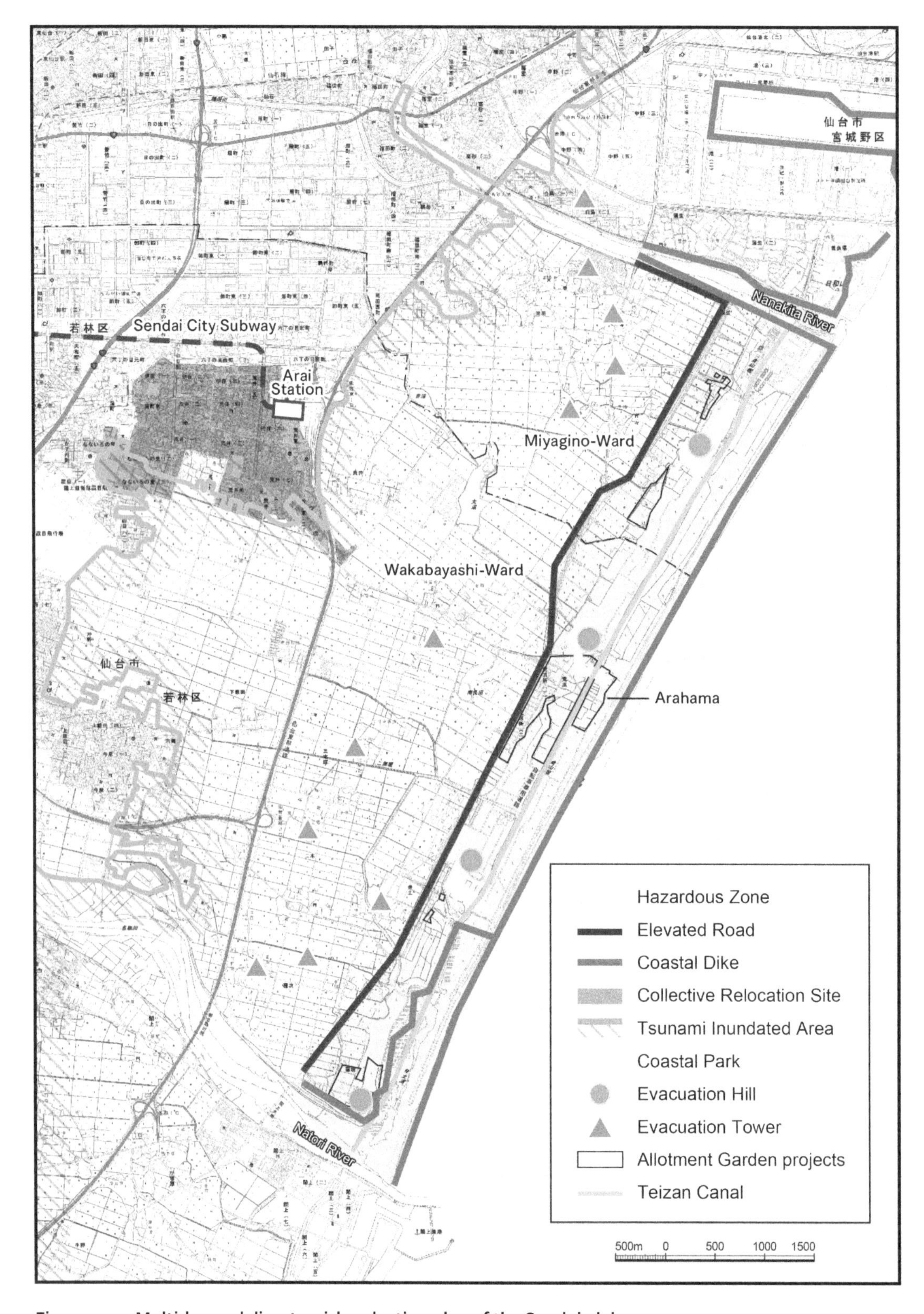

Figure 14.2 Multi-layered disaster risk reduction plan of the Sendai plain.
By author. The basemap is the digital topographic map published by Geospatial Information Authority of Japan.

The Teizan Canal (see Figure 14.2) extends north to south along the coastline between 400 and 500 meters inland. It was built from the Edo Period to the Meiji Era, extended to a length of 50 km, and was used to maintain the castle town of Sendai as well as in the transportation of goods. Japanese black pine trees were planted along the canal to protect farmlands from sea breezes and sand drift. The coastal forests slowed the speed of the tsunami and the time at which it arrived (Ohira et al., 2016). The Teizan Canal delayed the run-up of the tsunami, and helped increase draining functions for dilatational waves (Ishikawa, 2020). The Arahama area, where the Teizan Canal is located, was largely populated by people involved in the fishing industry; however, most of their houses were washed away in the tsunami of 2011 (see Figure 14.1).

Sea Level Rise Projections

The coastal areas of the Sendai Plain are low lying at between 0 and 2 meters above sea level. This terrain is not only vulnerable to tsunami, but also susceptible to inundation from external and internal water sources. Figure 14.1 shows the 2011 tsunami inundation area and the area lower than 1 meter; the area lower than 1 meter should be expected to flood due to sea level rise projections by the IPCC estimates. Attention should be paid to the fact that estimated sea level rise inundation is based on elevations and is not the result of a sophisticated longitudinal model focused particularly on sea level rise projection. This is because mitigation effects for sea level rise by coastal dikes reconstructed after the 2011 tsunami are currently somewhat poorly understood.

Even with a sea level rise of 1 meter, settlements emerging along natural levees formed by repeated river flooding will not be flooded (see Figure 14.1). Ancient settlements are located on this slightly higher ground, with groves of trees surrounding houses. These are called "*igune*" on the Sendai Plain. *Igune* protect houses from blizzards and coastal winds, and the trees are used for fuel and as building materials. Besides being the "the traditional scenery of people's hometowns," *igune* are also "a common social capital that leverages natural resources" (Ishikawa, 2020: 177). While the *igune* and coastal forests that had formed the cultural landscape of the area were greatly damaged by the tsunami, they also reduced its damage. The homes on higher ground that were surrounded by *igune* were not as badly damaged as those without (Koganezawa & Umikawa, 2012). Tsunami risk reduction measures, explained in the next section, take advantage of mitigation effects by local resources such as canals, coastal forests, and *igune*.

Design Synopsis

Structural and Non-structural Mechanisms

Figures 14.2 and 14.3 and Table 14.1 show the multi-layered disaster risk reduction measures taken against tsunami (Sendai City, 2011) and sea level rise (Sendai City, 2016). Moving progressively inland from the coast, these measures include reconstructing coastal dikes, establishing hazardous zones, regenerating coastal forests and *igune*, building embankments along the Teizan Canal and other rivers, building evacuation hills and towers, constructing elevated roads, and developing inland residential areas for people who cannot rebuild their housing within the hazardous zones (see Figure 14.3, above). Sendai, called the "City of Trees," is surrounded by rich natural environment. The Coastal Forest Regeneration Project is a long-term memorial reconstruction process that will regenerate this greenery landscape "hometown forest" in order to pass the assets of the people on to the next generation through multiple stakeholders' collaboration (see Figure 14.3, below).

Besides combining the existing blue (the Teizan Canal) and green infrastructure (coastal forests and *igune*), which are part of the natural ecosystem with the grey infrastructure (coastal dikes), managed retreat is achieved through collective relocation initiatives by the leveraging of land use regulations. Structural, non-structural, and hybrid mechanisms are all mixed, applied, and implemented throughout the area (see Table 14.1).

The concept of multi-layered disaster risk reduction in Japan was advocated by the Reconstruction Design Council (2011), which recommended a reconstruction plan to the Japanese Government. After experiencing an enormous tsunami, awareness emerged that the area could not be adequately protected using coastal dikes exclusively, and that additional disaster reduction measures would be required. The national government classified tsunamis into two categories: Level 1 (L1) for those tsunamis with a possible return period of 100 years, and Level 2 (L2) for larger-scaled events with a return period of 1,000 years, such as the 2011 tsunami. The idea is that L1 tsunami damage can be prevented by engineering solutions such as coastal levees, whereas L2 tsunami risk requires more comprehensive mitigation measures, including land use regulation.

Table 14.1 Program element of structural and non-structural mechanisms

Program element	*Structural*	*Non-Structural*	*Hybrid*
Coastal dike	X		
Canal	X		
Elevated road	X		
Evacuation tower	X		
Hazardous zone		X	
Managed retreat (collective relocation)		X	
Coastal forest			X
Igune			X
Evacuation hill			X
Coastal park			X
Allotment garden and agriculture farm			X

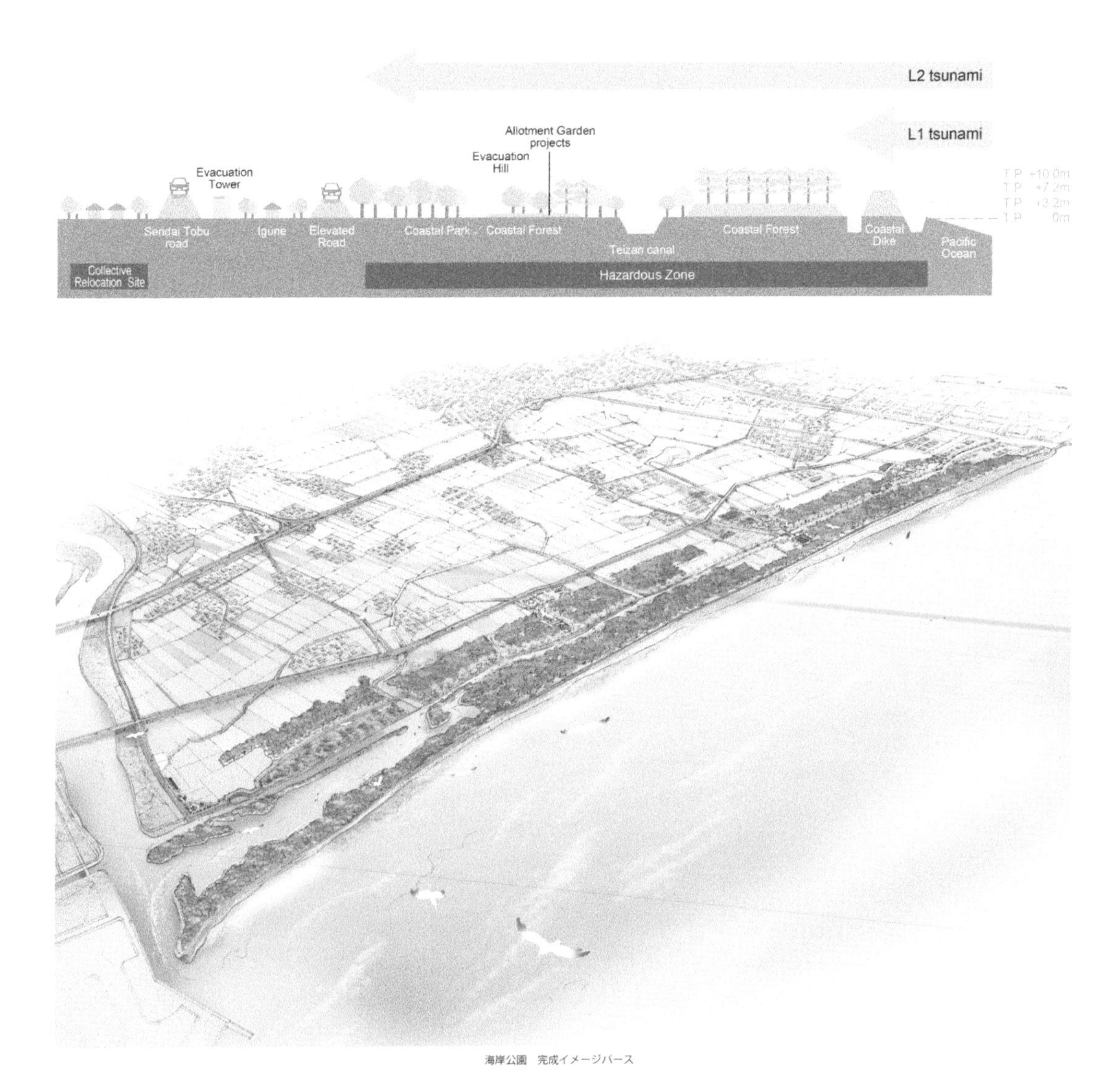

Figure 14.3 Cross-section of multi-layered disaster risk measures (above) and coastal forest regeneration project (below) of the Sendai plain.
Above: by author; below: aerial view image provided by Sendai City (Sendai City, 2013).

Using the traceable heights of previous tsunami and the results of simulations of earthquakes and tsunami with a high probability of occurrence, the water level of future tsunami was established for L1 tsunami in a manner that recognized that there would be overflow from the coastal dikes. Based on this premise, the height of the new dikes was decided, considering factors such as the environment, feasibility, maintenance, and management.

Coastal forests also received substantial amounts of damage; many trees fell, were bent, or broken. Nevertheless, much is expected of them as a major green infrastructure resource. Public sector entities such as the National Forestry Agency, Miyagi Prefecture, and Sendai connected with private sectors and civic groups, with citizens participating in the planting of coastal protection forests. The Teizan Canal was designed to maximize disaster reduction.

The construction of elevated roads was also implemented as part of Sendai City's Post-Earthquake Reconstruction Plan. A 10 km high embankment elevated road with a height of 7.0 meters (Tokyo Peil: T.P.) finished its construction in 2019. The road was built along the hazardous zone. Further, as a line of defense that follows coastal dikes and coastal protection forests, it was equipped with the function of reducing the power of the tsunami and ensuring the safety of settlements that were further inland and of mass relocation sites.

Areas where the depth of flooding would exceed 2 meters, even with the construction of coastal dikes, were designated as hazardous zones. According to the results of a survey on the damage done by tsunami carried out by the Ministry of Land, Infrastructure, Transport, and Tourism (MLIT), it was found that in depths of less than 2 meters the proportion of buildings that were completely destroyed decreased massively; thus, this was the basis for the establishment of a hazardous zone (MLIT, 2011). Flood waters of 2 meters or less resulting from L2 tsunami were set as an acceptable risk level. Residents living in the hazardous zone had the option of the government voluntarily purchasing their lands and providing them with a loan of up to 7,000,000 yen to purchase land and build a new house in the area that they relocated to. Since 2015, Sendai has collected plans from private businesses for how to use this purchased land, with a decision made to establish allotment garden projects including agriculture farms and recreational facilities on it.

Design Impact

What was the impact of the tsunami risk reduction? Is this also effective against sea level rise? First, let us evaluate the design's tsunami disaster reduction. Frequently occurring tsunami were controlled by coastal dikes. For the largest class of tsunami, such as the one in 2011, the risks were reduced by mobilizing land use strategies and establishing evacuation centers (Miyagi Coastal Local Coordination Committee, 2011). The regeneration of coastal protection forests continues; they weaken the energy of the tsunami, thereby slowing the time at which it reaches a given point and protecting homes by catching drifting debris (Shaw et al., 2012). Among these initiatives, the designation of the hazardous zone coupled with mass relocation initiatives to avoid risks were the most effective methods for ensuring that houses are not destroyed by tsunami and people do not die. The conversion of lands on which settlements are prohibited and the creation of recreational spaces within these zones have also been effective. Coastal parks and farms attract citizens from the city center and tourists from outside the region. This can lead to the creation of new economic opportunities.

Conversely, what are the negative impacts? A link between the historical settlements and its inhabitants has been broken. While coastal forests and *igune* play a role in disaster reduction, at the same time, they also constitute a living culture that the region has nurtured for many years. Having residents live in settlements is a requirement for the maintenance and passing on of living culture and the cultural landscape. After the restoration of green infrastructure, determining who will maintain and pass on these resources and how this will be done constitute major challenges. The uncertainty surrounding the dynamic recovery process requires incremental adaptive action (Kondo & Lizarralde, 2021).

But, how effective are these tsunami disaster risk reduction efforts against rising sea levels? The phenomenon in which the water level rises slowly during sea level rise resembles how inland waters create floods through breaking their banks. Sea level rise is sometimes referred to as a "slow tsunami," while tsunami themselves are actually, in essence, simply rapid sea level rise. However, the equivalence between the two is not fully accurate. Sea level rise has substantial impacts on sandy beaches and coastal levees. Therefore, new initiatives and approaches to coastal dikes that differ from those that deal with tsunami are necessary.

When the sea level rises, the incident wave height and wave run-up become higher (see Figure 14.4). In some places, the amplification factor is more than three times the sea level rise (Isobe, 2013). If the increase in sea levels causes the depth of the water to increase, buoyancy also increases, and the frictional resistance of coastal dikes decreases. Moreover, water may seep out from the bottom of the dike. The disappearance of sandy beaches increases the instability of the coastal dikes that stand on top of them. When the volume of overtopping increases, because of damage caused by scour behind the coastal dikes, harbor function is impeded through the obstruction of walkers and car traffic. In this way, sea level rise decreases the resistance of coastal dikes. Besides this, sea level rise massively increases the size of tsunami and high tides (Hoshino et al., 2016; Takayama et al., 2018). This does not mean, however, that one should simply add the sea level rise to tsunami height to determine coastal dike heights.

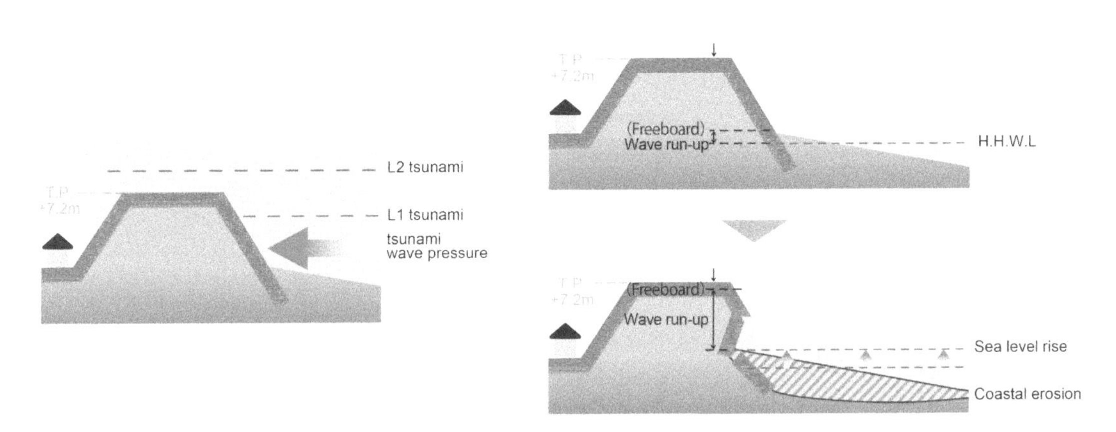

Figure 14.4 Different hazard features and risk between tsunami and sea level rise.
By author.

Conclusion

Innovation and Applicability

The revolutionary aspect of the multi-layered disaster risk reduction strategy adopted against tsunami in the Sendai Plain is an approach with a high level of redundancy which is one component of resilience. The multiple scenario-based adaptation approach implemented in Sendai mitigates tsunami differently depending on the level of tsunami risk, and could also be applied to the uncertainties in the magnitude of sea level rise. Green infrastructure, such as forest regeneration, was actively developed to support the existing grey infrastructure, like coastal dikes. This is an improvement in disaster reduction function by leveraging the existing natural environment to the greatest possible extent. The regeneration of coastal protection forests and *igune* is not only being realized by the public sector but also involves multiple stakeholders, including the regional community and individuals. The case is, in essence, a de-urbanization of tsunami-affected areas which enhances city-wide livability and urban amenity through a landscape approach combined with mitigation planning.

Hazard features of sea level rise, including physical behavior and the accretive nature, are different from those of tsunami, which urge landscape architects to develop alternative temporal–spatial design for sea level rise and place more focus on storing and living with water (e.g. such as *igune* and adaptive housing) rather than simply defense strategies against tsunami. Sea level rise will certainly occur in the future. Governments, communities, and academia must deepen discussions on what kind of relationship between places and people they will forge and how they should proceed to create them using step-by-step transitions.

References

Hada, Y., & Maeda, M. (2020). Change in population within estimated flood inundation areas in Japan and its prefectures. *Journal of Disaster Information Studies*, *18*(1), 107–114.

Hoshino, S., Esteban, M., Mikami, T., Takagi, H., & Shibayama, T. (2016). Estimation of increase in storm surge damage due to climate change and sea level rise in the Greater Tokyo area. *Natural Hazards*, *80*(1), 539–565.

Ichinose, T. (2017). Green infrastructure in reconstruction after the 2011 earthquake and tsunami: A case study of historical change on Awaji Island in Japan. In W. Yan & W. Galloway (Eds.), *Rethinking resilience, adaptation and transformation in a time of change* (pp. 253–265). Springer.

Intergovernmental Panel on Climate Change's Assessment Report. (2013). *Climate Change 2013: The Physical Science Basis*. Contribution of Working Group I to the Fifth Assessment Report of the Intergovernmental Panel on Climate Change, Cambridge University Press. Retrieved from www.ipcc.ch/report/ar5/wg1/

Ishikawa, M. (2020). *Green infrastructure: Toward the sustainability of earth environment*. Chuo University Press.

Isobe, M. (2013). Impact of global warming on coastal structures in shallow water. *Ocean Engineering*, *71*, 51–57.

Koganezawa, T., & Umikawa, K. (2012). The function of Tsunami risk management on the coastal forest and wind break forest in Sendai coastal region. *Bulletin of Miyagi University of Education*, *47*, 1–9.

Kondo, T., & Lizarralde, G. (2021). Maladaptation, fragmentation, and other secondary effects of centralized post-disaster urban planning: The case of the 2011 "cascading" disaster in Japan. *International Journal of Disaster Risk Reduction, 58*, 102219. Retrieved from www.sciencedirect.com/science/article/pii/S2212420921001850

Kossin, J. P., Emanuel, K. A., & Camargo, S. J. (2016). Past and projected changes in Western North Pacific tropical cyclone exposure. *Journal of Climate, 29*(16), 5725–5739.

Margolis, E. (2021, January 16, 2021). The true cost of the climate crisis on Japan. *The Japan Times*. Retrieved from www.japantimes.co.jp/life/2021/01/16/environment/cost-climate-change/

Ministry of the Environment (2001) *Impact of global warming on Japan 2001*. Retrieved from www.wwf.or.jp/activities/lib/pdf_climate/environment/WWF_NipponChanges_lores.pdf

Ministry of Land, Infrastructure, Transport and Tourism (MLIT). (2007). *White Paper on Land, Infrastructure, Transport and Tourism in JAPAN*. Retrieved from www.mlit.go.jp/en/statistics/white-paper-mlit-index.html

MLIT. (2011). *Survey of tsunami damage condition*. Retrieved from www.mlit.go.jp/english/white-paper/2011.pdf

Miyagi Coastal Local Coordination Committee. (2011). *Determining the necessary height of the coastal dike in Miyagi Prefecture*. Retrieved from www.csis.org/analysis/japan-chair-platform-operation-tomodachi-miyagi-prefecture-success-and-homework

Mori, N., Takahashi, T., Yasuda, T., & Yanagisawa, H. (2011). Survey of 2011 Tohoku earthquake tsunami inundation and run-up. *Geophysical Research Letters, 38*(7), 1–13.

Ohira, H., Hayashi, A., Yamashita, K., & Imamura, F. (2016). Tsunami damage mitigation effect by multiple defense system using coastal forest in iwanuma city. *Journal of Japan Society of Civil Engineers, Ser. B2 (Coastal Engineering)*, I_1459–I_1464.

Reconstruction Design Council. (2011). *Towards reconstruction: "Hope beyond the disaster"*. Retrieved from www.preventionweb.net/publication/towards-reconstruction-hope-beyond-disaster

Sendai City. (2011). *Sendai City earthquake disaster reconstruction plan*. Retrieved from www.preventionweb.net/files/25605_planenglish1.pdf

Sendai City. (2016). *Sendai City promotion plan of global warming countermeasures*. Retrieved from https://eird.org/cd/recovery-planning/docs/10-additional-resources/Sendai-City-Reconstruction%20Plan.pdf

Shaw, R., Noguchi, Y., & Ishiwatari, M. (2012). *Green belts and coastal risk management*. World Bank Group: Open Knowledge Repository (OKR). Retrieved from https://openknowledge.worldbank.org/handle/10986/16156

Takayama, Y., Ito, K., Tanaka, H., & Takahashi, K. (2018). The effect of sea level rise on tsunami hazard and the countermeasures by green infrastructure. *Journal of Japan Society of Civil Engineers, Ser. B3 (Ocean Engineering), 74*(2), I_169–I_174.

Balanced Design

15

FLEMING PARK, BALTIMORE, MD

David N. Myers and Isaac Hametz

Site Size and Location: Fleming Park, Baltimore, MD: 20.1 acres

Introduction/Rationale

Project Overview

The State of Maryland has over 3,000 miles of tidal shoreline along the Chesapeake Bay, including numerous tributaries along the Atlantic coastline, making this varied landscape vulnerable to sea level rise (Boesch et al., 2018). The relative sea level in Baltimore is likely to be between 0.8 and 1.6 feet above the year 2000 level, with a 5% chance that it will exceed 2.0 feet or higher (Boesch et al., 2018). Due to these conditions, the State of Maryland and its municipalities have taken an aggressive approach in developing strategies for both mitigation and adaptation to addressing climate change. The Maryland Coast Smart Council in the Department of Natural Resources was established for the purposes of adopting specific Coast Smart siting and design criteria to address impacts associated with sea level rise and coastal flooding on future capital projects (DNR, 2021).

The Baltimore–Washington metropolitan region is the largest developed area within the Chesapeake Bay and includes complex coastal landscapes with intertwining elements related to ecology, economy, and culture. Within this environment, there are a significant number of tidally influenced legacy landscapes built prior to current environmental regulations. Many of these are formerly industrial sites which have been converted to post-industrial uses but remain impacted by heavy metals and polycyclic aromatic hydrocarbons (PAHs). As a result, these waterfront sites and their encompassing communities are particularly vulnerable to both tidal and terrestrial inundation, which not only bring floodwaters, but can also release sediment entrained with pollutants.

For generations, front line communities like Turner Station have lived at the water's edge amidst the myriad of competing uses and aesthetic expressions. Situated between the marshes of Bear Creek, the Dundalk Marine Terminal, and a Baltimore-Gas and Electric substation, Fleming Park exists as a quintessential Chesapeake Bay edge landscape. By examining the strategies and tactics deployed to develop the

DOI: 10.4324/9781003183419-21

conceptual plans for Fleming Park, this chapter provides policymakers, practitioners, and the public actionable insights to guide their own efforts to adapt to a changing climate and rising seas.

Rationale

Spanger-Siegfried et. al. (2014) outline current tidal flooding and projections for 2030 and 2045. For cities along the Atlantic seaboard, Baltimore ranks eleventh for projected tidal events by 2045. "Baltimore is projected to face more than a 10-fold increase in the number of tidal floods it sees each year by 2045—to more than 225—because of sea level rise (compared with today's average)" (Spanger-Siegfried et al., 2014, p. 41). The National Oceanic and Atmospheric Administration (NOAA) predicts that Baltimore, due to climate change and sea-level change, will experience 15–25 nuisance flood events by 2030 and could see as many as 50–160 events by 2050 (NOAA, 2019). Spanger-Siegfried et al. (2014, p. 41) noted that the "city has already started work to protect its historic assets and prepare its economically vulnerable areas, such as Cherry Hill and Southeast Baltimore, where median family incomes are roughly one-third of those in the Inner Harbor neighborhood." While the All-Hazard Mitigation Plans completed in 2006 and 2011 did not address climate adaptation, plans created in 2013 and updated in 2018 addressed climate change hazards, including heat waves, sea level rise, increased precipitation, and flooding (Baltimore Office of Sustainability, 2018). Dupigny-Giroux et al. (2018) note that Maryland is expected to be the second most chronically flooded state in the nation by 2050. Recent nuisance flooding in Baltimore Harbor and Fells Point as well as pluvial flooding in nearby Northeast Baltimore neighborhoods (Rosenzweig et al., 2018) are examples of nearby extreme flooding events. As a result, it will be important to have a variety of short- and longer-term responses in addition to strategies that employ mutualistic multi-objective goals and benefits including, for example, utilizing dredge materials for wetland restoration and regeneration that can enhance affordability and acceptability of dredged material management and natural/nature-based solutions.

Design Synopsis/Description

Study Area

Fleming Park, under the jurisdiction of the Baltimore County Department of Recreation and Parks, is located on a peninsula of Bear Creek, a tributary of the north branch of the Patapsco River. This section of the Patapsco River serves as the primary artery of the Baltimore Harbor which is home to overlapping industrial, institutional, and recreational uses. In this environment, geomorphology and hydrology collide with economics and politics to shape the form and function of the waterfront. Fleming Park is a microcosm of this larger estuarine harbor complex, which is replicated in a variety of ways throughout the Chesapeake Bay, the largest estuary in the United States.

Fleming Park's 2,600 feet of shoreline and 20 acres of upland have served the historically majority African-American Turner Station community since it was established at the turn of the 20th century for housing African American steel workers who were barred from living in the housing available for white employees. The landscape of Fleming Park is characterized by sports fields, open lawn, and phragmite dominant wetlands. Views from Fleming Park look north over Clement Cove, southeast over the Francis Scott Key Bridge and the former home of Bethlehem Steel, which has been remade into a global logistics hub for Tradepoint Atlantic (including among its occupants an Amazon fulfillment center, Under Armour fulfillment center, and more). To the southeast, the viewshed covers the Baltimore Gas and Electric substation and the Dundalk Marine Terminal.

Design Process

The Fleming Park project has its roots in the collaborations between (1) the Turner Station Conservation Teams' (TSCT) more than two decades of volunteer service on the Maryland Department of Transportation Maryland Port Administration (MDOT MPA), (2) the Dredged Material Management Committee, (3) the Port's community outreach vehicle for its dredging program, and (4) Mahan Rykiel Associates' collaborative Design with Dredge research program. Combining TSCT's existing relationships with MDOT MPA and Mahan Rykiel's research on innovative reuse and beneficial use (IRBU) of dredged material produced an initial set of ideas about how sediment might be repurposed to regenerate coastal ecologies at Fleming Park as well as restore the community's connection to the waterfront. These ideas included using dredge material, often seen as waste, to create a new complex of diverse landscapes offering multiple benefits such as flood risk reduction, enhanced ecological function, and cultural resource conservation.

To explore design possibilities, stakeholders committed to an iterative and open design process. The foundation of this success rests on strong leadership of all stakeholders, from community partners to the design team. Community leaders, as part of Conservation Teams, in the Turner Station neighborhood have a long history of volunteering and citizen oversight of the Maryland Dredged Material Management Program. Capacity building and the community's knowledge of regulatory programs have provided a strong and critical foundation for success in partnering with the numerous stakeholders led by the design team. Led by Mahan Rykiel Associates, the design team held numerous community meetings to convey critical site information including environmental, historical, and regulatory information. Mahan Rykiel also employed the use of 3-D visualization, sponsored by the Maryland/D.C. Chapter of the Nature Conservancy (Rott, 2019) to communicate complex data and opportunities for change. The engagement of multiple local, state and federal agencies, as well as non-profit partners garnered support for project funding.

Design Strategy(s)/Structural and Non-Structural Mechanisms

The design strategies incorporate a proven technology that places thin layers of dredge material to achieve a renovated public park amenity that integrates environmental, economic, and social benefits for all project stakeholders. The illustrative Master Plan (see Figure 15.1) depicts a maritime themed playscape with ball fields and an improved circulation of walkways and boardwalks that knits together the entire park, intermingling multiple structural, non-structural, and hybrid mechanisms combating sea level rise (see Table 15.1). The restoration of a series of diverse aquatic ecosystem habitats and increased tree canopy provide for shoreline stabilization and resiliency.

Figure 15.1 The design for Fleming Park reconnects the community of Turner Station with its shoreline and returns ecological productivity of restored marshes to the inter-tidal zone using beneficially placed dredged material.

Table 15.1 Structural and non-structural mechanisms applied to the site's program

Program elements	*Structural*	*Non-structural*	*Hybrid*
Playgrounds	X		
Community centers and community facilities	X		
Recreational boardwalks	X		
Natural habitat improvement		X	
Soil amendments		X	
Material reuse and recycling		X	
Public parks & green infrastructure		X	
Marsh restoration			X
Walkways	X		

The strategies and co-benefits for Fleming Park include the following:

1. Reducing storm damage to property and infrastructure by restoring wetland ecosystems and stabilizing shorelines to attenuate wave/tidal action and storm surge (see Figure 15.2).
2. Promoting public health by capping toxic pollutants in the offshore benthic substrate of Fleming Park.
3. Restoring aquatic ecosystem habitats by amending the intertidal zone and nearshore environment of Fleming Park with thin layer placement of dredged material and planting of native species to create tidal flats, low marsh, and high marsh habitats (see Figure 15.2).
4. Stabilizing and enhancing shorelines by increasing the quantity and quality of wetland ecosystems, as well as by creating dual purpose boardwalk structures that prevent erosion and provide recreational opportunities (see Figure 15.2).
5. Promoting recreation by enhancing the quality of and access to public parkland, waterfront trails, playgrounds, and environmental education/observation areas (see Figure 15.3).
6. Supporting risk management adaptation strategies by coordinating outreach and educational programs with local community groups and government regulators.
7. Reducing the cost of dredging and dredged material placement or disposal for civic improvement objectives by implementing an urban thin layer placement project, which limits the need to handle, dewater, and process dredged material for beneficial use in the Baltimore Harbor.

Figure 15.2 The shallow waters of the peninsula allow for varying levels of applied thin layer dredge material affording a diversity of restored marsh habitats. The subtidal zone can accommodate a thick placement (up to ~23") of dredged material to improve the benthic substrate and cap pollutants. In the inter-tidal zone dredged material can be placed at variable thicknesses (~9"–23") to create low and high marshes that are intermittently inundated during high and low tides. Along the water's edge, an innovative boardwalk provides a hybrid response to tidal fluctuations and nuisance flooding.

Figure 15.3 The innovative layering of dredge material supports the establishment of higher landforms sculpted to afford a newly created maritime playscape. The playful shapes mimic both the gently sloping topography of the coastal plain and the shape of small peninsula found in the region. The nautical play structures invite exploration, the play area serves as a fun and educational destination

Design Impact

Environmental Benefits

The application of thin-layer placement of dredged material to Fleming Park is expected to provide 1,300 feet of enhanced shoreline and the restoration of about 11,000 square feet of substrate marsh zone, 17,000 square feet of low marsh, and 20,000 square feet of high marsh habitats (see Figure 15.4). Industrial land conversion practices in the Baltimore Harbor area have significantly decreased these habitat types and adversely impacted the hydrologic function, habitat value, and flood mitigation capacity of the surrounding area. The development of these marsh structures will provide for numerous ecosystem services afforded by wetland ecosystems from improved local ecosystem functioning to improved conditions for threatened/endangered plant and animal species. It will positively influence and improve public health by fostering opportunities for passive and active recreation.

These anticipated environmental benefits will support a wide range of both state and federal regulations and Chesapeake Bay restoration strategies. Critically, where benthic pollutants exist, the project is designed to cap off any hazardous substances which may have been deposited in near-shore sediments by industrial manufacturing processes common within the region. In these aquatic patches, the thin layer placement of dredged material and native plantings will bind pollutants in place and keep them from migrating to other areas in the watershed.

Economic Benefits

The structural systems put in place in Fleming Park will also provide direct and indirect economic benefits. Direct savings include cost reductions in stormwater management and nutrient management by filtering

Figure 15.4 Map of the Chesapeake Bay indicating community flood risk areas; environmental economic and social benefits are outlined on the right side of the diagram.

surface runoff from adjacent roads, as well as flood risk reduction from storm induced surges. In turn, this will provide indirect savings on mitigating future losses from storm damage. The amenities and structural systems provided also support local real estate values and developmental interests which have shown to be positively correlated with high quality open space. This is particularly important for underserved communities. Utilizing thin layer placement may also provide cost savings compared to traditional dredging and placement costs as hydraulically dredged sediment can be pumped directly to the site without need for dewatering or further processing, resulting in incremental cost savings as part of the Baltimore Harbor Channel Diversified dredging program.

Social Benefits

Fleming Park affords significant multiple social benefits. An improved and restored Fleming Park creates a destination for community gatherings, celebratory events, and both passive and active recreation. The positive social identity captured in historic photographs of fishing and crabbing from a boardwalk (Wheeler, 2018) can now return with a new water's-edge boardwalk integrated with diverse marsh habitats. Public landscapes strengthen social bonds among residents and park visitors and provide a landscape of civic pride and place identity. These benefits are particularly important to address the legacy of environmental injustice issues associated with neglect and discrimination which has disproportionately impacted historically African American communities such as Turner Station. Another social benefit of the overall process is the social capital and good will fostered by the partnership engagement between federal and state agencies. This has enhanced existing partnerships between community-based nonprofits, private industry, and the philanthropic community as well as increased local and regional capacity for risk management and dealing with the amount of work needed to address climate change. Here, positive action constitutes a commitment for change and thus contributes to success.

Conclusions

Innovations

The innovative use of thin layer placement of dredged material for a public park provides economic, environmental, and social co-benefits. As an example, to address nuisance flooding, valuable cultural infrastructure landscapes like Fleming Park found along the watershed edge achieve multiple objectives related to community resiliency, environmental justice, and economic development. It does so by proposing the beneficial use of dredged material from the Baltimore Harbor navigation channel to nourish the intertidal zones of Fleming Park. This nourishment is created by thin layer placement techniques to create enhanced wetland ecosystems including substrate zone improvements, low marsh, and high marsh areas. The newly created marsh zones are planted with native vegetation to enhance the environmental benefits of the habitat areas. Existing pile structures on site would be repurposed to contain sprayed in dredged material, which would reduce both costs and regulatory hurdles. The pile structures would also be repurposed to support a restored boardwalk to serve the recreational and social needs of the Turner Station community. In addition to the aquatic beneficial use of dredged material, the project proposes the innovative reuse of dredged material to create landforms for a children's play area, which would be capped with a rubberized play surface for both comfort and environmental protection. By combining IRBU techniques with multiple social, environmental, and economic purposes, the project optimizes efficiencies and streamlines regulatory pathways for future projects in the Baltimore–Chesapeake region.

Global Applicability

Multiple lessons can be gleaned from Fleming Park for its utility and applicability to broader geographic contexts. As a model of action, Fleming Park serves as a demonstration of the beneficial use of materials that have traditionally not been seen as a resource. Hametz and Davis (2019) note that projects like Turner Station are a model that expand traditional practice by incorporating research activism into adaptive management with strategic partnerships, providing a precedent for using dredged material in areas like the Baltimore Chesapeake Bay Region and other port cities in coastal communities. How can we use other resources, like dredged material, as beneficial aids to help with climate change? New models of adapting to climate changes are critical to applicability and adaptiveness to other environments. Solutions for how waste products can be turned into use-products help move the costs of environmental degradation and human activities to the benefit side of the ledger. A resilient and more regenerative model for adaptive strategies is the co-benefits model afforded by projects like Turner Station. Human appropriation of resources should be balanced with the appropriateness of attempts to both restore habitats impacted by the past and predicted future actions. Peninsula landscapes, developed along the bay and other coastal environments, would potentially benefit from this technique of raising land levels to provide mitigation for nuisance flooding from sea level rise and a method for recreating the diverse functions of restored or novel habitats.

Turner Station also demonstrates a commitment to addressing historic and long-standing environmental justice issues. The treatment of edge cultures (e.g. minorities, the disadvantaged, the indigenous, etc.) helps define the status of our social evolution (Myers, 2008). Edge communities, like Turner Station, have been underserved due to a legacy of political and social power centered away from its residents. Where public space provides critical social and institutional infrastructure, the Turner Station project demonstrates a commitment to protecting these communities and placing them front and center in adaptive strategies for addressing climate change. As citizens address nuisance flooding along the varied undulating physiography of bays and damaged estuaries across the globe, these landscapes interweave with the undulating milieu of histories, ecologies, and social context unique to each site. While peninsulas define the edge, they should be front and center in addressing early needs for a future faced by rising sea levels.

References

Baltimore City. (2020). *2020 nuisance flood plan*. Department of Planning Office of Sustainability. 126 pages. Retrieved from www.baltimoresustainability.org/flood-preparedness/

Baltimore Office of Sustainability. (2018). *Disaster preparedness and planning project (DP3): A combined all-hazard mitigation and climate adaptation plan*. City of Baltimore. Retrieved from www.baltimoresustainability.org/plans/disaster-preparedness-plan/

Boesch, D. F., Boicourt, W. C., Cullather, R.I., Ezer, T., Galloway, G. E. Jr., Johnson, Z. P., Kilbourne, K. H., Kirwan, M. L., Kopp, R. E., Land, S., Li, M., Nardin, W., Sommerfield, C. K., & Sweet, W. V. (2018). *Sea-level rise: Projections for Maryland 2018*, 27 pp. University of Maryland Center for Environmental Science, Cambridge, MD.

DNR. (2021). *Maryland Coast Smart Council*. Retrieved from https://dnr.maryland.gov/climateresilience/Pages/cs_Council.aspx

Dupigny-Giroux, L. A., Mecray, E. L., Lemcke-Stampone, M. D., Hodgkins, G. A., Lentz, E. E., Mills, K. E., Lane, E. D., Miller, R., Hollinger, D. Y., Solecki, W. D., Wellenius, G. A., Sheffield, P. E., MacDonald, A. B., & Caldwell, C. (2018). Northeast. In D. R. Reidmiller, C. W. Avery, D. R. Easterling, K. E. Kunkel, K. L. M. Lewis, T .K. Maycock, & B. C. Stewart (Eds.), *Impacts, risks, and adaptation in the United States: Fourth National Climate Assessment, Volume II* (pp. 669–742). U.S. Global Change Research Program, Washington, DC. https://doi.org/10.7930/NCA4.2018.CH18

Hametz, I., & Davis, B. (2019). Beyond services: Design with dredge. *Landscape Architecture Frontiers*, *7*(1), 94–109. https://doi.org/10.15302/J-LAF-20190109

Myers, D. (2008). Global climate change in Maryland: Loss at the margins of place. *Places: Climate Change and Place*, *20*(2), 46–49.

NOAA. (2019). 2018 *State of U.S. high tide flooding with a 2019 outlook*. NOAA Technical Report NOS CO-OPS 090. Silver Spring, Maryland June 2019. National Oceanic and Atmospheric Administration. U.S. Department of Commerce. Retrieved from https://tidesandcurrents.noaa.gov/publications/Techrpt_090_2018_State_of_US_HighTideFlooding_with_a_2019_Outlook_Final.pdf

Rosenzweig, B. R., McPhillips, L., Chang, H., Cheng, C., Welty, C., Matsler, M., Iwaniec, D., & Davidson, C. I. (2018). Pluvial flood risk and opportunities for resilience. *WIREs Water*, *5*(6), e1302. https://doi.org/10.1002/wat2.1302

Rott, N. (2019). *An eye-opener: Virtual reality shows residents what climate change could do*. Retrieved November 24, 2019, from www.npr.org/2019/11/24/779136094/climate-planners-turn-to-virtual-reality-and-hope-seeing-is-believing

Spanger-Siegfried, E., Fitzpatrick, M. F., & Dahl, K. (2014). *Encroaching tides: How sea level rise and tidal flooding threaten U.S. East and Gulf Coast communities over the next 30 years*. Cambridge, MA: Union of Concerned Scientists.

Wheeler, T. B. (2018, November 29). Project to revive shoreline park using dredged material wins support. *Bay Journal*. Retrieved from www.bayjournal.com/news/people/project-to-revive-shoreline-park-using-dredged-material-wins-support/article_73bbc2bc-9399-5014-a944-be6b2ad9b770.html

16

SANYA DONG'AN WETLAND PARK, HAINAN, CHINA

Kongjian Yu

Site: Hainan, China: 168 acres

Introduction/Rationale

Three decades of intense development have left Sanya Dong'an's landscape a visible example of the destruction that such development can bring. Nearly all of the waterways in the city's developed districts are currently highly polluted and littered with debris. Concrete flood walls were built to protect and reclaim land for development, but destroyed many mangroves and wiped out riparian habitat while simultaneously blocking tides from the sea- and storm-water from the higher ground. Further, the city's flood resilience has significantly decreased, causing the growing population, including seasonal tourists and migrants, to begin voicing their desires for a more livable and flood-proof city. Such problems have become common in many Chinese cities; over 65% of Chinese cities are suffering from flood inundation and over 75% of the surface water is contaminated. In addressing such overwhelming challenges, conventional gray, or structural, infrastructure solutions alone appear to be insufficient. Non-structural alternatives, or green infrastructure, are now being more readily applied as part of a "Sponge City" campaign.

The concept of "sponge city" originated from the reference to a "sponge's" water absorption functions and how similar urban absorption capabilities can increase the resiliency of cities. In 2003, in China, the term "sponge" was first used to refer to the flood and pollution regulating capacities of natural systems. The term posits that the natural wetlands along rivers (similar to a sponge) are able to help mitigate the disastrous effects of droughts and floods by regulating the inflow and outflow of river water while also cleaning pollutants (Yu & Li, 2003). It was originally used to argue that an integrated nature-based holistic solution should be taken to solve urban and rural water issues through the construction of ecological infrastructure, rather than conventional single-goal-minded grey infrastructure.

On July 21, 2012, a severe flood killed 79 people in Beijing, which drew the attention of the central government of China, making flooding a primary urban issue. Immediately after this flood occurred, a proposal

DOI: 10.4324/9781003183419-22

was sent to the top leadership of the central government and Beijing Municipal Government calling for increased "green sponge" mechanisms, instead of simply building more concrete flood walls to solve the urban water issue (Terreform, 2018, p. 124). On August 25, 2012, the Chinese Central Television's (CCTV) New Investigation program broadcast a 45-minute documentary called *Breathing Rivers* that featured Turenscape's (the author's place of work) approach to transform "grey into green" to recover the mother river and create more water-resilient cities (see www.turenscape.com/video/detail/26.html). Coincidently, on October 12, 2012, the CCTV then broadcast news related to Harbin Qunli Stormwater Park (Yu, 2011), which won the 2012 Award of Excellence from the American Society of Landscape Architects (ASLA), followed by an interview by ASLA CEO Nancy Sullivan and *Harvard Design Magazine* editor William Saunders, who highly praised Turenscape's stormwater resilient approach (see swww.turenscape.com/video/detail/31.html). Among others, these are the key events that cached the attention of the Chinese top leadership about the nature-based solution to solve urban water issues (Gies, 2018; Yu, 2021). Eventually, on December 12, 2013, General Secretary and state president Xi Jinping proposed to build "sponge cities" to retain water, cleanse the water, and recharge aquifers based on nature at the National Conference of Urbanization.

There was, then, a call for building sponge cities by President Xi and the Chinese State Council in 2013. In 2015, the municipal government and the Chinese Ministry of Housing and Urban and Rural Construction decided to make dramatic changes in Sanya City to demonstrate the sponge city concept, and turned to Turenscape which was known for its advocacy of sponge city and nature-based solutions for assistance. As a result, a series of demonstration projects were designed and executed, including the restoration and construction of sponge-like wetlands in the city to remediate stormwater and the transformation of greenspaces along major roads to be better adapted to the monsoon climate and sea level rise. Among many executed projects, Dong'an Wetland Park was the largest demonstration project and has played a key role in transforming Sanya into a climate-resilient city and in promoting the national campaign for a sponge city.

Design Synopsis/Description

Study Area

The size of the park is 68 hectares (168 acres) in size. It is a wetland on a river corridor that had been filled with urban debris (see Figure 16.1). The water was polluted and the wetland was degraded and overgrown with invasive water hyacinths (*Eichhornia crassipes*), which caused severe urban inundation in the surrounding communities, with foul odors and constant flooding, resulting in frequent complaints from residents. The site challenges were significant and the related problems had many facets including ecological, social, and cultural issues. The scale of landscape transformation required was large, the timeline was short, and the budget was limited, yet the practices demonstrated in this project needed to be widely replicable.

Figure 16.1 The pre-existing situation of the site: urban floods, water contamination, invasive species, filling of wetland by urban debris, lack of public access, etc., called for a dramatic landscape transformation.

Structural and Non-structural Mechanisms

Dong'an Wetland Park was envisioned as an integral part of the green infrastructure of a water-resilient city; therefore, the park was carefully planned after a systematic hydrological analysis of the entire metropolitan region using a method known as ecological security pattern analysis (Shearer, 2019; Yu, 1996). The plan of the park calls for more space for water, and for removing the concrete flood walls that had channelized and reduced the resiliency of the rivers, replacing that structural infrastructure with eco-friendly, non-structural embankments. It also integrates wetlands, ponds, rice paddies, greenways, parks, and coastal habitats into a holistic sponge system to store and cleanse water as well as recharge the aquifer. This green infrastructure also integrates interconnected pedestrian and bicycle paths for people to use. Table 16.1 shows the program of the design and the green and grey elements used to create the sponge city design.

Simple and Inexpensive Solutions Inspired by Ancient Wisdom

Inspired by the ancient farm-building techniques of cut-and-fill used in the Pearl River Delta area in China, the landscape architect employed three types of earthwork approaches to quickly transform the site into a water-resilient green sponge, without hauling earth to or away from the site, and only just a single piece of earth-moving equipment, as efficiently as possible (Yu, 2017; 2021). At the periphery of the park, the pond-and-dyke system was designed to retain and cleanse urban runoff from the surrounding communities. Each pond differs in terms of both depth and plant communities; each also functions as a

Table 16.1 Structural and non-structural mechanisms applied to the site's program

Program elements	*Structural*	*Non-structural*	*Hybrid*
Skywalk	X		
Elevated board walk	X		
Elevated circular road	X		
Permeable parking Retention	X		
Retaining wall	X		
Earthen mounds		X	
Dredged areas		X	
Bioswales		X	
Riparian zone		X	
Tree islands			X
Terraced landform			X
Pond-and-dyke landform			X

water-remediation experiment that produces data for further refinement of the techniques used. At the northeast edge of the park, where the elevation drop is most significant, terraces are created to stabilize the slope of the edge and catch the stormwater runoff from upstream urban areas.

In the center of the park, an island system was designed to create a lake scattered with other smaller islands (see Figure 16.2). On each island, a banyan tree was planted; its dense root system removes excess nutrients within the water, and the trees will eventually create a forest over the lake and cool off the lake (see Figure 16.3).

Multiplying and Integrating Space to Amplify Ecosystem Services

A large green space sited in the center of the city, Dong'an Wetland Park is intended to serve as multifunctional urban green infrastructure to (1) remediate stormwater, (2) create urban habitats for native species, and (3) provide recreational public space for local residents and an aesthetically pleasant attraction for tourists and locals (see Figures 16.3 and 16.4). At the periphery of the park, a porous landscape composed of dykes and ponds of different depths creates a diversity of habitats that retain and clean the water and nourish rich biodiversity, including native birds, fish, and amphibians. A network of pedestrian paths is designed along the matrix of dykes under the growing tree canopy, creating an immersive and intimate experience of a cool oasis right in the heart of this tropical city.

In the center of the park, the design has created three superimposed layers of landscape: at the bottom is a wetland and lake which function

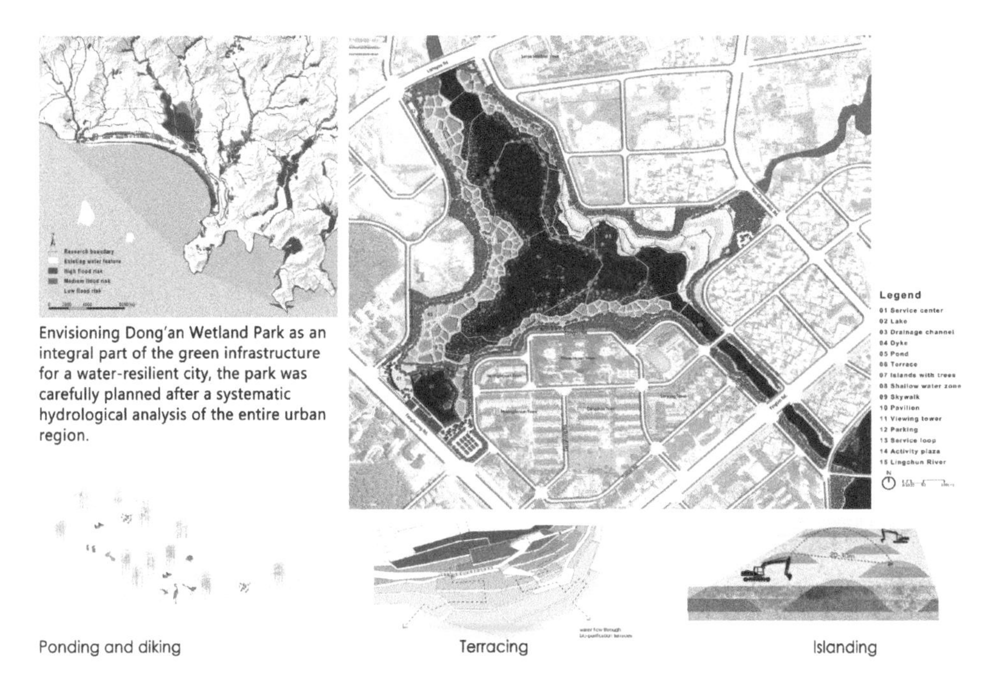

Figure 16.2 Planning and design strategies for the park. Envisioning Dong'an Wetland Park as an integral part of the green infrastructure for a water-resilient city, the park was carefully planned after a systematic hydrological analysis of the entire urban region. Three design strategies of simple earth work techniques – terracing, ponding-and-diking, and islanding – inspired by ancient wisdom were used to transform the site into a water-resilient green sponge in the center of the city.

Figure 16.3 The project not only addressed the water-associated problems of the surrounding communities, but has also become a refuge for native biodiversity, a pleasant public space, and a catalyst for urban redevelopment (property value increased 300% in two years).

Figure 16.4 A banyan tree is planted on each of the islands, with a dense root system that removes excess nutrients in the water, and eventually creates a lush forest over the lake. The islands are densely covered with water-adapted plants.

as a sponge to retain and cleanse stormwater; in the middle, the vegetation and banyan forest on the lake's islands become refuges for birds and other wild animals; and at the top, the skywalks over the tree canopy connect the surrounding communities and provide pleasant recreational spaces and views of the city.

Conclusions

Impacts, Innovations, and Global Applicability

As a demonstration project of the sponge city concept, Dong'an Wetland Park has proven to be a tremendous success. The majority of the park was built on a very compressed timeline of less than one year, and at a comparatively low cost (about one third of a normal city park in the region). The ecosystem services the park provides are significant in that it not only solved the water-associated problems of the surrounding communities, including urban inundation, sea level rise forethought, and contaminated surface runoff, it also became a significant refuge for native biodiversity which also attracts bird watchers and photographers. It is ranked as one of the most popular parks by residents and attracts thousands of visitors daily. It has been a catalyst for urban redevelopment, and the property values around the park increased by 300% two years after the project was built. The park has become an official demonstration site for the national Sponge City program and is featured in the mayor's textbook as an exemplar case; it has also drawn hundreds of mayors on visits organized by the Chinese Ministry of Housing and Rural Development.

References

Gies, E. (2018). Sponge cities: Restoring natural water flows in cities can lessen the impacts of floods and droughts. *Scientific American*, *12*, 80–85.

Shearer, A. (2019). The paradox of security. *Places Journal*, October 2019. Retrieved November 23, 2021, from https://doi.org/10.22269/191029

Terreform (Ed.) (2018). *Letters to the leaders of China: Kongjian Yu and the future of the Chinese*, with contributions by A. Weiwei, T. J. Campanella, Z. Lin, X. Ren, P.G. Rowe, M. Sorkin, D. Sui, J. Sze, Terreform, New York. Retrieved April 10, 2021, from https://doi.org/10.22269/191029

Yu, K. (2017). Green infrastructure through the revival of ancient wisdom. *American Academy of Arts and Sciences Bulletin*, *LXX*(4), 35–39.

Yu, K. (1996). Security patterns and surface model and in landscape planning. *Landscape and Urban Planning*, *36*(5), 1–17.

Yu, K. (2021). Sponge city: Planning and design and political design. In S. Pelsmakers & N. Newman (Eds.), *Everything needs to change: Architecture and the climate emergency* (pp. 47–55). RIBA.

Yu, K. (2011). Stormwater park for a water resilient city: Qunli National Urban Wetland. *Topos*, *77*, 72–77.

Yu, K., & Li, D. (2003). *The way to urban landscape: Communicating with mayors.* Beijing: China Building Industry Press: 149–153 (In Chinese).

17

HOUSTON–GALVESTON METROPOLITAN STATISTICAL AREA, LEAGUE CITY, TX

Galen D. Newman and Zixu Qiao

Site: League City, TX: 97 acres

Introduction/Rationale

The effects of sea level rise has had observable ecological, social, and economic impacts on the built environment on Gulf Coast communities, resulting in wetland loss, increased coastal erosion/inundation, and increases in the duration and frequency of flooding from storm surge (Horton et al., 2014). The National Oceanic and Atmospheric Administration (NOAA, 2015) predicts that (in a med-high scenario) the mean sea level will rise at least 0.82 inches per year in the US Gulf Coast, reaching 6.29 feet by 2100.

League City, TX, due to its location on the Texas Gulf Coast, is highly vulnerable to flood events and other issues related to sea level rise. For example, in 2008, Hurricane Ike wreaked havoc on Texas, causing 113 deaths and $29.5 billion in damage; approximately 200 of the damaged homes were located in League City, TX (Rego & Li, 2010). U.S. coastal counties, which comprise 17 percent of the land area in the United States and 52 percent of its population, typically have lower overall resilience and higher flood vulnerability (Beatley et al., 2009). Both in the United States and globally, total population is growing in vulnerable areas (e.g. the 100-year floodplain) and development and urbanization are also occurring in high hazard areas (Douglas et al., 2008). The impacts from the combined effects of rapid environmental change and the increasing severity of natural hazards have necessitated new approaches intended to address concerns related to sea level rise (Folke et al., 2010).

Several key factors can lead to unsustainable coastal development and reduced resilience, such as coastal population growth, demographic trends, desires to enjoy coastal living, and policies or financial systems that encourage coastal land development (Beatley et al., 2009). A lack of awareness of long-term risks and threats associated with living in high-hazard areas can contribute to precarious development patterns. Sprawl, loss of farmland, replacement of natural areas and open spaces

DOI: 10.4324/9781003183419-23

with impervious surfaces, and substantial losses of wetlands and other habitats that provide natural buffers from flooding can further exacerbate vulnerability (Newman et al., 2014, 2016a; Sohn et al., 2014). A growing body of evidence suggests that natural habitats such as wetlands, dunes, green infrastructure, sea grasses, coral reefs, and barrier islands can reduce the chronic risk of coastal flooding that stems from rises in sea level (Newman et al., 2016b). Thus, negligent undervaluing of natural ecosystems and their services can effectively compromise the safety of coastal communities (Berke et al., 2015). The process for the effective visioning of local climate change depends on a combination of variables that pertain to the planning, design, policy, and health impacts of sea level rise. As part of this process, we (1) identify future flood prone areas in accordance with current sea level rise projections on municipal and local scales, (2) spatially execute a master plan based on these findings, and (3) project future impacts of this master plan using landscape performance measures.

Design Synopsis

Study Area

According to Pielke (2007), storm frequency has increased to 14 instances per year in the United States since 1995, compared to an average of ten storms annually between 1950 and 1990. Moreover, most coastal communities are highly vulnerable to rising sea levels. Titus and Richmond (2001) assessed that 23,166 square miles along the Gulf and Atlantic coasts were situated approximately 1.5 meters or less above sea level. The most vulnerable states along the coasts include Florida, Louisiana, North Carolina, and Texas. NOAA (2015) predicts that sea levels will increase and storm surge will become more frequent along the Texas coast. In general, sea level is projected to rise by up to 6.29 feet by 2100 along the US Gulf Coast. Specifically, flooding and hurricanes are major concerns along the Texas Gulf Coast since the frequency of a normal hurricane along any 50-mile segment of the Texas coast is about one every five years, with a major hurricane occurring nearly every 15 years (Rego & Li, 2010). The Texas Gulf Coast often experiences extreme storm activity from hurricanes and tropical storms.

League City, TX, located along the Gulf coast near Galveston, is exposed to many hazards, all of which have the potential to disrupt the community, cause morbidity and mortality, and damage or destroy property. Of particular concern to the city are the effects of flood events. League City will be significantly inundated by storm surge from hurricanes of Category 3 and larger (see Figure 17.1). The city recognizes that it will continue to be exposed and subject to the impact of current hazards, as well as hazards that may develop in the future. Within League City, a site was chosen by city representatives and researchers for further exploration, planning, and analysis. First, the site is highly exposed to flooding and storm surge, and parts of it are located in both the current and future 100-year floodplains. The site is currently vacant, yet slated for urban development in the city's future land use plan. It is surrounded by relatively dense land uses with high hazard vulnerability.

Sea Level Rise Projections

Sea level rise was forecasted to surfaces using the FEMA 100-year flood elevations on Digital Flood Insurance Rates Maps (DFIRM). This method is consistent with methods used to support the rebuilding of structures that received FEMA's public assistance funds after Hurricane Katrina (U.S. Army Corps of Engineers [USACE], 2014). This approach delineates the extent of flooding using a 1% probability of occurrence, and subsequently adds the level of sea rise projected by NOAA. Data derived from the U.S. Army Corps of Engineers' (USACE) sea-level rise calculator provides alternative scenarios of sea level increases by 10-year increments up to 2100. By adding sea level rise to the base elevation of the 100-year floodplains, we determine the projected expansion of current flood zones (Berke et al., 2015). A limit in this approach is that adding sea level rise in this way may not account for other changes in climate (e.g., storm intensity that could affect storm surge heights). However, results show that by 2100, nearly 50% of League City projects will be covered by the FEMA 100-year floodplain. Should a 6 feet sea level rise occur, 76% of the land on the design site will be affected (see Figure 17.1), with the entire site being covered by the 500-year floodplain.

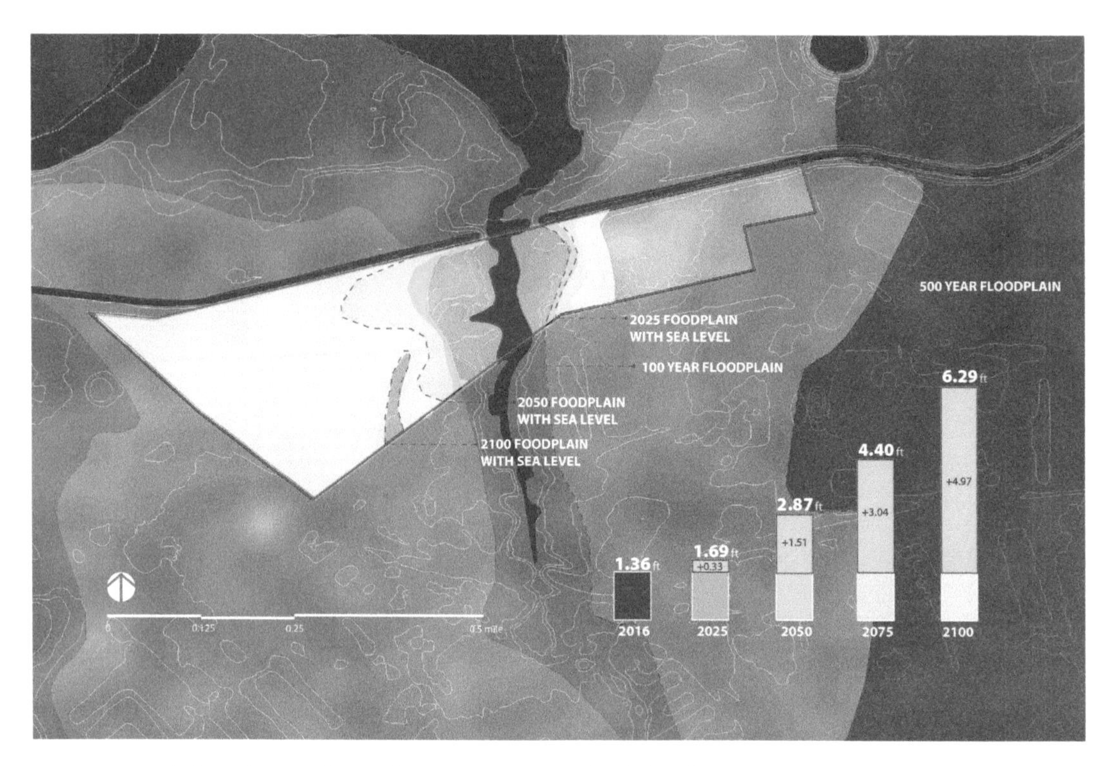

Figure 17.1 GIS-based projection of the FEMA 100-year flood plain by 2100 at the site scale in League City, TX.

Design Synopsis

Structural and Non-structural Mechanisms

The master plan develops and incorporates a series of adaptable flood attenuation mechanisms (both structural and non-structural) responsive to both current and future hazard exposure on a community scale. Structural mechanisms are engineered infrastructure used primarily to block and control heavy floods. Non-structural mechanisms primarily rely on natural systems and green infrastructure to reduce flooding, store stormwater, and soften the potential effects of frequent flooding events. Both of these mechanisms are applied throughout the study site, and together compose a protective system to defend the site from current and future flood issues while simultaneously providing recreational, housing, and economic opportunities (see Figure 17.2). For example, the designed green space bordering Clear Creek (a water body connecting to the Gulf of Mexico) protects the community from floods and surge and is designed as a park with an amphitheater, recreational pier, riparian edge, hotel and other cultural amenities (see Figure 17.3). It is connected to the designed green infrastructure system through strategically placed bio-swales, elevated trails, and eco-levees; engineered-based residential areas, commercial space, and transportation lines also act as multifunctional protective structures to help decrease flood vulnerability.

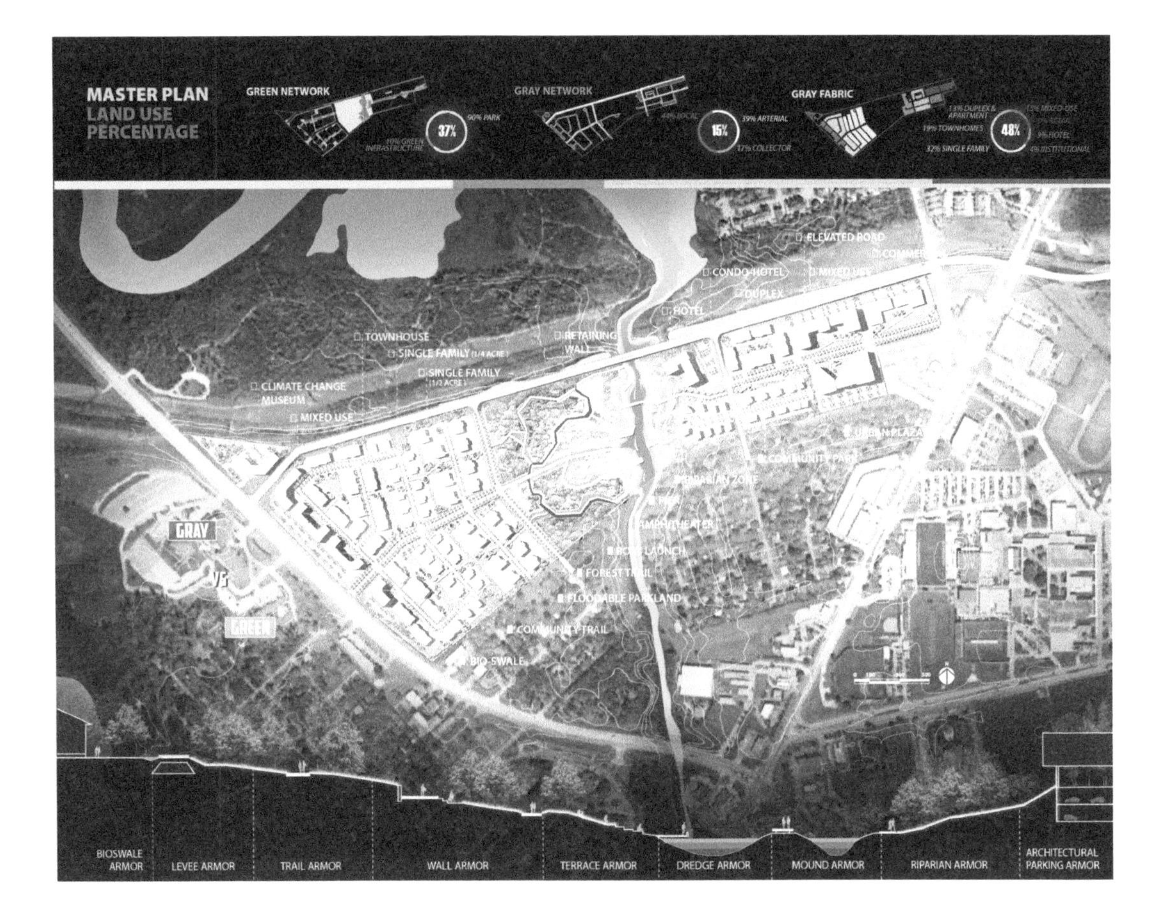

Figure 17.2 Master plan and section showing spatial functions and flood protection mechanisms at the site scale in League City, TX.

Table 17.1 Structural and non-structural mechanisms applied to the site's program

Program elements	*Structural*	*Non-structural*	*Hybrid*
Elevated architecture	X		
Elevated highway	X		
Sluice gate	X		
Sunken parking retention	X		
Retaining wall	X		
Earthen mounds		X	
Dredged areas		X	
Bioswales		X	
Riparian zone		X	
Green levee			X
Terraced landform			X
Mini-levee trails			X

The structural and non-structural typologies are strategically applied throughout the site into the green and gray network/fabric, to protect residents and deliver valuable ecological and economic benefits (see Table 17.1). To accomplish such a large undertaking, the design is to be implemented in three phases:

Phase 1) Retreat from flood – This phase focuses on placing development in areas with higher elevation area and integrating green infrastructure. The designed medium density commercial and mixed-use spaces are connected with existing arterials integrated into the surrounding residence but are strategically placed outside of flood prone areas to limit vulnerability. Public urban spaces with landscape features and permeable paving provide connections to neighbors and promote infiltration, retention, biological treatment, and evapotranspiration processes.

Phase 2) Flood mitigation – This phase develops lower density residences and green infrastructure to provide protection during frequent storms, as well as gray infrastructure to mitigate larger flood events. Diverse housing types bring in residents from different age groups and backgrounds. New institutional land uses such as a climate change museum provide engaging and educational opportunities for communities.

Phase 3) Flood control – This phase completes major installations of structural and gray infrastructure to create a multi-functional armor system that blocks and controls heavy floods and regulates hydrologic activity during extreme hazard events. Simultaneously, an interconnected circulation system including pedestrian trails, boat launch points, pedestrian bridges, and bicycle paths enhances local connection to the waterfront, attracts tourists, and creates economic opportunities.

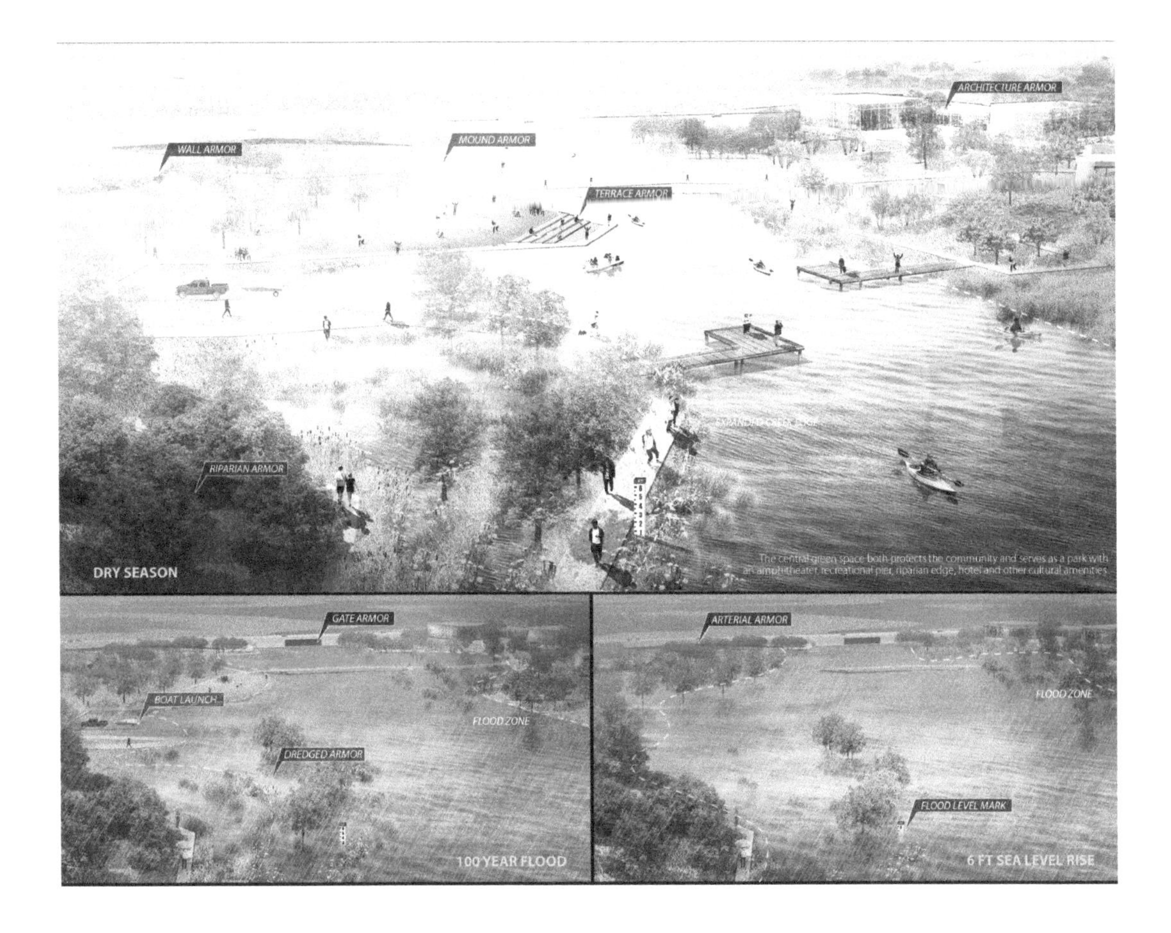

Figure 17.3 Birds' eye view of both a dry season and flood scenarios.

Design Impact

A large portion of the non-structural mechanisms integrated into the plan to increase resiliency are different types of green infrastructure. Often green infrastructure-based approaches are combined with modifications to other traditional engineered infrastructures as support mechanism to help control for frequent floods. Green infrastructure is now being recognized for its value as a means for adapting to the emerging and irreversible impacts of climate change (Foster et al., 2011). Green infrastructure approaches have become increasingly used to help to achieve resilience goals in the face of climate change. The climate adaptation benefits of green infrastructure are related to their ability to moderate the impacts of extreme precipitation. Benefits include stormwater runoff management, water capture and conservation, loss flood ponding/settling, flood prevention, storm-surge attenuation, defense against sea level rise, and floodplain management (Foster et al., 2011).

Many measures have recently been developed through landscape performance-related research to more scientifically evaluate impacts and seek to more accurately measure the effectiveness with which landscape solutions fulfill their intended purpose and contribute to sustainability. One such tool for measuring landscape performance is the

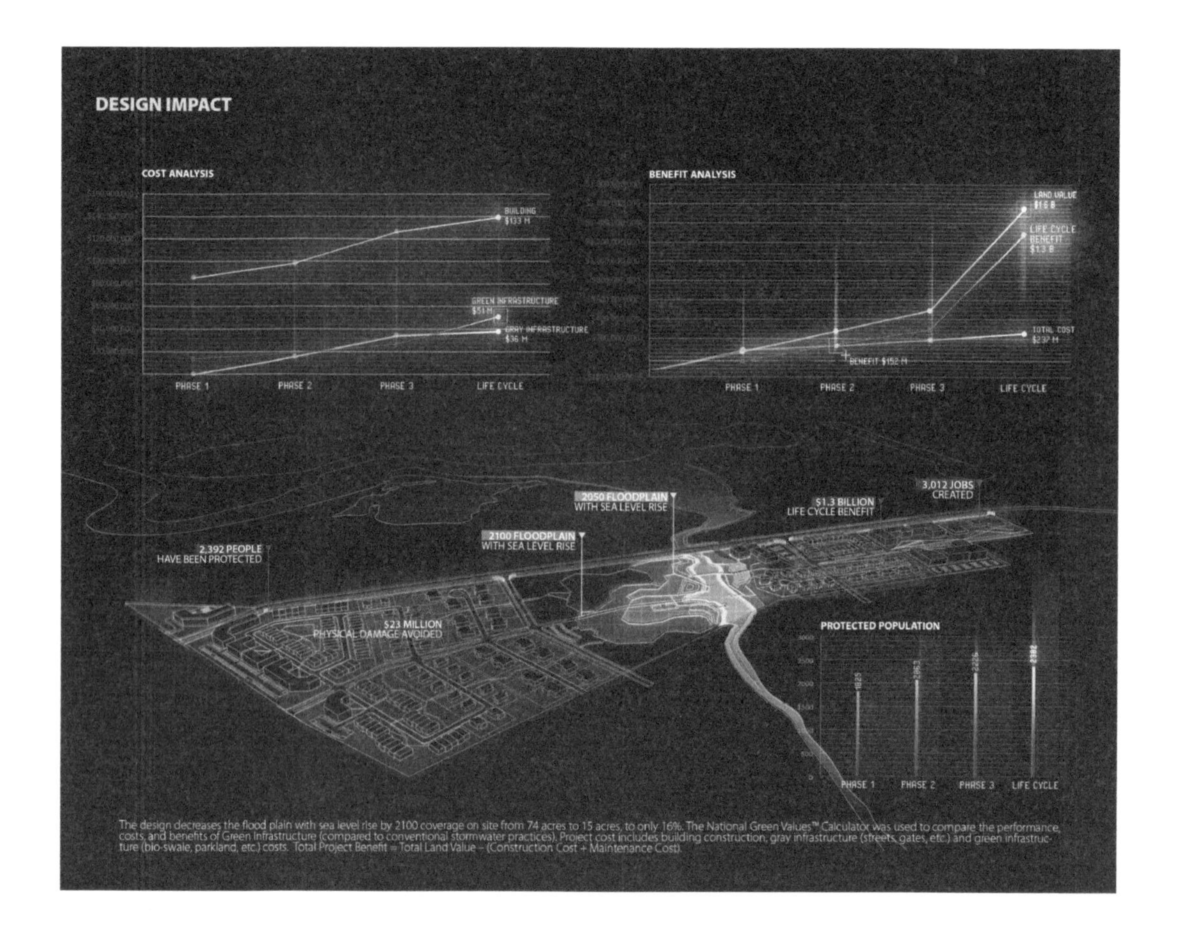

Figure 17.4 Design impact outputs from the National Green Values™ Calculator at the site scale in League City, TX.

National Green Values™ Calculator (Jayasooriya & Ng, 2014), a tool used in this research to project the performance, costs, and benefits of the green infrastructure utilized within the design (Online Appendix 1 describes the input and output data utilized in the Calculator). Compared with conventional approaches, the Green Stormwater Best Management Practices (BMPs) of the study site design decrease the site impermeable area by 26% and capture 30.3% of the runoff volume required. Simultaneously, the study site design can capture 221,921 ft^3 of runoff, creating $419,901 annual green benefits by reducing air pollutants and energy use, providing pollution treatment, increasing carbon dioxide sequestration, escalating the compensatory value of trees, and improving groundwater replenishment (these economic benefits reach $13,305,657 by 2100). Facilities proposed for the study site create not only economic and ecological benefits, but also enormous cultural and social benefits. The study site design decreases the 100-year flood plain by the year 2100 with sea level rise from 74 acres to 15 acres (from 76% coverage to only 16%) and 221,921 ft^3 of runoff can be captured. Also, nearly 2,400 new residents are protected, over 3,000 jobs are created, around $23 million in physical damage is avoided, and nearly $1.3 billion are generated by life cycle benefits by 2100 (see Figure 17.4).

Conclusions

Innovation and Applicability

This case study integrated the resilience planning scorecard, Geodesign tools, and landscape performance calculators to project current flood vulnerability, future flood plain alteration, and potential design impacts for a site in League City, TX. As part of the case study, we sought to determine how plan evaluation and landscape performance can assist Geodesign processes to improve resilience in neighborhoods experiencing high hazard exposure. The emergence of new approaches to the techno-scientific blending of integrated research, geography, and design (Wilson, 2014; Steinitz, 2012), makes the process presented in this paper a potentially useful method to improve decision making in support of a more resilient future. As indicated by this research, Geodesign, as a movement, is much more than a platform for utilizing GIS for spatial analysis. It can become a scientifically driven means of analyzing, measuring, predicting, and strategically determining the layout or layout options for geographic space, which can be supported through landscape performance metrics and resilience planning analytics.

The process presented here is a primarily digital (workflow-based) method of designing multi-scalar space that streamlines the analysis process directly into the design output through design concepts based on logic models developed by the designer/planner. A limit to this approach is that determinants of geographic arrangement are dependent upon the identified goals of the project, the needs of the region/community, the rationale used by the designer/planner, data availability, the development of innovative technological tools/programs which address contemporary issues, and the capability to operate these tools. To be relevant to current needs in hazard research, these logic models must be based on a key issue(s) and use technology as a means for beginning the process of solving this issue. Success will be limited by data availability, the designer's knowledge of science in the topic area, the designer's ability to successfully operate a multitude of (sometimes difficult or time consuming) technologies and their inherent computer languages, and his/her ability to keep up with the ever-changing world of computer programs and new and relevant tools for design and analysis.

In traditional planning/design, there are an infinite number of possibilities for the future development of a space. It is the planner/designer's responsibility to determine, based on these possibilities, what the best use of the space is. Perhaps the greatest strength of the framework presented here is that it provides a quantifiable, evidence-based rationale upon which to justify design choices. The framework's ability to predict future scenarios make it much more powerful than traditional planning/design, by mixing GIS with other technologies while maintaining the creative aspects of the undertaking, one in which the role of science for helping make decisions can be somewhat tempered. While theory or analyses can be used to reinforce claims on design decision making, the creative intent of the planner/designer can counterbalance some analytical positions, thereby making science the primary medium to improve the consistency of design decisions and validate them while allowing for the creative process to still occur.

References

Beatley, T., Rosenzweig, C., Solecki, W. D., Hammer, S., & Mehrotra, S. (2009). *Coastal resilience: Best practices for calamitous times.* Washington, D.C.: Island Press.

Berke, P., Newman, G., Lee, J., Combs, T., Kolosna, C., & Salvesen, D. (2015). Evaluation of networks of plans and vulnerability to hazards and climate change: A resilience scorecard. *Journal of the American Planning Association, 81*(4), 287–302.

Douglas, I., Alam, K., Maghenda, M., Mcdonnell, Y., Mclean, L., & Campbell, J. (2008). Unjust waters: Climate change, flooding and the urban poor in Africa. *Environment & Urbanization, 20*, 187–205.

Folke, C., Carpenter, S. R., Walker, B., Scheffer, M., Chapin, T., & Rockstrom, J. (2010). Resilience thinking: Integrating resilience, adaptability and transformability. *Ecology and Society, 15*, 20.

Foster, J., Ashley L., & Winkelman, S. (2011). The value of green infrastructure for urban climate adaptation. *Center for Clean Air Policy, 750*, 1–52.

Horton, B. P., Rahmstorf, S., Engelhart, S. E., & Kemp, A. C. (2014). Expert assessment of sea-level rise by AD 2100 and AD 2300. *Quaternary Science Reviews, 84*, 1–6.

Jayasooriya, V. M., & Ng, A. W. M. (2014). Tools for modeling of stormwater management and economics of green infrastructure practices: a review. *Water, Air, & Soil Pollution, 225*(8), 2055.

National Oceanic and Atmospheric Administration [NOAA] (2015). *Digital coast.* Retrieved from http://coast.noaa.gov/digitalcoast/

Newman, G., Kim, J. H., Berke, P., Merrill, J., Wang, Y., & Li, Q. (2016a). From idle grounds to ecological infrastructure: The resilient design of Manchester neighborhood in Houston. *Landscape Architecture Frontiers*, 4(5), 68–84.

Newman, G., Sohn, W. M, & Li, M. H. (2014). Performance evaluation of low impact development: Groundwater infiltration in a drought prone landscape in Conroe, Texas. *Landscape Architecture Frontiers*, 2(4), 122–133.

Newman, G., Guo, R., Zhang, Y., Bardenhagen, E., & Kim, J. H. (2016b). Landscape integration for storm surge barrier infrastructure. *Landscape Architecture Frontiers*, 4(1), 112–125.

Pielke, R. A., Jr. (2007). Future economic damage from tropical cyclones: Sensitivities to societal and climate changes. *Philosophical Transactions of the Royal Society, 365*(July), 2717–2729.

Rego, J. L., & Li, C. (2010). Storm surge propagation in Galveston Bay during Hurricane Ike. *Journal of Marine Systems*, 82(4), 265–279.

Sohn, W., Kim, J. H., & Newman, G. (2014). A blueprint for stormwater infrastructure design: Implementation and efficacy of LID. *Landscape Research Record, 2*, 50–61.

Steinitz, C. (2012). *A framework for geodesign: Changing geography by design.* Redlands, CA: ESRI.

Titus, J. & Richmond, C. (2001). Maps of lands vulnerable to sea level rise: Modeled elevations along the U.S. Atlantic and Gulf Coasts. *Climate Research, 18*, 205–228.

U.S. Army Corps of Engineers (USACE). (2014). Climate change adaptation: Comprehensive evaluation of projects with respect to sea-level change. Retrieved from www.corpsclimate.us/ccaceslcurves.cfm

Wilson, J. P. (2014). Towards geodesign: Building new education programs and audiences. In D. J. Lee, E. Dias, & H. J. Scholten (Eds.), *Geodesign by integrating design and geospatial sciences* (pp. 357–369). Springer International Publishing.

Scenario-based Design

18

AMSTERDAM AND WESTERN SCHELDT REGIONS, THE NETHERLANDS

Anne Loes Nillesen and Mona zum Felde

Study area: Greater Amsterdam region (2,500 acres) and Western Scheldt (20,000 acres).

Introduction/Rationale

A large portion of the Netherlands is positioned below sea level and subject to flood risk (see Figure 18.1, left) from coastal and riverine flooding. To occupy and develop the area, an extensive flood risk protection system was developed consisting of sandy dunes, dikes, dike-rings (around low-lying polders), and barriers. Waterboards and the Dutch Deltaprogramme are responsible for maintaining the flood risk protection system and developing long-term flood risk management strategies.

The Deltaprogramme currently uses sea level rise (SLR) scenarios that assume 0.35 to 1 meter SLR by 2100 (Deltacommissie, 2008); recent studies indicate this may be more severe. The Royal Netherlands Meteorological Institute (RNMI) published projections for accelerated and more severe SLR projecting a +2 or +3 (scenarios RCP4.5 and RCP8.5) meters increase by 2100 (Haasnoot et al., 2018, based on Le Bars et al., 2017).

The Deltaprogramme, as part of their adaptive flood risk management approach, initiated a program that explores the consequences of possible accelerated SLR and potential adaptation strategies (Staf deltacommissaris, 2020). The potential impacts of SLR are still being explored, but, without adaptation measures, it can impact (1) the peak water discharge and flood risk (and the lifespan of barriers), (2) the amount of saltwater seepage, (3) salinization and freshwater need/availability, (4) erosion and sedimentation processes, and (5) coastal foundations and the existence of intertidal areas (Haasnoot et al., 2018).

DOI: 10.4324/9781003183419-25

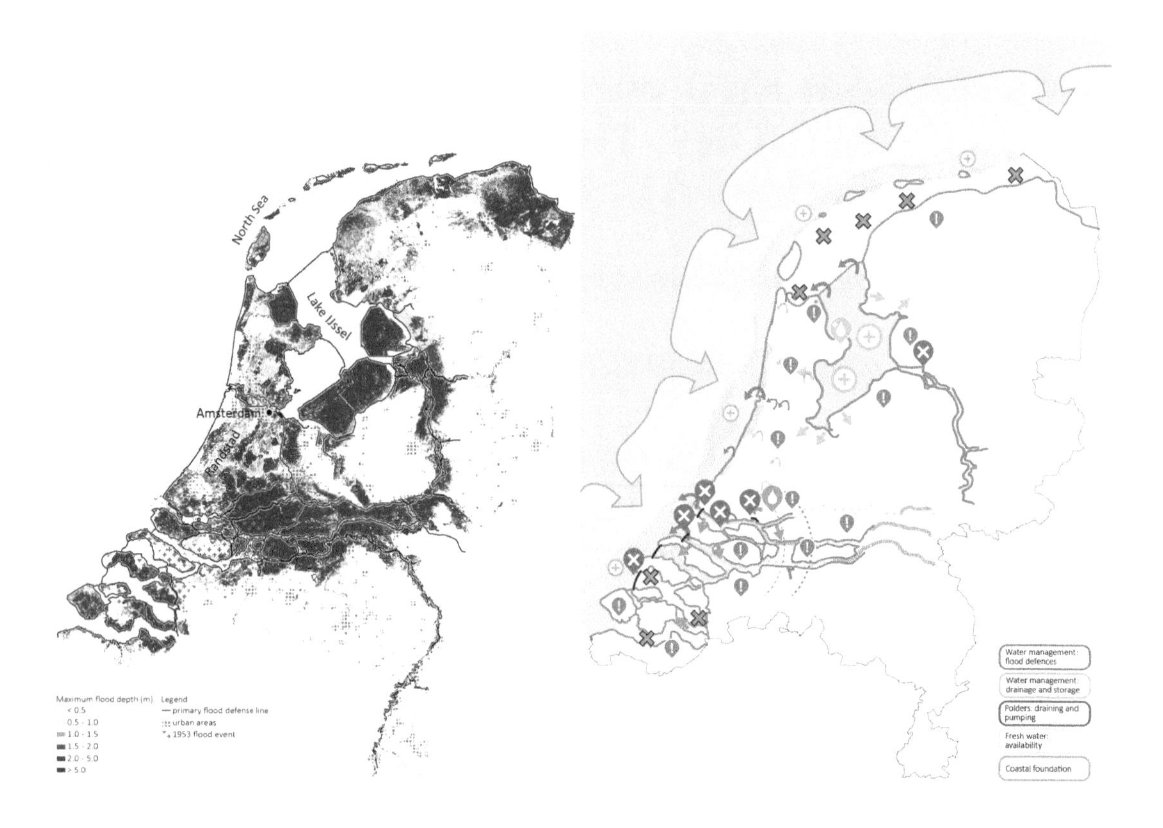

Figure 18.1 The map on the left shows the area subject to flood risk (map by Defacto Urbanism, based on LIWO, 2021 and van der Bie, 2019. The map on the right indicates possible impacts of SLR related to the water management system. Maps by Defacto Urbanism.

Design Synopses

Study Areas

Design studies are conducted to explore integral long-term options for combining water management with spatial programs such as housing, energy transition, ecology, and recreation. This takes place both on a national scale (exploring long-term strategies in relation to the countries spatial composition) and at the local scale (detailed integral design proposals). In this section, we will link the results of a national study with two local design studies for the Amsterdam and Western Scheldt region to demonstrate the local scale impacts of different structural, non-structural, and hybrid approaches to SLR adaptation (Table 18.1).

National Scaled Design

As part of the Deltaprogramme, differing long-term directions for extending the current water management system to address accelerated SLR are explored. In the Deltares report "Strategieën voor adaptatie aan hoge en versnelde zeespiegelstijging" (Haasnoot et al., 2019), four future directions are defined: protection, accommodation, coastal advancement, and strategic retreat. These directions are conceptual cornerstones used to facilitate a debate and research-by-design on the potential impact that adaptation strategies for accelerated SLR can have on the spatial and economic development in the Netherlands. For these four strategies, storyline and conceptual drawings (Figure 18.2)

Table 18.1 Structural, non-structural, and hybrid elements applied in the different study areas

Program elements	*Structural*	*Non-structural*	*Hybrid*
Long-term direction accelerated sea level rise: Protection			
Sandy coastline (maintained with sand suppletion)			X
Barriers to close river arms	X		
Water pumps	X		
Local peak water retention areas		X	
Fresh water storage			X
Long-term direction accelerated sea level rise: Accommodation			
Sandy coastline (maintained with sand suppletion)			X
Levee enforcement	X		
Water storage areas		X	
Transition to salt or draught robust crops		X	
Long-term direction accelerated sea level rise: Coastal advance			
Islands in front of the coast (first step in time)		X	
Sea wall to close new coastline (second step in time)	X		
Long-term direction accelerated sea level rise: Strategic retreat			
Building with nature		X	
Land use changes to accept salinity		X	
Combined peak water storage in the greater Amsterdam region			
Pumps and inlets to manage water	X		
Levee enforcement	X		
Flood proofing existing buildings	X		
Peak water storage areas		X	
Double dike system in the Western Scheldt area			
Double dike system			X

were developed that demonstrate some characteristic differences (Nillesen & zum Felde, 2021).

Protection Direction: Elements and Impacts

This direction resulted from a historic attitude towards water management that aims to facilitate demands from different types of land uses (with a focus on urbanization and agriculture) within technical water management infrastructure. The coastline will be sandy, where possible, and contain engineered structures and barriers where needed; this will require additional barriers in the now open rivers, as well as intense coastal sand suppletion. The river discharge towards the sea will require additional pumping as well as local peak water retention areas. Lake IJssel could be used to store extra freshwater, if needed, to compensate for salinization though seepage. Major inland and hinterland waterway connections will be closed off and transformed into sluices, impacting shipping. Also, ecology will be severely impacted since the ecological

Figure 18.2 Conceptual drawings representing characteristic elements of the four different long-term directions for addressing accelerated sea level rise: protection (top left), accommodation (top right), coastal advance (bottom left), and strategic retreat (bottom right).
Images by Defacto Urbanism based on workshops series and Haasnoot et al., 2019.

valuable tidal plains with brackish water within the estuaries will be closed off from the sea; without tidal influence and siltation the tidal plains will eventually vanish. Water from rivers and polders will need to be discharged via pumps into the sea.

Accommodation Direction: Elements and Impacts

Much like the protection direction, the current engineered system is extended but contains the open connections to the sea. The coastline will remain as it is, requiring upgrading. Many levees will need to be thoroughly reinforced. Freshwater will be scarcer, which can be addressed by non-structural measures such as freshwater buffers and salt or drought-robust crops. Freight transport and ecology profit from the open sea-connections. Dike enforcements of often densely built historic dike ribbons within coastal–riverine transition zones are needed. Existing "room for the river" projects that are based on reducing riverine water levels by creating extra space (Klijn et al., 2013) may become less effective. Salt intrusions from seepage and further salinization of the river arms will press the freshwater availability and drinking water inlets. For the central Netherlands, additional freshwater could be stored in lake IJssel. The increased water levels will also increase the seepage in polders, resulting in the need for more pumping capacity.

Coastal Advancement Direction: Elements and Impacts

This direction builds on the Dutch water management tradition of creating favorable conditions for urbanization. SLR is addressed by a non-structural seaward extension of the coastline requiring large amounts of sand, while adding space for functions such as housing, harbors, airports, sustainable energy, ecology, and recreation. The strategy is phased in and begins with the construction of several islands that help reduce storm-surge impacts, but may be closed with barriers if SLR progresses. The construction of such barrier islands and their related sand mining will have a major impact on coastal ecology. The islands offer opportunities for a wide range of functions that will need to be realized near the Randstad. However, these new areas may, for instance, be used for new functions such as airports or urban extensions, and will therefore need to be provided with costly high-end transport connections to be able to compete with the agglomeration effects of the current Randstad. The resultant newly created inner lake will influence the character and economy of the current coastal towns. The lake may have a positive effect on reducing salt seepage into the western Netherlands, but will remain brackish for a long period and therefore be unable to increase freshwater supplies. As with the closed shore, many ecological-rich intertidal planes may disappear, and the river and rainwater will need to be pumped out to be discharged. The new inner lakes can, however, function as a valuable buffer for peak water discharge.

Strategic Retreat Direction: Elements and Impacts

This direction aims at an integral water and land use approach in which the characteristics of the water system (water availability and flood risk), where feasible, are the leading consideration when considering land use type. This reduces the structural measures for pumping, water supply and sediment control. Building with nature, such as double dike systems and accepting salinity are an important element of this strategy. Consequence reduction for flood risk management will receive more attention, especially in deep positioned polders. Agricultural and natural land uses will encourage more natural processes and a shift towards salt- and drought-tolerant crops and aquaculture. The coastline will become more dynamic and the closed-off connections to the sea in the Southwest Delta may be reopened.

Design Example: Peak Water Storage in the Greater Amsterdam Region

Study Area

In the greater Amsterdam region SLR (as well as other climate change aspects such as more extreme rainfall) will further pressure the current discharge system, causing it to become more reliant on pumping. Currently, the capacity of the system is reached about once every 72 years (Vermeulen et al., 2017); with climate change and SLR coupled with increased urbanization, the threshold level will be reached almost yearly (based on expert judgment). One of the adaptation measures for continuing the closed system is peak water storage areas. A design study was commissioned by a taskforce to future proof the water system ("Toekomstbestendig watersysteem") that explores design options for a 2,500-acre integrated peak water storage area. Based on functional requirements (for extra housing, energy transition, nature, cultural heritage preservation, and recreational space) and the technical suitability for peak water storage, different designs for combined peak water storages were developed (Nillesen et al., 2021).

Structural/Non-structural Elements and Impacts

The structural measure is the water inlet. Pumps are generally readily available in polder areas since pumping is the default discharge option in the Netherlands. Also, compartmentalization levees and flood proofing of existing buildings are typically required. Though some structural elements are required, peak water storage areas are often considered non-structural measures since they are an alternative for increased pump discharge capacity.

Each of the functional combinations has its own characteristics and impacts. The cultural heritage peak water storage utilizes opportunities to accentuate the former military water inundation defense line (the UNESCO heritage "stelling van Amsterdam") and the historic natural Oer-IJ flow bed. New temporary nature areas can be created that strengthen the overall ecological structure and functionality. Though being impacted yearly by poor inlet water quality, these extra temporary nature areas can still support a more diverse ecology (Reker et al., 2006). For peak water events, elevated refugee spaces for small mammals are included in the design. They can function as recreational areas, a much-wanted function in this highly urbanized region. A recreational flood forest can provide shaded and cool recreational spaces, anticipating increasing temperatures in summer and heat island effects

Figure 18.3 Design of the (left) dry and (right) flooded combined peak water storage with an energy park (above) and the high-density urban area (middle), as well as designs for the water storing forest (below left) and low-density living area (below right).

(Klimaateffectatlas, 2020); a forest with this functional combination has already been realized in Leipzig (Leipziger Auwald, n.d.).

Other functions that are currently competing for development space are housing (target of 230,000 new houses in the Metropolitan region of Amsterdam by 2040 (Metropoolregio Amsterdam (MRA), 2020) and sustainable energy (Nationaal Programa Regionale Energie Strategie (NP RES), 2019). Both low- and high-density urban development can be well combined with peak water storage. Though the investment costs in urban areas will be high due to high land prices, the benefits of realizing a large-scale green space in urban areas are also substantial (Nillesen et al., 2020). The low-density housing water storage area could be combined with created natural space (Rebel Group, 2019). Regarding sustainable energy, both solar panels as well as windmills can well be combined with water storage. An additional benefit of the peak water storages is that they can be implemented in areas where the subsidence (partly drive by climate change) makes the current agricultural land use less profitable and therefore a less sustainable practice.

Design for a Double Dike system in the Western Scheldt Area

Study Area

The Western Scheldt is one of the estuaries that still has an open connection to the North Sea. The connected estuary is an important ecological area with several tidal plains. This open connection is also an important condition for the accessibility of the neighboring Antwerp

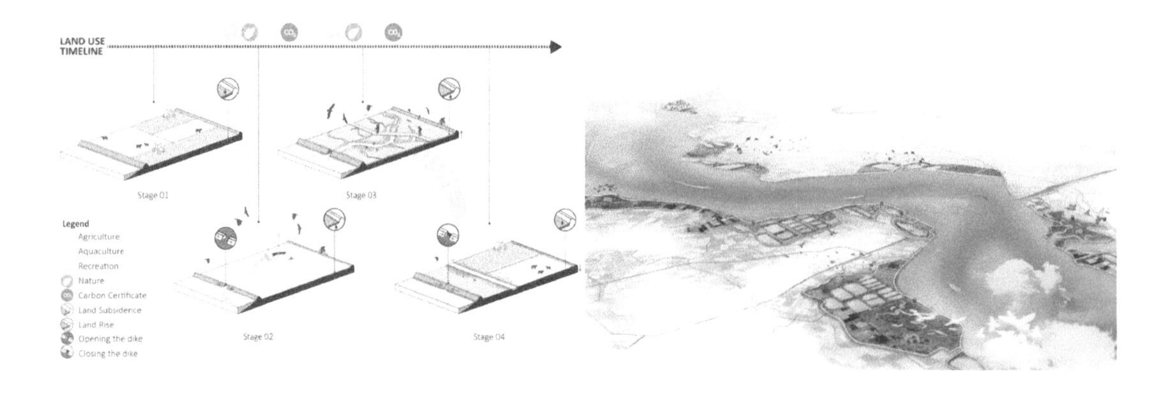

Figure 18.4 Image (left) showing the double dike zone transformation cycle and (right) birds' eye perspective. Images by Defacto Urbanism.

harbor in Belgium. However, the sea connection results in saltwater seepage into the Southwest Delta islands that have a freshwater-based agricultural economy. For the design in this area, controlled retreat is developed in cooperation with the World Wildlife Fund and NIOZ, the Royal Netherlands Institute for Sea Research.

Structural/Non-structural Elements and Impacts

One of the characteristics of the Southwest Delta landscape is that of parallel dikes which were historically developed (Meyer et al., 2015). The approach is based on the principle of tidal river management, like that applied in Bangladesh (Seijger et al., 2019), and based on allowing sediment rich water into polder areas to elevate them through sedimentation. In the Western Scheldt, by re-opening the current primary sea dike, the ebb and flow of the tide can enter behind the polders and deposit sediment. The second dike is and can remain lower than the primary dike since the water force will already be reduced by the primary, first levee and the created foreshore. By applying this principle, the area can slowly rise due to the silt that builds up with each tide; this, then, can grow with SLR. Along the Western Scheldt, this elevation includes about 1 to 2 centimeters per year (van Belzen et al., 2021).

The double dike area will create a valuable ecological intertidal zone. When elevated, the area can be be utilized again for agriculture (assuming the land use has disappeared). In the meantime, the intertidal zone can be converted to an ecological use, be used for aquaculture and saline crops, or recreational purposes. Although the implementation costs compared to the conventional solution (of strengthening the primary dike) can be higher, the returns on investment and additional ecological and recreational benefits are much higher in the long term (van Belzen et al., 2021).

Conclusions

Design Innovations and Global Applicability

The multidisciplinary research-by-design approach in which different conceptual orientations are used to reflect on the potential impacts of such a direction shows to be a valuable approach for flood mitigation of SLR. The approach secures an open mindset towards possible future development and provides valuable insights into system relations as well as impacts between the water management system and land uses. The local scaled designs have a valuable function in demonstrating that apparent contradicting spatial claims can be combined and lead to integral design solutions that improve the spatial quality of an area. This method is applicable and recommended for other areas where water system choices need to be explored to assist with decision making.

References

Deltacommissie (2008). *Working together with water, a living land builds for its future: Findings of the Deltacommissie 2008*. Deltacommissie. Retrieved from https://english.deltaprogramma.nl/documents/publications/2008/09/03/working-together-with-water

Haasnoot, M., Bouwer, L., Diermanse, F., Kwadijk, J., van der Spek, A., Oude Essink, G., Delsman, J., Weiler, O., Mens, M., ter Maat, J., Huismans, Y., Sloff, K., & Mosselman, E. (2018). *Mogelijke gevolgen van versnelde zeespiegelstijging voor het Deltaprogramma. Een verkenning*. [Possible consequences of accelerated sea level rise for the Delta Programme. An exploration.] Deltares rapport 11202230-005-0002. Retrieved from www.deltares.nl/app/uploads/2018/08/Bijlagen_Mogelijke-gevolgen-van-versnelde-zeespiegelstijging-voor-het-Deltaprogramma.pdf

Haasnoot, M., Diermanse, F., Kwadijk, J., de Winter, R., & Winter, G. (2019). *Strategieën voor adaptatie aan hoge en versnelde zeespiegelstijging. Een verkenning*. [Strategies for adapting to high and accelerated sea level rise. An exploration.] Deltares rapport 11203724–004. Retrieved from https://publications.deltares.nl/11203724_004.pdf

Klijn, F., de Bruin, D., de Hoog, M., Jansen, S., & Sijmons, D. F. (2013). Design quality of Room-for-the-River measures in the Netherlands: Role and assessment of the Quality Team (Q-team). *International Journal of River Basin Management*, *11*(3), 287–299. https://doi.org/10.1080/15715124.2013.811418.

Klimaateffectatlas (2020). *Kaartverhaal* hitte. [Map story heat.] Retrieved April 1, 2021, from www.klimaateffectatlas.nl/nl/kaartverhaal-hitte

Le Bars, D., Drijfhout, S., & de Vries, H. (2017). A high-end sea level rise probabilistic projection including rapid Antarctic ice sheet mass loss. *Environmental Research Letters*, *12*, Article 044013. Retrieved from https://iopscience.iop.org/article/10.1088/1748-9326/aa6512/meta

Leipziger Auwald (n.d.). *Lage und Größe*. [Location and area.] Retrieved April 1, 2021, from www.leipziger-auwald.de/front_content.php?idcat=7&lang=1

LIWO (2021). *Landelijk Informatiesysteem Water en Overstromingen*. [National Information System water and floods.] Retrieved April 1, 2021, from www.helpdeskwater.nl/onderwerpen/applicaties-modellen/applicaties-per/watermanagement/watermanagement/liwo/

Metropoolregio Amsterdam (MRA) (2020). *Afstemming* woningbouw *tot 2040*. [Alignment of house building up to 2040.] Retrieved April 1, 2021, from www.metropoolregioamsterdam.nl/afstemming-woningbouw-tot-2040/

Meyer, H., Bregt, A. K., Dammers, E., & Edelbos, J. (Eds.) (2015). *New perspectives for urbanizing deltas: A complex adaptive systems approach to planning and design*. Integrated Planning and Design in the Delta (IPDD). MUST Publishers. https://edepot.wur.nl/367890

Nationaal Programa Regionale Energie Strategie (NP RES) (2019). *Handreiking 1.1.* [Handbook 1.1.] NP RES. Retrieved from www.regionale-energiestrategie.nl/bibliotheek/res++media/downloads_getfilem.aspx?id=1125851&forcedownload=true

Nillesen, A. L., Koning, R., Stuurman, R., Dolman, N., & Gleijm, A. (2020). *Resilience by design Metropoolregio Amsterdam – landelijk gebied.* [Resilience by design Metropolitan Area Amsterdam – rural area.] Defacto Urbanism. Retrieved from d.efac.to/RbD%20MRA%20Eindrapport%20Defacto_web file.pdf

Nillesen, A. L., Lijdsman, L., & van den Bosch, G. (2021). *Casus Piekberging Amsterdam–Rijnkanaal /Noordzeekanaal.* [Case Peak storage Amsterdam–Rhine Canal/North Sea Canal.] Defacto Urbanism. Retrieved from http://d.efac.to/en/publications

Nillesen, A.L. & zum Felde, M. (2021). *Ruimtelijke ontwerp verkenning gevolgen versnelde zeespiegelstijging. Tussenresultaat eerste projectfase "work in progress".* [Spatial design exploration consequences of accelerated sea level rise. Interim result first project phase "work in progress".] Defacto Urbanism. Retrieved from d.efac.to/Ruimtelijke%20verkenning%20zeespiegelstijging_fase1_Defacto_webversie.pdf

Rebel Group (2019). Concept *eindrapport Werken met Natuur, Bouwsteen voor rivierengebied WNF.* [Draft final report Working with Nature, Building Block for the River Region WNF.] Rebel Group. Retrieved from www.researchgate.net/publication/40139039_Ruimte_voor_de_rivier_ruimte_voor_de_natuur_fase_1_verkenning

Reker, J., Helmer, W., Braakhekke, W., & Linnartz, L. (2006). *Tijdelijke natuur, permanente winst.* [Temporary nature, permanent profit.] Stroming & ARK. Retrieved from www.ark.eu/sites/default/files/media/25_jaar_ARK/Tijdelijke_Natuur.pdf

Seijger, C., Datta, D. K., Douven, W., van Halsema, G. & Khan, M. F. (2019). Rethinking sediments, tidal rivers and delta livelihoods: Tidal river management as a strategic innovation in Bangladesh. *Water Policy, 21,* 108–126. doi: https://doi.org/10.2166/wp.2018.212

Staf deltacommissaris (2020). *Nationaal Deltaprogramma 2021.* [National Delta Programme 2021.]. Staf Deltacommissaris. Retrieved from www.deltaprogramma.nl/binaries/deltacommissaris/documenten/publicaties/2020/09/15/dp2021-nl-printversie/DP2021+NL+printversie.pdf

van Belzen, J., Rienstra, G. U., & Bouma, T. J. (2021). *Dubbele dijken als robuuste waterkerende landschappen voor een welvarende Zuidwestelijke Delta.* [Double dikes as robust flood defence landscapes for a prosperous Southwestern Delta.] NIOZ Report 2021–01. NIOZ Royal Netherlands Institute for Sea Research. Retrieved from https://doi.org/10.25850/nioz/7b.b.kb

van der Bie, R. (2019, November 18). *Watersnoodramp 1953: CBS brengt schade in kaart.* [Flood disaster 1953: CBS maps out damage.] CBS. Retrieved from www.cbs.nl/nl-nl/corporate/2019/47/watersnoodramp-1953-cbs-brengt-schade-in-kaart

Vermeulen, C., Versteeg, R., & van den Brink, M. (2017). *Slim Watermanagement. Faalkansanalyse Noordzeekanaal/Amsterdam Rijnkanaal bij wateroverlast.* [Smart Water Management. Failure probability analysis of the North Sea Canal/Amsterdam Rhine Canal in the event of flooding.] HKV & HydroLogic PR3393.10. Retrieved from www.agv.nl/contentassets/af47e62321754920892b2867ccac27c4/swm-fka-nzk-ark-hoofdrapporttoelichting-agv.pdf

19
MIAMI, FLORIDA

Maria Debije Counts

Site: Miami-Dade County, FL: 40 acres

Introduction/Rationale

While sea level rise (SLR) projections can vary, proactive measures for planning and design purposes will render much of Miami, Florida inundated by 2100. Miami was identified as the most economically vulnerable city to SLR globally, according to a UN National Climate Assessment (Melillo et al., 2014), highlighting the increased risk of Miami's unique coastal character and biodiversity. In addition to SLR, rain-induced flooding hazards also contribute to the city's vulnerability and inundation-related issues (Wdowinski et al., 2016). For example, sewage spills into storm drains, waterways, and open grounds as sea levels rise and drain outlets are overtopped.

Rising waters are projected to occur over the next several decades. The National Oceanic and Atmospheric Administration (NOAA) and the U.S. Army Corps of Engineers (USACE) have run various models projecting ranges from low to extreme scenarios for the South Florida region with a minimum of 0.16 ft and maximum of 10.4 ft of relative SLR by 2100 (U.S. Army Corps of Engineers, 2019). In a recent study, the average rate of SLR in Southeast Florida after 2006 rose to 9 ± 4 mm/year, a significant increase from the pre-2006 rate of 3 ± 2 mm/year (Wdowinski et al., 2016). Another study incorporating the digital elevation model (DEM) derived from airborne light detection and ranging (LIDAR) projected a 1.5 m (4.9 ft) of SLR for the same time period (Zhang, 2011) in Miami (see Figure 19.1).

In addition to SLR, short-term fluctuations from hazard events such as storm surges and extreme rainfall events are a critical concern for the future of Miami. Miami's porous limestone bedrock enhances its flood risk. Water from below-ground which percolates up through the bedrock, coupled with a shallow water table, renders the ground extremely saturated and susceptible to flood risk. A recent study examining rainfall, tidal flow, and SLR found that the rain-induced water table is rising and is a primary driver of flooding events; areas below 1.5m North American Vertical Datum (NAVD) in Miami were shown to be vulnerable to exceptionally large rainfall events (Sukup et al., 2018).

DOI: 10.4324/9781003183419-26

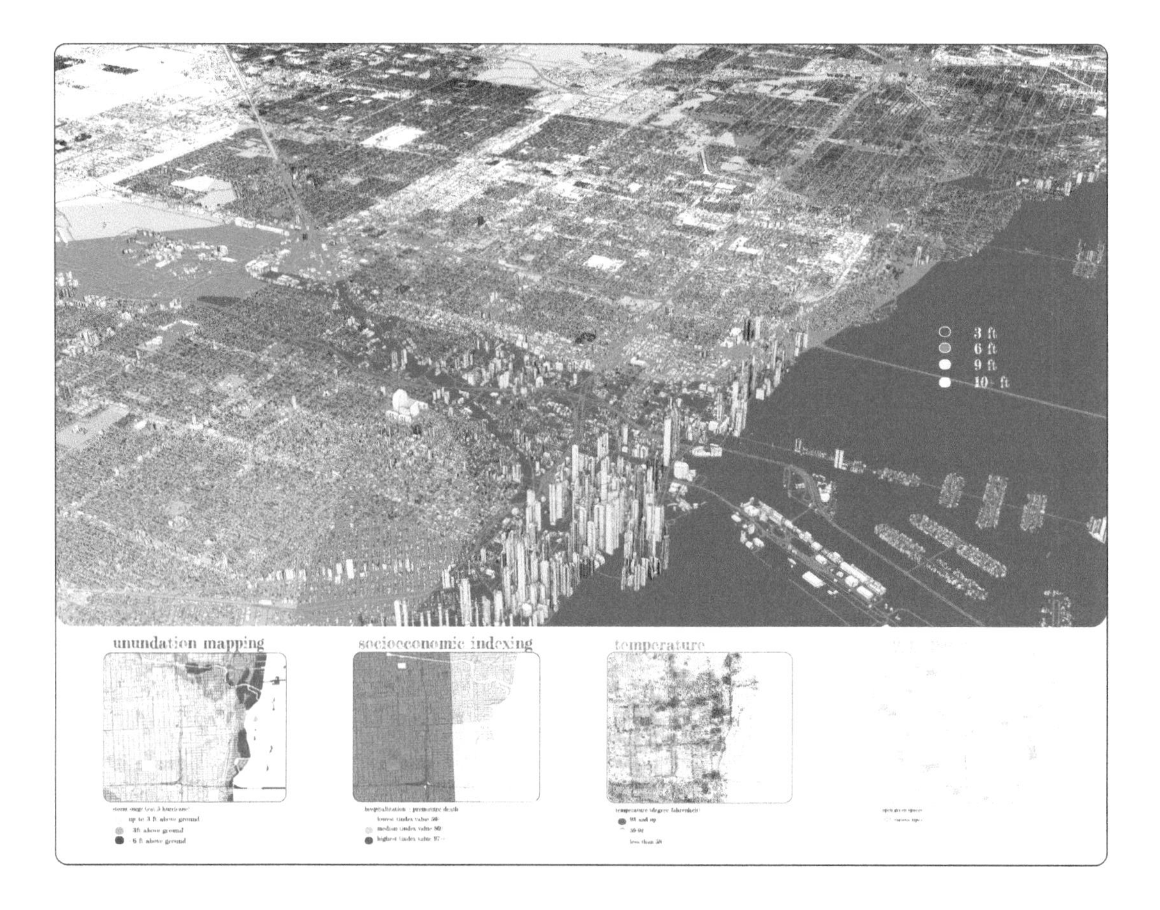

Figure 19.1 Site context aerial of Miami site proposal area by Ryan Rodriguez. Plan illustrations depicting inundation projections and existing site conditions analysis of flood risk, socio-economic indexing, temperature, and open green spaces left to right by Christina Currais, Emilie Catala, Derrek Roncek, and Sarah Belfer.

Underground freshwater is at risk for being infiltrated with saltwater, as much of Miami-Dade County sits below six feet in elevation along its coastline. These factors are of great concern for the areas, as out of the five most populous counties in Florida, four are coastal and comprise 2.7 million people in Miami-Dade County alone (United States Census Bureau, 2019). Further, Miami-Dade County is expected to reach 4.1 million people by 2045 (Bureau of Economic Business Research, 2019).

Design Synopsis

Study Area

While SLR averages range for the region, on average, Miami will need to plan for roughly 5 feet in rise by 2100 in addition to short-term events such as rainfall and storm surges. As with most coastal cities, significant investment will need to be allocated for the re-imagining of its coastline. A series of resilient landscape-based master plan solutions that integrate a variety of adaptable structural, non-structural, and hybrid mechanisms for Miami are both proposed and analyzed through performance modeling to combat these issues through design interventions. Much of Miami-Dade County has been heavily developed and is not currently a "blank slate" for future development (i.e. not much vacant land),

Table 19.1 Breakdown of programmatic elements for all master plan typologies by mechanism type (structural, non-structural, and hybrid)

Program elements by strategy	*Mechanisms*		
1.0 Constructed wetlands	*Structural*	*Non-structural*	*Hybrid*
Marsh		X	
Constructed wetland		X	
Bioswale		X	
Irrigation ditch		X	
2.0 Stabilized edge			
Seawall with back fill			X
Edging-rip rap			X
Site-engineered berms			X
3.0 Artificial islands and pier			
On-structure deck	X		
Pier	X		
Artificial island platform	X		

as is the case for many other coastal global cities facing SLR issues. Each master plan scenario was developed at the scale of 40 acres.

Structural, Non-Structural, and Hybrid Mechanisms

The flood and SLR mitigation mechanisms utilized (see Table 19.1) for the Miami case study include three design strategies: (1) constructed wetlands, (2) stabilized edge, and (3) artificial islands and pier. Because the mechanisms are primarily landscape based, when adapted to Miami, each varied not only by form, but also by function in terms of site performance, economic benefits, recreation, and other programmable possibilities.

For assessing all three scenarios, the National Green Values™ Calculator (Jayasooriya & Ng, 2014) was applied to calculate the Green Infrastructure Best Management Practices (BMPs) and measure the projected performance of integrating Green Stormwater Infrastructure (GSI) benefits and overall design impact. Stormwater capture and reuse, carbon sequestration, groundwater recharge, additional reduced construction, and maintenance costs throughout the lifetime of the proposed design were assessed for each proposed site. The Climate Positive Design Scorecard (Climate Positive Design, 2021) tool was used to measure emissions and climate positivity that weighed emissions against carbon sequestration potential and their net impact in metric tons over the next 50 years.

Master Plan Typology 1.0: Constructed Wetlands

Overview

This non-structural emphasis typology (see Figure 19.2) consists of wetlands, large berms, and open space attached to the mainland. Inland flooding is mitigated by providing resistance and sequestration

Figure 19.2 Non-structural SLR landscape proposal and illustrations in plan, section, perspective, and aerial inundation projections by Christina Currais.

of storm surge through the design development of contouring that generates opportunities for swales that amplify a series of strategically placed highs and lows designed to capture and transport excess rainfall and water from storm-surge events. Nutrients are stored in the sediment and can be used for biofiltration, storing high levels of carbon, and supporting local wildlife. Most of the site is designed with low slope ratios (in addition to a permeable generous path network ranging from 6′ to 10′ and 20′ wide walks) to provide outdoor rooms, making up approximately 12 acres of a combination of lawn and open recreational area. A small wood deck also provides access from the larger park to the smaller wetland zones.

Design Impact

BMPs including native planting, bioswales, and permeable paving applied to this site result in a total water volume capture potential of over 1.87 million gallons, compared to 14,258 gallons required for a site of its size; this is over 13,000% more capacity than is required. One hundred percent of the site is designed to be at a minimum of 6 feet in elevation with 77% of the site above the maximum SLR projection average of 10 feet. While the total projected cost for the implementation and maintenance for the project is 21.1% higher with these BMPs than without, the GSI benefits increase the real estate value of the site by an estimated 289.2%. The project would also be climate positive despite the wood decking, paved areas, and lawns negatively contributing to carbon dioxide emissions totaling 27,163 kg CO_2-eq. The park achieves a net impact of −25,216.2 metric tons of CO_2 over a 50-year lifespan. The design also results in 0.2 kg/ft² of total emissions and the sequestration per area is equal to 14.7 kg/ft². Space for outdoor active and passive flexible rooms are aquatic zones rich with biodiversity and space to introduce water-access-related activities such as kayaking, paddle-boarding, and more.

Master Plan Typology 2.0: Stabilized Edge

Overview

This hybrid emphasis typology (see Figure 19.3) is designed to be built on *terra firma*, with a bulkhead to the east and stabilized rip rap to the north and south where the ground meets the water. Earthen-berm mounds arranged vertically with loose slopes serve as a protective barrier along the water's edge. Micro-climate opportunities for native planting and rain gardens are able to thrive and attract biodiversity. Deep soils provide opportunities for robust native planting. The overall circulation meanders in and out of the berms, creating multiple experiences for visitors to enjoy. A series of plazas are situated at strategic moments throughout the site to provide for larger gatherings and scenic overlooks.

Design Impact

The BMPs (based on green infrastructure such as rain gardens, native vegetation, permeable sidewalks, and trees) applied to this site result in a total water volume capture potential of 2.8 million gallons, compared to the 244,389 gallons required for a site of its size (over 1,000% more

Figure 19.3 Hybrid SLR landscape proposal plan and inundation projections by Aliannys Hernandez. Section and illustrative perspective by Emilie Catala.

capacity than is required). Over 75% of the site is designed to be above 6 feet in elevation with over 55% of the site above the maximum SLR projection of 10 feet in rise. While the total projected cost for the implementation and maintenance for the project is 41.3% higher with BMPs than without, the GSI benefits increase the real estate value of the site by an estimated 1,566.5%. The project would take 1 year to become climate positive. The lawns, water play zones, and pavement contribute negatively to carbon dioxide emissions totaling 324,114 kg CO_2-eq, and the park achieves a net impact of −21,082 metric tons of CO_2 over a 50-year lifespan. The design results in 0.4 kg/ft^2 of emissions, but the sequestration per area is equal to 12.5 kg/ft^2. The experience of the site is enriched through a variety of activities with over 25 acres of programmable space, 18 of which are permeable pavement creating opportunities for exercise loops, nooks, and community events. The berms provide different age groups with experiential learning and outdoor natural play and engagement points of contact. Heavy planting can be conducted within this scheme, as it can have the heaviest of the weight-bearing capacities of all three scenarios.

Master Plan Typology 3.0: Artificial Islands and Pier

Overview

This structural emphasis typology (see Figure 19.4) is composed of 4 acres of pier, 6 acres of floating artificial islands, and 20 acres as a mid-section that serves as a platform connecting the land to the

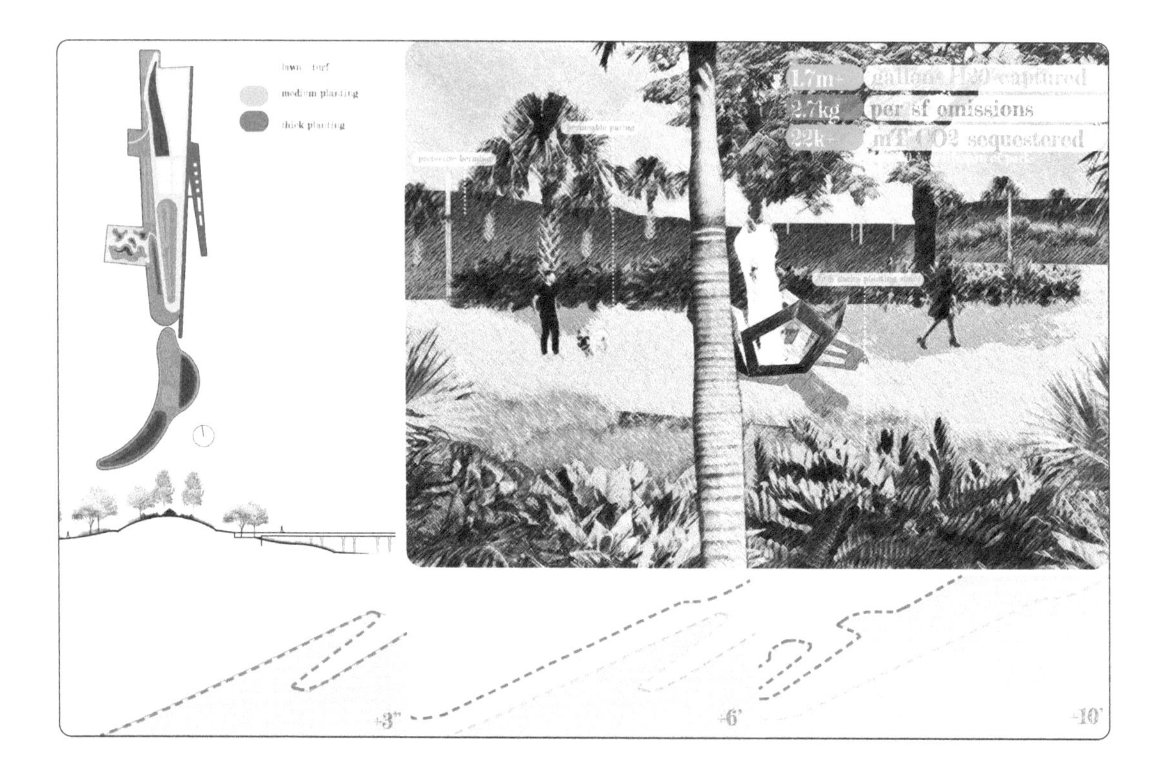

Figure 19.4 Structural SLR landscape proposal plan, perspective, and inundation projections by Derrek Roncek. Section by James Cadenas.

floating elements. The linearity of the proposal lends itself well to highly structured and organized spaces, with elevation as a series of terraces that protect the city from storm-surge and SLR, while offering water collection for irrigation of planting material. The floating barrier serves as a living breakwater to disrupt tidal inundation. Due to the on-structure elements, soil depths are thin, respectively. Different prospects are shaped mostly for passive use with a variety of angular views.

Design Impact

The green infrastructure applied to this site results in a total water volume capture potential of over 1.7 million gallons, compared to 155,049 gallons required for a site of its size and type; this is over 1,100% more capacity than required. Over 33% of the site is designed to be above 10 feet in elevation with 25% of the site floating. The total projected cost for the implementation and maintenance for the project decreases the total construction and maintenance costs by 25% with the BMPs added, compared to conventional approaches. GSI benefits increase the real estate value of the site by an estimated 234%. The project is estimated to take eight years to become climate positive. The lawns (artificial on-structure turf), pavement, and pedestrian pier walks contribute negatively to carbon dioxide emissions totaling 4 million kg of CO_2. The park achieves a net impact of –22,108 metric tons of CO_2 over a 50-year lifespan. The design results in 2.7 kg/ft^2 of emissions, with the sequestration area being equal to 15.3 kg/ft^2. Most of the site is programmable, with only the island (6 acres) currently not designed for occupation. The pile-supported platforms require significant investments for power and other amenities. Utilities are challenging in this typology, as they are not connected to land, occur over the water, and are furthest away from the city's main infrastructure connections. With just under 8 acres of paving, the site provides spaces for outdoor passive and active engagement. Just over 5 acres of artificial turf are usable for urban outdoor lawn space, while earthen mounding creates innovative uses of planted zones, wind protection, and the ability to plant trees and other plant species with deeper roots than a typical green roof would allow. The wood-decking pier is intentionally modular for program flexibility. Organized sports like basketball, volleyball, tennis, and others conducive to a flat, lightweight activity could be implemented over time. The pier lends itself well to water connection, boat slip storage, and water sports.

Conclusions

Innovation

When designed to perform, landscapes can serve communities tackling SLR on an environmental level, but also an economic and social one as well. Results from testing the projected performance of structural, non-structural, and hybrid mechanisms for Miami's coast show that all three types of landscape-based solutions can address these issues.

From an environmental standpoint, the non-structural and hybrid scenarios offer the greatest opportunity for biodiversity, soil depth, and space for development. In addition, strategies that address the financial costs related to protecting the city show promise to significantly benefit through sustainable building, adaptive housing, nature-based solutions to SLR, and other related approaches. As a social generator, while the stabilized edge and berm master plan is almost twice as costly to implement as the other two, it shows over 700% greater increase as regards infrastructure benefits and has the most activities for the greatest range of recreational uses from passive to active. As different levels of investment are required for each scenario, it is important for any city to carefully consider their local needs and immediate context as no solution is a one-size-fits-all.

The typology with the highest water volume capture potential was the hybrid typology with 2.8m gallons compared to 1.87m gallons for the wetlands and 1.7m gallons for structure typology. The constructed wetlands also resulted in the greatest percentage of land above 10 feet (77% of site) of protection from SLR and storm surges along the shoreline. By comparison, the hybrid typology was 55% and the structure typology 33%. The structure typology had the highest emissions of all projected at 2.7 kg/ft^2 compared to 0.2 kg/ft^2 for the non-structural and 0.4 kg/ft^2 for the hybrid typology. The master plan with the best net impact of carbon sequestration over the next 50 years was the non-structural typology by a margin of roughly 3,000 metric tons of CO_2 and taking nearly no time to be climate positive after implementation.

Global Applicability

In the case of Miami, policies related to coastal land development will need to simultaneously address SLR and flooding issues. Public awareness of short-term and long-term water-related risks and threats for the economic and environmental stability and longevity of the city need to be improved for support of the magnitude of efforts that can make a difference. Solutions all show different merit. As the city grows, so too does the need for access to safe drinking water, city infrastructure, housing, and outdoor public space for its swelling population. Sustainable coastal development strategies will be vital to ensure Miami is livable for years to come.

Many of the typologies discussed as well as the performance tools utilized are applicable for not only other coastal areas, but inner-city parks as well. Some of the benefits identified may assist not only with SLR, but also with frequent and extreme storm events. Runoff, reducing urban heat temperatures, native planting strategies, diverse microclimate creation, expanded biodiversity, and carbon sequestration are simply a few of the landscape-based benefits to combat climate change issues in better ways. Landscape-led solutions come from the design of the site first. The mechanism and the way in which the mechanism is applied impact the outcome of the site performance. The performance of each outcome is not only one of environmental concern, but also of public health, safety and welfare.

References

Bureau of Economic Business Research (2019). *New Americans in Miami-Dade County. New American Economy Research Fund.* Retrieved from https://research.newamericaneconomy.org/report/new-americans-in-miami-dade-county/

Climate Positive Design. (2020). *Why climate positive design?* Retrieved from: https://climatepositivedesign.com/about/

Jayasooriya, V. M., & Ng, A. W. M. (2014). Tools for modeling of stormwater management and economics of green infrastructure practices: A review. *Water, Air, & Soil Pollution, 225*(8), 2055. Retrieved from https://greenvalues.cnt.org/index.php#calculate

Melillo, J. M., Richmond, T. T. C., & Yohe, G. W. (Eds.). (2014). Climate Change impacts in the United States: The Third National Climate Assessment. *U.S. Global Change Research Program*. Retrieved from www.globalchange.gov/browse/reports/climate-change-impacts-united-states-third-national-climate-assessment-0

Sukup, M., Rogers, M., Guannel, G., Infanti, J. M., & Hagemann, K. (2018). High temporal resolution modeling of the impact of rain, tides, and sea level rise on water table flooding in the Arch Creek basin, Miami-Dade County Florida USA, *Science of the Total Environment, 616–617*, 1668–1688.

United States Census Bureau. (2019). *Population estimates*. Retrieved from www.census.gov/quickfacts/fact/table/miamibeachcityflorida,miamidadecountyflorida,FL/PST045219

U.S. Army Corps of Engineers (USACE). (2019). *Climate change adaptation: Comprehensive evaluation of projects with respect to sea-level change*. USACE Curve Calculator. Retrieved from https://cwbi-app.sec.usace.army.mil/rccslc/slcc_calc.html

Wdowinski, S., Bray, R., Kirtman, B., & Wu, Z. (2016). Increasing flooding hazard in coastal communities due to rising sea level: Case study of Miami Beach, Florida. *Ocean and Coastal Management, 126*(1), 1–8. 10.1016/j.oceoaman.2016.03.002

Zhang, K. (2011. Analysis of non-linear inundation from seal-level-rise using LIDAR data: A case study for South Florida. *Climatic Change, 106*, 537–565. https://doi.org/10.1007/s10584-010-9987-2

20

CHRISTCHURCH, CANTERBURY REGION, AOTEAROA, NEW ZEALAND

Nada Toueir and Gillian Lawson

Site: Ōtautahi/Christchurch, Aotearoa/New Zealand: 1,426 km2

Introduction/Rationale

The impacts of climate change on Aotearoa, New Zealand have become increasingly evident. Located in the South Pacific Ocean, its group of islands are highly exposed to sea level rise (SLR). According to the Intergovernmental Panel on Climate Change (IPCC, 2018), global warming may reach 1.5°C in the next 30 years, which will lead to higher sea levels and expose coastal areas to more severe flooding. Between 1901 and 2010, the global mean sea level has increased by 0.19m, with ocean warming likely to be greater in the Southern Ocean (IPCC, 2018). In Lyttelton Harbour (south of the city of Christchurch), higher SLR levels have been recorded (Eaves & Doscher, 2016). Since the 2010 and 2011 earthquakes, the City of Ōtautahi (Māori name) Christchurch (English name) has begun planning for adaptation and mitigation against flooding with a 'Climate Smart Strategy 2010–2025' and a 'Long Term Plan' that is revised every three years. By 2030, the City of Christchurch is committed to spending $416 million toward stormwater and flood protection infrastructure (Christchurch City Council, 2018).

Ōtautahi Christchurch is a flat coastal low-lying city with high groundwater levels. Due to its geomorphology, the impacts of SLR on Ōtautahi are noticeable on the physical landscape. The city is vulnerable to flooding and is subject to recurrent hazards such as liquefaction due to earthquakes, river overflow after major rain events, extreme tidal variations and SLR due to climate change (Hughes et al., 2015). The city was originally primarily swamps that were drained to make use of its fertile soils for agricultural and horticultural purposes (Brown et al., 1995). Ōtautahi is located on the eastern shore of the South Island with three main rivers traversing it: the Waimakariri River, the Ōtakaro Avon River and the Heathcote River (from north to south respectively). The rivers flow into estuaries along Pegasus Bay before connecting to the South Pacific Ocean at Brooklands Lagoon and the Avon–Heathcote Estuary. Both inlets are important zones for their ecological and hydrologic values (Brown et al., 1995; Eaves & Doscher, 2016). The neighbourhoods

DOI: 10.4324/9781003183419-27

that are directly adjacent to the estuaries include Brooklands, North and South New Brighton, Redcliffs and Sumner.

Design Synopsis

Study Area

The Ōtautahi Christchurch coastal environment has undergone major geomorphic change due to a series of major earthquakes from 2010 to 2011. This created localised uplift and subsidence within the urban environment, altering vulnerability to flood or storm surge inundation for many residents (Eaves & Doscher, 2016. After the earthquakes in September 2010 and February 2011, the Christchurch City Council (CCC) implemented residential red zones, where residents were financially compensated to voluntarily relocate to less vulnerable areas. The proposed residential red zones included areas along the Ōtakaro Avon River, starting at the eastern border of the city centre and ending at the Avon–Heathcote Estuary and Brooklands Lagoon (CERA, 2011). These areas are to be converted into public green spaces for recreational activities and to provide ecological sanctuaries for native fauna and flora (Regenerate Christchurch Te Kowatawata, n.d). In addition, the CCC created a Flood Management Area (FMA) that identified areas at risk of inundation, where building is no longer permitted (Christchurch City Council, n.d.).

South of the city, Te Waihora Lake Ellesmere is a shallow brackish coastal lake that is separated from the ocean by a 28 km long shingle barrier. The lake is prone to recurrent floods from tidal change and major rain events, hence affecting adjacent land (Zarour, 2019). The coastal areas along Pegasus Bay and Te Waihora play an important role in providing rich and diverse habitats for migratory birds. Both the Avon–Heathcote Estuary and Te Waihora are separated from the ocean by sand pits, mudflats and salt marshes that are enriched by semi-diurnal tides. Many bird species, both migratory and local, are found in both inlets (Crossland, 2013; Henderson-Fitzgerald, 2012). Te Waihora Lake Ellesmere is a shallow lake surrounded by agricultural land, and when it floods, due to the low-lying and flatness of the area, the extent of the inundation can spread quickly to adjacent land. Under Water Conservation Orders, artificial drainage channels are used to control the flooding. Over time, the quality of lake water has rapidly declined, and measures have been set in place by the Selwyn District Council to preserve the lake. Te Waihora is of great cultural and ecological importance where a diverse fauna and flora have existed for centuries (Zarour, 2019).

Sea Level Rise Projections

A projected SLR of 1.0 meters by 2115 is expected to result in increased storm inundation, greater frequency of extreme tidal levels and the progressive retreat of the shoreline in low lying areas in coastal Canterbury. The areas affected will be around the fringes of the Avon–Heathcote Estuary, Brooklands Lagoon and Te Waihora Lake Ellesmere due to their low topography. Sumner and Redcliffs, in the lower reaches of the Avon and Heathcote Rivers, farmland adjacent to the Brooklands Lagoon and small settlements on the edge of Te Waihora Lake Ellesmere will be inundated to varying extents. The risk of inundation along the New Brighton dune system is expected to have only minimal effect, if any, as the elevations are above storm surge levels. Along the Sumner and Clifton Beach revetments, a general lowering of the beach profile will occur due to scouring at the base, with inundation likely due to low points in the road structure in the future, with Clifton Beach facing coastal squeeze between cliffs and the ocean (Tonkin & Taylor Ltd, 2013). The inundation impacts on the lower Avon and Heathcote tidal estuary appear to aggrade its inner edges and erode its outer edges due to wave action across its surface.

Previous Floods and Damage

Following the Darfield earthquake in 2010, flooding was observed in areas of liquefaction and in subsequent large storms (Quigley & Duffy, 2020). Recurrent liquefaction lowered ground surface elevations in liquefaction-affected areas by >30 cm to >1 m. The effect of floodplain lowering was observed most profoundly adjacent to urban streams, where high tides locally inundated former floodplains. Earthquake-induced damage to stormwater pipelines and the consequent impacts on the connectivity and capacity levels of the pipeline stormwater network contributed to an increased flood hazard in Christchurch. Christchurch experienced several intensive rainstorms in 2014 and 2017, resulting in widespread flooding of properties in river suburbs that in some instances exceeded historical flooding depths and spatial extents due to floodplain subsidence.

Design Strategy(s): Structural and Non-structural Mechanisms

Debates related to climate change and risks of SLR often focus on the impacts to human settlements and agricultural land. However, flora and fauna species will also be adversely affected along coastal shorelines. A design studio project in Ōtautahi Christchurch focused on SLR and migratory shorebirds that fly along the East Asian Australasian Flyway (between Siberia and Alaska to Australia and Aotearoa/New Zealand) each year. There is considerable concern as the population of migratory shorebirds has declined by 40% around the world as stopover sites for feeding and resting disappear along coastlines (Iwamura et al., 2014). For instance, populations of great knot *Calidris tenuirostris*, red knot *Calidris canutus* and bar-tailed godwit *Limosa lapponica* are decreasing at rates of 5%–9% per year (Amano et al., 2010; Wilson et al., 2011). Shorebird biology and behaviour is known to vary in relation to changes in food supply and foraging patterns, particularly where they over-winter, as a result of climate change

(Durant et al., 2009; Paxton et al., 2014). An ecologist with Christchurch City Council, Andrew Crossland, confirmed in 2021 that migratory bird species, were shifting to alternative feeding areas within the Avon–Heathcote Estuary and Te Waihora Lake Ellesmere, in response to SLR and changing coastal conditions.

Students at Lincoln University were therefore asked to focus on one migratory bird species and design a multi-species habitat in eastern Christchurch and nearby inter-tidal areas that would prioritise shorebird protection and conserve existing tidal flats for these vulnerable animals facing rising sea levels. This chapter presents four projects focused on habitat conservation for four migratory bird species – the Arctic skua, *Stercorarius parasiticus*, bar-tailed godwit, *Limosa lapponica*, red knot, *Calidris canutus* and red-necked stint, *Calidris ruficollis.* Each project uses dynamic landforms (Hill, 2015), trapping sediment, constructing mounds, islands and basins, to protect inter-tidal foraging and roosting sites. By designing the physical environment to maintain a range of shorebird feeding opportunities and minimise favouring of one species over another, the design work would improve the survival of multiple migratory bird species in Aotearoa New Zealand. This chapter looks at the application of SLR design solutions to protect tidal habitat areas for four different migratory birds that stop in Ōtautahi Christchurch to rest and feed.

Project Location

Avon–Heathcote Estuary near the Southshore Spit Reserve in south New Brighton, east Christchurch.

Description

The Arctic skua, *Stercorarius parasiticus*, breeds in the Arctic and subarctic tundra and coastal moorland from May to August then migrates to

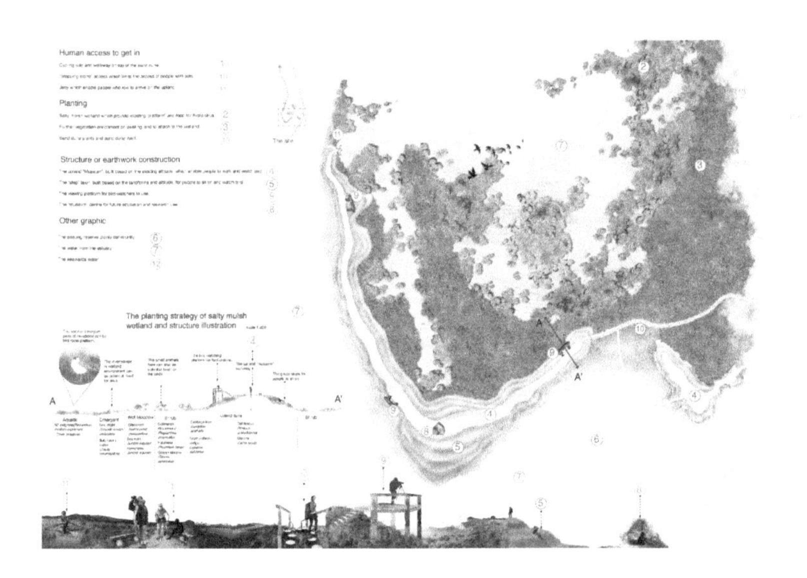

Figure 20.1 Master plan for Southshore Spit Reserve in south New Brighton.
With permission of M. Zhang.

Aotearoa New Zealand in September for the winter (Szabo, 2013). Saltmarshes provide a roosting platform for the skua who mostly scavenges food from other terns or gulls. The first project explored in this chapter proposes a tiered viewing terrace around a reconfigured coastal wetland habitat where sediment could be trapped and accumulate in the Avon–Heathcote Estuary (see Figure 20.1). A gradient of plant species from marine seagrass to saltmarsh species could be progressively inundated as the sea level rises.

Project Location

Avon–Heathcote Estuary in McCormacks Bay, in the suburb of Redcliffs, east Christchurch.

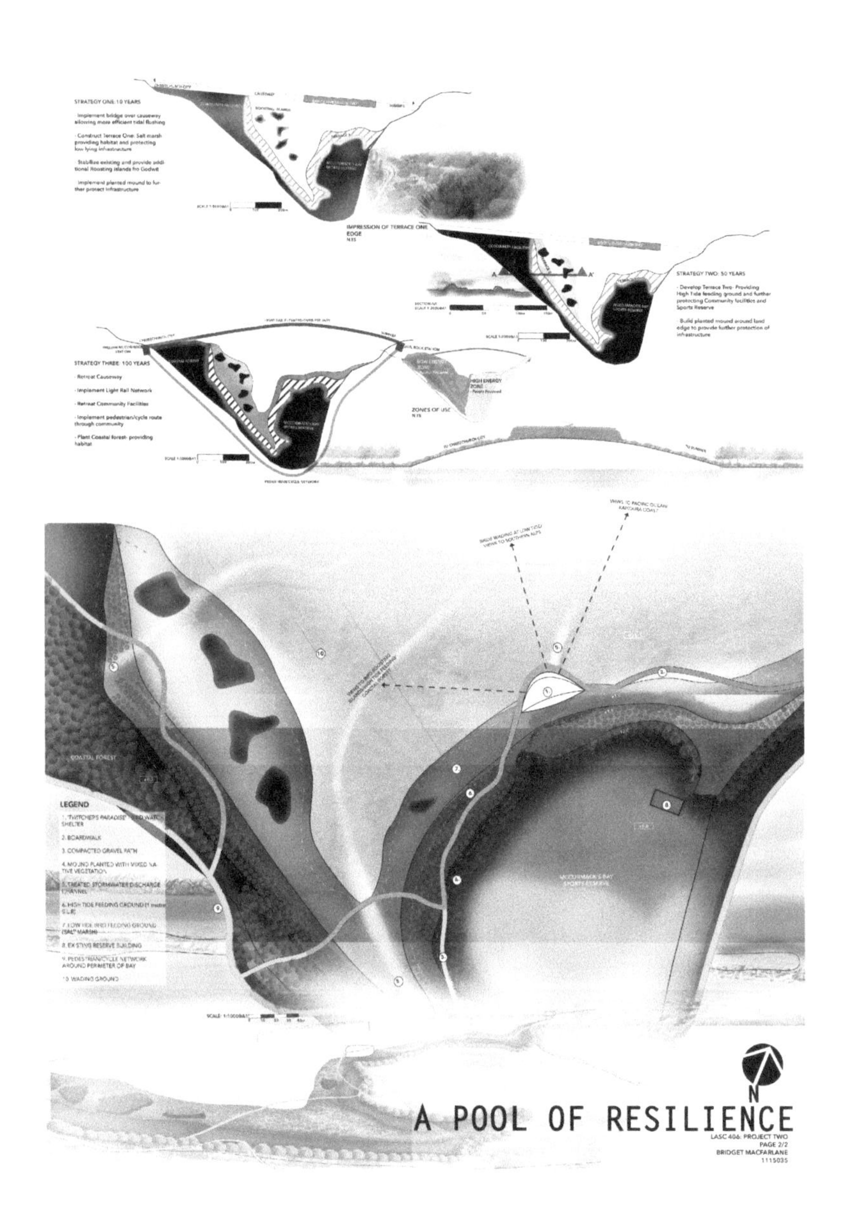

Figure 20.2 Design development and master plan for tidal mudflats at McCormacks Bay, on the Avon–Heathcote Estuary. With permission of B. McFarland.

Description

The bar-tailed godwit, *Limosa lapponica*, breeds in upland and coastal tundra in western Alaska. Godwits are fully protected in Aotearoa New Zealand, as they are considered to be at risk due to habitat loss. Global climate change is predicted to affect these birds at all stages of their annual migratory cycle. Their breeding habitat in the Alaskan tundra may be adversely affected by invasive trees and shrubs. Peak invertebrate emergence in feeding areas may occur before chicks are hatched. Changes in synopic weather patterns may disrupt their flyway routes. Intertidal foraging in over-wintering, staging and post-breeding sites may be affected by SLR. Also, godwits roost on shell banks and sand spits with other wading birds (Battley, 2013; Woodley, 2013). Another project in McCormacks Bay (adjacent to the Avon–Heathcote Estuary) proposes mounds as roosting islands surrounded by tidal mudflats for wading birds to feed on molluscs, crustaceans, snails, worms and other aquatic invertebrates (see Figure 20.2). The design suggests retreating community sports facilities from low lying open space, hence freeing up construction material for building mounds. The surrounding parkland is edged with coastal herbs and shrubs that reduce human interference frightening the godwits while foraging. It elevates the previously flood-prone causeway to allow improved flushing of estuarine water into the tidal flats for increased invertebrate populations.

Project Location

Te Waihora Lake Ellesmere foreshore, near Motukarara, south of Christchurch.

Description

The red knot, *Calidris canutus*, or lesser knot (compared to the great knot), is the second most common migratory shorebird in Aotearoa NZ, arriving in September. It is a flocking sandpiper, feeding in flocks on coastal tidal sandflats or mudflats. It is nondescript for most of the year before moulting into red plumage and hence known as the red knot. They breed in far-eastern Siberia in Russia and over-winter in Australia and in good numbers in the South Island of Aotearoa New Zealand. Its conservation status is classified as 'vulnerable' due to the loss of habitat in stopover sites and, although tidal flats in Aotearoa New Zealand have less reclamation pressure than other parts of the world, human impacts on roosting sites are still detrimental to this bird (Battley, 2013). This project proposes reintroducing saltwater wetland 'islands and basins' to slow inundation of nearby farmland on Te Waihora Lake Ellesmere (see Figure 20.3). The lake edge retreats inland as sea level rises and is planted with endemic grasses and cabbage trees, *Cordyline australis*, with a boardwalk and walking tracks to restrict damage by off-road vehicles to roosting sites as sea level rises.

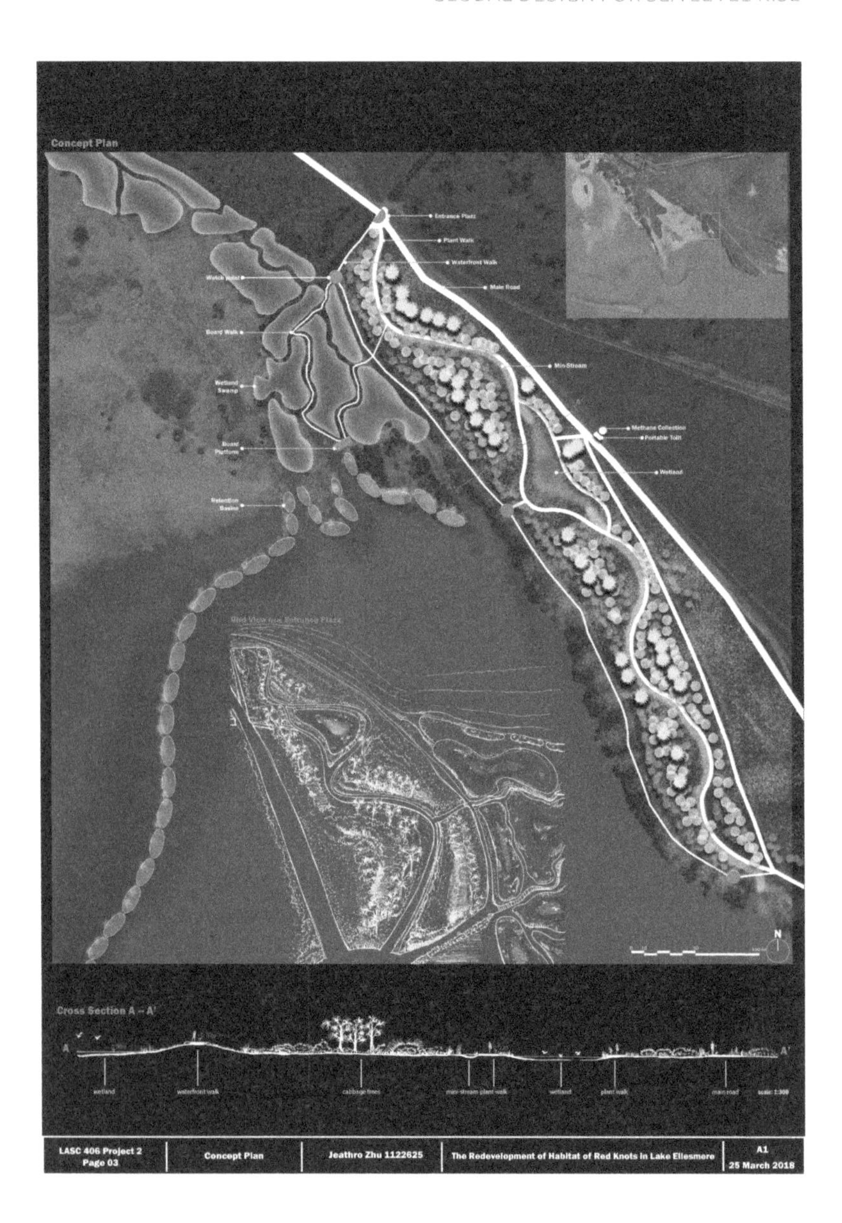

Figure 20.3 Master plan for mudflats near Motukarara at Te Waihora Lake Ellesmere. With permission of J. Zhu.

Project Location

Te Waihora Lake Ellesmere foreshore, near Green Park Huts, south of Christchurch

Description

The red-necked stint, *Calidris ruficollis*, is the smallest of the migratory wading birds, about the size of a sparrow. It lays its eggs in grass-lined depressions on the ground in low tundra in north-eastern Siberia and north-western Alaska. Like most migratory wading birds using the East Asian–Australasian Flyway, red-necked stints are threatened by coastal pollution, reclamation and hunting along their migration route. Most arrive in Aotearoa/New Zealand in September to November and leave in March to April. They feed on small invertebrates such as small gastropods, crustaceans (amphipods, ostracods), fly larvae and pupae obtained by probing with a sewing machine action (Miskelly, 2013). This final design proposes channelling stormwater through tidal flats and mounding key locations for viewpoints that celebrate the arrival of migratory waders in Te Waihora Lake Ellesmere (see Figure 20.4). These viewpoints are connected by elevated walkways that entice visitors to watch and listen to the birds as they feed but as sea level rises, these mounds become refuges for roosting birds.

Projected Design Impacts

Ōtautahi Christchurch is the largest city in Aotearoa New Zealand built on a floodplain. Christchurch Council City undertook a study in 2003 to

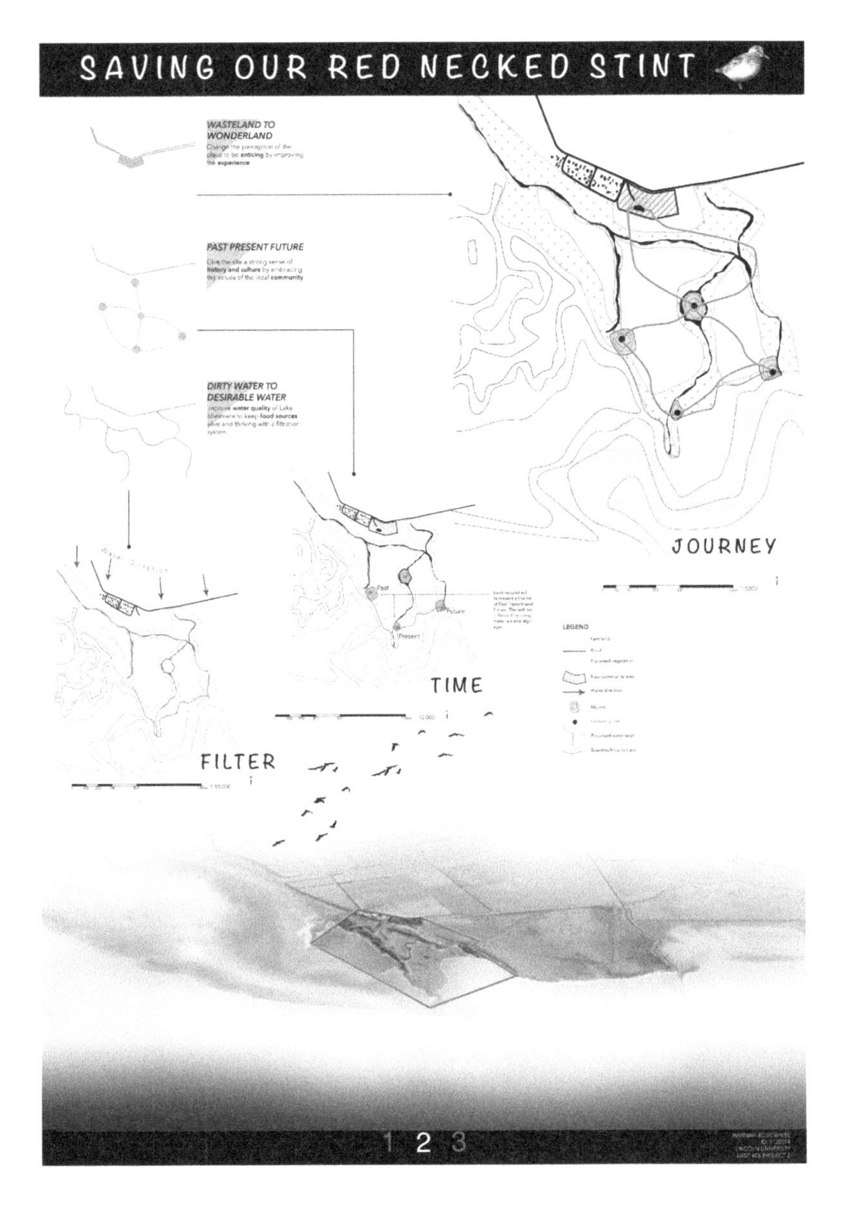

Figure 20.4 Design development for tidal flats near Greenpark Huts at Te Waihora Lake Ellesmere.
With permission from H.-R. White.

assess how potential risks due to climate change could be managed (Ministry of the Environment, n.d.). Only minimum floor levels for buildings in ponding basins were deemed necessary at the time and were incorporated into the City Plan. After the earthquakes in 2010 and 2011, gravel stop-banks were constructed along much of the Ōtakaro Avon River to temporarily mitigate the post-earthquake flood hazard (Quigley and Duffy, 2020, p.19). These stop banks have led to increased sediment build-up within the river channel, which could increase flood hazards but also be beneficial to estuarine deposition for maintaining shallow shorebird tidal flats. Implementing dynamic landform strategies are often missing as alternatives for adaptation to SLR (Hill, 2015). Working with sediment flows in these fragile environments is a challenging task. The impacts of creating higher ground in tidal zones, such as wherever land reclamation has taken place, will change sediment patterns as sea level rises. Protection of mudflats and sandbanks, however, from inundation and contaminants that affect estuarine invertebrate populations that are a food source for many migratory shorebirds, may occur as human settlements and farms retreat from the coastal foreshore. According to Andrew Crossland, an ecologist with Christchurch City Council, migratory bird species, particularly South Island pied oystercatchers (*Haematopus finschi*), are shifting to alternative feeding areas within the Avon–Heathcote Estuary and Te Waihora Lake Ellesmere, in response to sea level rise or changing coastal conditions.

In this chapter, two projects proposed positive changes to saltwater wetlands through retreat and earthen mounds in the Avon–Heathcote Estuary (see Table 20.1) to overcome negative impacts of earthquake-induced changes for shorebirds and waterbirds. For the Arctic skua, *Stercorarius parasiticus* and bar-tailed godwit, *Limosa lapponica*, increased island refuges and convoluted edges of tidal flats would assist in maintaining foraging areas as sea level rises. Two other projects proposed coastal retreat and refuges (see Table 20.1) for the red knot, *Calidris canutus* and red necked stint, *Calidris ruficollis* in Te Waihora Lake Ellesmere that could have positive impacts on shorebirds, as already seen

Table 20.1 Mechanisms utilised within the designs for Ōtautahi/ Christchurch

Program elements	*Structural*	*Non-structural*	*Hybrid*
Retreat	X		
Earthen mounds		X	
Saltwater wetlands		X	
Elevated access	X		
Elevated viewpoints	X		
Tidal flats		X	
Dredged areas		X	
Riparian zone		X	

at Brooklands Lagoon due to positive earthquake-induced changes. All four projects fostered safe visitor access on elevated walkways and viewing platforms to increase public awareness of the importance of conserving stopover sites for migratory birds on the East Asian–Australasian Flyway. Greater attention given by landscape architects to designing these coastal environments, specifically for shorebirds foraging for invertebrates and avoiding predators, will improve migratory birds' energetic state during their non-breeding phase prior to their long migration back to their northern hemisphere breeding grounds (Paxton et al., 2014).

Conclusions

Innovation and Applicability

The case of coastal Ōtautahi Christchurch illustrates the vulnerability of an earthquake-prone city built on a floodplain of alluvial silt, clay and gravel. SLR not only affects human settlements and farm production areas, but also flora and fauna species along our coastal foreshores. A landscape architectural design studio aimed to develop design proposals that focused primarily on the conservation of feeding and roosting habitats of migratory shorebirds in eastern Christchurch at the southern end of the East Asian–Australasian Flyway. Migratory birds are threatened by land reclamation pressures, contaminated marine invertebrate populations, human interference of roosting sites by dogs and off-road vehicles and rising water levels over mudflat and sandflat foraging sites. Some shorebird species, such as the bar-tailed godwit and red knot, are considered to be 'at risk' and 'vulnerable'.

Application of these strategies will depend on local knowledge of natural coastal processes; sediment movement, especially where landfill and structures have changed flow patterns; and the strength of conservation measures for tidal flats and coastal wetlands in the face of land reclamation and human recreation pressures. Changing coastal landscapes could be greatly improved through designing with natural coastal processes for migratory birds navigating the East Asian–Australasian Flyway from Siberia and Alaska, through east Asia, to Australia and Aotearoa New Zealand (Wikramanayake et al., 2020). The loss of hundreds of Ramsar stopover sites including coastal wetlands in Hebei, Shandong, Tianjin and Jiangsu provinces in China (Xia et al., 2017), Mai Po Inner Deep Bay in the Pearl River estuary (Wikramanayake et al., 2020) and Western Port in south-eastern Australia (Hansen et al., 2015), are seeing and predicting significant shorebird losses due to inundation and accretion under a 1.5m SLR scenario. Increasing public awareness of the impacts of SLR on coastal habitats of flora and fauna would be a worthwhile step in climate-proofing the East Asian–Australasian Flyway.

References

Amano, T., Szekely, T., Koyama, K., Amano, H., Sutherland, W. J. (2010). A framework for monitoring the status of populations: An example from wader populations in the East Asian–Australasian flyway. *Biological Conservation*, 143, 2238–2247.

Battley. P. F. (2013). [updated 2017]. Lesser knot. In C. M. Miskelly (Ed.), *New Zealand Birds Online*. Retrieved from www.nzbirdsonline.org.nz

Brown, J., Beetham, D., Paterson, R., & Weeber, H. (1995). Geology of Christchurch, New Zealand. *Environmental and Engineering Geoscience*, *1*(4), 427–488.

Canterbury Earthquake Recovery Authority (CERA). (2011). *Canterbury Land Information Map*. Retrieved from https://ceraarchive.dpmc.govt.nz/documents/canterbury-land-information-map

Christchurch City Council. (2018). *Long term plan 2018 to 2028*. Richmond, Tasman District Council. Retrieved from https://ccc.govt.nz/the-council/plans-strategies-policies-and-bylaws/plans/long-term-plan-and-annual-plans/older-plans/ltp-2018-2028/

Christchurch City Council. (n.d.). *Flood management.* Retrieved from https://ccc.govt.nz/environment/water/water-flooding/flood-management/

Crossland, A. C. (2013). Wetland bird monitoring at the Avon–Heathcote Estuary and Bromley Oxidation Ponds, Christchurch: August 2009 to July 2010. *Notornis*, *60*(2), 151–157.

Durant, J. M., Hjermann, D. Ø., Frederiksen, M., Charrassin, J. B., Maho, Y. Le, Sabarros, P. S., Crawford, R. J. M., & Stenseth, N. C. (2009). Pros and cons of using seabirds as ecological indicators. *Climate Research*, *39*(2), 115–129.

Eaves, A., & Doscher, C. (2016). Coastal modelling of sea level rise for the Christchurch coastal environment. *Lincoln Planning Review*, *7*(1–2), 3–15.

Hansen, B. D., Menkhorst, P., Moloney, P., & Loyn, R. H. (2015). Long-term declines in multiple waterbird species in a tidal embayment, south-east Australia. *Austral Ecology*, *40*, 515–527.

Henderson-Fitzgerald, M. (2012). *Recommendations for Establishing a Community Volunteer Bird Monitoring Program at Styx Mill Conservation Reserve*. Christchurch, New Zealand: The Styx Living Laboratory Trust.

Hill, K. (2015). Coastal infrastructure: a typology for the next century of adaptation to sea-level rise. *Frontiers in Ecology and the Environment*, *13*(9), 468–476.

Hughes, M. W., Quigley, M. C., van Ballegooy, S., Deam, B. L., Bradley, B. A., & Hart, D. E. (2015). The sinking city: Earthquakes increase flood hazard in Christchurch, New Zealand. *GSA Today*, *25*(3), 4–10.

Intergovernmental Panel on Climate Change (IPCC) (2018). Global warming of 1.5° C: Summary for policy makers. Retrieved from www.ipcc.ch/site/assets/uploads/sites/2/2018/07/SR15_SPM_version_stand_alone_LR.pdf

Iwamura T., Fuller R. A., & Possingham, H. P. (2014) Optimal management of a multispecies shorebird flyway under sea-level rise. *Conservation Biology*, *28*(6), 1710–1720.

Ministry of the Environment (n.d.). *Impacts of sea level rise on the Avon River, Christchurch.* Retrieved from www.mfe.govt.nz/publications/climate-change/impacts-sea-level-rise-on%C2%A0-avon-river-christchurch%C2%A0/impacts-sea-level

Miskelly, C. M. (2013). Red-necked stint. In C. M. Miskelly (Ed.), *New Zealand Birds Online*. Retrieved from www.nzbirdsonline.org.nz

Paxton, K. L., Cohen, E. B., Paxton, E. H., Nemeth, Z., & Moore, F. R. (2014). El Niño-southern oscillation is linked to decreased energetic condition in long-distance migrants. *PLoS ONE* *9*(5), e95383. doi:10.1371/journal.pone.0095383

Quigley, M., & Duffy, B. (2020). Effects of earthquakes on flood hazards: A case study from Christchurch, New Zealand. *Geosciences*, *10*(3), 114.

Regenerate Christchurch Te Kowatawata. (n.d). *Flood risk in the residential red zone.* Retrieved from https://engage.regeneratechristchurch.nz/flooding

Szabo, M. J. (2013). [updated 2017]. Arctic skua. In C. M. Miskelly (Ed.) *New Zealand Birds Online*. Retrieved from www.nzbirdsonline.org.nz

Wikramanayake, E., Or, C., Costa, F., Wen, X., Cheung, F., & Shapiro, A. (2020). A climate adaptation strategy for Mai Po Inner Deep Bay Ramsar site: Steppingstone to climate proofing the East Asian–Australasian Flyway. *PLoS ONE*, *15*(10), e0239945. https://doi.org/10.1371/journal.pone.0239945

Wilson, H. B., Kendall, B. E., Fuller, R. A., Milton, D. A., & Possingham, H. P. (2011). Analyzing variability and the rate of decline of migratory shorebirds in Moreton Bay, Australia. *Conservation Biology*, *25*, 758–766.

Woodley, K. (2013). [updated 2017]. Bar-tailed godwit. In C. M. Miskelly (Ed.), *New Zealand Birds Online.* Retrieved from www.nzbirdsonline.org.nz

Xia, S., Yua, X., Millington, S., Liu, Y., Ji, Y., Wang, L., Hou, X. & Jiang, L. (2017). Identifying priority sites and gaps for the conservation of migratory waterbirds in China's coastal wetlands. *Biological Conservation* 210 (2017), 72–82.

Zarour, D. (2019). The effects of high lake levels due to climate change on lakeside communities and adjacent land use: Case study: Lake Ellesmere/Te Waihora. Thesis. Lincoln University.

Part 3

Innovative Solutions for Sea Level Rise

MECHANISMS OVERALL INDEX

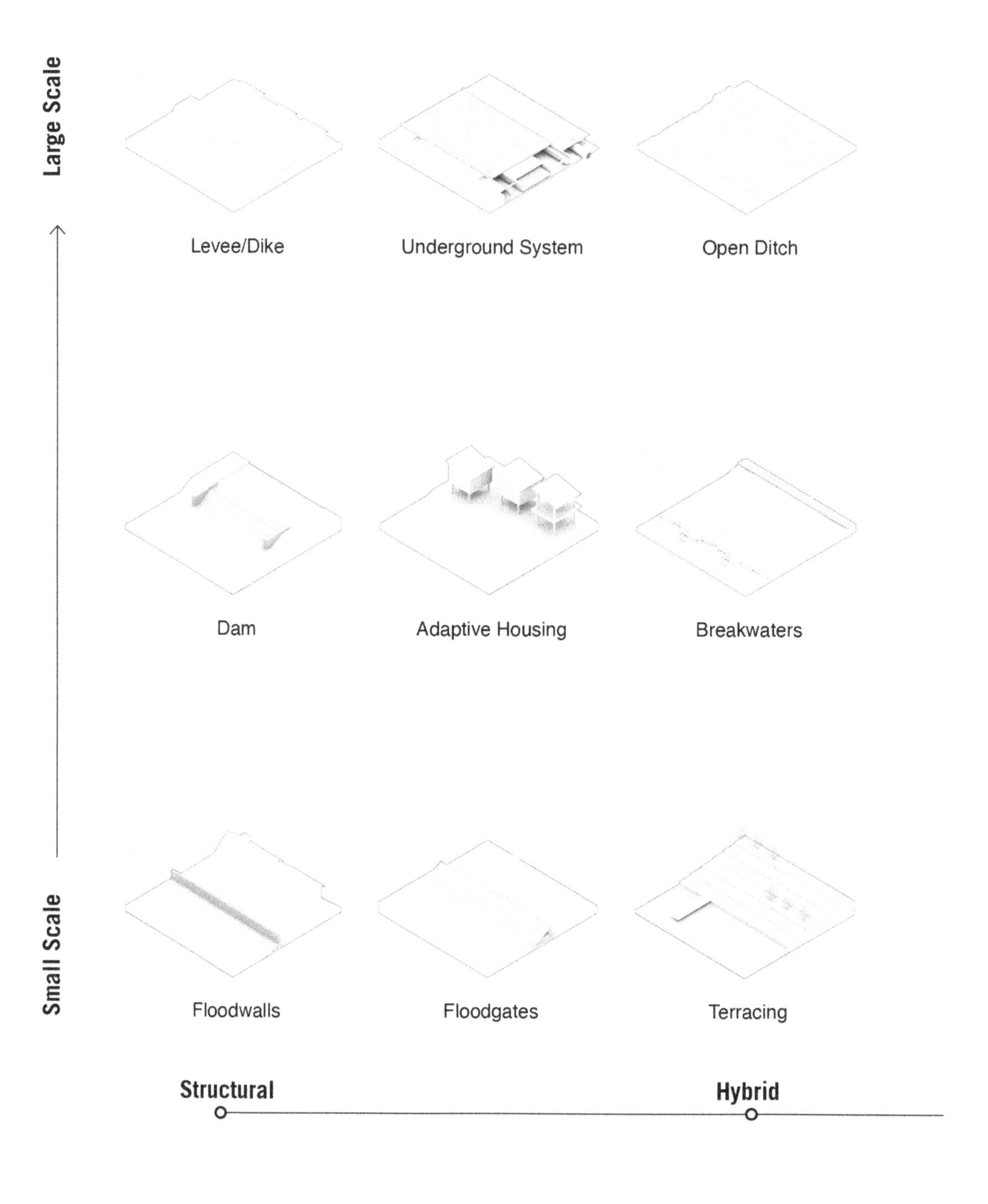

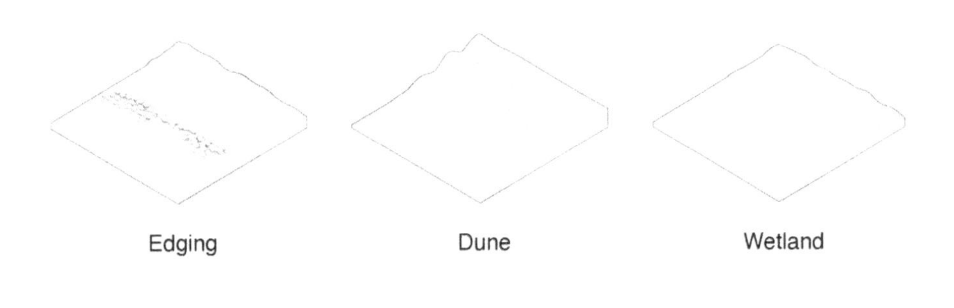

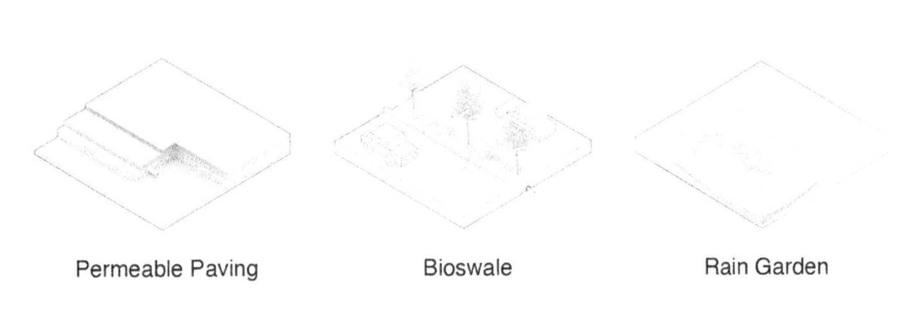

Hybrid **Non-Structural**

21

STRUCTURAL MECHANISMS

Zixu Qiao and Galen D. Newman

INDEX

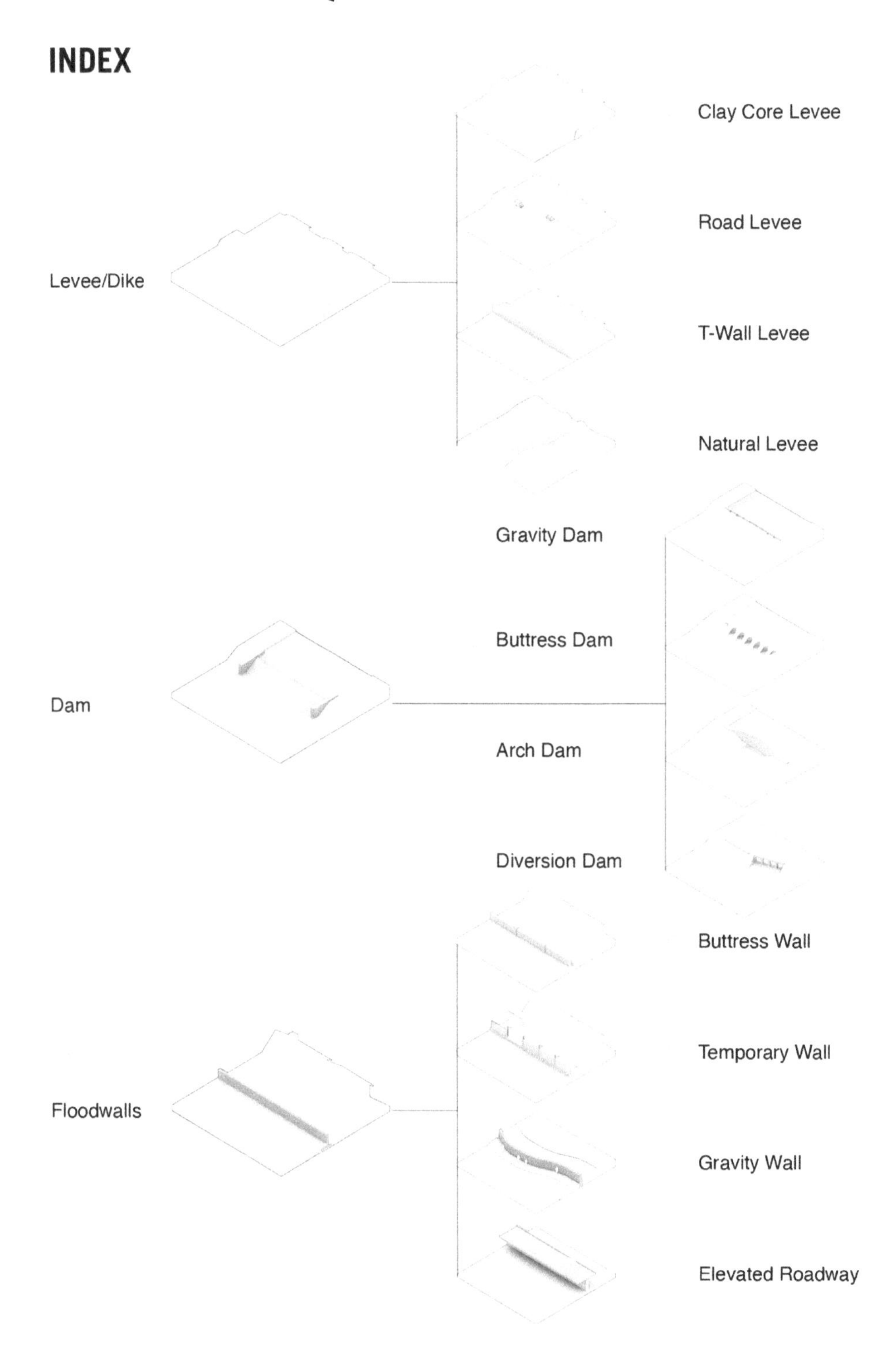

DOI:10.4324/9781003183419-29

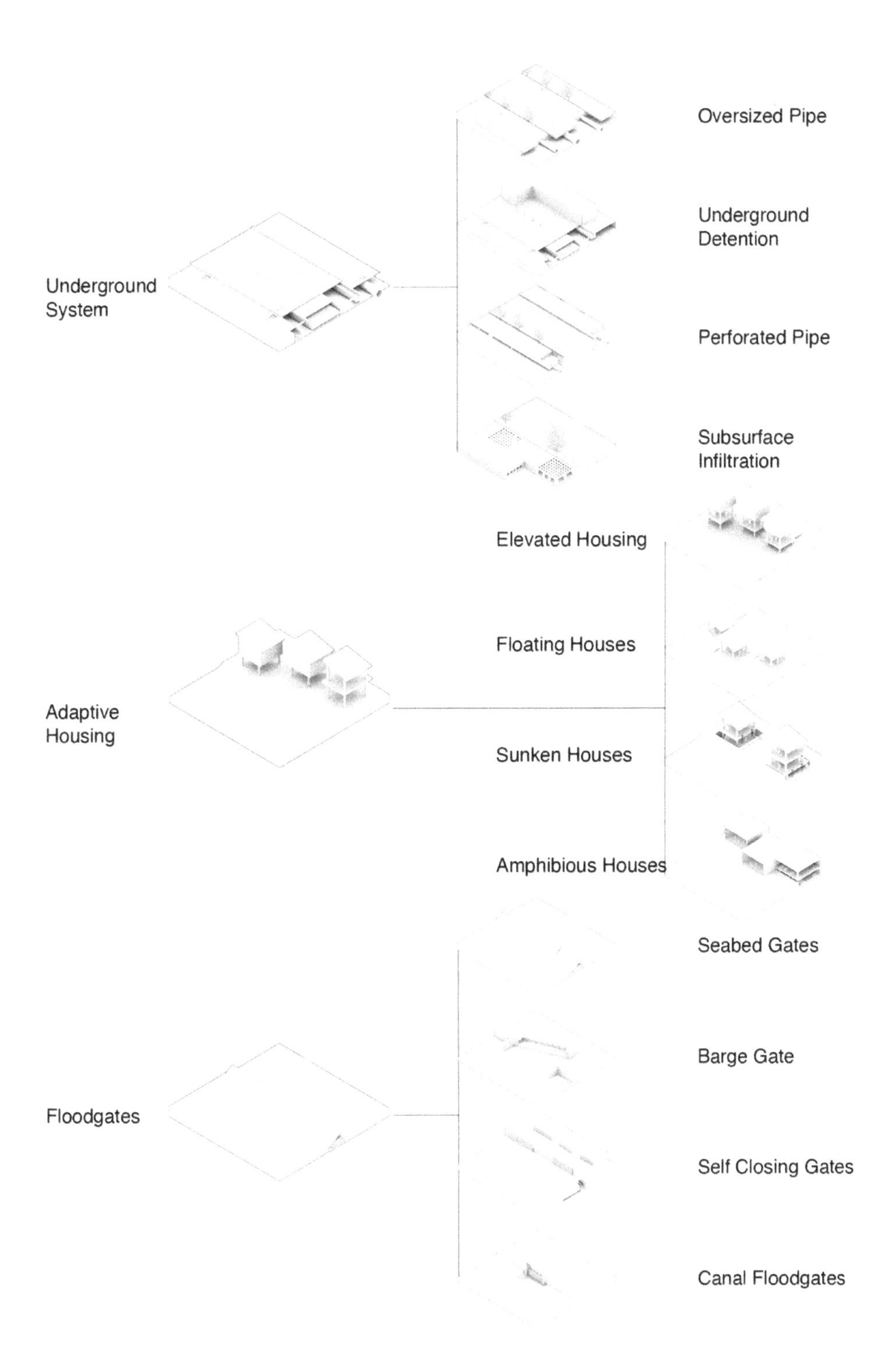
Oversized Pipe
Underground Detention
Underground System
Perforated Pipe
Subsurface Infiltration
Elevated Housing
Floating Houses
Adaptive Housing
Sunken Houses
Amphibious Houses
Seabed Gates
Barge Gate
Floodgates
Self Closing Gates
Canal Floodgates

A. Levee/Dike

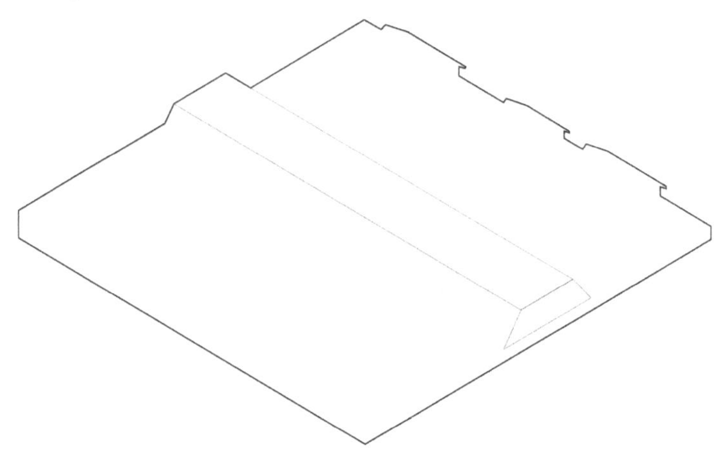

Figure 21.1

Man-made levees or dikes are artificial embankments which are built along the edges of a river or coastline to protect land from flooding and overflow (Van Zandt et al., 2020). Typically, levees are man-made hydraulic engineered structures located adjacent to a water body, along the coastline to protect land on another tangent side. In cities such as New Orleans, levees are designed to prevent inundation from hurricane surges. Dikes have similar functions and are structurally constructed similar to levees, but are much more common in areas such as the Netherlands. While the terms are used, oftentimes, interchangeably, levees protect land that is normally dry, but that may be flooded as water levels rise; dikes protect land that would naturally be underwater most of the time. Natural vegetation with fibrous root systems such as grasses are sometimes planted atop a levee's bank so that erosion will be kept to a minimum. Typically, dikes and levees have a maximum settled height of 6 feet and a minimum levee rest width of 5 feet.

Location

Riverside, coastline

Ability to Address Coastal Hazards

Storm surge
Wave force
Flooding
Erosion

Cost

● ● ○ ○ ○

Compared with structural mechanisms

● ● ● ● ○

Compared with overall mechanisms

Scale

● ● ● ● ●

City/Regional

A1. Clay Core Levee

The most inexpensive levees and dikes are constructed using clay, silt, or sand atop a clay core, often on a foundation of erodible substrata (Wu et al., 2011).

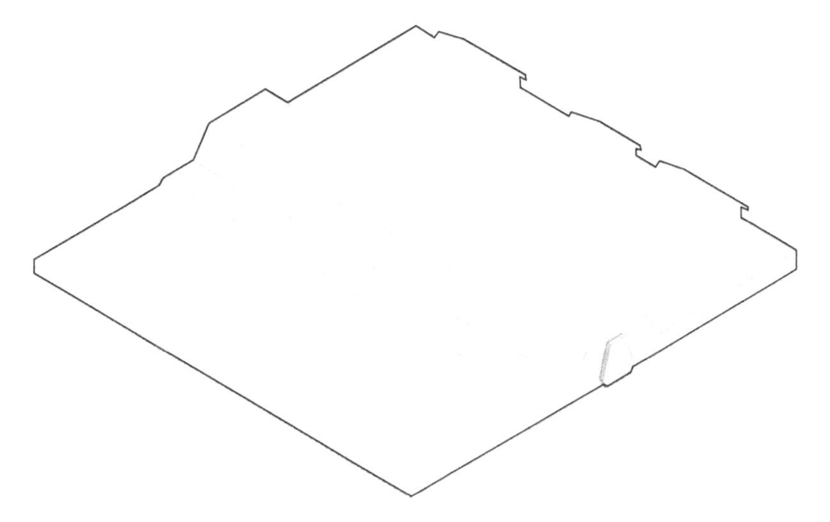

Figure 21.2

A2. Road Levee

To save the space, roadways can be elevated or built atop of an earthen levee, doubling as levees and transportation corridors.

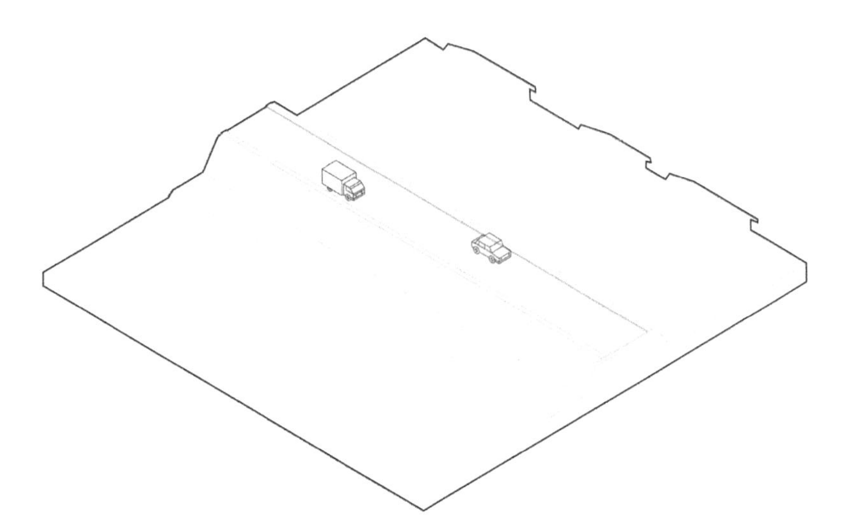

Figure 21.3

A3. T-Wall Levee

T-walls are solid concrete walls, shaped like inverted T-shaped blockades (Kim & Newman, 2029). They consist of a concrete foundation, an upward extending high flood wall panel, a long metal pile, and a wide metal sheet pile. T-walls (and I-walls) are often used when space is limited for an earthen levee.

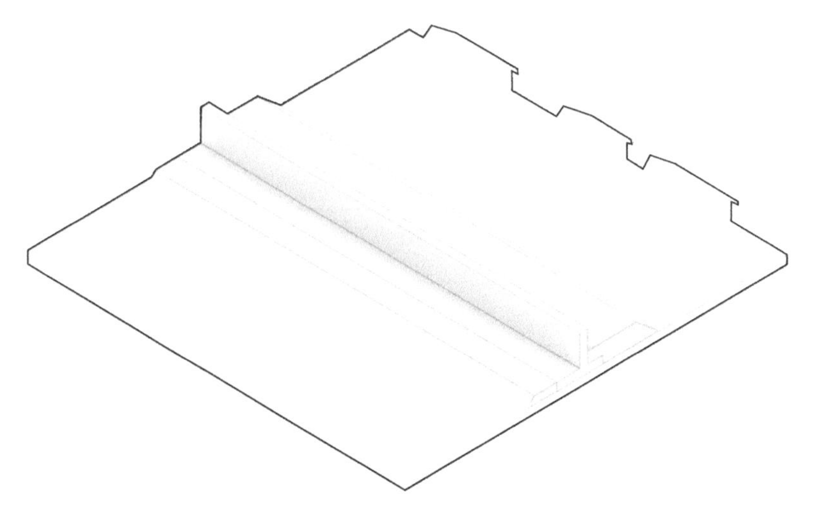

Figure 21.4

A4. Natural Levee

While not a structural mechanism, we are including natural levees here to simply have them listed with the levees. Natural levees are formed by the process of overbank flood sedimentation through time, depending on the process of flood inundation within the floodplain. Like artificial dikes, their function is to reduce the overflow of flooding.

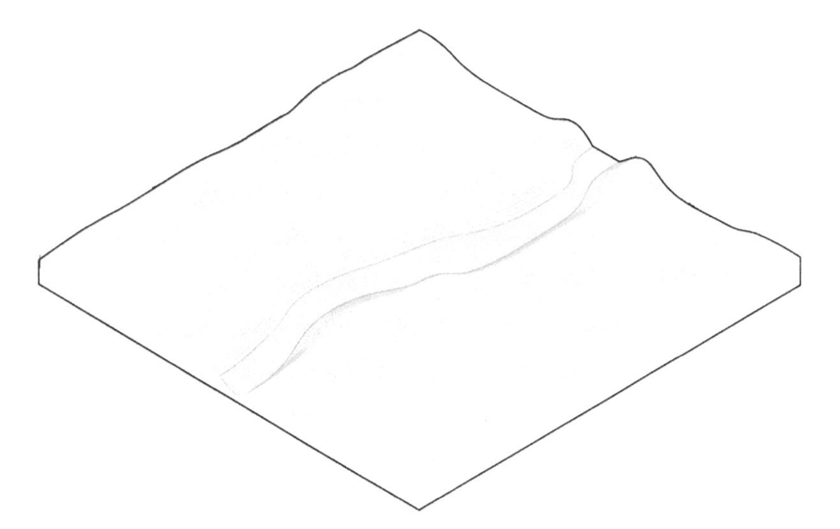

Figure 21.5

B. Dam

A dam is a barrier for preventing the flow of water. Dams are built to provide water for human consumption, for irrigating arid and semiarid lands, or for use in industrial processes. They also can be used to increase the amount of water available for generating hydroelectric power, to reduce peak discharge of floodwater created by large storms or heavy snowmelt, or to increase the depth of water in a river in order to improve navigation and allow barges and ships to travel more easily (Jackson et al., 2020).

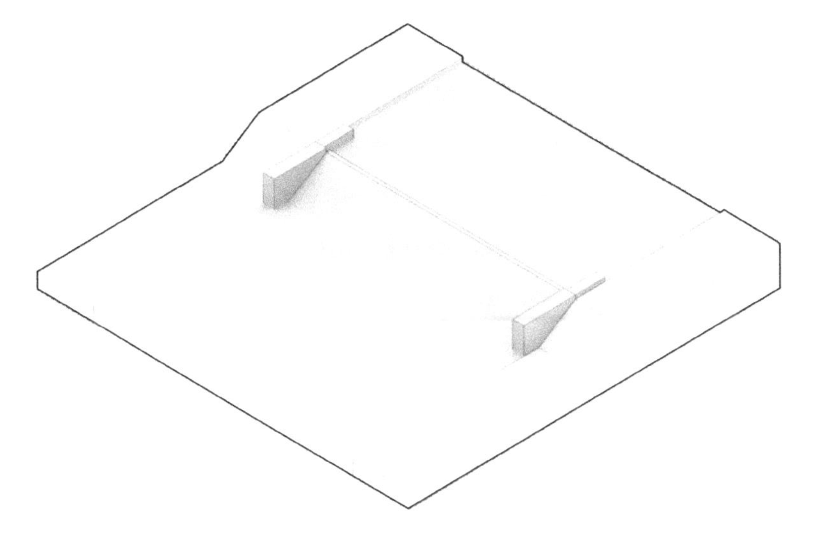

Figure 21.6

Location

Across a stream, a river, or a lake

Ability to Address Coastal Hazards

Storm surge
Wave force
Flooding
Erosion

Cost

• • • • ○

Compared with structural mechanisms

• • • • ○

Compared with overall mechanisms

Scale

• • • • •

City/Regional

B1. Gravity Dam

A gravity dam is a structure designed to withstand loads by its own weight and by its resistance to sliding and overturning on its foundation (Boes & Hager, 2003).

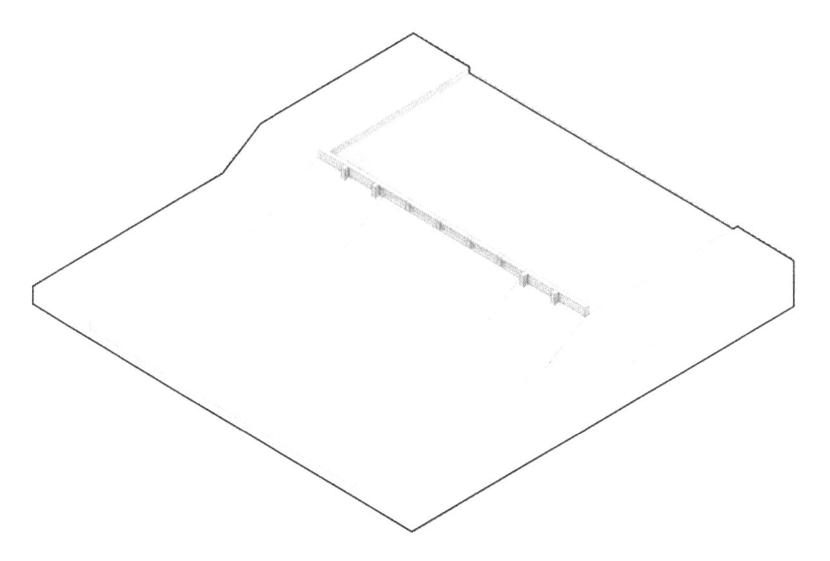

Figure 21.7

B2. Buttress Dam

Buttress dams are concrete or masonry structures usually comprising inclined panels or arches supported by buttresses (Boes & Hager, 2003). Typically, buttress dams are made of reinforced concrete and can be designed as either curved or straight.

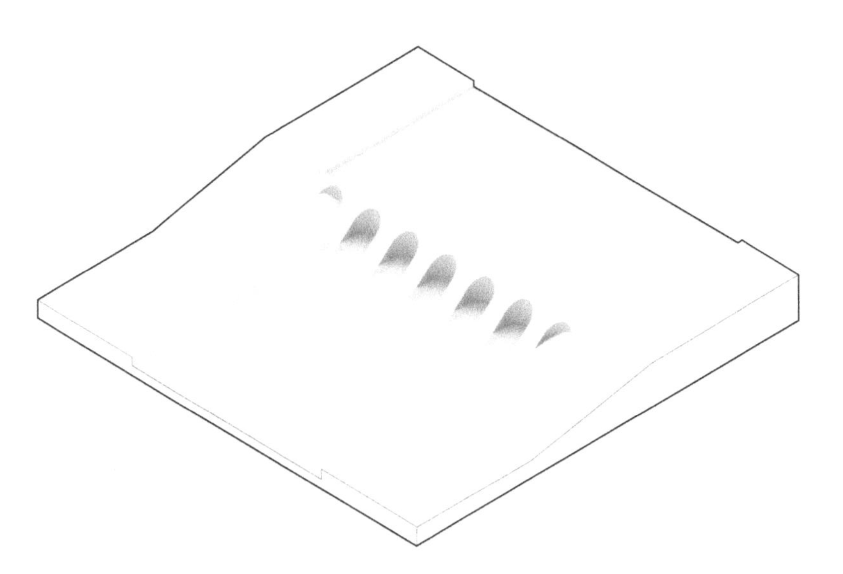

Figure 21.8

B3. Arch Dam

Arch dams are normally curve shaped concrete walls. They are suitable for river valleys or narrow gorges but require large amounts of concrete for construction.

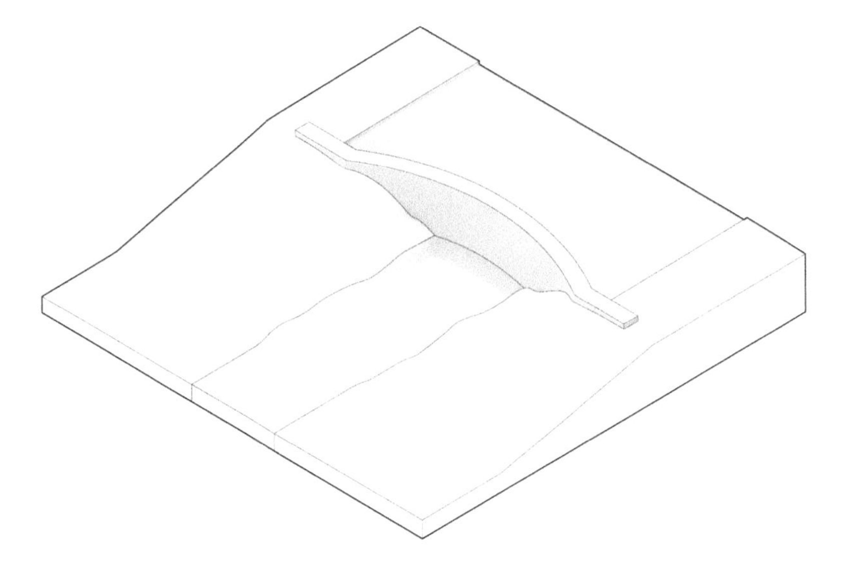

Figure 21.9

B4. Diversion Dam

Diversion dams are designed to divert water from a stream or a river. They are used to divert all or part of the water from a given waterway in such a manner that it can be controlled and used beneficially for uses such as irrigation, develop renewable energy systems, or recreational activities (Roozbeh, 2020).

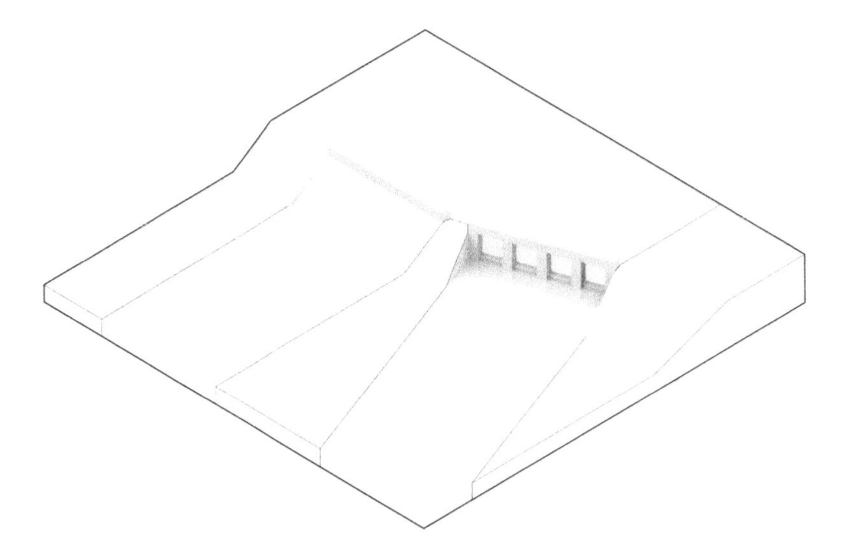

Figure 21.10

C. Floodwalls

Similar to a levee, floodwalls are built to prevent the inundation of high-level water; however, they are generally in areas requiring limited space. A floodwall can either be permanent or temporary, is usually small in scale (e.g. retaining wall or terrace) and sometimes is coupled with a smaller scaled floodgate to control water flow. Compared to levees, floodwalls are also generally more resistant to erosion.

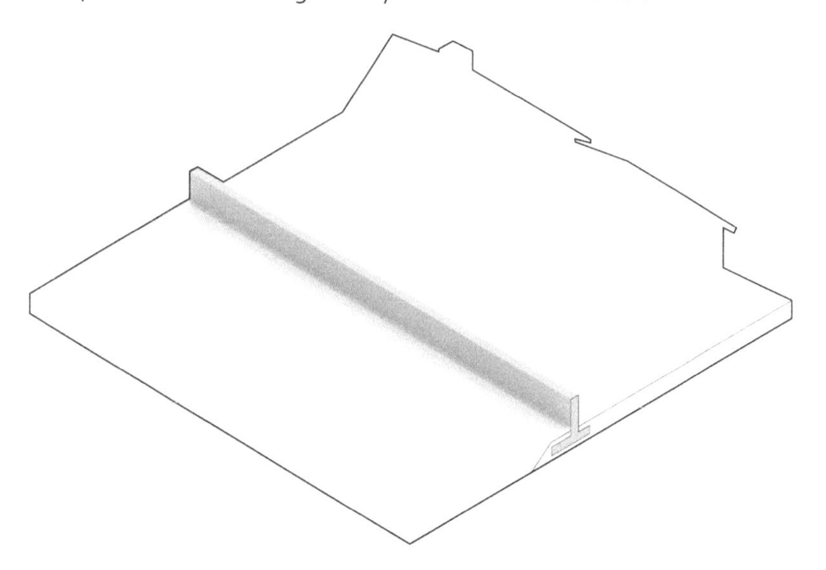

Figure 21.11

Location

Riverside, Coastline

Ability to Address Coastal Hazards

Storm surge
Wave force
Flooding
Erosion

Cost

Compared with structural mechanisms

• • • ○ ○

Compared with overall mechanisms

• • • • ○

Scale

• • • ○ ○

Community/City/Regional

C1. Buttress Wall

A buttress is a structure for reinforcing or supporting a floodwall which is typically used to construct a fixed or permanent floodwall.

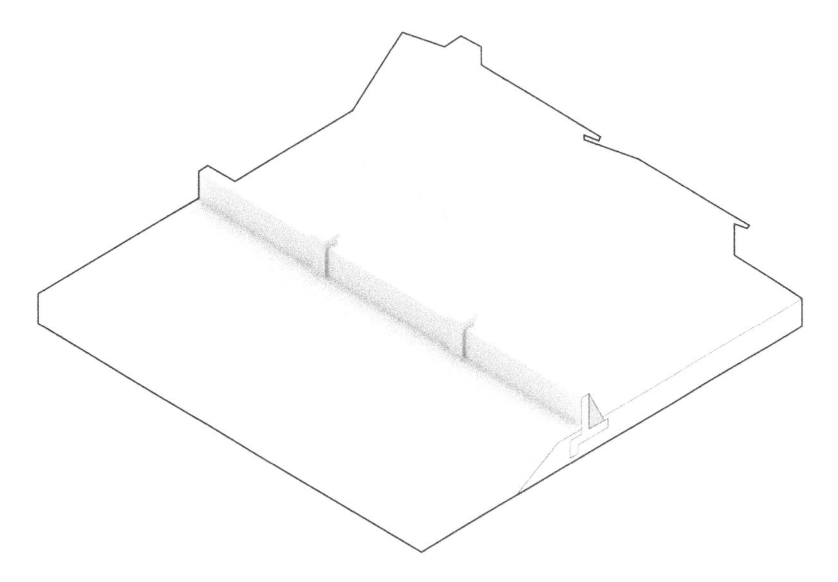

Figure 21.12

C2. Temporary Wall

Temporary flood walls are designed to accommodate construction worksite dewatering, flood control, and other critical or rapid-deployment situations requiring effective spill containment (Newman et al., 2016).

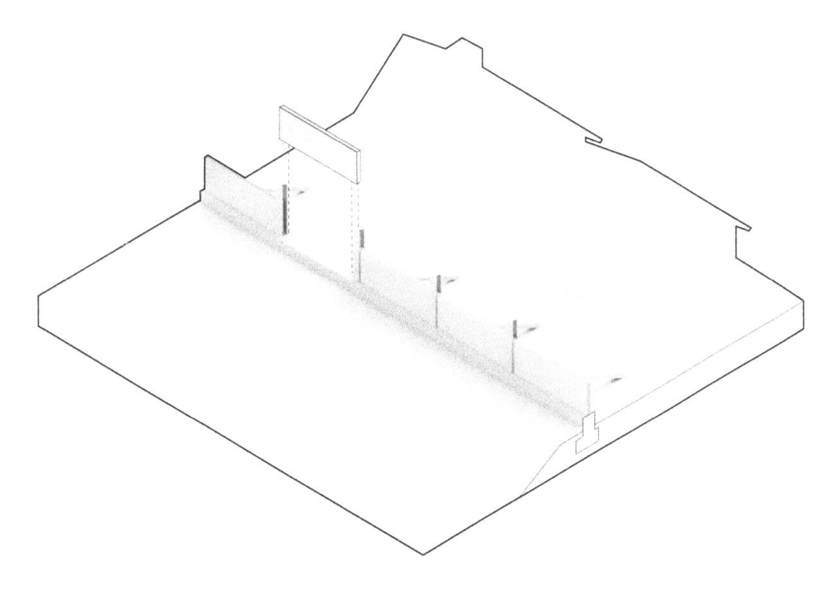

Figure 21.13

C3. Gravity Wall

One of the least complexly constructed floodwall structures, gravity walls are weighted down by their own gravity at the bottom. Structural stability is based on the mass of the wall; the higher the wall, the more weight that is needed on its bottom.

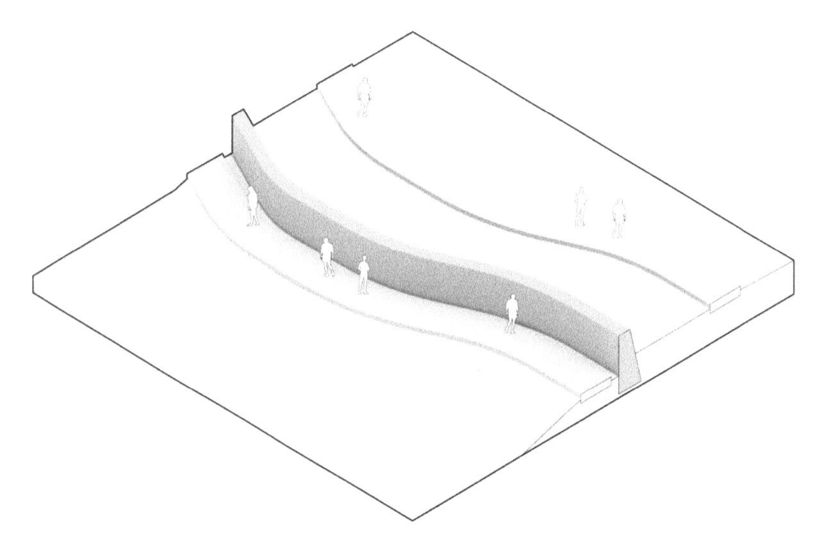

Figure 21.14

C4. Elevated Roadway

The lower portion of the structural composite of a roadway is used as a floodwall to resist flood water. Transportation operation occurs atop the wall.

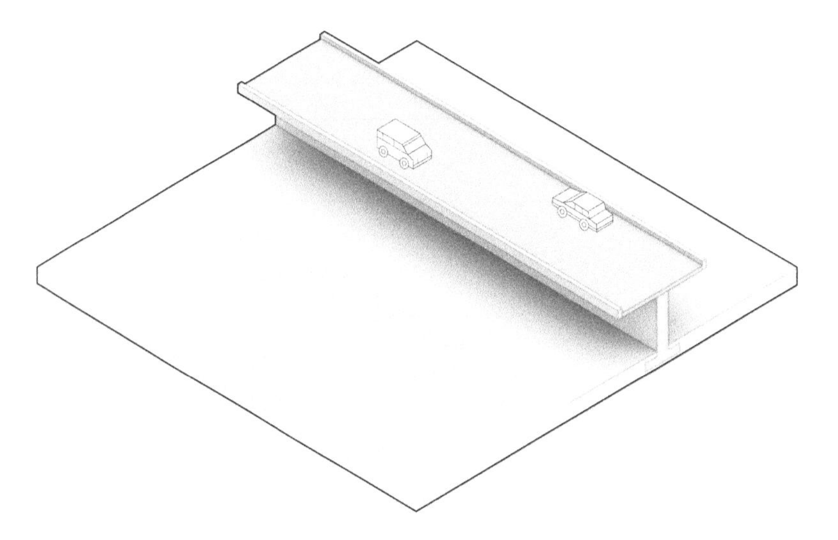

Figure 21.15

D. Underground System

Underground systems are typically utilized within urban areas with limited space to systematically control floodwaters and rainwater. The underground facilities act like a sewer to capture water from the street level. Once the collection device is filled to capacity, the flow of rainwater is normally then transported to the sea or rivers.

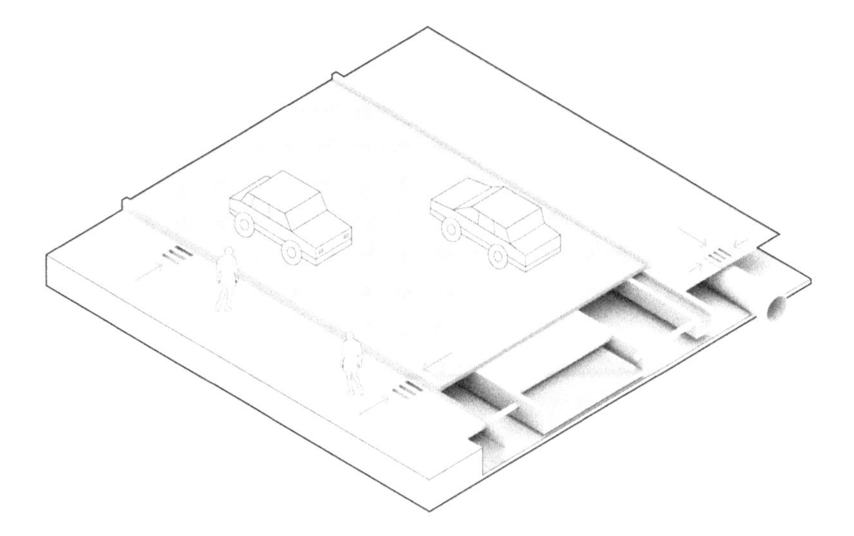

Figure 21.16

Location

Urban, Community, Underground

Ability to Address Coastal Hazards

Storm surge
Wave force
Flooding
Erosion

Cost

Compared with structural mechanisms

● ● ● ○ ○

Compared with overall mechanisms

● ● ● ● ○

Scale

● ● ○ ○ ○

Site/Community/Regional

D1. Oversized Pipe

Ideally, the larger diameter of the pipe, the more rainwater or grey-water it can carry. The optimum balance between drain line diameter and water flow volume should be accurately calculated to determine pipe size.

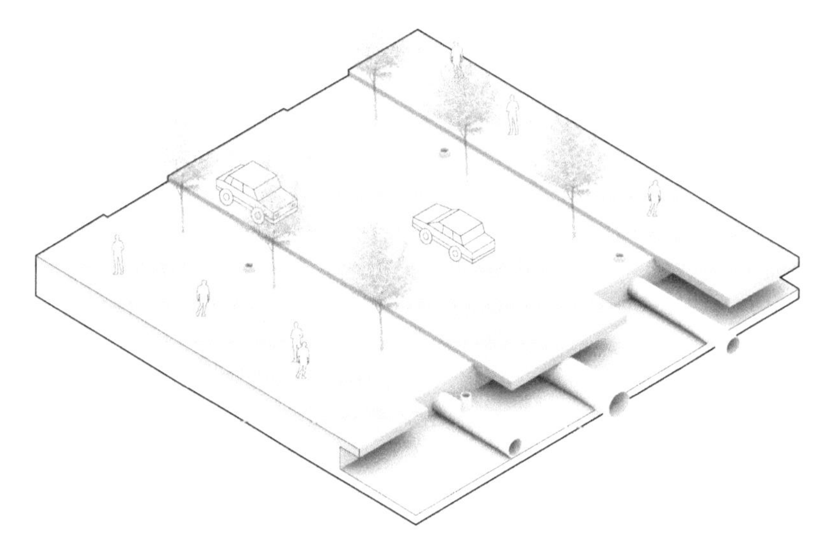

Figure 21.17

D2. Underground Detention

Underground detention is used to store excess stormwater runoff, decrease runoff volume and flow rates, enhance water quality, and assist with erosion control. This approach allows for more developable land while also supporting runoff capture in already developed areas.

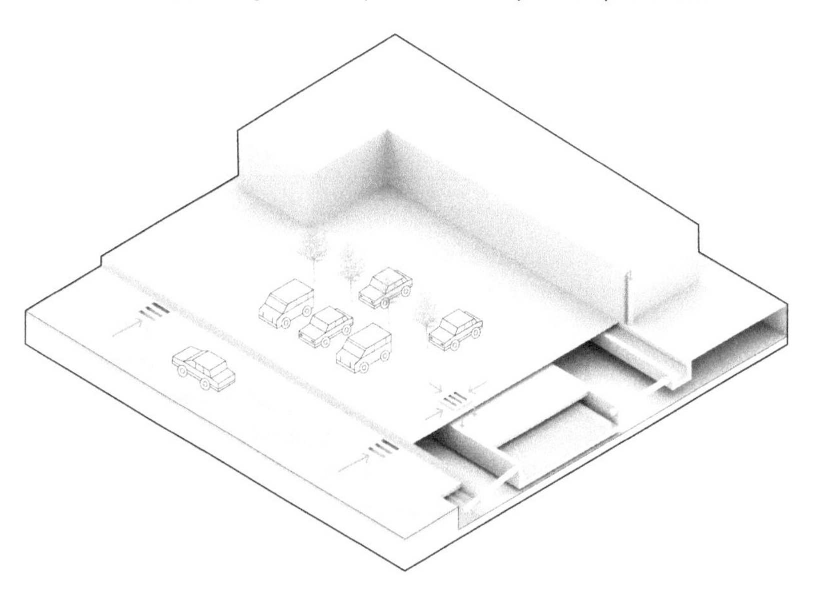

Figure 21.18

D3. Perforated Pipe

Perforated pipes are designed so that water can enter and exit through a myriad of small holes along the drainage pipe. This allows the excess stormwater to slowly drain into the ground and be released to multiple areas.

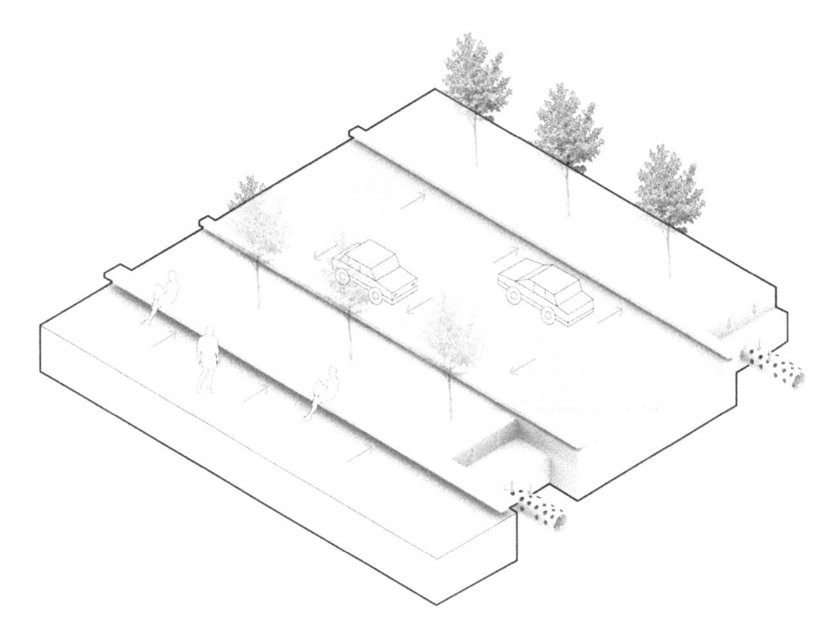

Figure 21.19

D4. Subsurface Infiltration

Subsurface infiltration consists of an engineered layer of pervious soil and vegetation with storage pipes located beneath landscaped or paved surfaces. It is typically used for temporary water storage and infiltration of stormwater runoff into the subsurface or aquifer.

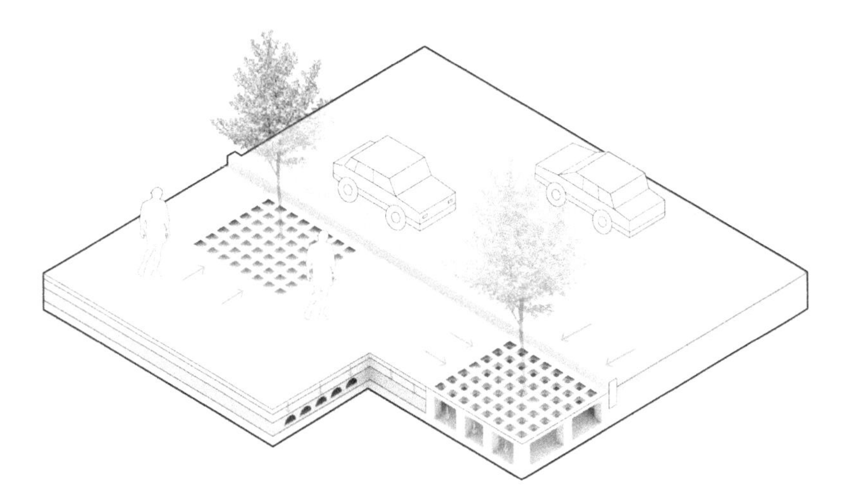

Figure 21.20

E. Adaptive Housing

The adaptive housing is designed to allow for flooding to occur while still remaining inhabitable as they are adaptable to surrounding environmental conditions such as flooding or extreme weather conditions. In the context of sea level rise, the architecture built near rivers and seas are normally elevated, tilted, or floatable to avoid flood damage.

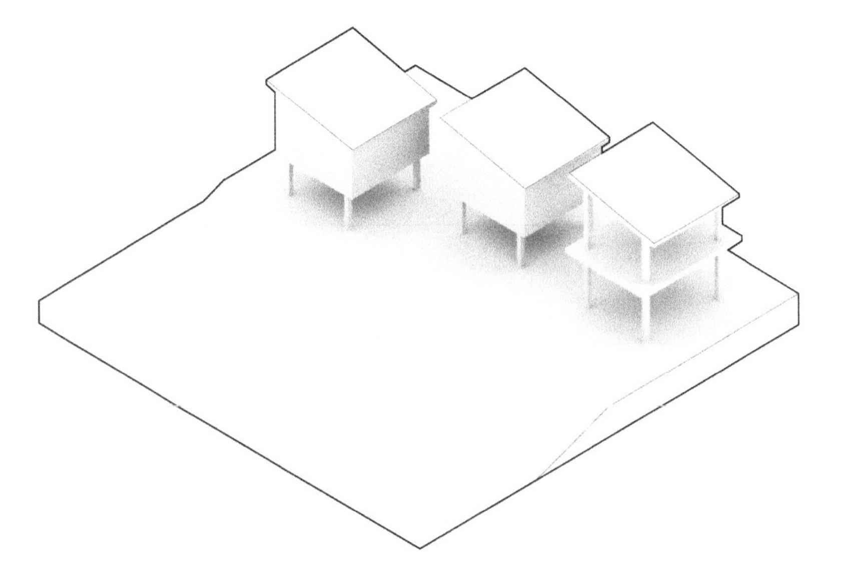

Figure 21.21

Location

Coast, river, lake

Ability to Address Coastal Hazards

Storm surge
Wave force
Flooding
Erosion

Cost

Compared with structural mechanisms

● ● ● ○ ○

Compared with overall mechanisms

● ● ● ● ○

Scale

● ● ● ○ ○

Site/Community

E1. Elevated Housing

Elevated houses are built to avoid floodwater through the allowance of flooding below their bottom floors; the bottom floor is elevated beyond the highest floodwater in the inundated area. Typically small in scale, the area of such houses is normally built on a bare reinforced concrete frame system of about 20–25m², which is sufficient for basic activities of a household of 2 to 5 people during a flood (Ngo et al., 2020).

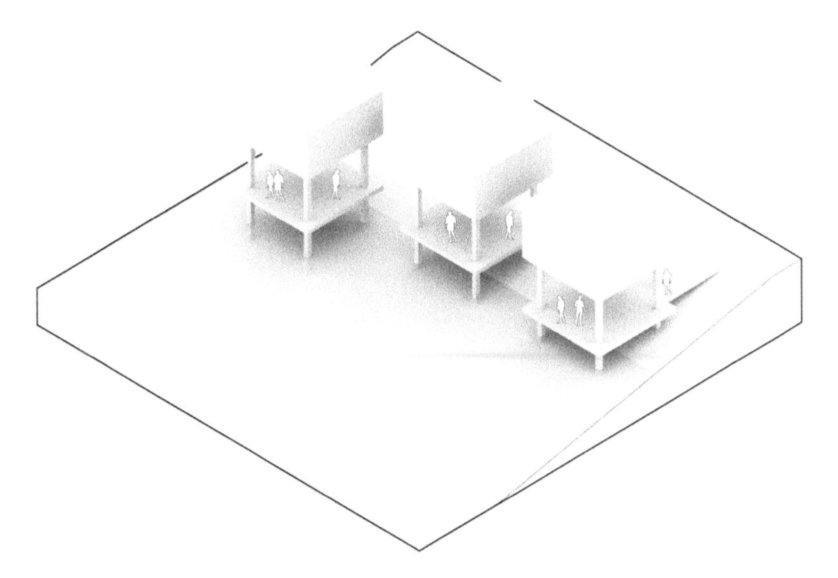

Figure 21.22

E2. Floating Houses

Floating houses are designed to adapt to rising water levels through the ability to rise as floodwater rises and are typically built within an existing water body. When the water/sea level rises, the house is able to float and move upwards.

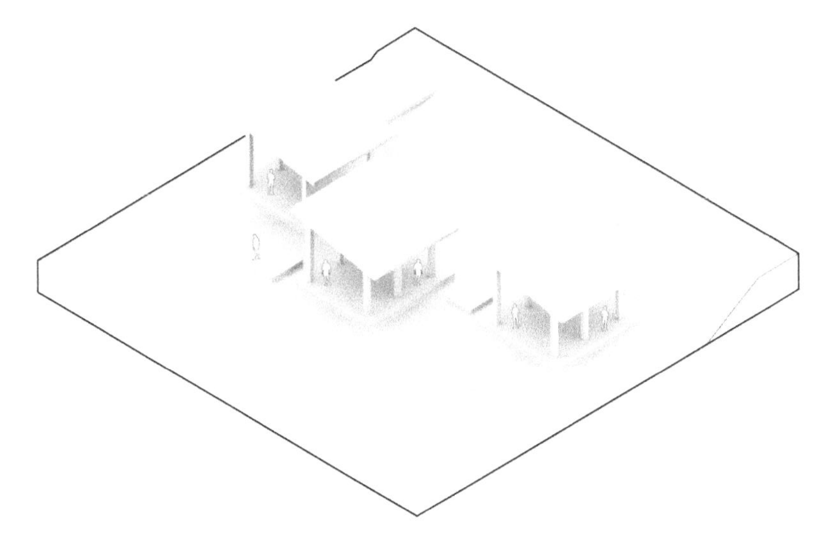

Figure 21.23

E3. Amphibious Houses

Similar to the floating house, amphibious housing is built to adapt to rising water. Instead of permanently within a body of water like a floating house, the amphibious house is built above the water, and is designed to float only as the water or sea level rises.

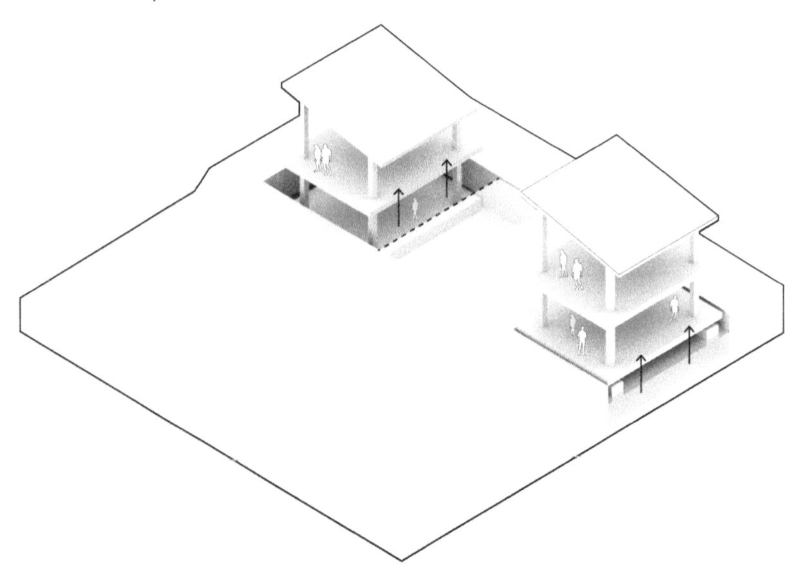

Figure 21.24

E4. Sunken Houses

Sunken houses are, basically, multi-story houses that are evacuated on the lower buildable areas and allow the bottom floors to be flooded. They are built, normally, around half under the water and require a strong foundation. In some urban designs, sunken houses have even been used programmatically as museums.

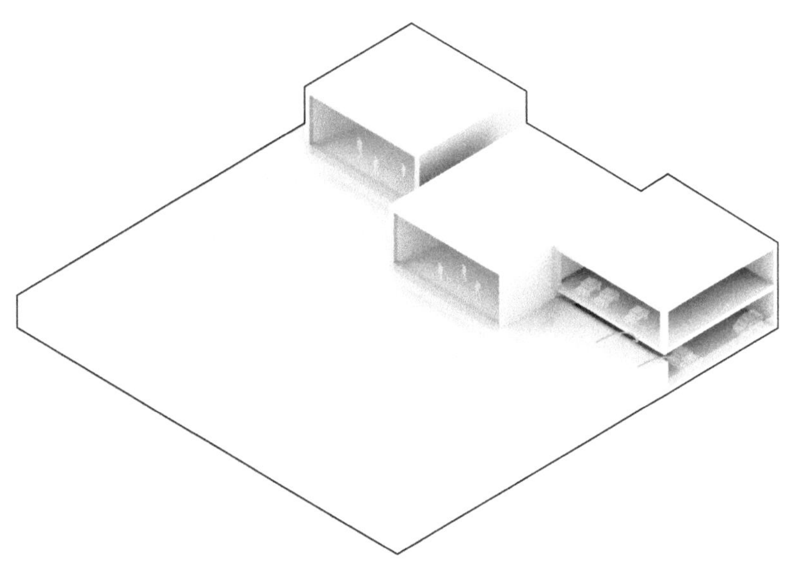

Figure 21.25

F. Floodgates

Floodgates are used for controlling or releasing the flow of water into or out of a given area. Often, they are used in connection with a levee, dam, or smaller-scaled flood barrier such as a floodwall. The size/scale of the floodgate can vary but they are normally designed to set the crest height of a spillway within a dam, control the water level of a creek, or block surge waters from a community.

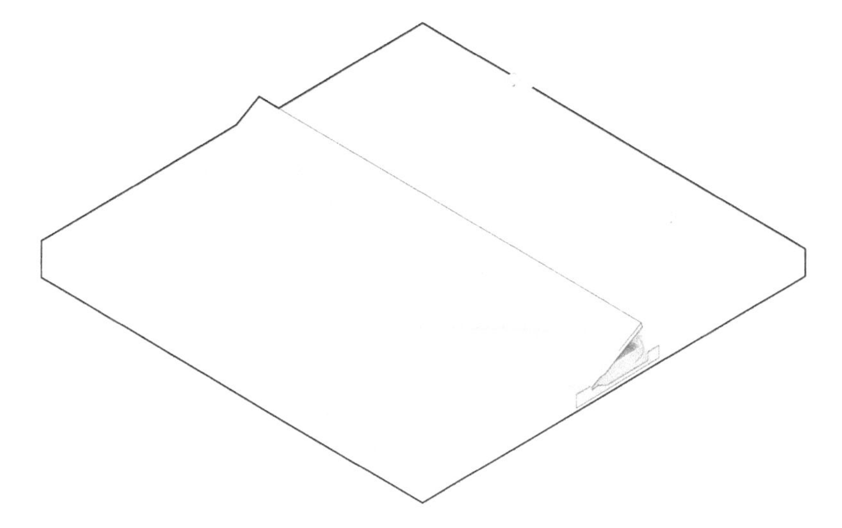

Figure 21.26

Location

Coast, river, lake

Ability to Address Coastal Hazards

Storm surge
Wave force
Flooding
Erosion

Cost

Compared with structural mechanisms

● ● ○ ○ ○

Compared with overall mechanisms

● ● ● ○ ○

Scale

● ● ● ○ ○

Site/Community/Regional

F1. Seabed Gates

Seabed gates are used frequently in places such as Venice, Italy. When not in use, they allow areas to fill; when needed, compressed air is pumped in, expelling the water and forcing the gate to pivot upward until it breaches the surface and acts as a seawall.

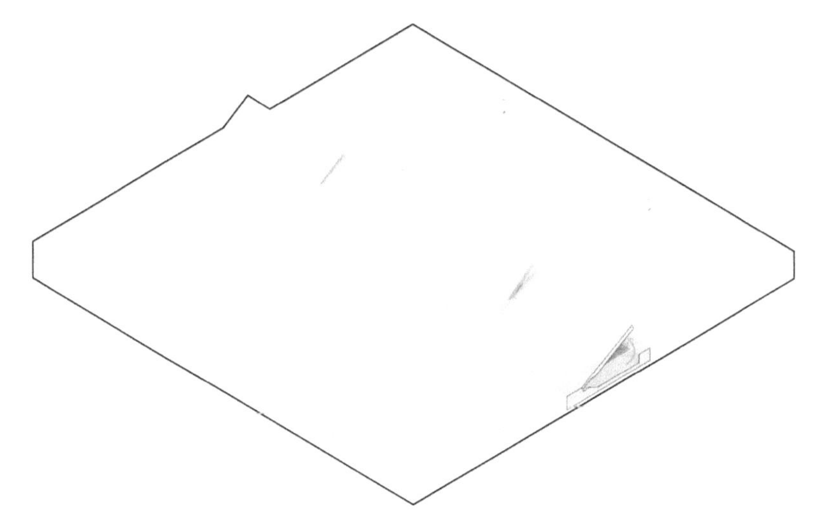

Figure 21.27

F2. Barge Gate

The structure of a barge gate is designed to close bypass channels used by ships when the main gate is closed for maintenance. Although the risk of a barge gate failing is comparatively small, just a 1 in 318 chance per year, they are extremely high-cost in regards to regular maintenance.

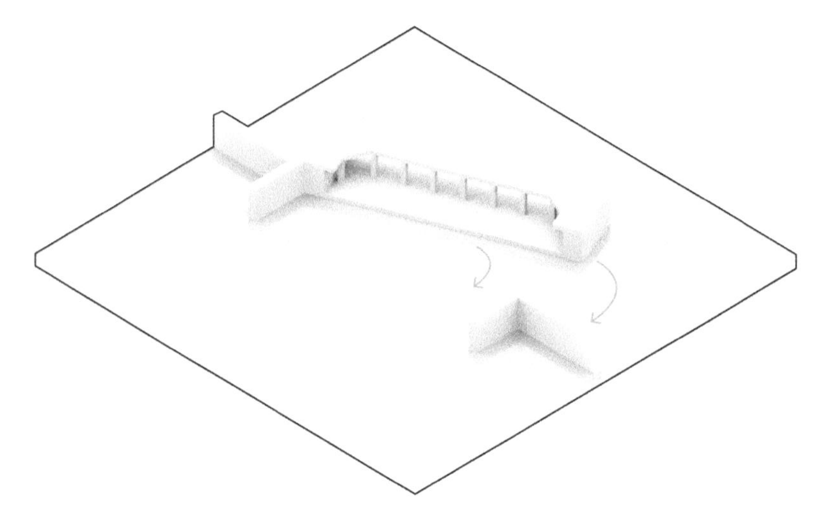

Figure 21.28

F3. Self-Closing Gates

Self-closing gates are relatively passive flood prevention systems requiring no human intervention. They are much smaller than seabed gates and can be used for riverbanks, public areas, or residential houses. In essence, they are small-scaled sluice gates that act as mini-seawalls when needed.

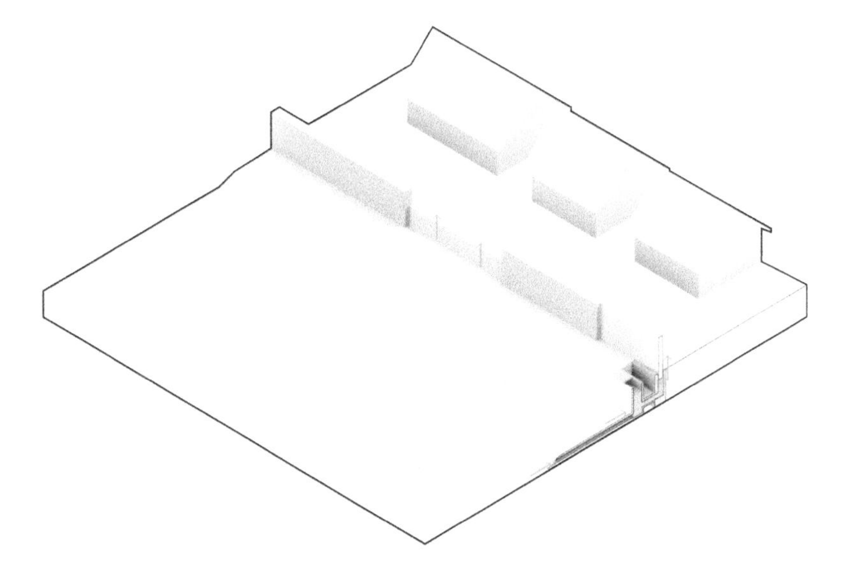

Figure 21.29

F4. Canal Floodgates

Canal floodgates, sometimes referred to as sluice gates, are relatively small floodgates typically built on canals that can be raised or lowered and used to block rising water. They are temporary dams which can be opened and closed as needed.

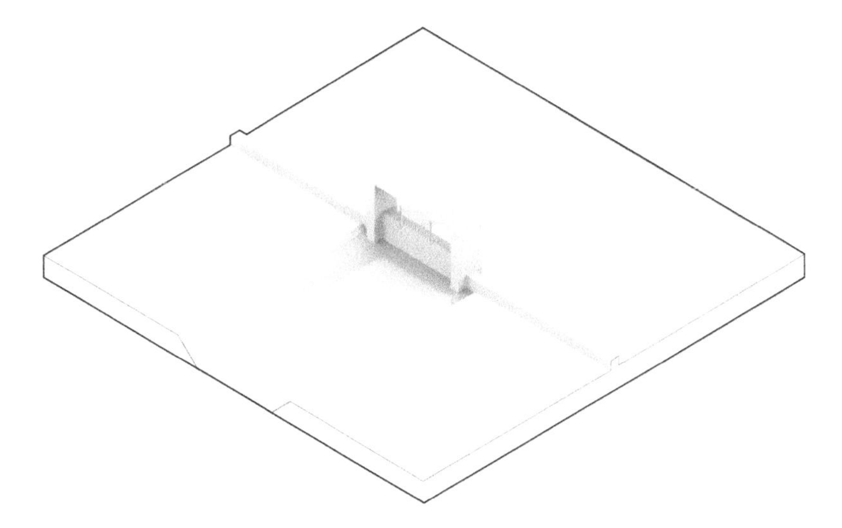

Figure 21.30

Conclusions

While structural mechanisms can be a powerful amenity in lowering flood risk, decreasing vulnerabilities, and counteracting the probable impacts of eventual sea level rise, they can also require large areas of space to be implemented and can be extremely expensive. For example, while dikes and levees can protect large tracts of land from floodwaters, they also occupy a significant amount of linear space. Further, if not planned correctly, extending the heights of dikes and levees to combat rising sea levels can exacerbate these issues, as they need to be implemented at a height tall enough to provide a required protection level while anticipating this level will rise in the future. They can also be particularly difficult to implement in already developed areas. The ability to block incoming tides and floodwaters make dikes and levees one of the best structural defense mechanisms against flooding. However, overtopping of such lines of defense can cause excess drainage necessities for pumping floodwaters out of the areas enclosed by the dikes. Compounding this, the forcing of floodwaters to remain within the flooded body of water can result in increased downstream flooding in unprotected or less well protected areas. Maintenance can also be costly as breakages or fails in these mechanisms can result in serious inland damage.

Dams can have similar positive and negative issues as dikes and levees. However, they have the ability to control water flow allowance for the production of hydropower, a relatively green energy. The regulation of water levels through damming can also allow for targeted irrigation and the capabilities to trap water containing hazardous materials so that communities are not threatened. While also threatened by breakage threats and cost issues, sediment buildup is also a major issue related to dams. Further, damming up natural bodies of water can cause ecological imbalances or completely alter natural land coverage of areas no longer receiving hydrological flow.

Floodgates and floodwalls can suffer from many of the issues related to dams, albeit on a much smaller scale. Floodwalls are a bit more flexible in that they can be much more easily removed than the permeant floodwalls. Both are available at multiple heights and help protect the surrounding areas through the blockage of water without significant alteration to inland areas. Relatedly, and also similar to dams, floodwalls allow water level depths of small water bodies to be adjusted to desired levels.

Finally, adaptive houses provide a way of living with floods that adjusts itself as the sea level rises. While expensive, such approaches allow for both the enjoyment of water and protection from it. In some cases, depending on how many adaptive houses are needed, costs can exceed even damming or floodgates. These housing types also allow for development within water, so no new land is needed. However, more advanced construction techniques are still needed to prevent failing of flotation of such houses during extreme flood events such as storm surge.

References

Boes, R. M., & Hager, W. H. (2003). Hydraulic design of stepped spillways. *Journal of Hydraulic Engineering*, *129*(9), 671–679.

Jackson, D. C., & Brown, J. G. (2020, March 24). Dam. *Encyclopedia Britannica*. Retrieved from www.britannica.com/technology/dam-engineering

Kim, Y. J., & Newman, G. (2019). Climate change preparedness: Comparing future urban growth and flood risk in Amsterdam and Houston. *Sustainability*, *11*(4), 1048.

Newman, G., Kim, J. H., Berke, P., Merrill, J., Wang, Y., & Li, Q. (2016). From idle grounds to ecological infrastructure: The resilient design of Manchester neighborhood in Houston. *Landscape Architecture Frontiers*, 4(5), 68–84

Ngo, L. M., Kieu, L. T., Hoang, H. Y., & Nguyen, H. B. (2020). Experiences of housing adapted to sea level rise and applicability for houses in the Can Gio District, Ho Chi Minh City, Vietnam. *Sustainability*, *12*(9), 3743.

Van Zandt, S., Masterson, J., Newman G., & Meyer, M. (2020, June 29). *Engaged Research for Community Resilience to Climate Change.* First Edition. Cambridge, MA: Elsevier. ISBN: 9780128155752

Wu, W., & ASCE/EWRI Task Committee on Dam/Levee Breaching. (2011). Earthen embankment breaching. *Journal of Hydraulic Engineering* *137*(12), 1549–1564.

22

HYBRID MECHANISMS

Zixu Qiao and Galen D. Newman

INDEX

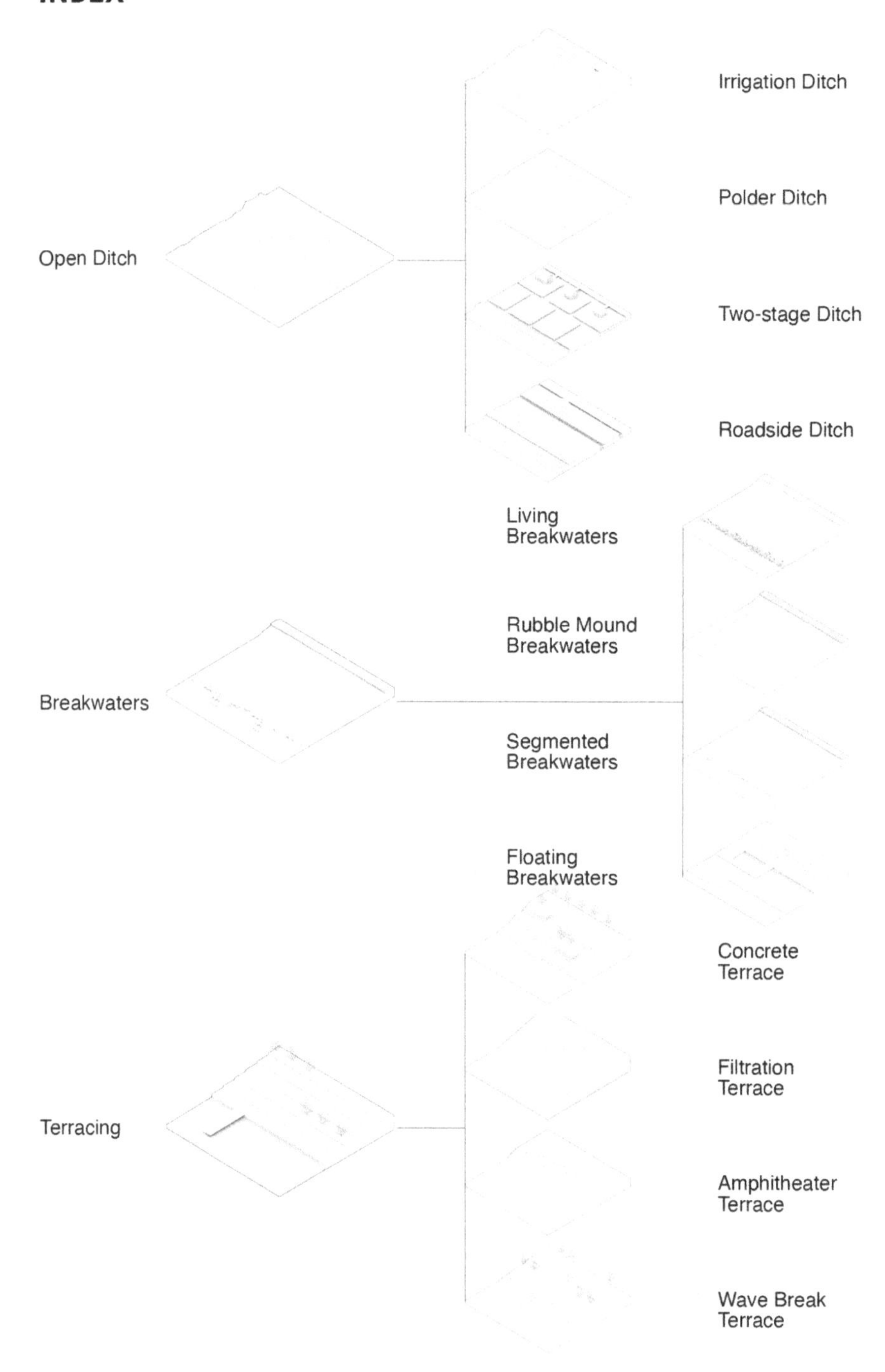

DOI: 10.4324/9781003183419-30

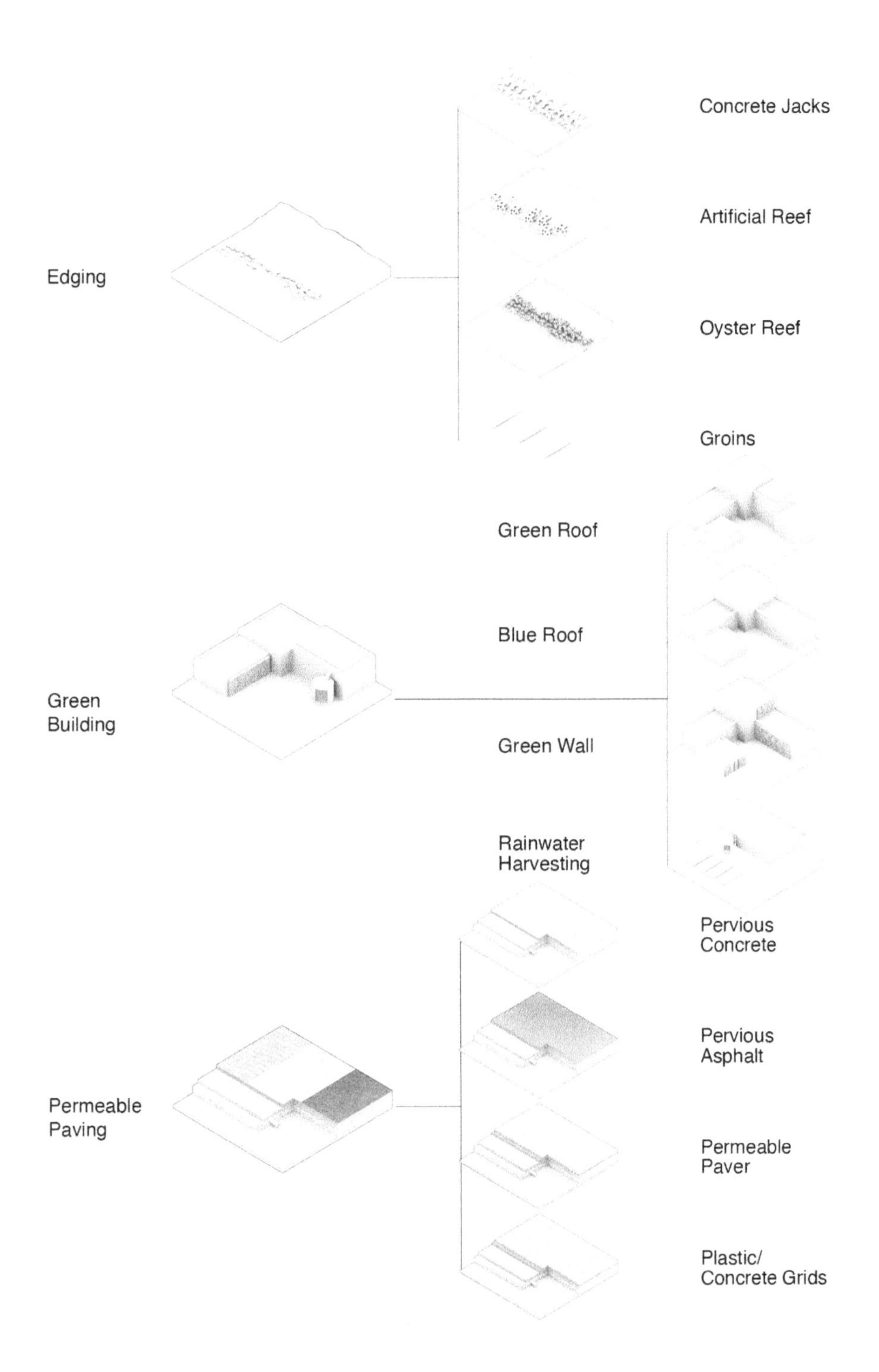
Concrete Jacks
Artificial Reef
Edging
Oyster Reef
Groins
Green Roof
Blue Roof
Green Building
Green Wall
Rainwater Harvesting
Pervious Concrete
Pervious Asphalt
Permeable Paving
Permeable Paver
Plastic/ Concrete Grids

G. Open Ditch

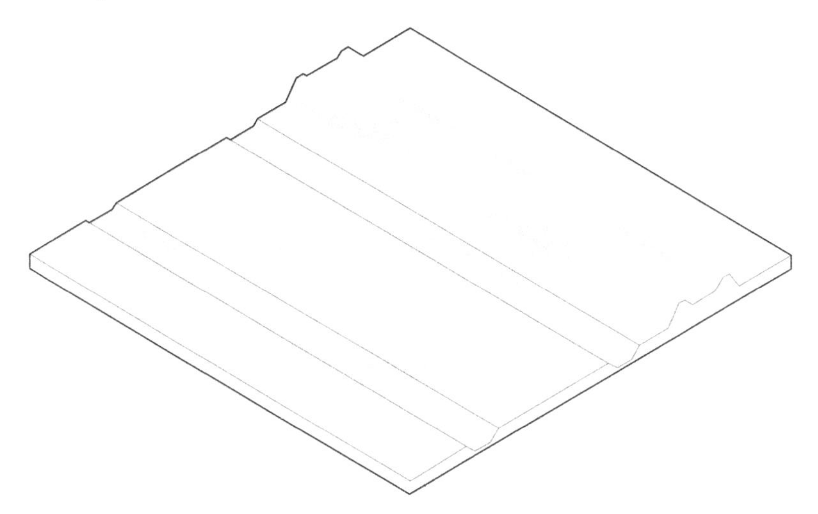

Figure 22.1

An open ditch, also referred to as a drainage ditch, is a narrow and uncovered channel that cuts into the ground on one side of a road or field, typically for carrying wastewater, drainage, or excess irrigation. Open ditches are more often used in rural or agricultural communities than in urban areas. Typically, the open ditches are unlined and not paved, making them easier to maintain and less expensive compared to covered pipes; although, paved ditches lined with concrete or rock typically perform better. Like levees and other similar engineered mechanisms discussed in the previous chapter, paved ditches may cause erosion issues and can also fail, resulting in increased maintenance and repair costs. Open ditches are also an important remaining refuge for biodiversity, when increased vegetation is applied (e.g. bioswales) and are commonly used in countries such as the Netherlands (Mukete et al., 2013).

Location

Agricultural, suburban, rural (sometimes urban)

Ability to Address Coastal Hazards

Storm surge
Wave force
Flooding
Erosion

Cost

● ● ○ ○ ○

Compared with other hybrid mechanisms

● ○ ○ ○ ○

Compared with overall mechanisms

Scale

● ● ● ● ○

Regional, local

G1. Irrigation Ditch

Irrigation ditches are artificial channels that typically deliver and supply water to areas such as farms or seek to help drain lands from natural creeks or rivers.

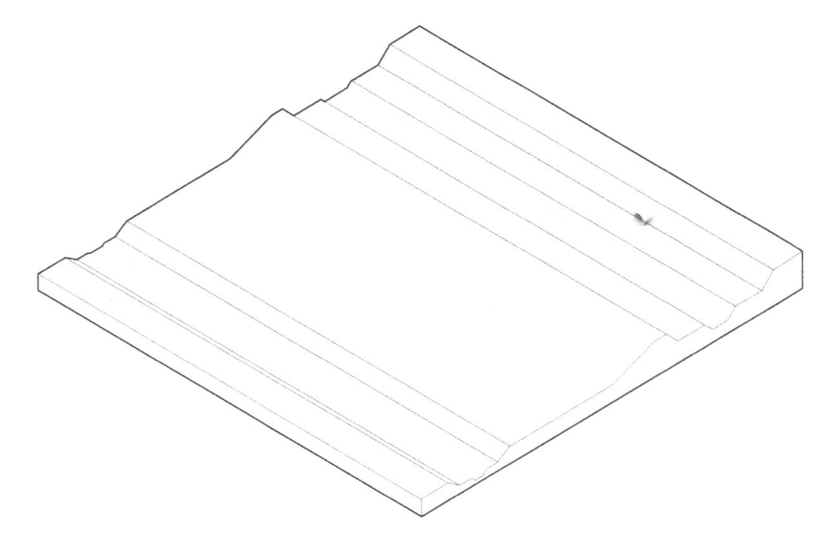

Figure 22.2

G2. Polder Ditch

Tx1Polders are low-lying tracts of land enclosed by embankments (primarily dikes) to form artificial hydrological components that are separated from surrounding waters and are drained by pumping (Newman, 2015).

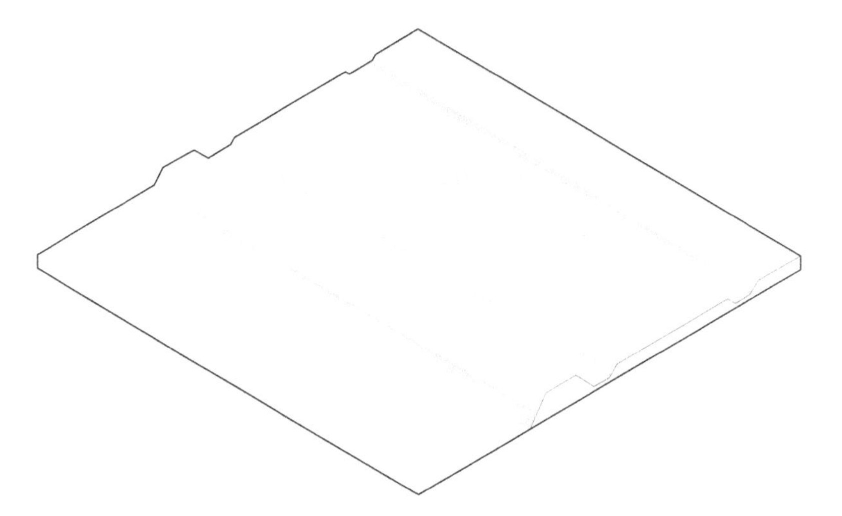

Figure 22.3

G3. Two-stage Ditch

Two-stage ditches are drainage ditches that have been modified by adding functional amenities such as benches that serve to help drain floodplains. This form of ditch is more consistent with fluvial formations and processes, and can therefore lead to greater channel stability (Purdue, 2020).

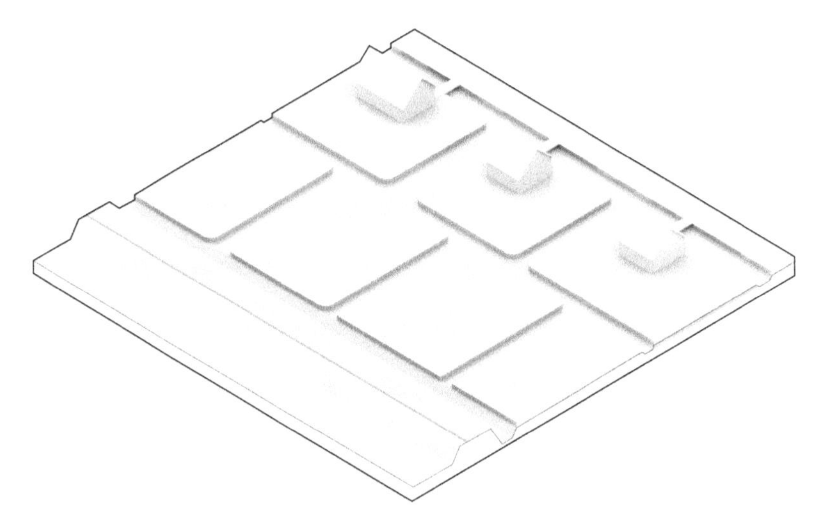

Figure 22.4

G4. Roadside Ditch

Roadside ditches are open channels that align with roadways and are used for draining stormwater, reducing floodwaters, and draining excess runoff from transportation routes (Van Zandt et al., 2020).

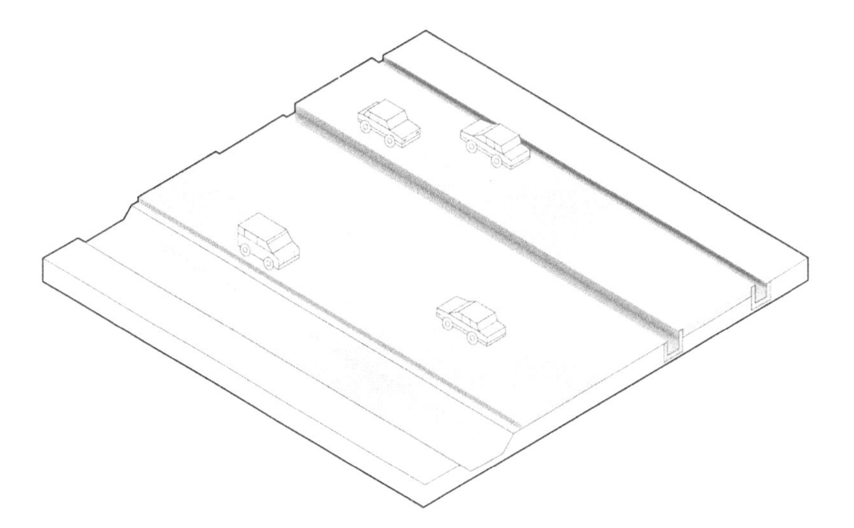

Figure 22.5

H. Breakwaters

Breakwaters are typically artificial (but can also be living) offshore structures which are constructed at or in close proximity to the shoreline to protect coastal areas from the effects of storm surge and help to reduce coastal erosion. The typical breakwater is constructed of concrete or stone, but there are many new breakwaters practices which are made with natural habitat components, such as oyster reefs and coral reefs.

Figure 22.6

Location

Coastal

Ability to Address Coastal Hazards

Storm surge
Wave force
Flooding
Erosion

Cost

• • ○ ○ ○

Compared with other hybrid mechanisms

• • ○ ○ ○

Compared with overall mechanisms

Scale

• • ○ ○ ○

Regional

H1. Living Breakwaters

Living breakwaters have the same function as traditional breakwaters, but they also incorporate natural habitat by providing opportunities for settlement and colonization by species such as oysters or corals or by creating complex structural components that provide shelter and habitat for various marine and aquatic species (CTCN, 2021).

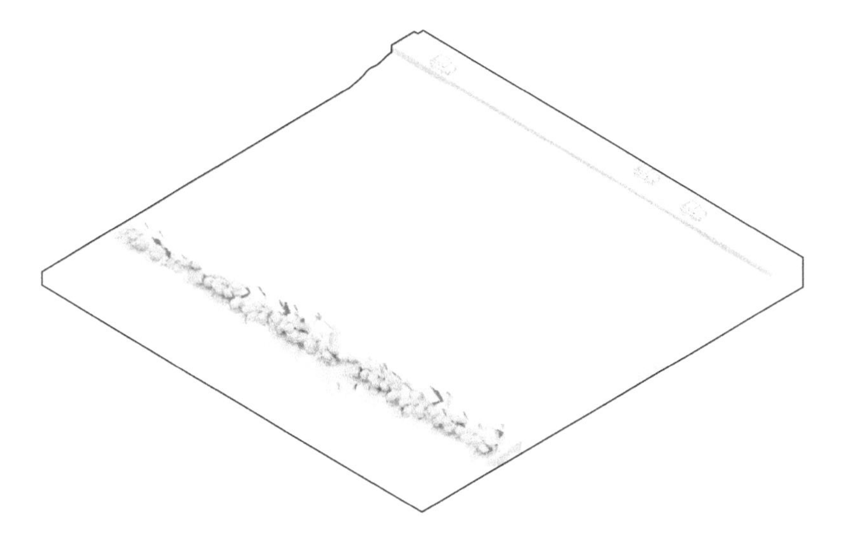

Figure 22.7

H2. Rubble Mound Breakwaters

Rubble mound breakwaters absorb wave energy by using structural voids. They consist of a toe structure, an armor layer of rock or concrete above geotextile, and granular underlayers applied atop the sediment core and toe structures.

Figure 22.8

H3. Segmented Breakwaters

Segmented breakwaters help absorb wave water and block storm surge but also allow some wave transmission into the shore. They help to allow for sediment transfer into the shore while seeking to retain some of the current wave action already in place.

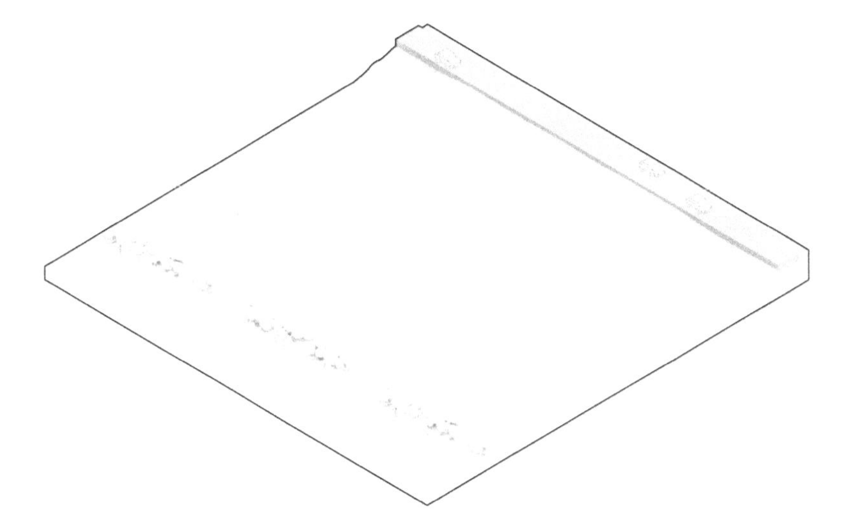

Figure 22.9

H4. Floating Breakwaters

Floating breakwaters are an alternative solution to protect areas from wave or surge inundation. Compared with fixed breakwaters, they have less interference with water circulation and are easier to construct in deeper-sea areas.

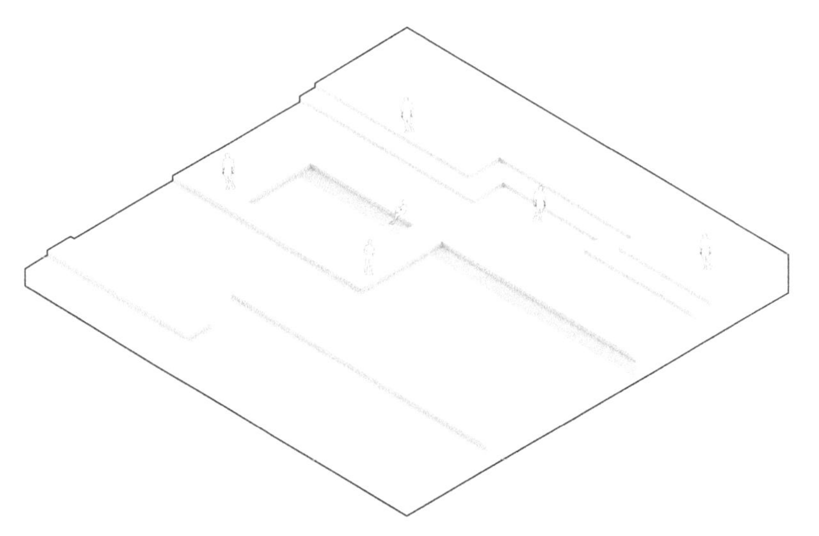

Figure 22.10

I. Terracing

Terracing involves a number of level flat platforms resembling steps which can deter different levels of inundation but allow for recreational use in dry times. In urban areas, terracing is normally used to replace steep slopes, prevent rainfall runoff, and decrease soil erosion while simultaneously being used as layers of floodwall/retaining walls to block storm surge or sea level rise at the coastline.

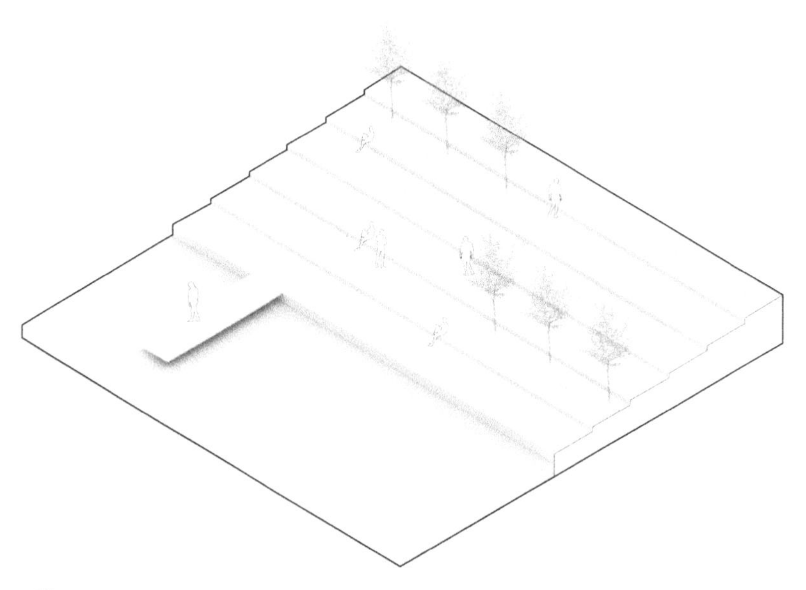

Figure 22.11

Location

Riverside, coastline

Ability to Address Coastal Hazards

Storm surge
Wave force
Flooding
Erosion

Cost

Compared with other hybrid mechanisms

● ○ ○ ○ ○

Compared with overall mechanisms

● ● ○ ○ ○

Scale

● ● ○ ○ ○

Community/Site

I1. Concrete Terrace

As stated in its title, concrete terraces are constructed with concrete or stone. Depending on their location, they can be used as engineered solutions for blocking floodwaters, and can act as hybridizations of terraced retaining walls or terraced floodwalls.

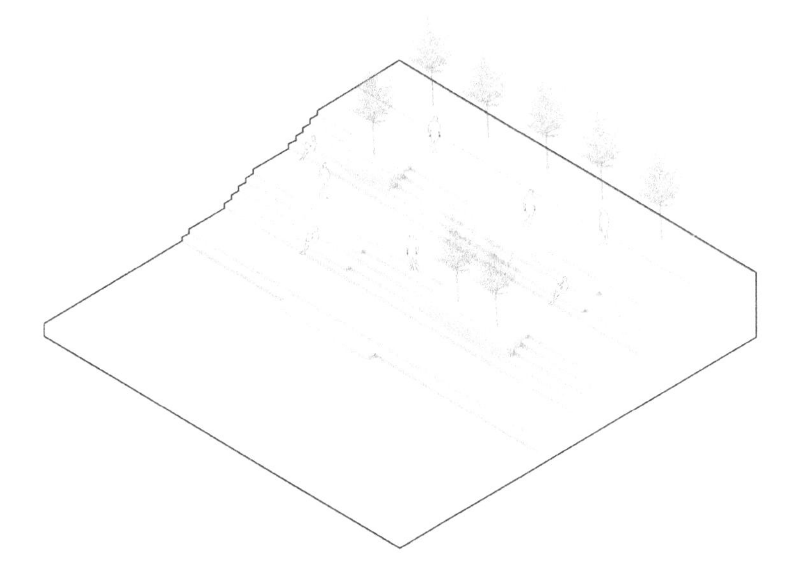

Figure 22.12

I2. Filtration Terrace

Filtration terraces are covered with vegetation and serve as landscape features integrated within coastal parks or green spaces. Consisting of newly terraced slopes, they can also be used to form shallow ponds, reduce rainwater runoff, and help retain sediment.

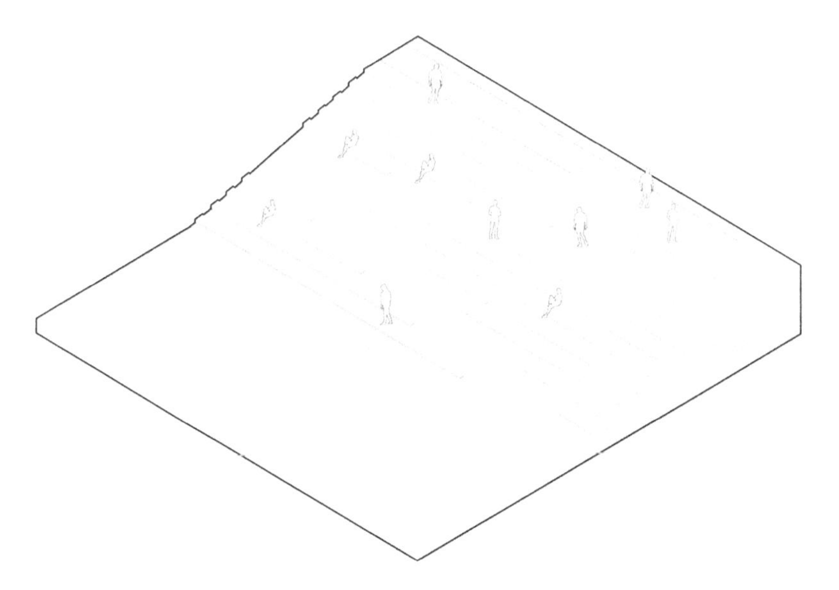

Figure 22.13

I3. Amphitheater Terrace

Amphitheater terraces are sunken outdoor spaces with a central area for functions or events. Terraces surrounding the central space are typically used as outdoor seating. They can be constructed with concrete and stone or mixed with structural components and vegetation such as grasses.

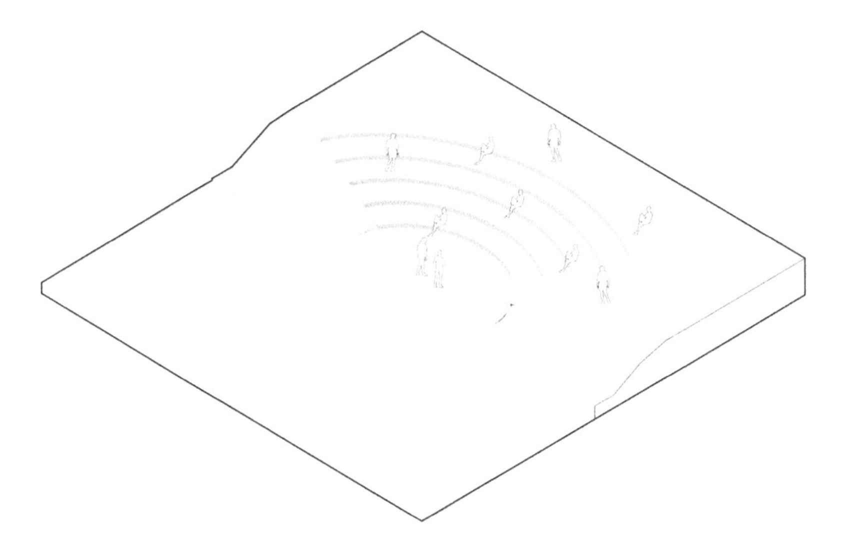

Figure 22.14

I4. Wave Break Terrace

Wave break terraces have similar functions as breakwaters. Compared with breakwaters, their scale is much smaller. They are normally installed within coastal urban parks and green spaces instead of outside of the shoreline.

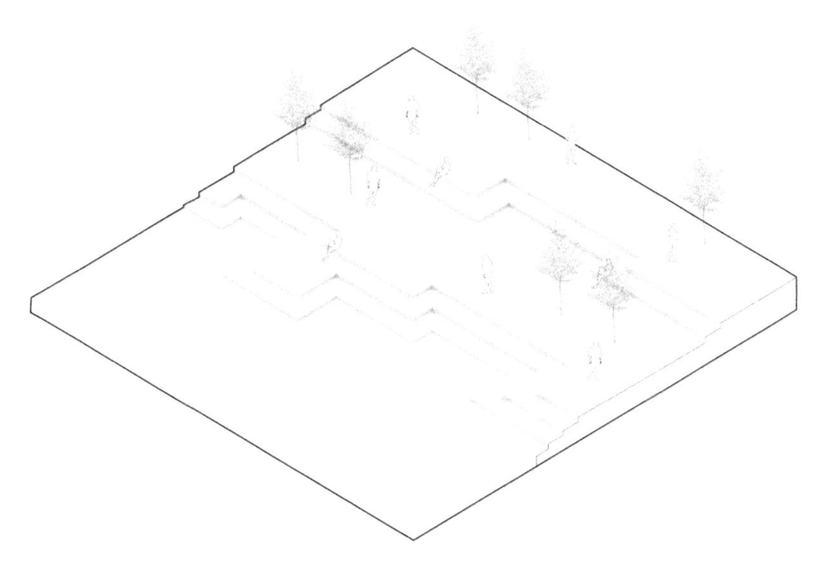

Figure 22.15

J. Edgings

Edgings are designed to protect shorelines and coastal areas from waves and beach erosion in the form of reinforced seawalls and small-scaled breakwater type elements. The constructions and materials of edgings are similar to breakwaters including concrete, stone, and natural habitat components, such as oyster reefs.

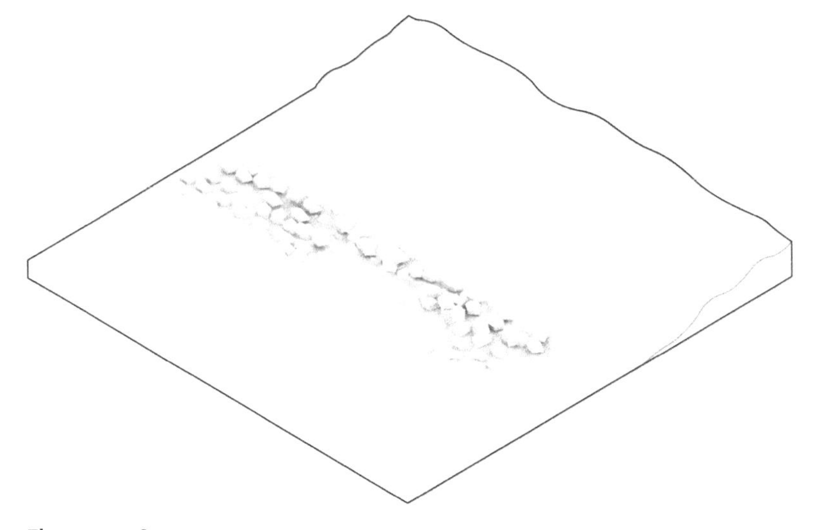

Figure 22.16

Location

Coastal

Ability to Address Coastal Hazards

Storm surge
Wave force
Flooding
Erosion

Cost

Compared with other hybrid mechanisms

• • • ○ ○

Compared with overall mechanisms

• • ○ ○ ○

Scale

• • • • ○

Regional

J1. Concrete Jacks

Concrete jacks, also called tetrapods, are made of concrete mixed with a high content of cement and hard aggregates for durability. They are extremely heavy and can stabilize coastlines in extreme storms and hurricanes, and help to limit sea level rise impacts.

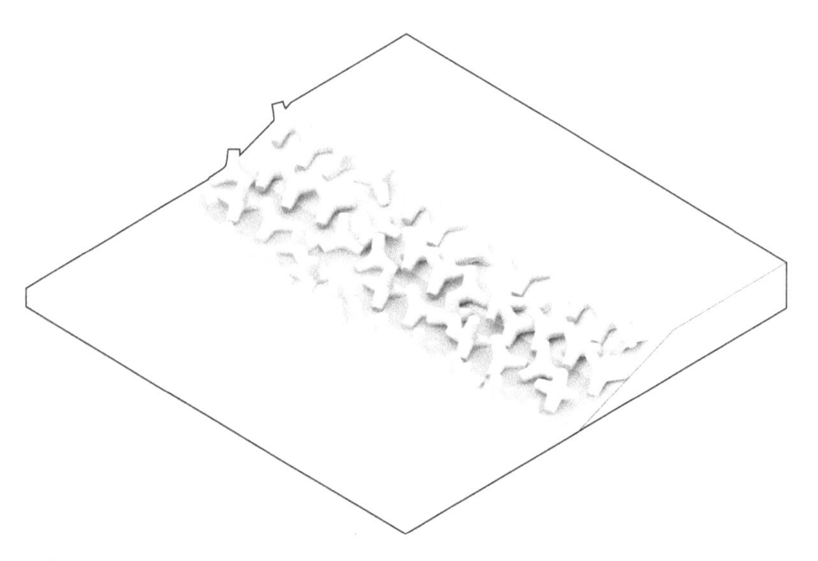

Figure 22.17

J2. Artificial Reefs

Artificial reefs are constructed of pre-cast artificial units which are made of reinforced concrete or steel. Basically, they are wide-crested submerged breakwaters that can provide shoreline stabilization by mimicking the functionality of natural reefs (Harris, 2009).

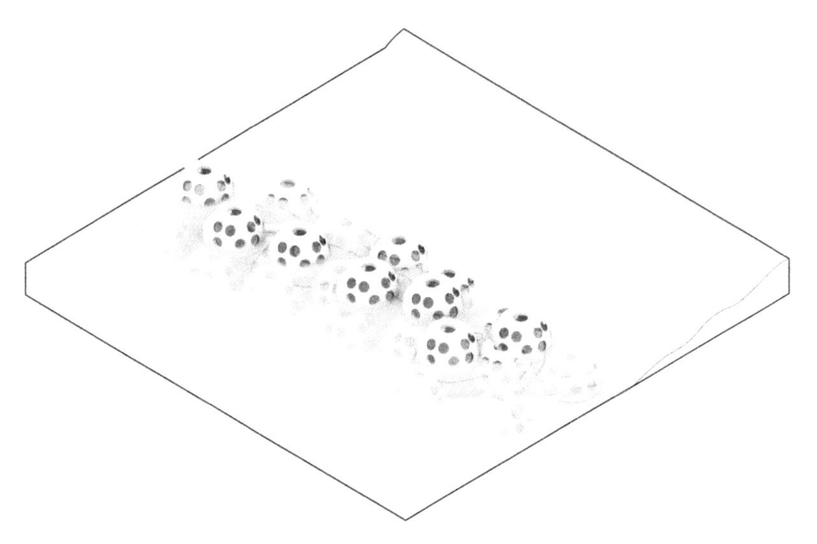

Figure 22.18

J3. Oyster Reefs

Oyster reefs consist of clusters of oysters that form habitats in estuaries. They also have the function of breaking up wave impacts and play important roles in maintaining water quality and providing habitat for juvenile fish and other marine organisms (Kilgen & Dugas, 1989).

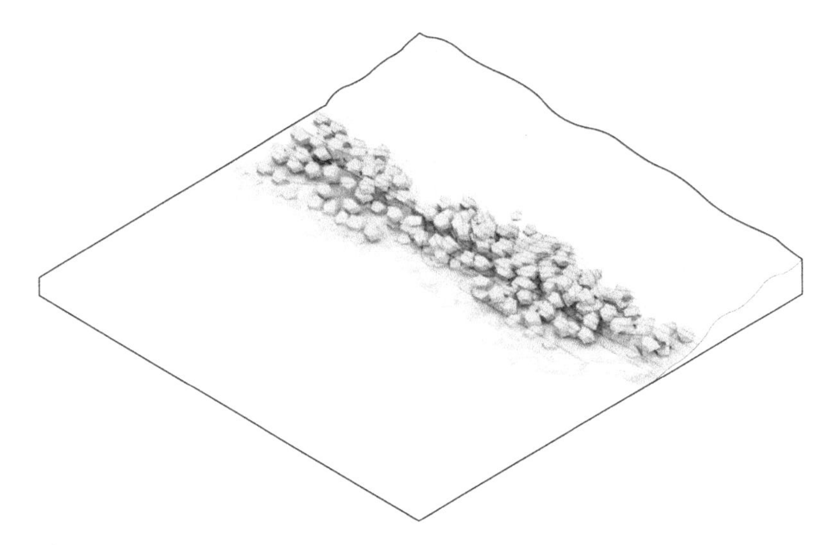

Figure 22.19

J4. Groins

Groins are engineered shoreline protection structures. Different than other edging and breakwater structures, they are a group of structures perpendicular to the shoreline which help to increase and accrue sediment to elongate shorelines.

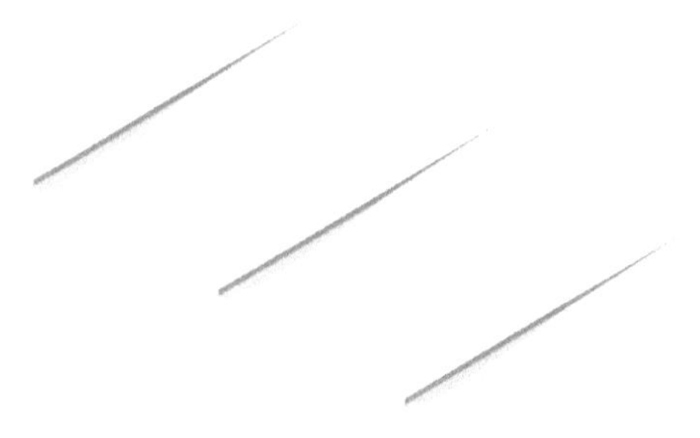

Figure 22.20

K. Sustainable Buildings

Sustainable buildings, also called green buildings, are buildings which have lower impacts on the environment by reducing the consumption of energy, water, and other resources. In this book, we focus on their functions of saving and capturing water.

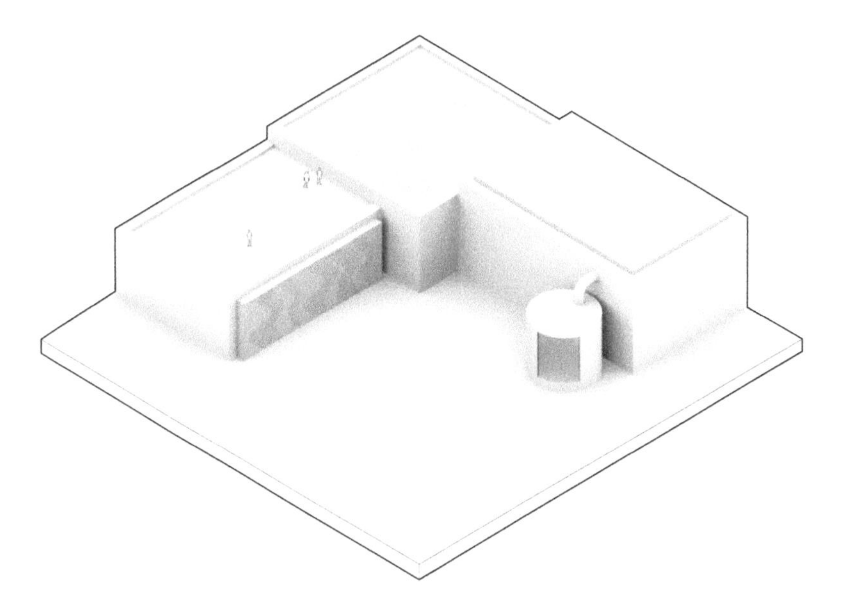

Figure 22.21

Location

Urban/Suburban

Ability to Address Coastal Hazards

Storm surge
Wave force
Flooding
Erosion

Cost

Compared with other hybrid mechanisms

• • • ○ ○

Compared with overall mechanisms

• • ○ ○ ○

Scale

• • • ○ ○

Site/Community

K1. Green Roofs

Green roofs are building tops with vegetated plants atop the conventional roof, albeit with particular structural envelopes. Besides their benefits in reducing building energy consumption and rooftop temperatures, green roofs also help reduce stormwater runoff in urban environments and also assist in reducing pollutant loads in stormwater runoff.

Figure 22.22

K2. Blue Roof

Blue roofs refer to the combination of "blue" and "green" roof technology. Traditional green roofs usually use drainage layers to reduce stormwater runoff. However, blue roofs are designed to capture stormwater and control the amount of water released.

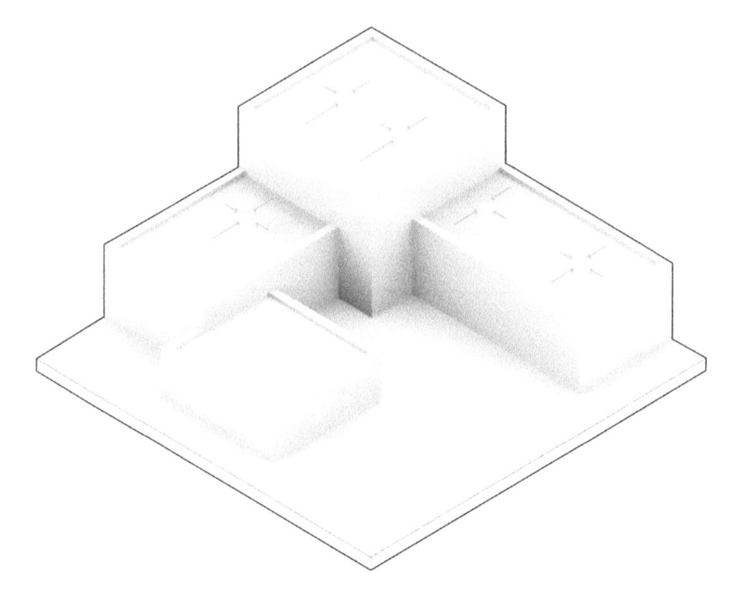

Figure 22.23

K3. Green Wall

Green walls are vertical structures that are covered with vegetation and have a myriad of benefits for stormwater management. Stormwater can be reused for the purpose of irrigating green walls, which, in turn, increases on-site infiltration and evapotranspiration (Lau & Mah, 2018).

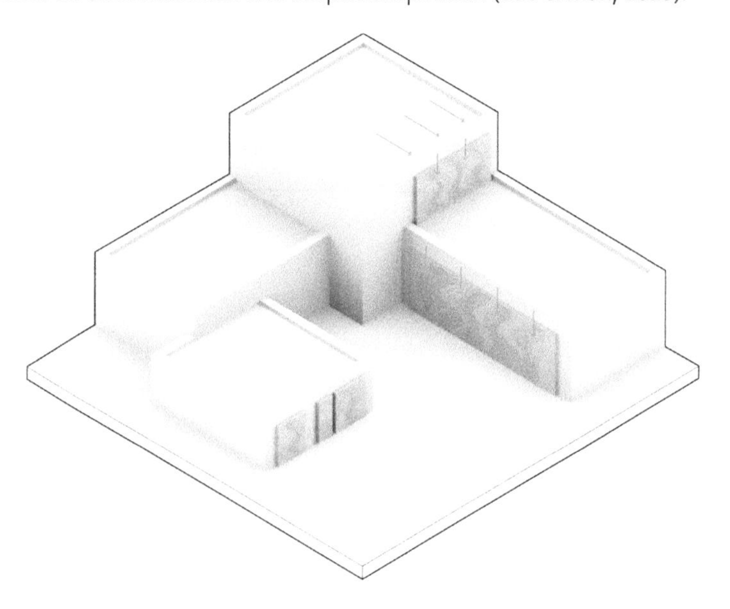

Figure 22.24

K4. Rainwater Harvesting

Rainwater harvesting is a stormwater management system which captures, stores, and purifies the stormwater runoff, typically through connecting downspouts with cisterns or rain barrels. The scale of rainwater harvesting systems can vary from community to homesteads.

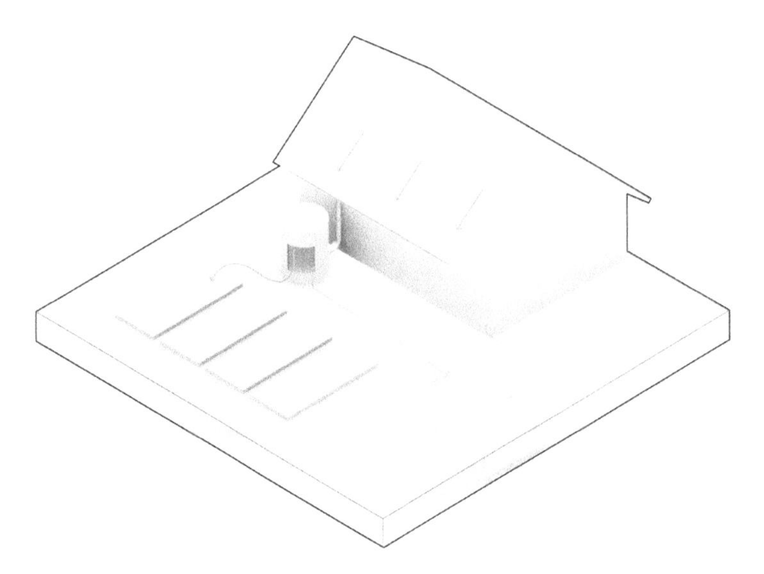

Figure 22.25

L. Permeable Paving

Permeable paving is made by applying porous materials in typically impervious areas which allow stormwater to pass through and permit stormwater to infiltrate storage areas such as underlying reservoirs (Kil et al., 2016). Such paving techniques work with other infrastructure such as bioswales, raingardens, underground systems, etc. to decrease stormwater volume.

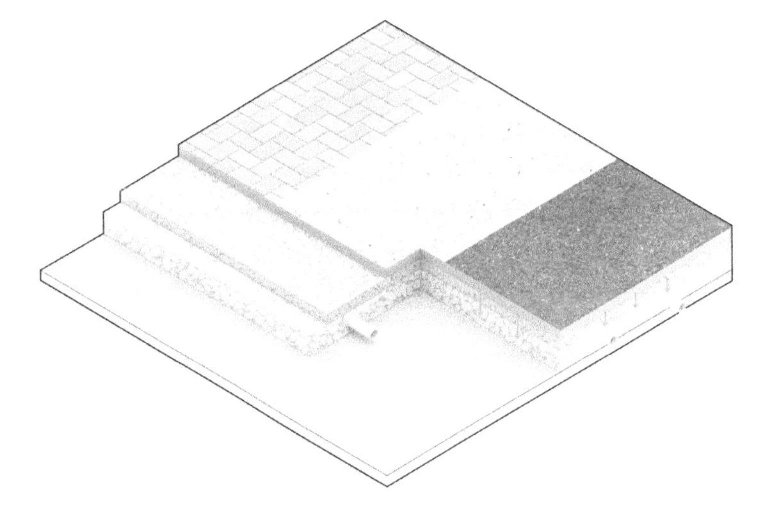

Figure 22.26

Location

Urban

Ability to Address Coastal Hazards

Storm surge
Wave force
Flooding
Erosion

Cost

Compared with other hybrid mechanisms

● ○ ○ ○ ○

Compared with overall mechanisms

● ○ ○ ○ ○

Scale

● ○ ○ ○ ○

Site/Community/Regional

L1. Pervious Concrete

Pervious concrete is a special type of concrete with a high porosity, made from a mixture of cement, water, coarse aggregate, and a minimal amount of fine aggregate (e.g. sand) (New York Engineers, 2019).

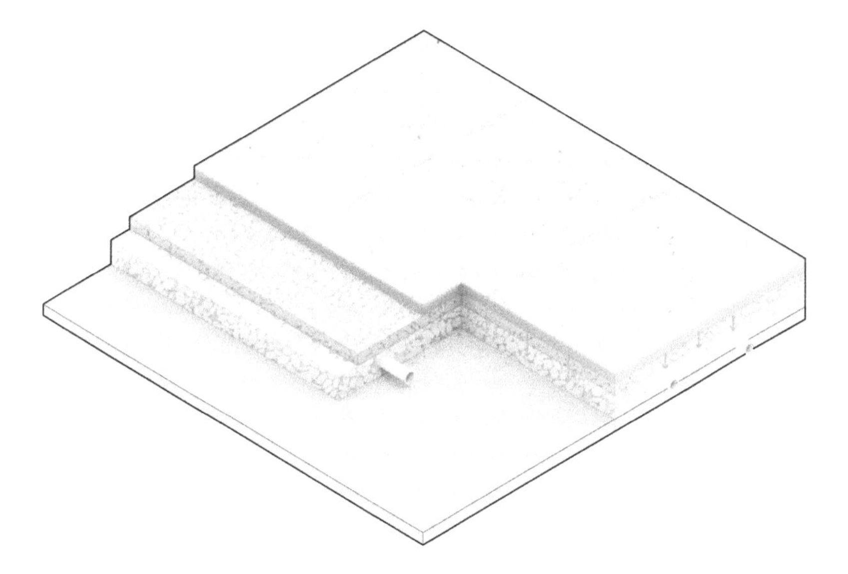

Figure 22.27

L2. Porous Asphalt

Porous asphalt can efficiently reduce runoff volume and stormwater pollutants on driveways or roadways. In colder climates, it has also been shown to reduce the need to apply road salt for de-icing in the winter (Houle et al., 2009).

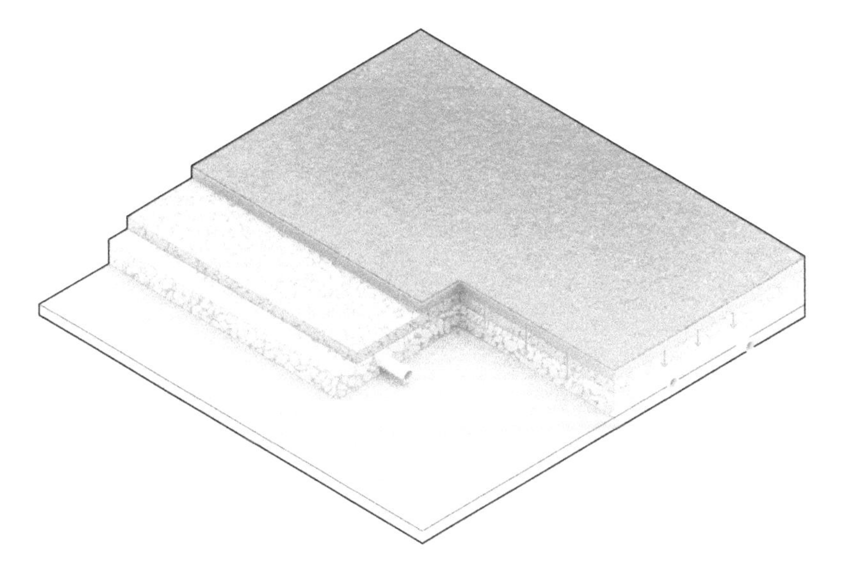

Figure 22.28

L3. Permeable Pavers

Permeable pavers are typically composed with permeable bricks or other tile-like paving systems. Because the size of each tile or paver can be quite small, permeable pavers are normally applied as sidewalks or for personal, home-scaled use.

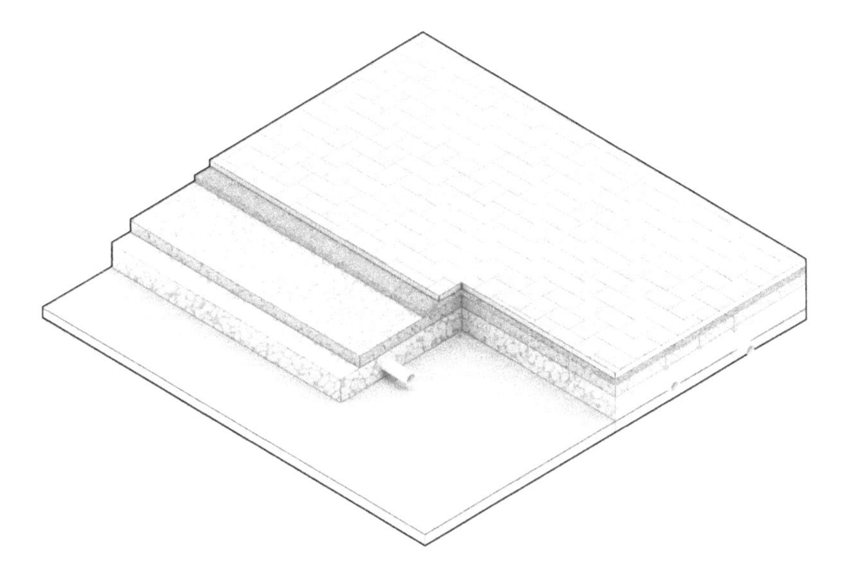

Figure 22.29

L4. Plastic/Concrete Grids

Plastic/concrete grids have extremely high permeability to help absorb rainwater and runoff nearly instantly. They are primarily used in parking lots.

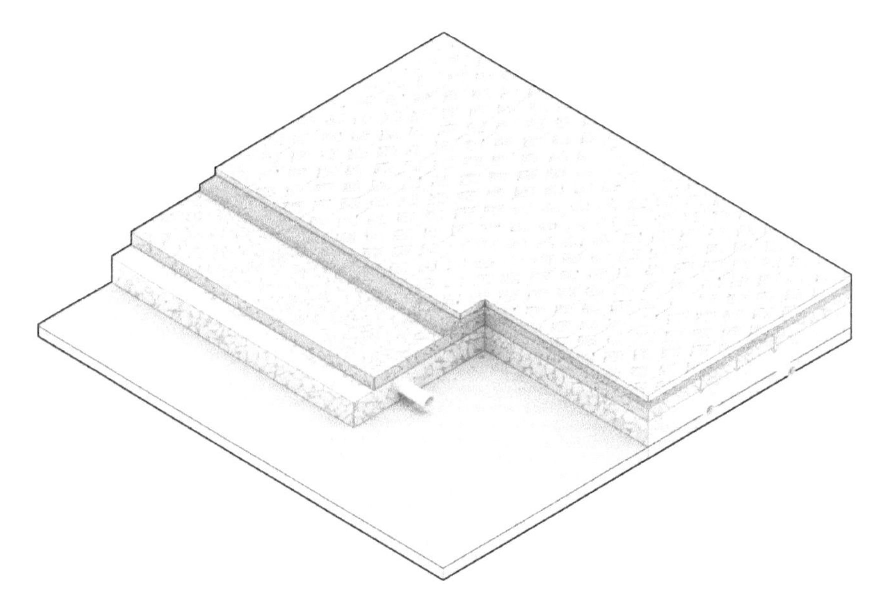

Figure 22.30

Conclusions

Despite each hybrid mechanism's differing capabilities to combat flooding and sea level rise, each also has its relative strengths and weaknesses. For example, while open ditches can easily and cheaply convey water and pollutants to different areas, they are also subject to heavy erosion and can clog up due to debris without continued maintenance. Overtopping and inability to transport enough water during heavy flood events are also a common occurrence.

Breakwaters have a large degree of flexibility in their potential to accommodate small changes in seabed/beach levels and to dissipate wave energy, allowing them to reduce wave loads on existing structures and the tendencies for scouring. Compared to typical large-scaled engineered mechanisms, breakwaters also have a relatively low cost of construction and maintenance. However, if the toe construction of a breakwater is not acutely thought out and constructed properly, such mechanisms can result in a sliding down of the armor layer, and, ultimately, slip surface failure within the core. While this hydraulic instability in the armor layer can result in ineffectiveness, other, more common obstacles are created with the use of breakwaters such as increased dangers for boating and fishing activities.

While breakwaters offer strong protection options from wave and sea level-based impacts along the coast, edging approaches, such as artificial and oyster reefs, advance the amenities of breakwaters by also providing shelter, habitat, and food for numerous species within near-shore environments. They, however, can also pose dangers to swimmers, surfers, and boaters if not interacted with appropriately. Further, other edging devices such as groins may result in increased local erosion of the seabed or sand loss within deep water due to the resultant new sediment deposits and transferal processes.

Sustainable buildings, while construction costs can vary immensely depending on attributes, can offer contributions such as decreases in albedo or ambient urban temperature, increased environmental services, more efficient water capture and reuse options, and ease of buildability. Such structures also often need specialized and continual maintenance. In many cases, sustainable structures are accompanied by permeable paving materials, as a complete sustainable ensemble. Such paving systems decrease the pressure on underground drainage systems and nearby stormwater management structures in a fairly cost-effective manner, depending on the materials chosen for construction. They also, however, require additional maintenance which is not often necessary for traditional paving approaches.

References

Climate Technology Centre & Network (CTCN). (2021). *Naturally resilient communities*. Retrieved from www.ctc-n.org/technologies/breakwaters

Harris, L. (2009). Artificial reefs for ecosystem restoration and coastal erosion protection with aquaculture and recreational amenities. *Reef Journal*, *1*(1), 235–246.

Houle, K., Roseen, R., Ballestero, T., Briggs, J., & Houle, J. (2009). Examinations of pervious concrete and porous asphalt pavements performance for stormwater management in northern climates. *World Environmental and Water Resources Congress 2009*, Kansas City, Missouri, May 17–21, pp. 1–18.

Kil, S. H., Lee, D. K., Kim, J. H., Li, M. H., & Newman, G. (2016). Utilizing the analytic hierarchy process to establish weighted values for evaluating the stability of slope re-vegetation based on hydroseeding measures in South Korea. *Sustainability*, *8*(1), 58.

Kilgen, R. H., & Dugas, R. J. (1989). *The ecology of oyster reefs of the northern Gulf of Mexico: An open file report*. NWRC-open file rept. 89–03. Washington, DC: National Fish and Wildlife Service.

Lau, J. T., & Mah, D. Y. S. (2018). Green wall for retention of stormwater. *Pertanika Journal of Science and Technology*, *1*, 283.

Mukete, B., Vermaat, J., & Straalen, N. V. (2013). Variability in microhabitats prevalence in low lying peat polder ditches of the Netherlands. *Applied Ecology and Environmental Research*, *11*(4), 629–643.

Newman, G. (2015, October 16). Dune integration for Galveston Island: Issues and options. In B. Kothuis, A. Brand, A. Sebastian, A. Nillesen, & S. Jonkman (Eds.) *Delft Delta Design: Houston Galveston Bay Region* (Ch. 35, Reflections Section, pp. 124–125). Deltas, Infrastructure, and Mobility Initiative (DIMI): Delft University of Technology. Delft, Netherlands: Delft University Publishers. ISSN: 978 94 6186 490 1

New York Engineers. (2019). *What is pervious concrete?* Retrieved from www.ny-engineers.com/blog/what-is-pervious-concrete

Purdue.Edu (2020). *Conservation drainage – two-stage ditches*. Retrieved from https://engineering.purdue.edu/watersheds/conservationdrainage/ditch.html

Van Zandt, S., Masterson, J., Newman G., & Meyer, M. (June, 29, 2020). *Engaged research for community resilience to climate change*. First Edition. Cambridge, MA: Elsevier. ISBN: 9780128155752

23

NON-STRUCTURAL MECHANISMS

Zixu Qiao and Galen D. Newman

INDEX

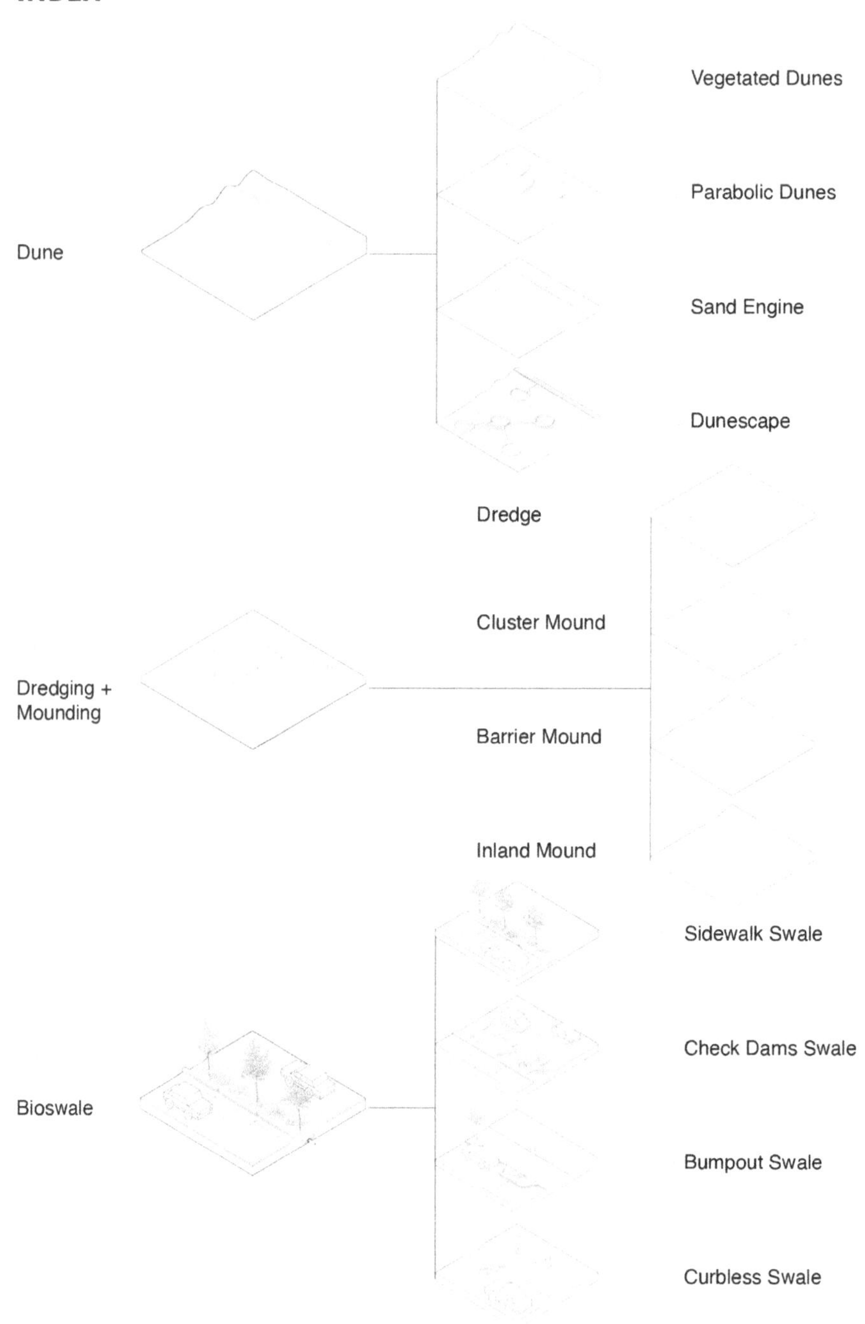

DOI: 10.4324/9781003183419-31

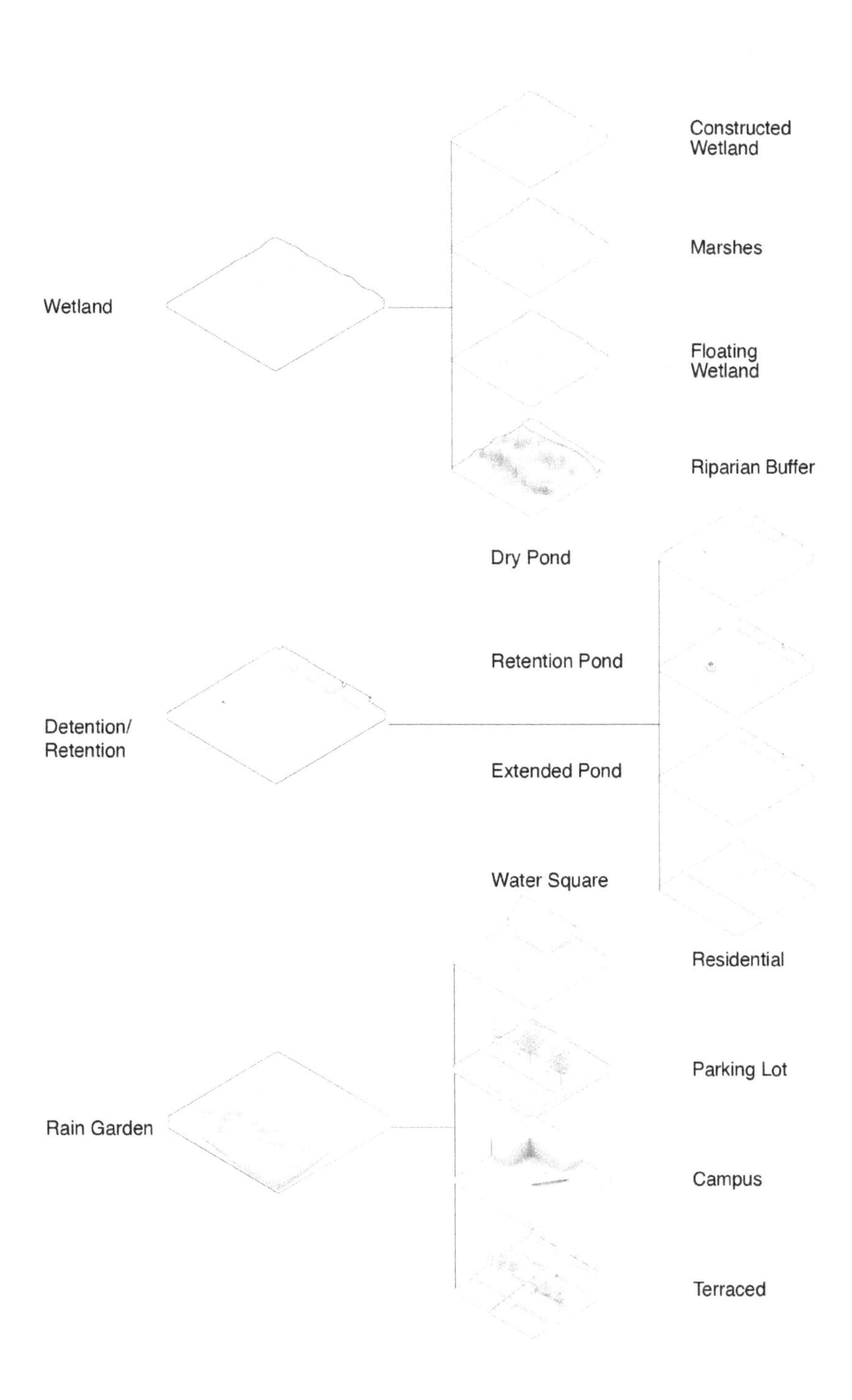
Constructed Wetland
Marshes
Wetland
Floating Wetland
Riparian Buffer
Dry Pond
Retention Pond
Detention/ Retention
Extended Pond
Water Square
Residential
Parking Lot
Rain Garden
Campus
Terraced

M. Dune and Sand

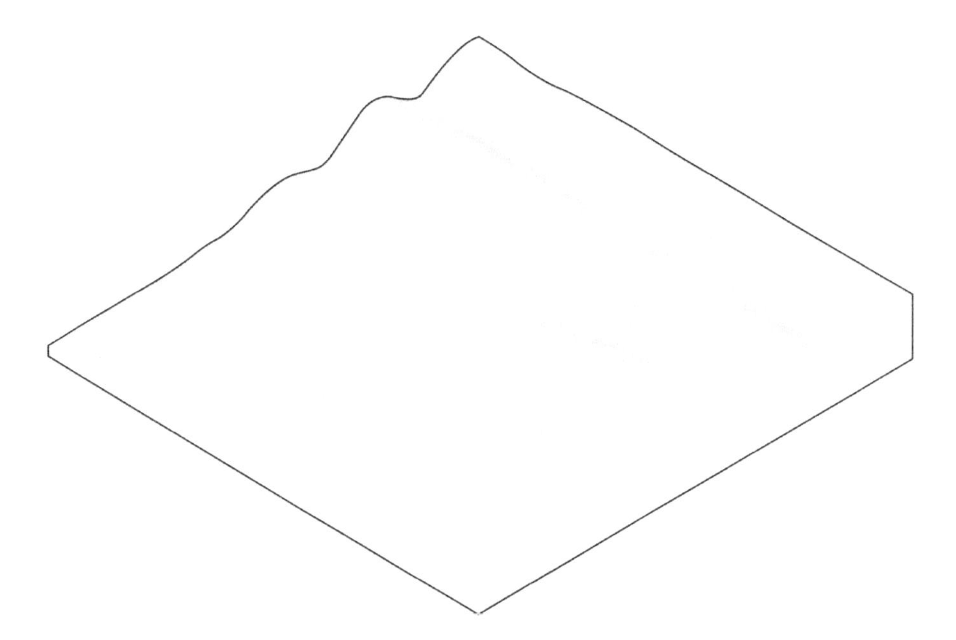

Figure 23.1

Dunes can be man-made or naturally composed through wind and wave action. Coastal dunes and sand deposits are typically artificial or human interventions which are designed as barriers to protect coastal areas from the effects of storm surge, wave attacks, and to help reduce coastal erosion or elongate beachline areas. The size and morphology of coastal dunes is dependent on the complex interactions between controlling winds, sediment supply, and the geomorphology of the nearshore and beach environments (Sloss et al., 2012).

Location

Coastal

Ability to Address Coastal Hazards

Storm surge
Wave force
Flooding
Erosion

Cost

● ● ● ○ ○

Compared with other non-structural mechanisms

● ○ ○ ○ ○

Compared with overall mechanisms

Scale

● ● ● ● ○

Regional, local

M1. Vegetated Dunes

Vegetation (typically grasses when applied to dunes) influence wave-induced dune erosion processes through modifying both the above- and below-ground characteristics of the dune through leaf and complex root structures. Such natural structures are abundantly present in most coastal dunes and can enhance the capability of a dune to withstand erosion and wave and tidal action (Figlus et al., 2014).

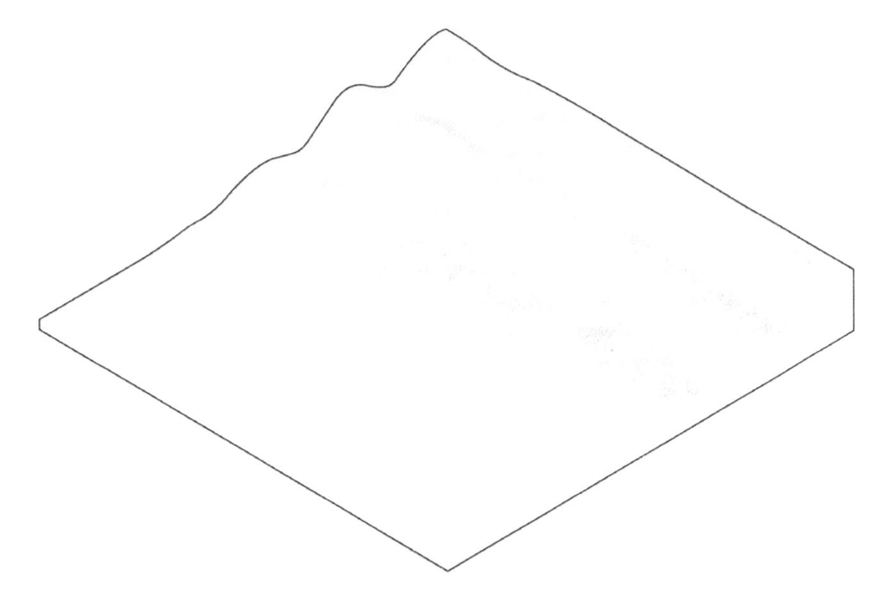

Figure 23.2

M2. Parabolic Dunes

Also called U-shape dunes, these are naturally formed dunes which are typically associated with colder environments (Koster, 1988) and humid sea and lake coastlines (McKenna, 2007). Vegetation naturally forms along the dune's ridges in most cases.

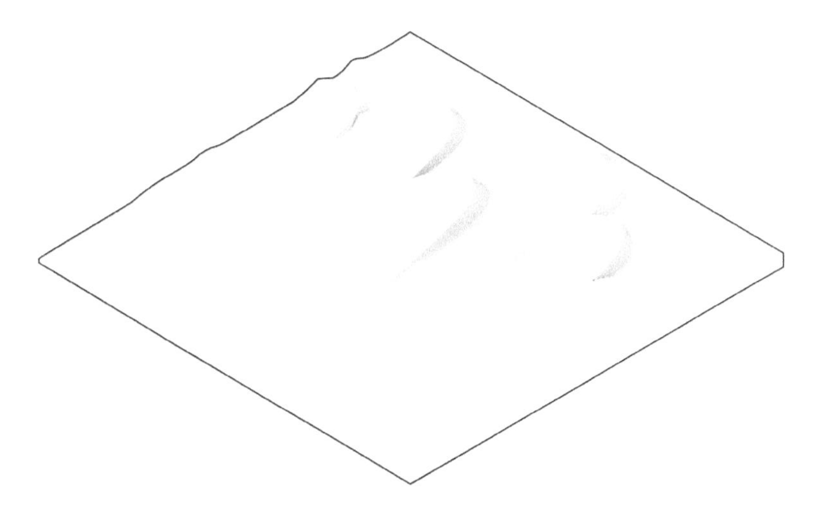

Figure 23.3

M3. Sand Engine

A sand engine is a large volume of dredged sand which is strategically deposited onto a coastline area to help protect it from sea level rise and storm surge. Areas with an abundance of sediment utilize natural tidal processes to deposit sand along coastlines to elongate beach areas, provide beach nourishment, or create barrier islands. Such approaches have been successfully applied in the Netherlands.

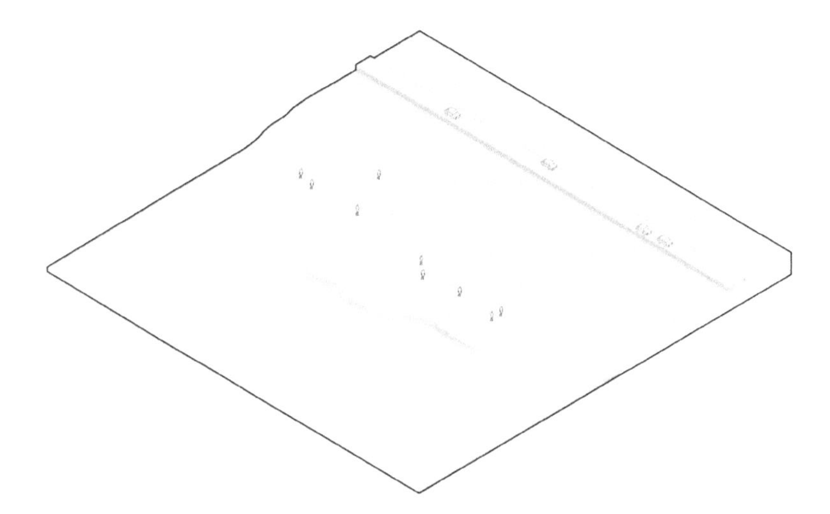

Figure 23.4

M4. Dunescape

A dunescape describes a collection of a series of dunes and dune types which comprise an entire landscape. It is, essentially, a combination of protective dunes and an open space network providing enhanced habitat for plants and animals while also offering tourism possibilities.

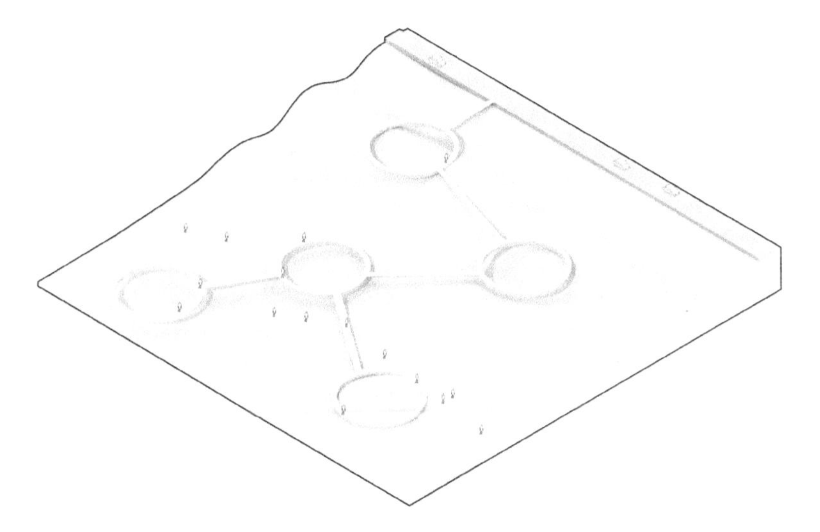

Figure 23.5

N. Dredging and Mounding

Dredging is a flood management method which involves the removal of silt from the river bed and the side of the river, and then mounded elsewhere on the riverbank (Sohn et al., 2014). This approach may also entail straightening/widening a channel or deepening its bottom. Dredging and mounding can reduce the water levels, improve general flood drainage, and reduce the extent of flooding.

Figure 23.6

Location

Riverside

Ability to Address Coastal Hazards

Storm surge
Wave force
Flooding
Erosion

Cost

● ● ● ○ ○

Compared with other non-structural mechanisms

● ● ○ ○ ○

Compared with overall mechanisms

Scale

● ● ● ○ ○

Regional

N1. Dredge

Dredging is the removal of sediments and debris from the bottom of lakes, rivers, harbors, and other water bodies (Newman et al., 2014). Typically, dredging includes excavation, suction, and ploughing. Excavators are normally used to dig out sediment to improve the capacity of a water body.

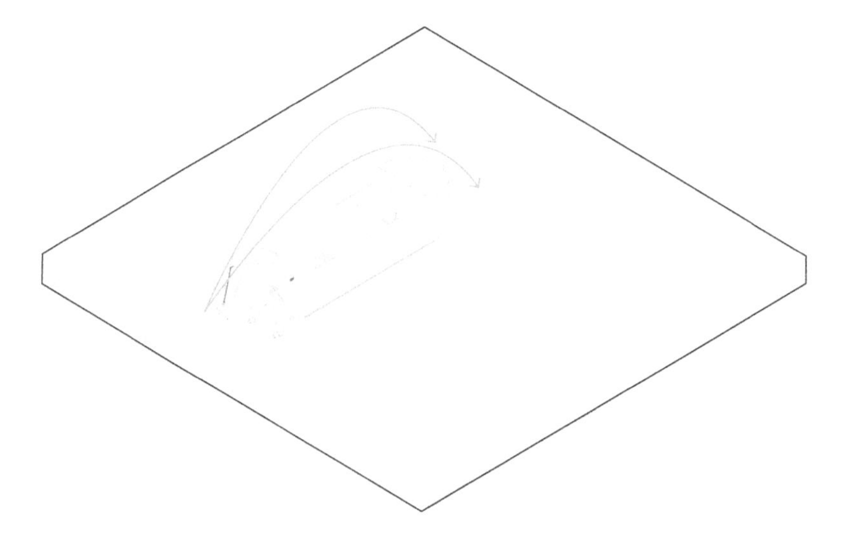

Figure 23.7

N2. Clustered Mound

Clustered mounds are normally human-made accumulations of dug out sediments placed in groups. Such approaches allow for the lessening of wave impacts through the mounding and the simultaneous deepening of other water bodies from the dredge source (Newman et al., 2016).

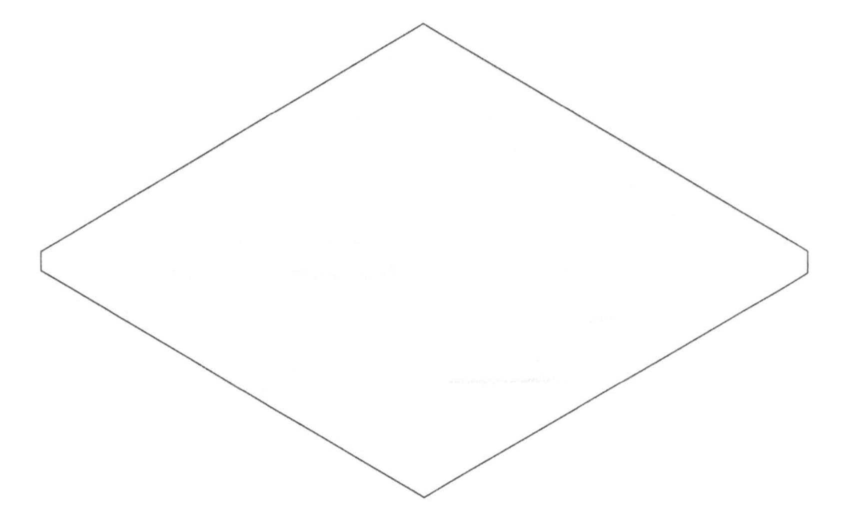

Figure 23.8

N3. Barrier Mound

Similar to breakwaters discussed in the previous chapter, barrier mounds are constructed close to the shoreline edge of a coast or river to protect from flooding and surge. Offshore barrier mounds can also be non-structural through inflatable materials that pop up only during storm events.

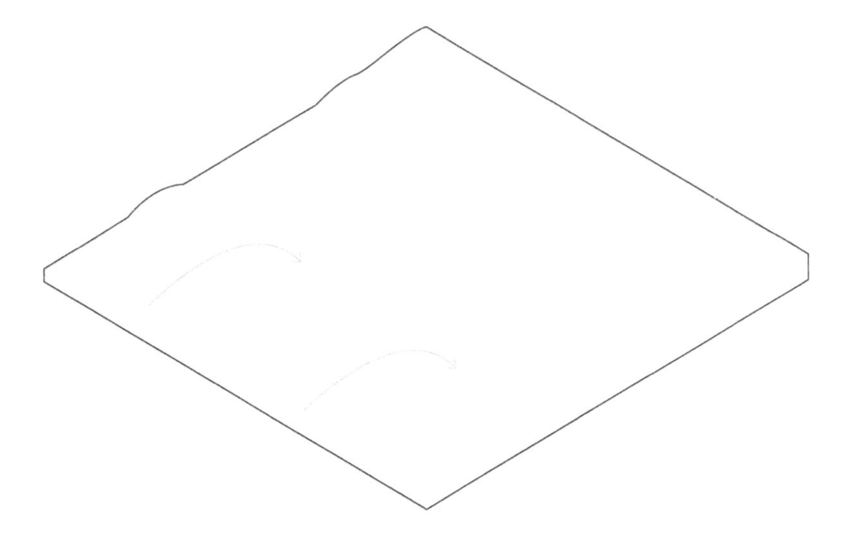

Figure 23.9

N4. Inland Mound

Inland mounds are made by dredging sediments from the bottom of a river or the edge of a shoreline and applying the sediments on coastal areas. Such mounds can have a variety of core types including non-structural materials such as hardened clay or structural core materials such as T-walls (Newman et al., 2017).

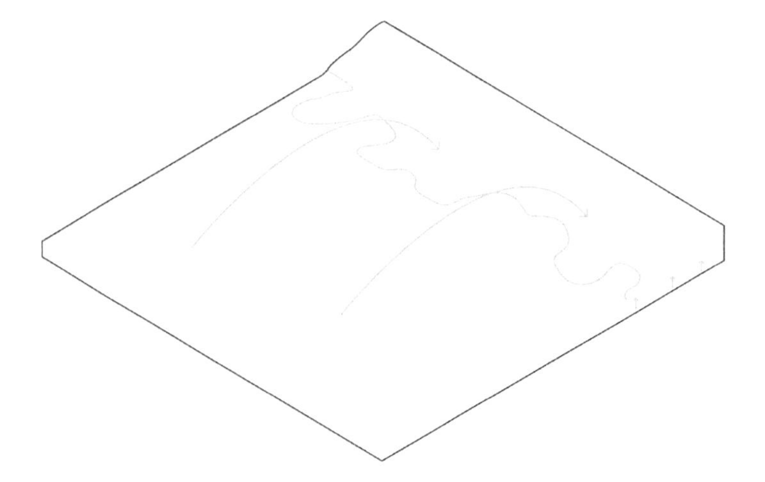

Figure 23.10

O. Bioswale

Bioswales are vegetated swales with a porous bottom that can collect, convey, filtrate, and filter stormwater runoff, and reduce flood potential (Kim et al., 2017). Typically, bioswales are composed of multiple layers including native vegetation, mulch, soil composition to maximize bio-retention, gravel, perforated underdrain pipes, and overflow structures. They are the eco-friendly enhancement of a traditional stormwater piping system.

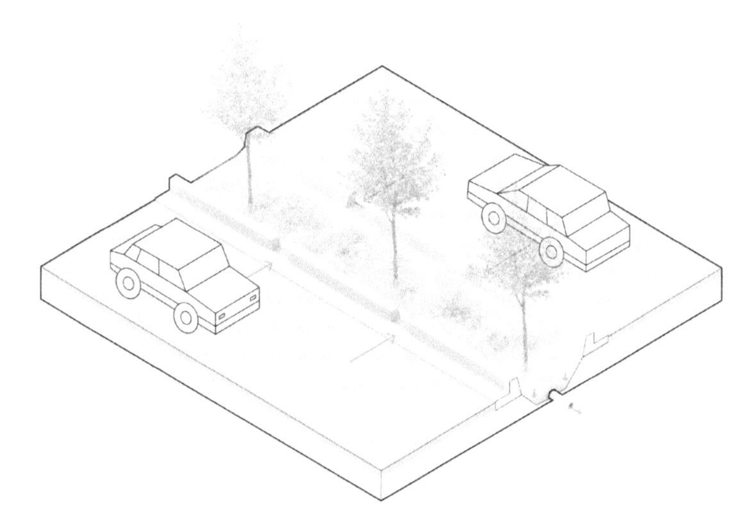

Figure 23.11

Location

Urban/Suburban

Ability to Address Coastal Hazards

Storm surge
Wave force
Flooding
Erosion

Compared with other non-structural mechanisms

● ○ ○ ○ ○

Compared with overall mechanisms

● ○ ○ ○ ○

Scale

● ● ○ ○ ○

Site/Community/Regional

O1. Sidewalk Swale

Sidewalk swales are vegetated landscape depressions on the side of road networks or within rights of way. Such bioswales capture and treat stormwater runoff from sidewalks and roadways while conveying it to necessary storage areas or allowing for infiltration.

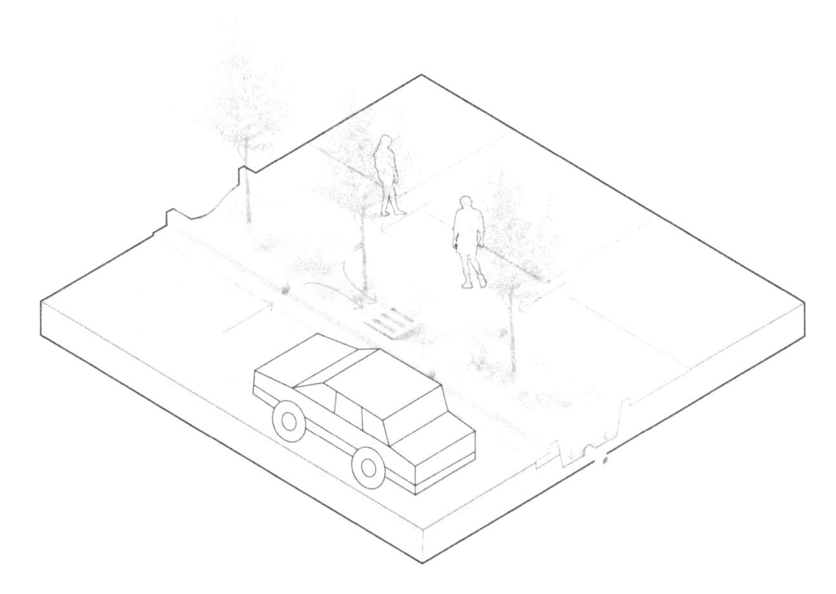

Figure 23.12

O2. Check Dams Swale

Check dams are small concrete or rock dams constructed across bioswales which lower the speed of concentrated flows and enhance stormwater treatment and infiltration. They can be created by simple walls or smaller scaled gabions.

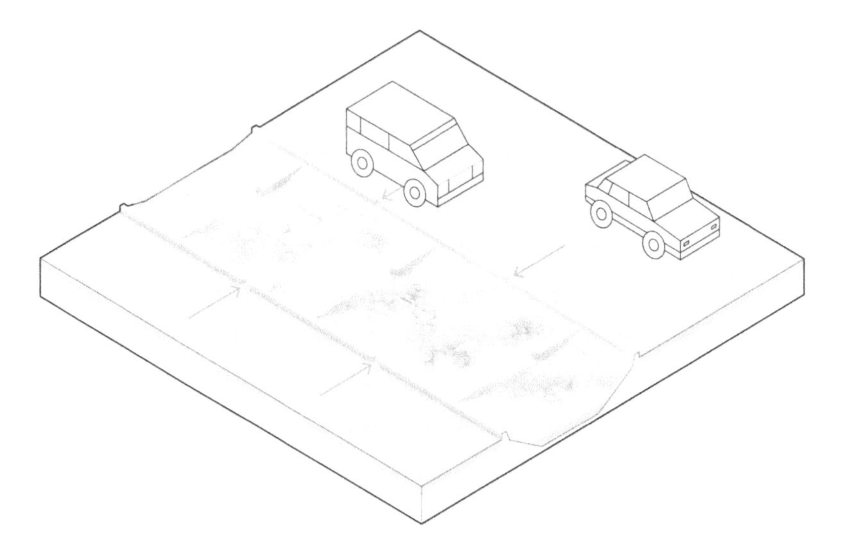

Figure 23.13

O3. Bumpout Swale

A bumpout swale is typically a vegetated curb extension area which is used to slow down traffic but has several inlets or curb openings which direct runoff into a vegetated patch.

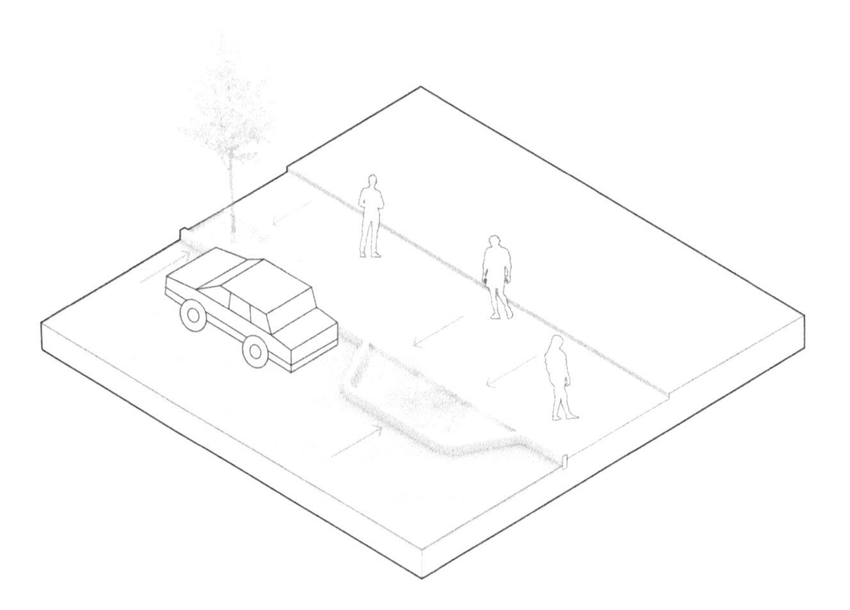

Figure 23.14

O4. Curbless Swale

Curbless swales are most appropriate when used along streets at highway medians or in suburban and low density residential areas. They are simply open, vegetated ditches which are parallel to the ground plane, with no separating device.

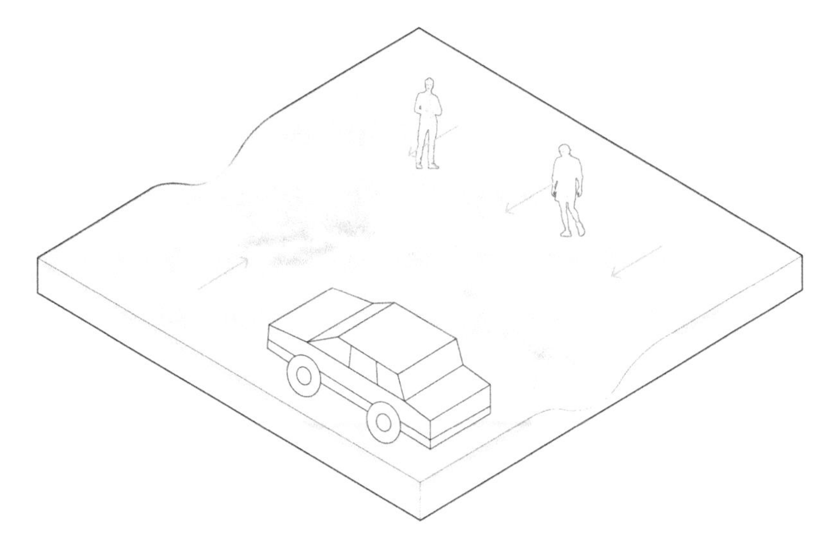

Figure 23.15

P. Wetland

Coastal wetlands help absorb wave water and block storm surge, thereby protecting the inland from flood and erosion while also providing benefits to biodiversity. According to the United States Environmental Protection Agency, a one-acre wetland can typically store about 3 acre-feet of water, or one million gallons (Shepard et al., 2011). However, sea level rise could result in major coastal wetland loss through over-inundation. Therefore, the preservation of wetlands should be a priority.

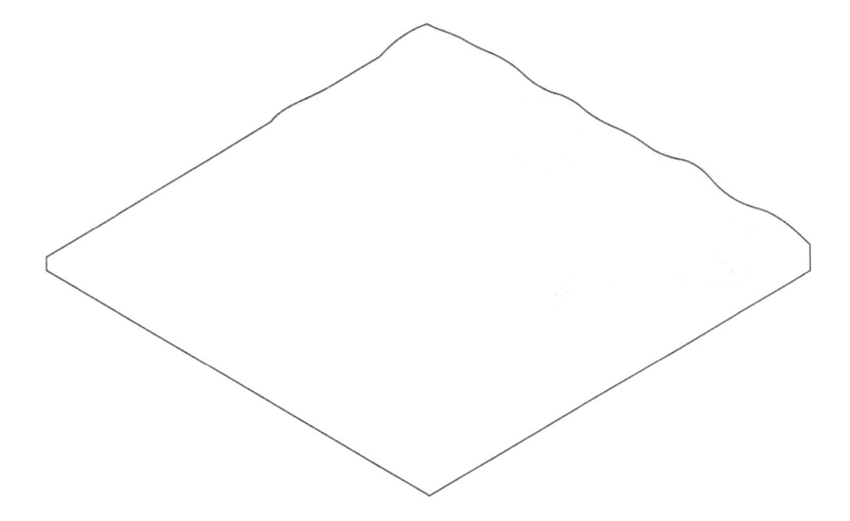

Figure 23.16

Location

Coastal

Ability to Address Coastal Hazards

Storm surge
Wave force
Flooding
Erosion

Cost

Compared with other non-structural mechanisms

● ● ● ○ ○

Compared with overall mechanisms

● ● ○ ○ ○

Scale

● ● ● ● ○

Regional

P1. Constructed Wetland

Constructed wetlands are an alternative method of creating coastal wetlands through the construction of artificial habitat which is mostly composed of vascular plants and algae communities. They act as treatment systems that use natural processes involving wetland vegetation, soils, and their associated microbial assemblages to improve water quality (Meyer at al., 2018).

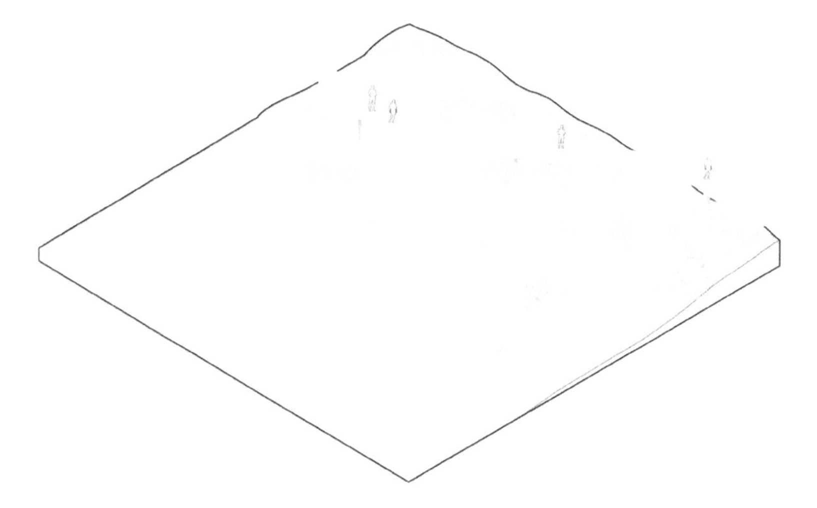

Figure 23.17

P2. Marshes

A marsh is a type of wetland which is inundated with water for long periods of time. They act as areas of low-lying land which are flooded in wet seasons or at high tide, but typically remain waterlogged at all times (Masterson et al., 2019). Marshes also slow down floodwaters and filter pollution from flood- and stormwaters.

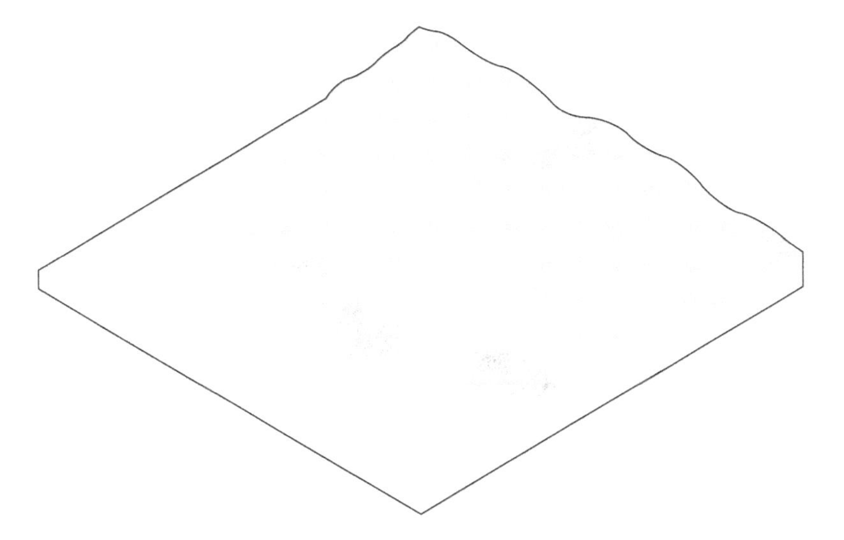

Figure 23.18

P3. Floating Wetland

A floating wetland island is a man-made raft that floats on the water's surface and houses native wetland plants (Tanner & Headley, 2011). They are container gardens which float atop the surface of the water and are composed of any wetland marsh plants except trees and shrubs.

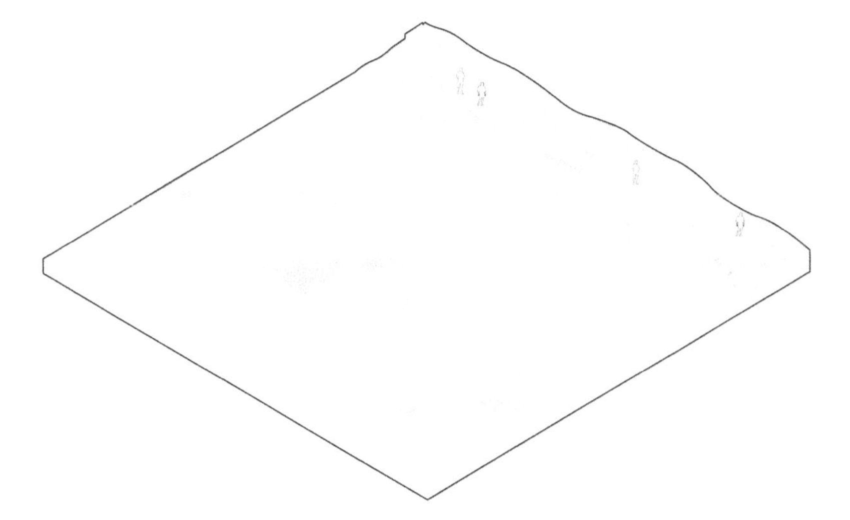

Figure 23.19

P4. Riparian Buffer

Riparian buffers are vegetated edges along rivers, streams, or other water bodies' banks. They act as a buffer between water bodies and development which prevents pollutants from runoff into water, controls erosion, provides habitat, and acts as floodable land to protect developed areas outside of the buffer zone from flood damage (Kim & Newman, 2019).

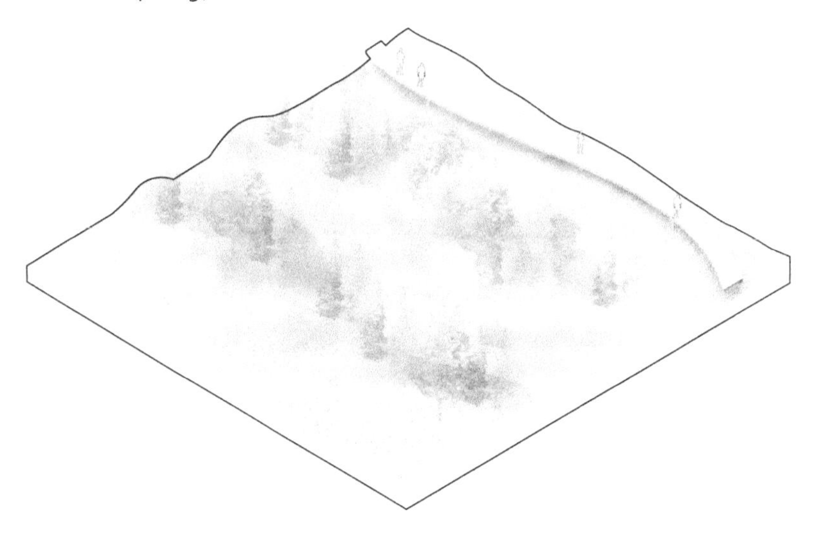

Figure 23.20

Q. Detention/Retention

A stormwater detention/retention pond is an open basin which provides storage of rainwater runoff during storm events. Unlike retention ponds, detention ponds can be dry during the year and serve other functions. Detention ponds are designed to capture stormwater runoff, reduce flood damage, and also reduce the peak flow downstream. Retention ponds, inversely, store water year-round.

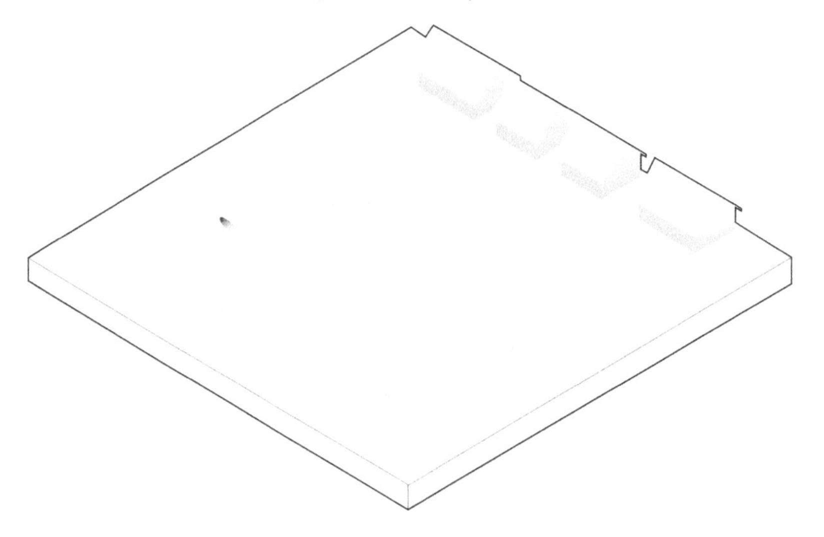

Figure 23.21

Location

Urban/Suburban

Ability to Address Coastal Hazards

Storm surge
Wave force
Flooding
Erosion

Cost

Compared with other non-structural mechanisms

● ○ ○ ○ ○

Compared with overall mechanisms

● ○ ○ ○ ○

Scale

● ○ ○ ○ ○

Site/Community

Q1. Dry Detention Pond

A dry pond is an impoundment pond that is used for short-term detention of stormwater runoff from developed areas, then releases the stormwater at a controlled rate until the pond empties into designated areas.

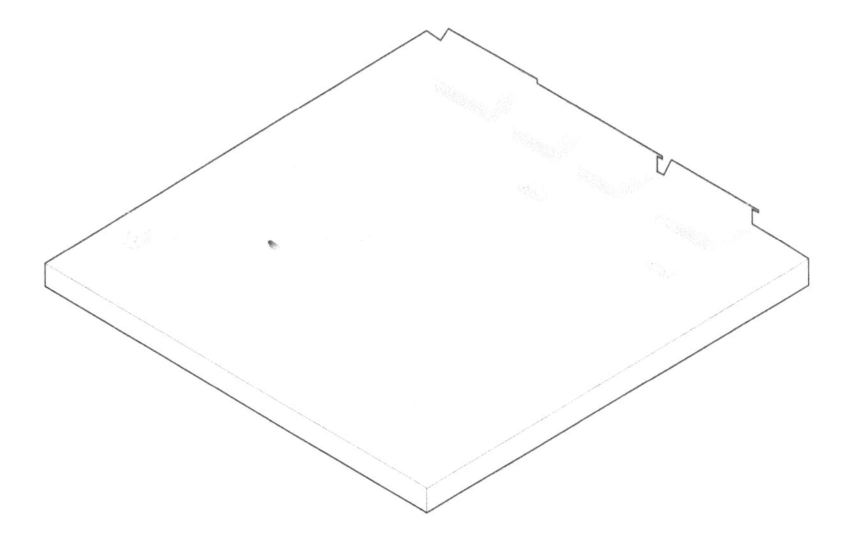

Figure 23.22

Q2. Retention Pond

A retention pond is essentially a wet detention pond that always retains a certain amount of water within the basin to control both stormwater quality and quantity.

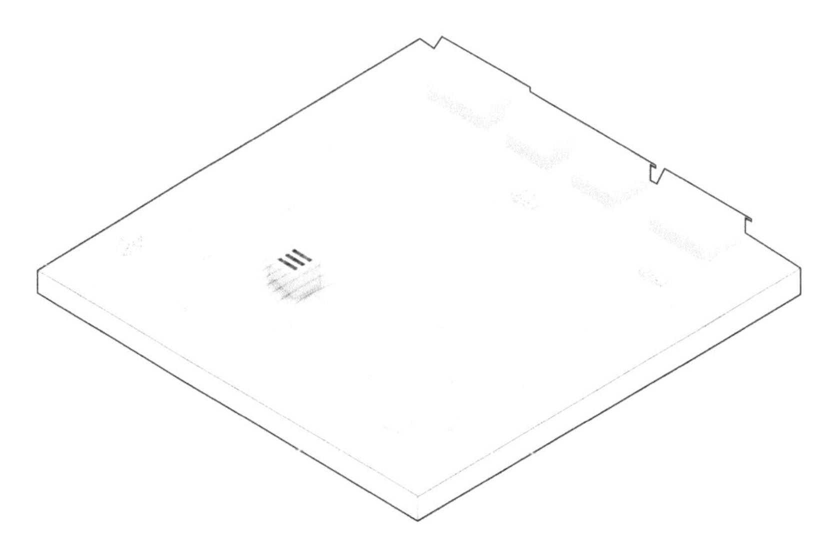

Figure 23.23

Q3. Extended Detention Pond

Extended detention ponds provide a storage volume above the invert of the lowest outlet, to temporarily detain a portion of stormwater runoff for an extended time period (Extended Detention Basin, 2020).

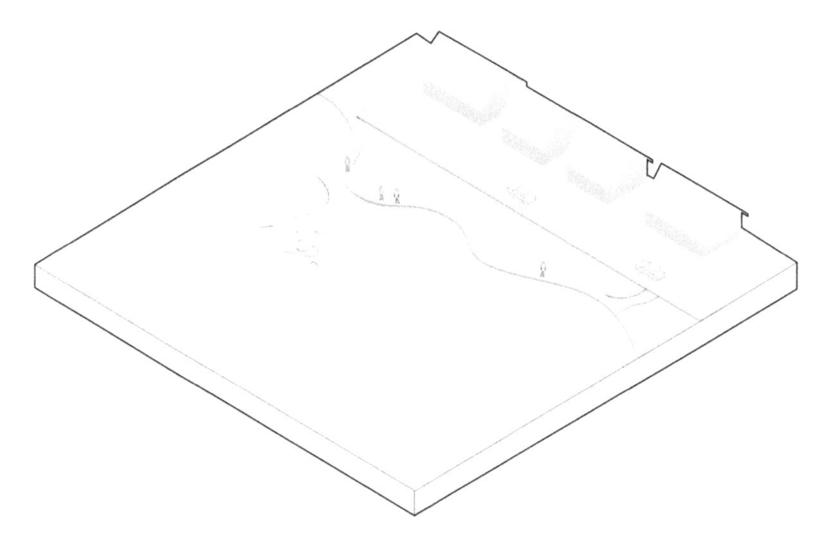

Figure 23.24

Q4. Multi-use Detention Pond

These ponds are modernly designed detention ponds with a multi-use program or facility. For example, when the basin is not flooded, it could be used as a sunken plaza or playground (after a rainfall event).

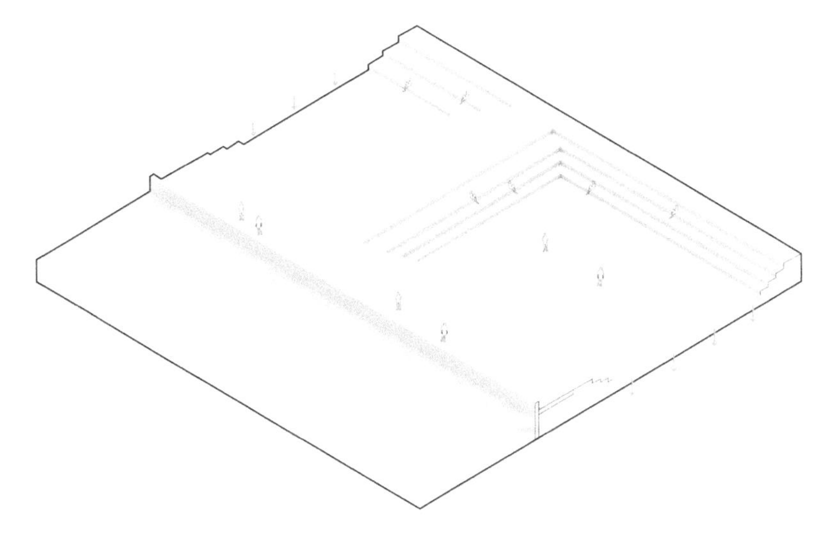

Figure 23.25

R. Rain Garden

A rain garden is a depressed landscape area planted with native grasses, shrubs, and perennials, which captures and filters stormwater runoff from streets, rooftops, groundscapes, etc. Like shallow bowls, rain gardens lie below the level of their surroundings and are designed to absorb rainwater that runs off of a surface (Stone et al., 2019).

Figure 23.26

Location

Urban/Suburban

Ability to Address Coastal Hazards

Storm surge
Wave force
Flooding
Erosion

Cost

Compared with other non-structural mechanisms

● ○ ○ ○ ○

Compared with overall mechanisms

● ○ ○ ○ ○

Scale

● ○ ○ ○ ○

Site/Community/Regional

R1. Residential Rain Garden

Residential rain gardens are household-scaled landscapes which capture the runoff from sidewalks, rooftops, or driveways near houses or are used to capture overflow from a rainwater harvesting system such as a rain barrel or downspout system.

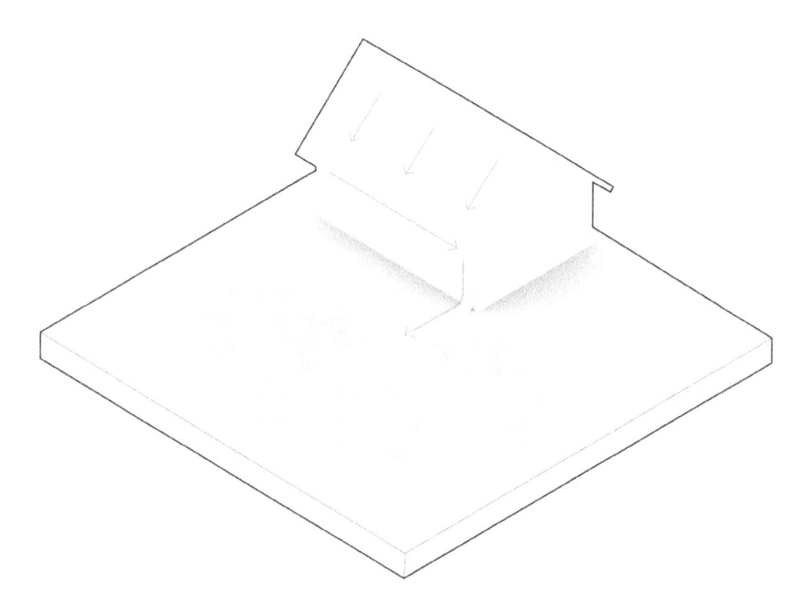

Figure 23.27

R2. Parking Lot Rain Garden

These rain gardens are located along the sides or within the middle of parking lots to reduce flooding through the absorption of stormwater runoff from impervious surfaces.

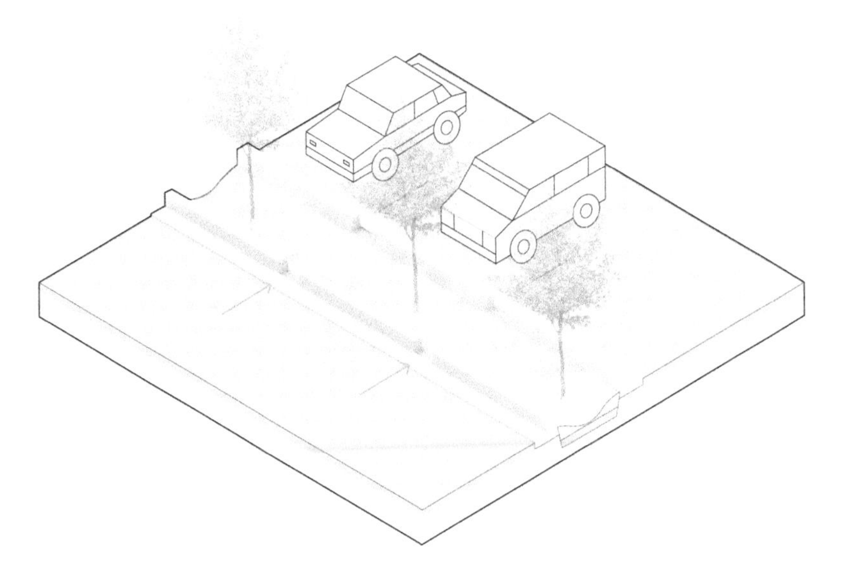

Figure 23.28

R3. Campus Rain Garden

More and more rain gardens are being applied on school campuses at the university or grade school level. Besides their ecological and hydrological benefits, such rain gardens also encourage student involvement on campuses and can act as living research labs.

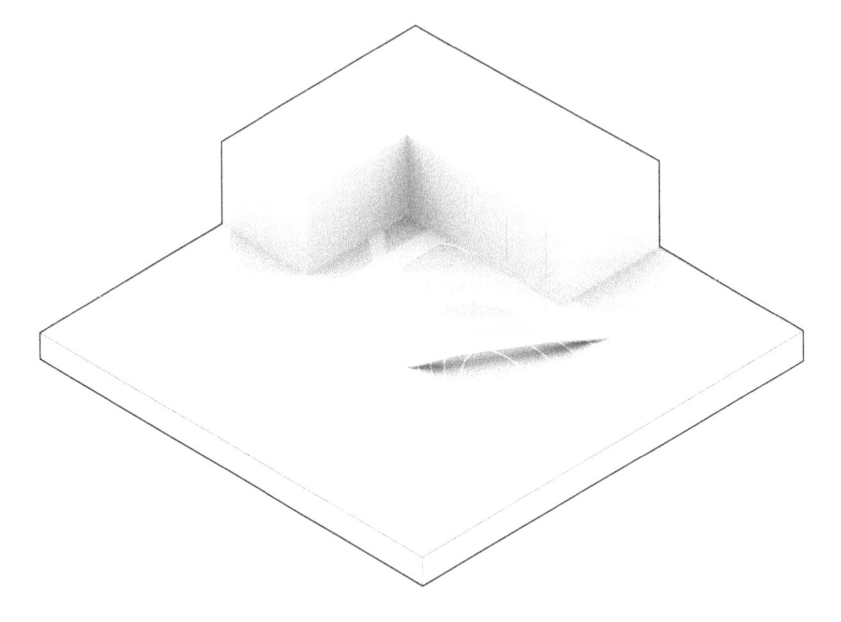

Figure 23.29

R4. Terraced Rain Garden

Terraced rain gardens are typically built on steep slopes with retaining walls or berms to hold soil. Terraced rain gardens are larger than normal rain gardens. They act as a series of rain gardens which interweave as a stepped ensemble to hold and filter water at different levels of elevation.

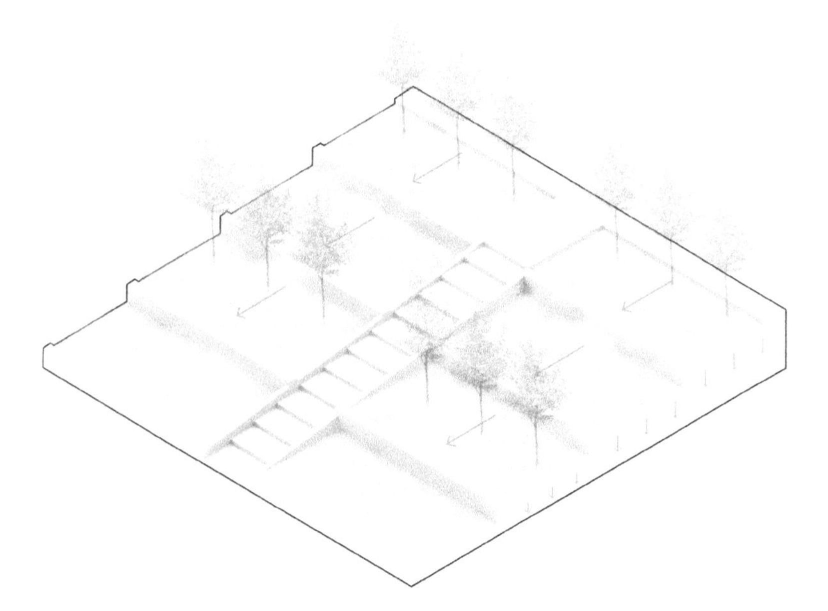

Figure 23.30

Conclusions

Most non-structural mechanisms utilized to defend against flooding and sea level rise are a much lower-cost alternative when compared to structural mechanisms. For example, the utilization of dunes and sand deposits provides a low-cost adaptive management strategy for increasing critical dune habitat while protecting areas from increased sea level rise that is built by naturally created materials and processes. Dunes and sand-related mechanisms, however, are much more vulnerable to damage from flood events than most structural mechanisms but are also cheaper to repair. Dune vegetation is also sensitive to disturbance and can be heavily affected by humans. The potential for dune recovery is dependent on the sediment supply in each area and on the intensity of human impact. While dredging can provide a repository for sediments to create dunes or other types of mounded protective landscapes, such approaches can also have significant negative impacts on riverine or aquatic ecosystems. Further, while dredging can, in many cases, reduce flooding duration, it cannot always fully prevent flooding or flood damage.

Bioswales help limit local flooding from stormwater, can transprt floodwaters into designated areas, and require less maintenance than turf grass because they need less water and typically no or limited fertilization. Bioswales can provide aesthetic enhancements for areas such as highways and are generally less expensive when used in place of underground piping. Again, however, the significance of flood prevention is limited when compared to many structural mechanisms, like dunes and dredging approaches. The capacity to attenuate flooding varies based on the size of the bioswale. This characteristic is also shared by rain gardens which are attractive, easy to maintain, flexible and able to fit into many landscapes, and easy to construct. Due to these strengths and benefits, non-structural mechanisms are best utilized as an ensemble, mixing both large- and small-scaled mechanisms into an entire flood-proofing system.

References

Extended detention basin. (2020). Massachusetts Department of Environmental Protection. Retrieved from https://megamanual.geosyntec.com/npsmanual/extendeddetentionbasin.aspx

Figlus, J., Sigren, J., Armitage, A., & Tyler, R. (2014). Erosion of vegetated coastal dunes. *Coastal Engineering Proceedings, 1*. https://doi.org/10.9753/icce.v34.sediment.20.

Kim, Y. J., & Newman, G. (2019). Climate change preparedness: Comparing future urban growth and flood risk in Amsterdam and Houston. *Sustainability, 11*(4), 1048.

Kim, J. H., Newman, G., Feng, H., Merrill, J., & Park, J. (2017). Sustainable urbanism for a metropolitan corridor: An evidence-based urban design for Park 10 in Houston, Texas. *Landscape Architecture Frontiers, 5*(5), 96–109.

Koster, E. (1988). Ancient and modern cold-climate aeolian sand deposition: A review. *Journal of Quaternary Science, 3*, 69–83.

Masterson, J., Meyer, M., Ghariabeh, N., Hendricks, M., Lee, R. J., Musharrat, S., Newman, G., Sansom, G., & Van Zandt, S. (2019). Interdisciplinary citizen science for hazard and disaster education. *International Journal of Mass Emergencies and Disasters, 37*(1), 6–24.

McKenna, W. (2007). An evolutionary model of parabolic dune development: From blowout to mature parabolic, Padre Island National Seashore, Texas. Unpublished M.Sc. Thesis, Louisiana State University.

Meyer, M., Hendricks, M. Newman, G., Horney, J., Berke, P., Masterson, J., Sansom, G., Cousins, T., Van Zandt, S., & Cooper, J. (2018). Participatory action research: Tools for disaster resilience education. *International Journal of Disaster Resilience in the Built Environment, 9*(4/5), 402–419.

Newman, G., Sohn, W. M, & Li, M. H. (2014). Performance evaluation of low impact development: Groundwater infiltration in a drought prone landscape in Conroe, Texas. *Landscape Architecture Frontiers, 2*(4), 122–133.

Newman, G., Guo, R., Zhang, Y., Bardenhagen, E., & Kim, J. H. (2016). Landscape Integration for Storm Surge Barrier Infrastructure. *Landscape Architecture Frontiers, 4*(1), 112–125.

Newman, G., Brody, S., & Smith, A. (2017). Repurposing vacant land through landscape connectivity. *Landscape Journal, 36*, 37–57.

Shepard, C. C., Crain, C. M., & Beck, M. W. (2011). The protective role of coastal marshes: A systematic review and meta-analysis. *PloS One, 6*(11), e27374.

Sloss, C. R., Shepherd, M., & Hesp, P. (2012). Coastal dunes: Geomorphology. *Nature Education Knowledge, 3*(10), 2.

Sohn, W., Kim, J. H., & Newman, G. (2014). A blueprint for stormwater infrastructure design: Implementation and efficacy of LID. *Landscape Research Record*, *2*, 50–61.

Stone, K., Horney, J., Newman G., Karaye, I., & Casaillas, G. (2019). A spatial analysis of possible environmental exposures in recreational areas impacted by Hurricane Harvey flooding, Harris County, Texas. *Environmental Management*, *64*(4), 381–390.

Tanner, C., & Headley, R. (2011). Components of floating emergent macrophyte treatment wetlands influencing removal of stormwater pollutants. *Ecological Engineering*, *37*, 474–486.

24

THE *URBAN PERICULUM*

A landscape at risk from sea level rise

Galen D. Newman and Dongying Li

Global Rising Seas

Coastal resilience is one of the most pressing and challenging issues which landscape architects face today. As the contents of this book have shown, flood risk will continue to increase due to the severity and frequency of storms and sea level rise, posing significant global challenges especially in coastal cities. This condition is even more dire considering that nearly one half of the world's population (44%) lives in coastal regions within 150 kilometers of the sea (Dedekorkut-Howes et al., 2020). Further, it is estimated that population densities in coastal regions are about three times higher than the global average (Lee, 2014). Relatedly, storms and hurricanes are predicted to increase in intensity and frequency along the coasts, where, in regards to the U.S., over half of the population lives (Burger et al., 2017).

Global sea level rise rates have accelerated in recent decades, rather than increasing linearly (Tang and Lukenda, 2019). Global mean sea level has risen by 8 inches (20 centimeters) since 1870, with nearly 3 inches gained since 1992 (NASA, 2017). The most recent 2021 IPCC report showed that the ocean had warmed fastest over the past century in the recent 10,000 years, which explained 50% of the sea level rise between 1971 and 2018. However, comparing 1992–1999 and 2010–2019, the rate of ice sheet loss increased by four times, and has become the primary cause of global mean sea level rise (Masson-Delmotte et al., 2021). Future projections show sea level rise of up to 1.88 m (high emission scenario) in 2015 relative to the level in 1995–2014. The report warns that a tipping point is drawing near and a 2-meter to 5-meter sea level rise cannot be ruled out depending on ice sheet processes (Masson-Delmotte et al., 2021).

As a result, coastal cities are presently facing unprecedented challenges associated with climate change. Sea levels are rising along nearly all coasts, worldwide and will impact millions of people, damage significant amounts of infrastructure, and disrupt multiple ecosystems globally. Coastal cities are threatened by frequent flood events, increasing wave heights, reduction of tidal flats and wetlands, and damage to

DOI: 10.4324/9781003183419-32

shoreline infrastructure. Communities within these areas, therefore, need designs and plans that will drive community resilience through sustaining ecologies, economies, and social activities. All future long-term resilience plans should recognize that the climate is changing, at least to some degree, and should seek to develop solutions in which to cope with these change's projected effects.

Typical Strategies for Addressing Rising Seas

Typical approaches to mitigating sea level rise are often classified into three primary strategies: strategies: protection, accommodation, and retreat (Lee, 2014). Protection often seeks to block floodwaters through large-scaled methods and includes structural mechanisms such as dikes or levees. This approach utilizes engineering-based structures to block the inflow of sea water to protects facilities and critical infrastructure that are difficult or impossible to move or relocate. The goal of this strategy should be to guard the maximum amount of land from flood effects with the minimum amount of necessary infrastructure. Relatedly, non-structural protection mechanisms such as the use of natural sedimentation and large-scale vegetation patches such as riparian zones are also sometimes employed. Coastal green spaces can act like sponges, reducing water flow during flood events, thereby protecting populations and infrastructure (Newman et al., 2021). Such approaches are relatively low-cost, are ecologically friendly, and utilize natural processes such as wetland restoration, sand dunes, forests, or waterfront parks as functions for these zones.

Accommodation seeks to reduce the impact of sea level rise through changes in both human behavior and infrastructure distribution, while maintaining existing uses of coastal areas (Atoba et al., 2021). Through this strategy, existing infrastructure is often modified to accommodate more adaptive land uses, the ground level can be raised, drainage facilities can be improved, or beachlines can be elongated through sand nourishments.

The retreat strategy seeks to mitigate flood risks simply by relocating developments or infrastructure further from the coastline. Such a strategy discourages new development in high-risk coastal areas while encouraging it within low flood risk inland areas, usually at higher elevations. It is, in essence, a method in which to develop out of harm's way. Retreat, however, can be extremely time-consuming (especially when relocating a community), require long-term phasing for implementation, and can be quite expensive in that new development within a lower risk site may need to be accompanied by a relocation policy or require new infrastructure. However, if planned proactively, this strategy can be the most effective adaptation to the uncertainty of future sea level rise (Malecha et al., 2020).

While the traditional protect, accommodate, and retreat strategies have been applied globally, through various combinations, there appears to be a greater emphasis on the use of structural measures for the accommodation of the impacts of sea level rise and coastal flooding compared to ecosystem-based measures when applying these strategies. An important issue with regards to the reliance on structural measures is the uncertainty around how much (and until when) these measures will be effective in protecting populations (Kim and Newman, 2020). The long-term socioeconomic implications are also unknown. More transformative approaches are required for planned adaptation of cities and communities to sea level rise and coastal flooding. There is certainly a need for a more integrated and comprehensive approach to sea level rise adaptation. Retreat from the ocean in some parts of a city (based on sound climate risk assessment), while fortifying existing defense in other parts and creating land use layouts which accommodate the population can all be effective; however, more research is required in order to capture the trade-offs and synergies between these strategies and their cumulative benefits (Newman et al., 2020).

The *Urban Periculum*: A New Framework

Despite growing attention to coastal resilience in the context of rising seas and climate hazards, planning and design professions rely heavily on FEMA flood plain designations for risk framing and the application of protect, accommodate, or retreat strategies. Although the 100- and 500-year flood plains are practically easy to interpret and follow, research has questioned their accuracy and reliability regards mapping flood damage probability. For example, a recent study suggested that, using an updated model, nearly 41 million Americans live within a 1% annual probability floodplain, which is more than three times higher than the estimate (13 million) based on FEMA flood maps (Wing et al., 2018). Given the uncertainties in hydrologic processes and uncertainties in anthropogenic emissions and climate change trajectory, researchers argue that floodplain boundary would be better represented as a continuous map of flood probabilities, rather than a single line (Bradley et al., 1994). The framing of 100- and 500- year floods, in addition to suggesting that risks are infrequent and static, do not fully account for the compounding effects of sea level rise and storm surge in coastal areas. Such an approach also may lead to misconceptions that sites and areas are in isolation and neglect the fact that design decisions impact broader ecological and hydrological processes. Therefore, when designing in the coastal area, a new framework is needed for risk characterization that is dynamic, holistic, and future oriented.

The term "urban periphery" is a common term often used to describe the landscape on the edge of a city. The urban periphery is composed of the spaces at the interface between core cities and the outer, less dense suburbs (MacCormack, 1979). While not necessarily referring to a city's edge, the term *periculum* is a Latin word referring to both risk and danger (MacCormack, 1979). It has its roots in the term *periclum*, a term used sometimes applied law studies, which also entails aspects of hazards, peril, responsibility for damage, and liability along with hazard and danger (MacCormack, 1979). As a term applied to landscape architecture, the *urban periculum*, as we define it here, refers to the collection of high flood risk landscapes which are threatened by current hazard events as well as future sea level rise and, as a result, require innovative solutions to help mitigate and counteract such circumstances. The *urban periculum* is characterized by land which is composed of coastal and riverine areas susceptible to the impacts of sea level rise, storm surge, and flooding, comprising a set of global irregularly shaped, but often large in size, landscapes which require creative and complex structural, non-structural, and hybrid solutions (see Figure 24.1). These landscapes, however, do not only include spaces within only a beachline or riverine edge; they are composed of entire built and ecological communities and include those aspects of the built environment which reside within and are adjacent to beach and riverine edges. Flood risks across the global *urban periculum*, as shown, are projected to amplify. This landscape, therefore, requires long-term foresight dependent upon urban analytics and monitorization, adaptable development approaches, and combinations of both hard and soft infrastructure.

Anticipating current and future risks within the *urban periculum* requires adaptative design and planning to mitigate social, economic, and physical damage. The recognition that many coastal urban communities are under impending threats will assist policy makers and designers in redefining the water-related problems. Such assistance could transform the entire process from emergency response to integrative co-existing. Take the Gulf Coast as an example; with a conservative projection of a

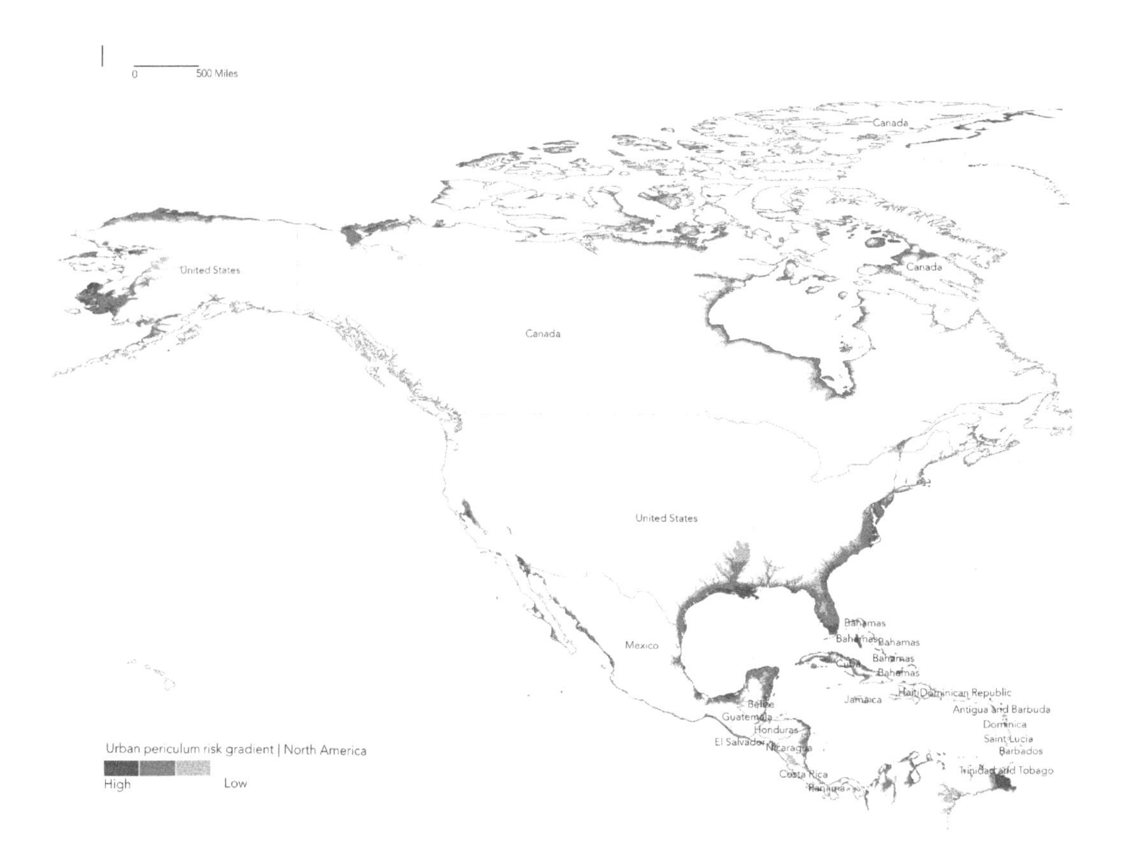

Figure 24.1 The global coastal landscapes of *urban periculum* (North America). The boundaries of *urban periculum* are dynamic and everchanging (as represented by a color/probability gradient).

10-ft sea level rise, areas up to 12–15 miles off shore will be inundated. Beyond a single line that marks flood plain, a section study that reveals the macro and micro relationships between the built environment and probabilities of water influx and tidal influences shows variations in risks within the *urban periculum* (See Fig. 2). In addition to absolute sea level rise caused by warming of the sea water and glacier melting, urban subsidence can also significantly contribute to relative sea level rise. As such, design for the *urban periculum* should pay attention to not only the changing aerial landscape but also the uncertainties to the vertical dynamics of the rising sea level, flood elevation, and the gradual setting of the urban land.

Figure 24.2 10 ft Sea Level Rise Inundation and Risk Gradient by Section along the Houston-Galveston., TX Coast.

Although we define the term '*urban periculum*' to recognize the severity of impending threats to many cities and communities, we by no means suggest a pessimistic attitude toward sea level rise. Quite the contrary, we advocate for a proactive approach to predict and mitigate the negative consequences and the utilization of locally appropriate strategies. In face of the vastly uncertain challenge, diversity, flexibility, and redundancy of solutions should be built into the infrastructure system. During emergencies, failure in one of the critical components of infrastructure would cause a system collapse. For example, a flood inundation dynamics mapping during historical hurricanes offer insights into the flood pathways as coastal areas were struck by storm surge, revealing the highly susceptible areas and weak links in storm infrastructure (see Figure 24.3). Many of these areas also coincide with high socially vulnerable communities. With the identification of vulnerable physical and social infrastructure, local interventions can be prioritized to enhance the robustness of the critical infrastructure and provide multiple layers of defense.

Although we have so far primarily focused on environmental modifications for the *urban periculum*, risk assessment approaches, the design process, and solution development should also seek to prioritize environmental justice and equity. Vulnerable populations often reside in low-lying areas, experience more acute and chronic environmental stressors, and have fewer coping resources and capacities. As many policies and designs amplify, rather than reduce inequalities, processes

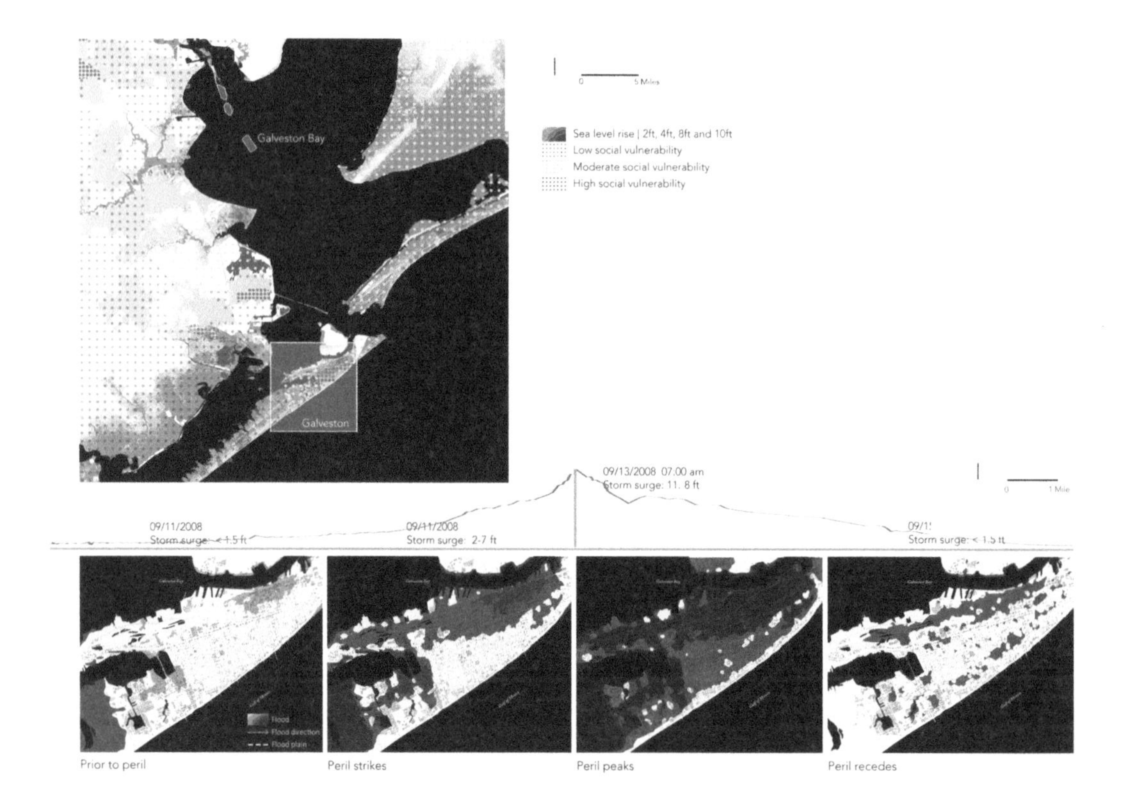

Figure 24.3 Peril impending within the City of Galveston during Hurricane Ike in 2008.

that involve authentic civic participation and address the long-standing inequalities that have been imprinted in the built environment through policies and developmental patterns are essential. Multiple chapters in this book provided examples of how the incorporating of non-structural elements such as public green space, or the process of developing shared solutions of such elements, can reshape civic identity, reinforce shared ownership, and serve as catalysts for social change toward more just cities.

Promoting Resilience within the *Urban Periculum*

Overall, local governments worldwide are using various strategies to address sea level rise and coastal flooding. Unfortunately, most of these responses are only reactive and were developed in an ad hoc manner following a specific event. There is an increasing recognition of the need for more comprehensive and proactive approaches to flood and sea level rise mitigation. This book showcased research and innovative design applications into this topic, reflecting and combining practice, education, landscape performance, community engagement, knowledge from existing studies within particular locations, and strategies applied in a piecemeal or logical manner which are founded on comprehensive pre and post evaluations. This is the best approach to effective designing for the *urban periculum* in the long term. Further, such an approach involving both collaborative and interdisciplinary based design can improve the ability of the *urban periculum* to recover from storms and sea level rise. Resilient design of the *urban periculum* must incorporate risk analysis, performance analytics, and mixed mechanisms. Through showcasing these processes through this book, we advocate taking steps to protect landscapes, increase adaptation, and mitigate disastrous outcomes associated with sea level rise from a global perspective.

As noted, despite the urgency needed to address sea level rise, current actions are primarily limited to singular, mostly structural approaches, and are quite varied across localities (Noor et al, 2021). Adaptation to shifting sea levels is a growing concern for coastal management authorities, engineers, ecologists, urban planners and designers (Moosavia, 2017). Currently, a shift is occurring from engineered-based defense systems to more ecologically integrated or green infrastructure-based systems. This shift has created more opportunities for landscape architects in helping to combat climate change through designing structures that are able to perform beyond basic engineering objectives, while also providing both social and ecological benefits. Many new studies have pointed out the importance of landscape-related solutions in informing the design of coastal infrastructure (Stone et al., 2019). While there are limited projects which demonstrate or seek to quantify the most effective design approaches, this book acts as a primary collection displaying such innovative approaches, many of which are quantified according to their impacts.

In regards to landscape architecture and the design of the *urban periculum*, sea level rise should act as an engine for innovation. Such creativity is vital in responding to its effects and leveraging it to maximize any inherent benefits; it is in the face of adversity that creativity becomes a critical factor, not just through responding to a crisis, but developing new ways to cope with such crises (Copley et al., 2015). Effective, yet flexible, design can play a critical role in the processes by which adaptation strategies are applied. For example, while structural mechanisms for mitigating sea level rise are often critical to dealing with flood related concerns, management strategies must increase the use and integration of non-structural (and hybrid) solutions for solving issues associated with sea level rise. These more ecological adaptation strategies in lieu of or in combination with engineered structures are necessary to both maximize protection and lessen risk. The anticipated effects of sea-level rise, increasing storm surges, and projected coastal erosion require more collaboration between engineers, ecologists, and designers for the provision of creative and advanced landscape-based solutions.

This is no question that large-scaled issues related to extreme flooding often require the reinforcement of coastal areas through large and small scaled structural infrastructure. This is particularly needed in lower-lying areas of elevation to protect the growing populations from the impacts of climate change. In fact, the global low elevation coastal population could rise by more than 50% between 2000 and 2030, from 625 million to 880 million; China, India, Bangladesh, Indonesia and Vietnam are the top countries with the highest exposure to impacts of sea-level rise on coastal population (Moosavia, 2017). In most of these countries, engineered coastal structures are considered as the primary mode for protecting communities from flood risks.

However, as shown, there can be multiple negative impacts of only using structural infrastructure, especially on marine and coastal habitats, including loss of biodiversity and ecosystem degradation. Structural mechanisms such as breakwaters and seawalls are often constructed to increase safety and reclaim land from the sea, but the environmental impacts and economic viability of utilizing these offshore reserves are seldom examined. Additionally, levees along the lower parts of channels require consistent assessments to evaluate their viability against sea level rise. In many areas, pumps are used to discharge excess standing water when levees are constructed. The pumping capacity of low-lying areas must then be constantly upgraded to keep up with changing increased needs. This approach, then, inevitably requires future upgrades, especially when considering operations such as the closing of outdated tidal gates, increasing deluge-style precipitation events, and accelerating sea level rise.

Efforts to modify structural infrastructure in the *urban periculum* should be evaluated based on sea level rise trends in extreme precipitation events and assessed in regards to their economic, ecologic, and risk reduction capabilities. Current and new landscape performance tools should also seek to address these issues. The increased consideration of green infrastructure and nature-based adaptation measures to reduce effects from sea level rise must be included as an alternative or additional/integrated approach. Long-term adaptation policies for managed retreat or setback limits for new development could also be applied to new buildings in low-lying areas that do or will increasingly suffer from erosion. This could reduce the flood risk to coastal areas in the short term while simultaneously creating buffer or riparian space along the coast which could be reused as green infrastructure to help fight against sea level rise and erosion. Integrated assessment methods alongside the implementation of greener adaptation strategies are urgently required in consideration of the *urban periculum* worldwide in order to ensure future resilience.

References

Atoba, K., Newman, G., Brody, S., & Highfield, W. (2021). Buy them out before they are built: Evaluating the proactive acquisition of vacant land in flood-prone areas. *Environmental Conservation*, *48*(2), 118–126.

Bradley, A., Potter, K., Price, T., Cooper, P., Steffen, J., & Franz, D. (1994). Flood analysis in DuPage county using hydrological simulation program: FORTRAN model. *Transportation Research Record*, *1471*, 41–46.

Burger, J., O'Neill, K. M., Handel, S. N., Hensold, B., & Ford, G. (2017). The shore is wider than the beach: Ecological planning solutions to sea level rise for the Jersey Shore, USA. *Landscape and Urban Planning*, *157*, 512–522.

Copley, N., Bowring, J., & Abbott, M. (2015). Thinking ahead: Design-directed research in a city which experienced fifty years of sea level change overnight. *Journal of Landscape Architecture*, *10*(2), 70–81.

Dedekorkut-Howes, A., Torabi, E., & Howes, M. (2020). When the tide gets high: A review of adaptive responses to sea level rise and coastal flooding. *Journal of Environmental Planning and Management*, *63*(12), 2102–2143.

Kim Y., & Newman, G. (2020). Advancing scenario planning through integrating urban growth prediction with future flood risk models. *Computers, Environment, and Urban Systems*, *82*, 101498

Lee, Y. (2014). Coastal planning strategies for adaptation to sea level rise: A case study of Mokpo, Korea. *Journal of Building Construction and Planning Research*, *2*, 74–81.

MacCormack, G. (1979). VII. Periculum. Zeitschrift der Savigny-Stiftung für Rechtsgeschichte: Romanistische Abteilung, *96*(1), 129–172.

Malecha, M., Kirsch, K., Karaye, I., Newman, G., & Horney, J. (2020). Advancing the toxics mobility inventory: Development of a toxics mobility vulnerability index and application in Harris County, TX. *Sustainability: The Journal of Record*, *13*(6), 282–291.

Masson-Delmotte, V., Zhai, P., Pirani, A, Connors, S. L., Péan, C., Berger, S., Caud, N., Chen, Y., Goldfarb, L., Gomis, M. I., Huang, M., Leitzell, K., Lonnoy, E., Matthews, J. B. R., Maycock, T. K., Waterfield, T., Yelekçi, O., Yu, R., & Zhou, B. (Eds.) (2021). Summary for policymakers. In: *Climate Change 2021: The Physical Science Basis*. Contribution of Working Group I to the Sixth Assessment Report of the Intergovernmental Panel on Climate Change (IPCC) Cambridge University Press. In Press.

Moosavi, S. (2017). Ecological coastal protection: Pathways to living shorelines. *Procedia Engineering*, *196*, 930–938.

NASA. (2017). *Rising seas*. Retrieved February 20, 2020, from www.nasa.gov/goddard/risingseas

Newman, G., Malecha, M., & Atoba, K. (2021). Integrating ToxPi outputs with Arc GIS dashboards to identify neighborhood threat levels of contaminant transferal during flood events. *Journal of Spatial Sciences*, 1–13. http://doi.org/10.1080/14498596.2021.1891149

Newman, G., Shi, T., Yao, Z., Li, D., Sansom, G., Kirsch, K., Casillas, G., Horney, J. (2020). Citizen science-informed community master planning: Land use and built environment changes to increase flood resilience and decrease contaminant exposure. *International Journal of Environmental Research and Public Health*, *17*(2): 486.

Noor, A., Casillas, G., Luo, Y., McDonald, T., Wade, T., Zhu, R., Newman, G., Chui, W., & Rusyn, I. (2021). Environmental impacts of Hurricane Florence flooding in eastern North Carolina: Temporal analysis of contaminant distribution and potential human health risks. *Journal of Exposure Science and Environmental Epidemiology*, *31*, 810–822.

Stone, K., Horney, J., Newman G., Karaye, I., & Casaillas, G. (2019). A spatial analysis of possible environmental exposures in recreational areas impacted by Hurricane Harvey flooding, Harris County, Texas. *Environmental Management*, *64*(4), 381–390.

Tang, H., & Lukenda, J. (2019). Rising seas: Adaptable planning strategies for coastal urban greenways: Case studies in the US and China. In *Proceedings of the Fábos Conference on Landscape and Greenway Planning*, *6*(1), 17.

Wing, O. E., Bates, P. D., Smith, A. M., Sampson, C. C., Johnson, K. A., Fargione, J., & Morefield, P. (2018). Estimates of present and future flood risk in the conterminous United States. *Environmental Research Letters*, *13*(3), 034023.

Index

Note: Page locators in *italic* refer to figures and page locators in **bold** refer to tables.